The
FOUR
WITNESSES

The REBEL, the RABBI, the CHRONICLER, and the MYSTIC

Robin Griffith-Jones

HarperSanFrancisco
A Division of HarperCollins*Publishers*

THE FOUR WITNESSES: *The Rebel, the Rabbi, the Chronicler, and the Mystic.* Copyright © 2000 by Robin Griffith-Jones. All rights reserved. Printed in the United States of America. No part of this book may be used or reproduced in any manner whatsoever without written permission except in the case of brief quotations embodied in critical articles and reviews. For information address HarperCollins Publishers, Inc., 10 East 53rd Street, New York, NY 10022.

HarperCollins books may be purchased for educational, business, or sales promotional use. For information please write: Special Markets Department, HarperCollins Publishers, Inc., 10 East 53rd Street, New York, NY 10022.

HarperCollins Web site: http://www.harpercollins.com

HarperCollins®, 📖®, and HarperSanFrancisco™ are trademarks of HarperCollins Publishers, Inc.

FIRST EDITION

Library of Congress Cataloging-in-Publication Data

Griffith-Jones, Robin.
　　The four witnesses : the rebel, the rabbi, the chronicler, and the mystic / Robin Griffith-Jones.
　　—1st ed.
　　　　p.　cm.
　　ISBN 0–06–251647–7 (cloth)
　　ISBN 0–06–251648–5 (pbk.)
　　1. Bible. N.T. Gospels—Criticism, interpretation, etc.　　I. Title.

BS2555.2.G695　2000
226'.06—dc21　　　　　　　　　　　　　　　　　　　　　　　　　00-020330

Designed by Kris Tobiassen

00　01　02　03　04　❖/RRD　10　9　8　7　6　5　4　3　2　1

To four children:
David and Louisa,
Honor and Ellie,
with my love.

Contents

Acknowledgments

For translations of the Old Order (my term for the Old Testament or the Hebrew Bible), I have drawn on the Revised Standard Version (RSV) and the Jerusalem Bible. Except where stated, the translations from the New Order (New Testament) are my own; readers may recognize some debts to the RSV. Some passages from the Old Order have been abbreviated. In addressing or describing members of a group, whether Jews, Christians, or pagans, the Bible often writes of men: *he, him,* and *his.* Where possible, I have changed these instances to the plural: *they, them,* and *their.* Quotations from the Old and the New Order are in italics. Where our witnesses have drawn on the Old Order's Greek translation, I have done the same.

For further texts I have made use gratefully of the following editions: W. G. Braude, *The Midrash on Psalms,* 1959; H. Chadwick, *Origen: Contra Celsum,* 1953; R. H. Charles, *Apocrypha and Pseudepigrapha of the Old Testament,* 1913; J. H. Charlesworth, *The Old Testament Pseudepigrapha,* 1983 and 1985; B. D. Chilton, *The Glory of Israel: The Theology and Provenience of the Isaiah Targum,* 1982; H. Danby, *The Mishnah,* 1933; A. Diez Macho, *Neophyti I: Targum Palestinense,* 1970; I. Epstein, *The Babylonian Talmud,* 1935–52; C. T. R. Hayward, *The Jewish Temple* (for Sira's Son [Ben Sira]), 1996; E. Levine, *Targum to the Five Megillot (Codex Vatican Urbanati I),* 1977; E. Lohse, *Die Texte aus Qumran,* 1971; A. D. Nock and A. J. Festugière, *Corpus Hermeticum,* 1945; K. Niederwimmer, *Die Didache,* 1989; G. Vermes, *The Complete Dead Sea Scrolls in English,* 1997. A valuable survey of evidence is in E. Schurer, *The History of the Jewish People in the Age of Jesus Christ,* new edition, 1973–87.

Almost all other translations from Greek and Latin are my own. A famous series of texts (in the original language with an English translation) is available as the Loeb Classical Library: the works of Josephus, Lucan, Philo, Philostratus, Pliny, Suetonius, and Tacitus are all published in the series.

Among the more important passages quoted from non-biblical texts, readers will find the chief descriptions of the morning sacrifice, the Temple and the Feast of Shelters in the *Mishnah,* "Tamid," "Middoth" and "Sukkah"; the sayings ascribed to Hanina are at "Aboth" 3.10.

The elaboration of Psalm 118.19 is in Midrash Tehillim, Braude, vol. 2, 242–5. The "Song of the Four Nights" is in the *Targum Neophyti* of Exodus 12.42 (with one emendation made by many editors). The varying hopes for the arrival of the Anointed are ascribed to Rabbi Joshua b. Levi in the Babylonian Talmud, b. Sanh 98a.

Papias's account of Mark and Matthew is in Eusebius, *Ecclesiastical History*, 3.39.15–16, of Quadratus at 4.3.2–3, and of John at 3.39.1–7. Tacitus' account of the fire at Rome and the Christians is in *Annals*, 15.38-44, the legend of Nero's revival at Sybilline Oracle 4.138-148 (Charlesworth, vol. 1, 387). Lucan extols Nero at *Pharsalia*, 1.45ff. The recipe for exorcism is abbreviated from the *Paris Magical Papyrus*, 3017ff. Of our various accounts of Vespasian in Alexandria, the fullest is in Tacitus, *Histories*, 4.82.

The stories of Abraham and the devil is in the Talmud, b. Sanh 89b, and of Moses' infancy in Josephus at *Antiquities*, 2.205ff. The visions we cite of "Baruch" are in 2 Baruch (The Syriac Apocalypse of Baruch), 1-10 (Charles, vol. 1, 621ff).

Josephus's supplement to the *Antiquities, Against Apion*, has prefaces at 1.1.1-3 and 2.1.1. Thessalus' account of his consultation has been published by H. V. Friedrich, *Thessalus von Tralles*, 1968. Philostratus tells of Apollonius in Nero's Rome in the *Life of Apollonius*, 4.43ff, and Pliny writes to the emperor about the Christians in his *Letters*, 10.96.

Rabbi Akiba's discussion of Israel's blessedness is at *Sayings of the Fathers* (*Pirke Aboth*, 3.19, Charles, vol. 2, 701). Philo speaks often of the Word; the mention of its priestly role is taken from *On Dreams*, 1.215. The dialogue of Hermes and Tat is in *Corpus Hermeticum* 13 ("On Rebirth"). The prayer cited from *The Teaching of the Missionaries* (*Didache 10*) has often been translated; the text is at Niederwimmer 193. Passages quoted from Qumran include 4Q246 (The Son of God Fragment), 1Q20.18–25 (the Genesis Apocryphon, on Abraham), and 1QS.3.12ff (The Community Rule).

Scholars and students of the New Order will recognize many of the views taken in *The Four Witnesses;* they will know, too, how many other solutions have been proposed to the questions through which we have threaded our path. For I have traversed some of the most hotly disputed terrain in scholarship. To take just one example from each gospel: the history, structure, and role (within our witnesses' own work and in their churches' life) of Mark's ending, Matthew's "Wisdom," Luke's Mission (Acts), and John's opening hymn are all subjects of ongoing, fruitful scholarship. The reader will find such topics discussed in any good contemporary commentary on the gospels. I am glad to acknowledge how much this book owes on every page to the great scholars of the last hundred years. Just two examples from so many: Matthew's "Wisdom" was brought to prominence by M. J. Suggs, *Wisdom, Christology and Law in Matthew's Gospel*, 1970; John's use of trial motifs throughout the first half of his gospel is the theme of A. E. Harvey, *Jesus on Trial*, 1976.

Less familiar is the function that we have found the gospels share: they unveil truths normally kept from human view. The strategies, in turn, are rarely discussed with which our witnesses "open their readers' eyes." Commentaries will outline to readers a good many more traditional views on the gospels' function. But to assess *The Four Witnesses* as a whole, readers should turn first and foremost to our four witnesses themselves: to the gospels of Mark, Matthew, Luke, and John.

Preface

The Four Witnesses brings to fruition a plan I have nursed for ten years. At their start I was assistant minister in a public housing project in Liverpool. I expected to learn there of deprivation and hardship. I learned far more about the gospels. Parishioners who had never studied them—who had never studied any texts at all—knew better than I did the power of the stories they contained.

From Liverpool I moved to Oxford University to be chaplain at Lincoln College there. I had gone from one extreme to the other. My students were among the most knowledgeable and privileged young people in England. In Oxford I taught and wrote in the study occupied by John Wesley 250 years ago. Years before his journey to America, Wesley was a professor at Lincoln College. He started there a club that was mocked for its 'methodical' prayer. Within a century the Methodist Church would span the world.

But my students' eyes were not on the stories themselves. They were looking for "the historical Jesus." They would boil down the gospels' different stories into one: to dish up a single, digestible Jesus—and so would lose the flavor of these four wonderful courses. The gospels offer us a far more inviting, exciting, and nourishing meal than any such reduction can encourage us to look for. In *The Four Witnesses* that whole meal is here to be enjoyed.

The gospels claim to relay truths to which no words are really adequate. This book's readers will see how elusive the gospels' Jesus can be. How then are we to speak of him? At Lincoln I learned what our gospels' writers knew two thousand years ago: some truths that cannot be spoken can be "sung." The gospels resort to poetry; over and again we will watch our writers circle some deep, dark insight, looking for words and ways to do it justice. Most of us now take more readily to music. I am privileged to have moved to the Temple Church in London; we listen here, every Sunday, to one of the finest church choirs in the world.

Readers will see, then, more quickly than I did myself, how much *The Four Witnesses* owes to the life of my last ten years. This is a personal book. To almost every question raised here, a dozen other answers could be given; and in different settings, would be. If *The Four Witnesses* gives rise to discussion—and sometimes, no doubt, to different answers—I will be well pleased. It is such talks with those around me at Oxford, after all, that have hammered my ideas into the shape they hold now. To Chris Rowland, Oxford's Professor of the Interpretation of Holy Scripture, I owe more than he would ever claim; he has been an inspiring guide and the loyalest of friends. Dr. Jeremy Duff and Dr. Teresa Morgan have scrutinized most of the book; their many comments and suggestions have been invaluable. Claerwen Frost has emerged from Oxford's libraries with some intriguing references. And further afield: Without the support of Felicity Bryan, my British agent; David Kennard, the legendary public television producer with whom I am developing a docudrama TV series based on the book; and John Loudon, my editor at HarperSanFrancisco, the book would not have been written at all.

Thirty years ago, our church in Liverpool was new. Lincoln College, by contrast, was founded in 1427; it was already three hundred years old when John Wesley arrived. The Temple Church was built by the Crusaders, three centuries earlier still. From 1200 to 2000, I am heir to an ancient tradition in an ancient community that is inspired afresh, in every generation, to do justice to the gospels' extraordinary stories. The ideas explored in this book will be new to many readers. In some ways, however, they are the oldest ideas of all. In *The Four Witnesses* we hear the questions, so often forgotten, that faced the gospels' writers themselves. We hear, too, their answers. And, most important of all, we can experience for ourselves the strategies with which those writers brought readers to the same answers in their turn.

From one generation to the next, our community hands on its oldest insights to its youngest members. I dedicate this book to four children. I hope they will grow up to see in the gospels all that I treasure there, and more. David and Louisa, Honor and Ellie: Drawn from the first millennium's first years, here is my present to you and to your generation for these decades that open the third.

—Robin Griffith-Jones
New Year's Day 2000

Prologue

CHAPTER 1

The Four Greatest
Stories Ever Told

Welcome to *The Four Witnesses*. I hope you will enjoy reading this book as much as I have enjoyed writing it. Of one thing you can, I think, be confident: You are the sort of reader for whom I have been writing. For you know the book's title and theme, you have picked it up and looked inside. To have just that much interest in Jesus and the gospels—even if you have never opened the gospels themselves—is enough; it is the enjoyment of such readers as yourself that I have had in mind. You may in the past have found Jesus enthralling or frightening, comforting or simply bemusing. There are good grounds within the gospels themselves for every such response. You may know the story of Jesus like the back of your hand; you may know just its outline; or you may give it a thought only when Easter and Christmas come around. Jesus himself asked, *"Who do you say I am?"* If his question has ever intrigued you—if it has ever just caught your imagination—then this book has been written for you.

Matthew, Mark, Luke, and John: The names stand on the title pages of the gospels, four of the most influential books in the world. But who were these four writers? Where did they write and when? For whom? Here in these four short books, as the motto has it, is "The Greatest Story Ever Told." The description is familiar enough, but it is oddly misleading. The story told in each gospel is certainly as gripping and dramatic as any we could hope to hear. But the gospels give strikingly different versions of the same events.

"Who do you say I am?" Jesus himself poses the question. Each gospel offers its own answer. Here are four takes on the extraordinarily exciting and poignant story of Jesus, perhaps the most famous life ever lived on earth. Faced with four such versions, some readers have read just one gospel and left the others aside; others have looked for a summary that merges everything in the four accounts into a single biography; others again

have contrasted the different gospels' stories to see what single sequence of events and teaching, however meager, might underlie them all. But a further, more satisfying—and finally more exciting—possibility lies open: to take each one of the four stories on its own terms. Each portrays Jesus from a particular angle and with particular questions in mind. Some are questions to which the story of Jesus had already given rise within a few years of his death; others are questions—deep questions as vivid now as they were then—to which, so his followers thought, this Jesus offered the answer.

Confronted as readers with all four gospels, we might think of ourselves as detectives on a case. To understand and assess the depositions put before us, we need (as any such detective needs) to know who these witnesses are, what makes them tick, what are the needs and purposes of their own that shape the evidence they offer. In *The Four Witnesses* we will hear afresh the story of Jesus. We will hear, too, of the decades that gave rise to these four gospels. Rome burned, Jerusalem was destroyed, the church felt the first pains of persecution. In *The Four Witnesses* a whole empire comes before our eyes: from rural Galilee to Rome itself, greatest city of the ancient world; from Jewish fishermen to the Emperor. When the cast of this drama comes alive, so can the stories come alive that were written to encourage those who were living, thinking—and suffering—through these dangerous years.

The differences among our four witnesses do not lie just in details. Most telling are the distinctive flavor and shape of each gospel. Each gospel is remarkable in itself and is all the more striking when seen beside its neighbors. We need to look at them in turn. One of our most rewarding tactics will be to watch our authors edit the stories that they knew from those who had written before them. Each turns and shapes the stories to meet the needs of his own church. Readers need not be surprised, then, that we explore Mark's gospel before Matthew's. For Mark's gospel, it seems likely, was finished first, some thirty years after Jesus' death; here in *The Four Witnesses* we shall start with his evidence. Matthew and Luke both used Mark's testimony, as well as other sources, when writing their own. We introduce them next. Finally, John: He stands slightly apart. His community had developed a different style of storytelling; if he did have any of our other three gospels before him as he wrote, he remolded their stories freely.

Mark tells a dark story. All Europe and half of Asia Minor were in the power of Rome's emperor, backed by the most powerful army ever known and revered throughout his empire as a god. But there is another emperor: God himself. And Mark proclaims his viceroy: Jesus. Jesus had challenged the power of his own people's leaders, of demonic powers, of Rome itself and had been hung up on a cross to die. So much, it seems, for his claims and his kingdom. He dies, abandoned and in agony, with words of despair on his lips: *"My God, my God, why have you deserted me?"*

The leader had died, his pupils were scattered. Those young men had joined Jesus for the excitement and revolutionary purpose of this new master's way. How little they understood! They would follow him to the death, they said, and at the crucial moment they ran away. But this was not the end of the story. These pupils insisted that

Jesus was once more alive. Their conviction led them to bear brave witness to this extraordinary "Lord." Some paid dearly for their courage. The Greek word for *witnesses* has become part of the English language, referring to those whose testimony cost them their lives: the *martyrs*.

These followers of Jesus spread throughout the empire and took their message with them. Within twenty years of Jesus' death, they were in Rome. Here in the empire's capital is the setting for Mark's gospel.

The crisis that Jesus' pupils faced had to be faced again by Mark's young church. In 64 C.E. a fire swept through Rome. Arson was suspected, and the Christians were soon blamed. Jesus' warning echoed down the years: *"All those,"* he had said, *"who want to follow after me must take up their cross and follow me."* The Christians in Rome were rounded up, tortured, and killed. Where in these terrible days was the victory of Jesus, mysterious rival to the emperor's power? Jesus asked, *"Do you still not understand?"* Mark knows his readers need all they help they can get if they are to open their eyes and *see*.

Mark's story sounds simple enough. His storytelling is abrupt and unadorned; the Greek in which he writes is basic. We can still hear the accent of a story, once told in a different language and translated into Greek by missionaries, such perhaps as Mark himself, who would never be mistaken for its native speakers. But such translation was essential. Greek was a cosmopolitan language, the empire's lingua franca, in which the gospel must be heard if it was ever to spread. We first hear of the Jewish Mark as a young man at home in Jerusalem. We might imagine him writing his gospel, decades later, as an immigrant to Rome. He would have been based in the outskirts of the city. Most of Rome's Jews lived across the river Tiber from the city's center, engine of the empire and unparalleled in wealth and power, just as families from Europe in the twentieth century might live in Queens and cross the river to make their living in Manhattan. Such modern immigrants master English; it was just as important then for missionaries such as Mark to write in Greek.

Jesus had been an artisan in a distant province of the empire. His pupils had been country people. His movement, it seemed, had been nipped in the bud. Few grandees in Rome would have heard of his claims; fewer still, if any, acknowledged them. But the forces of Rome, claimed the church should take care. For Jesus' followers maintained allegiance to their master still. Those in Rome made little fuss; they worked in the city and may well have served its elite, as an army of manual and clerical workers serves Manhattan's businesses now. The followers of Jesus crossed the Tiber, as thousands of others, and gazed on the city's marble temples and on the mansions of nobles and of government from which its vast empire was run. But this handful of Jesus' devotees remained quite clear: The emperor to whom all Europe did obeisance was not the king in whose hand this empire really lay. These "Christians" might suffer for the fire of 64 C.E., but there was suffering far worse still in store for those who resisted the reign of God and his Anointed, his "Christ." In Mark's stern, stark story we hear a rebel speak.

Matthew has other cares in mind. His gospel was finished ten years after Mark's. Jesus had been Jewish. So is our Matthew. Here is a rabbinical writer, a master of rich, allusive stories that draw on the ancient themes of Judaism and interpret them afresh. Jesus and his followers were dividing the synagogues of Matthew's city over one question: Was this Jesus a prophet or a fraud? His followers were making heady claims. They prompted the synagogues' leaders to ask, Could such people with such an allegiance be members of the synagogue at all? Jesus' followers were wondering in their turn, should they be attending synagogue? And if not, where did those stand before God whose allegiance to the synagogues was still secure? There was uncertainty on both sides and an increasingly angry suspicion.

Our Matthew is a wise, experienced teacher. He is steeped in the Law [Torah] and traditions of Judaism and has been a leader of its people in Antioch, greatest city of Rome's Asian domains. But a moment of decision has been reached. *"Who,"* asked Jesus, *"do you say I am?"* Matthew's answer is leading him and all who follow his teaching away from the synagogues and into a community of their own: the church.

Matthew builds his gospel in careful sections of miracles and teaching; he offers his readers a new Book of the Law shaped on the Law received from Moses that Moses in turn had received from God. Matthew highlights prophecies and their fulfillment at every turn: Here in Jesus is the promised Immanuel, "With-Us-God." The Law itself, declares Matthew, with all that it foretold, has been brought to its innate conclusion by a stately, commanding Jesus whose standing puts even Moses' in the shade.

So who can this Jesus be, who *must* he be, to wield the extraordinary authority that his followers claim for him? Matthew draws an answer from Judaism that puts the break with Judaism beyond doubt: Jesus is indeed "God with us," here and now. *"All authority,"* says the risen Jesus, *"has been given to me in heaven and on earth. . . . And look, I am with you always, every day, until the aeon's completed end."*

Luke writes out of a different world. The relation of Jesus and his fellow Jews is close to Luke's heart, too, but he writes for the gentile powers that be, for the likes of *"Your Excellency Theophilus,"* to whom his gospel is addressed. The Roman Empire had history on its side: ever-increasing domains, peace at last within its borders, imperial control so "beneficent" that an emperor's birthday could be hailed as the "gospel" [good news] of a savior for the world.

Luke built history around the story of a different savior. Any "Theophilus" had good reason to be nervous of this Jesus' followers, famous for their fiery language of freedom and of a world turned upside down.

Luke's story spans two books: the gospel and its sequel, the Mission (traditionally known as the Acts of the Apostles), which tells of the tumultuous foundation of the church. The gospel opens in the Jerusalem temple; Jesus is yet to be born. The Mission ends decades after his death; the last scene shows his missionary Paul in Rome. This Jesus dies at the midway point of a larger story, with mercy for those around him and with confidence in God.

Once more, Rome: Luke sees here far more than just another city that the church has reached in its westward spread across the Mediterranean. The world had turned on its axis: from an old order to a new; from Jerusalem, ancient center of the Jewish world, to the new hub, Rome itself, capital of the emperors who, by Luke's time, had razed Jerusalem and its Temple to the ground. Luke chronicles the events of fifty years. But of one thing he is sure: The history of which he tells is like no other history ever told.

Within our Luke's horizon lies a huge cast of rich and poor, men and women, Jews and gentiles. He has the historian's eye for the great sweep of history and for its most telling detail. No wonder this gospel has been linked with Paul's companion, the physician Luke. The writer has the compassion of a doctor—so has his Jesus. This is the "revolution" that Luke's savior brings: of compassion offered to all those, whoever and wherever they may be, who acknowledge the place of Jesus and his church in God's plan.

These first three gospels have distinctive emphases but are clearly of a kind. John has cast his narrative into a quite different shape. Around just a few miracles, elaborately told, John builds long—and riddling—conversations between Jesus and his friends, his opponents and those whom he heals, feeds, and shocks. John is a mystic, a poet. He has an insight to convey that is almost too deep, too bewildering to speak of: The "Word" that God spoke in the life of Jesus is the same word with which God began all things at creation's start. For God *spoke:* "Let there be light." This was the "Word" that led to Adam and Eve, to the Garden of Eden and Adam's tasks there of tending the garden and naming God's creatures. And Jesus, claims John, was and is this very same Word, the perfect and total expression of God's will. How were John's readers to grasp such a claim? *"In God's truth I tell you,"* says his Jesus, *"unless people are born again from above, they cannot see the kingdom of God."* As the readers must undergo this rebirth, John himself sets out to induce it. With his story's long, riddling dialogues and set-piece miracles, John, in the boldest strategy of all, is to be the midwife of his readers.

This Jesus is in control throughout his suffering and death; they are his choice, made in obedience to his Father's will. And this is the same Jesus who weeps at the grave of his friend; his last moments on earth are spent commending his mother and his dearest friend to each other's care. At the moment of his death, he himself declares, *"It is completed."* That completion becomes clear as light rises on Easter morning. The reborn readers are shown the source of their rebirth: Mary sees the "gardener" and hears him speak her name. "Adam and Eve" are once more in Eden. All creation is restored.

"Who," asked Jesus, *"do you say I am?"* Our authors' answers differ widely; it is far from clear that they are consistent with one another at all. We are confronted, it seems, not with the one but with the four greatest stories ever told. We must dig deeper into the reasons for their distinctive emphases and for the differences among them. Our work as detectives is under way. We will above all be *listening,* to the stories that our

witnesses tell of Jesus, and to the way in which they tell them. For any witness, first and foremost, must be attentively heard. What is true of the stories we ourselves tell is true of the gospels' stories, too: To a careful listener, narrators reveal as much about themselves as about the "facts" of the stories they tell.

In *The Four Witnesses* we will probe the gospels one by one. You may well find one of them—from this summary or from your knowledge of the texts themselves—more intriguing or attractive than the rest. The books in which we present their testimony can be read in any order and one by one. There is a thread, of course, and in the long run you may wish to see its course, running through all four gospels and through this book itself. The last chapter is important, however much of the rest you read first time around. It is at the end of our search, when we have all four stories before us, that we can see what unites them, the engine that drives them all.

We will start, in chapter 2, by looking at some key moments in the week of Jesus' death. We see them in this opening section without the filters through which our authors themselves view and present them; we give space instead to the hopes and beliefs of Judaism that underlay the festival of which the gospels speak. A rapid survey then steers us, in the terms and order offered by Luke in the Mission (Acts), through the thirty years that divide Jesus' death from the completion of our first testimony: the gospel of Mark. This survey introduces some people and places that dominate our story of the church's early years: the great cities of Antioch and Ephesus, and the central figures of Simon Peter and his pupil Mark; Mark's cousin Barnabas, a mysterious Seer John who spoke of Rome's destruction; and above all, Paul, the fiercest opponent of the church who became its most famous missionary.

We will then address the gospels themselves, one by one, in the order in which they are likely to have been completed. Occasionally, we will turn aside to look more closely at the texts we have inherited from that mysterious Seer John and from Paul. The Seer wrote a Book of Unveiling, now the last book of the New Order and known as Revelation or the Apocalypse. From Paul we have a collection of letters: dense, fervent, and central to the church's history and beliefs. Paul may have had a deep and direct effect—in different ways—on both Matthew and Luke. And more important for our purpose, his own life casts light on a side to our witnesses that we could not otherwise hope to see. It is help of which we will make full use. For as we thread our path through the gospels themselves, we may well wonder whether our work as detectives will ever bear fruit. Our four witnesses seem so far apart. To Jesus' question each offers his own answer with conviction and urgency. But the four depositions diverge so widely that an aggressive attorney could discredit them all. It is Paul and the Seer who offer us the clue we need: the perspective from which we can see the four gospels' unity.

From the Seer we learn of *unveiling*: of the disclosure of truths so strange and elusive, as the Seer believes, that we are powerless without God's help to see them. From Paul we hear how central to his mission was *presence*: the presence of the missionary himself. For he was not relaying a doctrine to his churches; he was representing a person. These discoveries may seem remote from the gospels. But we shall find that the gospels, too, are designed to unveil a truth that their story—if wrongly heard—can easily and dangerously disguise. And these gospels, we shall see, were written not just to be the story of a person, but to be themselves that person's active presence in the church. It is in the last pages of the gospels that our four witnesses seem most drastically to differ; precisely here these extraordinary clues, offered all along by Paul and the Seer, can be seen for what they are—the key to our mystery. Only in the last chapter, as we present the stories of Easter, will the evidence before us fall into place at last.

Let us change our metaphor for a moment. Our four gospels, we might say, give us four portraits of one Jesus, painted by quite different artists from different schools of painting and with different viewers to inform and enthrall. To give depth to these paintings we provide in *The Four Witnesses* a setting for each gospel, a frame for each portrait.

We will look first, of course, for information about the artists themselves, the four individuals immortalized by the gospels that have reached us in their names. We always look more comfortably at a painting if a neighboring plaque declares the artist's name and dates and nationality. Our portraits of Jesus, however, are not signed. The four writers to whom they are ascribed are shadowy figures; they have left not a word of autobiography behind. We will pursue what slight records we have of four men with these names and what grounds for linking them with the gospels. This search presents an intriguing puzzle. The trail is faint. There are strange breaks in its path from our texts to any Mark, Matthew, Luke, and John of whom we know.

Our hunt, however, leads us to an unexpected clearing. We were looking for four individuals; what we find are four traditions, ongoing communities within and for whose members, over decades and even generations, these texts were compiled, re-edited, and brought to their final forms. To discover our witnesses is to discover the varied life of the church across half the Mediterranean and the most exciting, formative—and dangerous—decades of its early life.

We will still speak, in each case, of a controlling intelligence that has shaped the gospel; we will use *Mark, Matthew, Luke,* and *John* to speak of the texts' "authors" as well as of the texts themselves. For each gospel has a sustained, coherent character of its own: Mark's we can think of as distinctively "Markish," Matthew's as clearly "Matthean." This character is first and foremost revealed in the perspective from which each gospel was written: Here was that tradition at work, from master to pupil and to pupil's pupil, within which each gospel was shaped. But of each tradition we might well ask: Was there at one point a single genius, a teacher whose insight shaped his church's life for generations to come? Such a figure might have stood at the tradition's start, writing just months or years after Easter; he then would have stamped his wisdom on all that followed. Or he may have been the final editor of the text we have today; he would have inherited both the material on which he worked and (almost certainly) the style in which he worked on it, and then by an inspiration given to him alone, he would have enclosed its various stories in a compelling, overarching whole.

No depth of inquiry will uncover for certain four such single, identifiable writers. But their trace is scattered throughout these texts. To do them justice we must speak of them as individuals and by name. And it may well be that the church has remembered those names aright, in the titles by which their stories have been known for over eighteen hundred years, from the second century until now: the Gospels according to our four teachers, shadowy but unforgettable, Mark, Matthew, Luke, and John.

Our detective work is taking a new direction. We can now search the gospels for the varied contexts in and for which these four portraits were painted. There is more to be discovered on this search than we could ever have expected to find. We hear for ourselves the hopes and fears of those early communities—small, beleaguered groups on fire with commitment to their new life.

A painted portrait is rarely designed just to depict the sitter's appearance. For one thing, the artist must catch in paint the sitter's character. For another, the painting must be well suited to its intended setting and to the function it will serve there. The gospels, we might think, were intended simply to describe what actually happened. To do justice, however, to our four artists' skill, we must see how carefully each has caught the sitter's character and how boldly he has explored the function that his portrait could fulfill.

There is a wonderful story to be heard in our gospels, and their setting offers a glimpse of some unforgettable moments in the history of the West: Rome in flames, mad Nero watching the blaze, Jerusalem destroyed, dire civil war—and amid it all the gradual, inexorable spread of this new sect, the church. But there is more, too: There is the role that our authors intended their stories to fulfill. Description, we shall find, is not the half of it. *"Who do you say I am?"* Each gospel offers its own answer to Jesus' question and works with compelling skill to bring that same answer within its readers' grasp. Our own readers can watch those strategies at work and relish the care and courage with which they were pursued. And more: Some readers may find that our authors' strategies are still effective today, that we, too, can experience the mysterious discovery into which the gospels invited their readers nearly two thousand years ago.

To restore these portraits to their settings, to specify what is general and flesh out what is left unsaid, to discover how the stories functioned once and can function again—this is to set out on a detective's trail of the most exhilarating kind. Almost all the chief evidence is there before us, within the gospels themselves; it is for us to read this evidence correctly, to see what the gospels really have to tell us. The rest of the evidence we need is soon introduced from the history and scriptures of Judaism; here are ancient stories whose effect on later generations we will readily understand even if we may not feel it at work on ourselves. From these marvelous stories Jesus and his pupils inherited the language of their hopes: the language of slavery and freedom, exile and return, sacrifice and reconciliation.

We can then set out to make sense of our four differing testimonies, to see the stories at work in the communities for which they were written. On the way we will encounter individuals and cultures far more foreign than we had expected—and yet with hopes, fears, needs, and questions that we will recognize as our own. For the gospels are intrinsically civic. They speak of communities as important for their readers as our own are for ourselves. We rely upon the stability of our own communities, of their membership, rules, and public standing. Only when these are challenged, rivaled, and starting to shift do we realize how important they have always been—and how threatening their realignment can be.

We will be watching the birth pangs of a new community. This was an urgent, passionate—and often painful—business. New loyalties had to be forged and old loves foregone; the coordinates of members' lives had to be redrawn. In these birth pangs are history and biography and the echo of a rich, poetic world in which the ancient hopes of Judaism are recast.

Some readers will have mastered already the insights and trends of modern scholarship. They might wonder why in *The Four Witnesses* we take as point of entry the functions of our texts and the churches they were written to serve. Many books set out on the search for Jesus and glance in passing at such communities and roles. But to relish those roles, perhaps even to recreate them, is a far less familiar approach. It is well to explain, here at the start, the grounds for our procedure.

First and foremost, our witnesses wrote stories, and to hear their own concerns we must hear the stories as they wrote them. They reach us as four "clocks." Each has a mechanism unique to itself; each works perfectly. Many readers, looking for "the truth" about Jesus, have felt encouraged to take the clocks apart and itemize their cogs and bars. Chief victims of such a search are the clocks themselves: They do not work anymore. Each clock, in turn, was beautifully enclosed, in a case that could tell us much about its makers and the customers for whom they made it. These cases were the first parts of the clocks to be dismantled and put aside. There is much to be reassembled, much that is beautiful and finely crafted.

In *The Four Witnesses* we leave the clocks ticking. In this way the gospels can appeal once more to those who value them as literature. Our four narratives tell of the same life and largely of the same incidents within that life. But in the following pages we will see this apparently simple story put to powerful use in four quite different ways. Other authors might have found themselves constrained by the narrative, its conventions and its rigid shape. Our own writers, however, discovered possibilities of which we, their later readers, have almost completely lost sight. We do not look for such an achievement as theirs, and so we do not find it. It is time to bring that achievement back to light.

In each case we will watch carefully our own use of the gospels' testimony. We will be deducing a history from within the gospels of which the gospels themselves do not speak. Above all, we will be using the apparent success of this method to justify the premise on which it depends: that we can discover from the gospels the needs of the churches for whom they were written. This circular inquiry, on principle, is always open to question; and in its pursuit, different scholars find significance in quite different clues. Here lies a good part of the search's fascination. To reconstruct the church's life from the gospels is to walk through an enthralling hall of mirrors. Many historians have measured and assessed the mirrors' angles of reflection, and some have finally found that the "original" of their strange refracted image is neither Jesus' face nor the early church's, but their own. Our own search is no more immune to this danger than any other. In the course of *The Four Witnesses,* we will invite readers to assess for themselves how successfully we are weaving our way through the corridor of ever-shifting possibilities.

We will be speaking throughout of the gospels' own "readers": those whose benefit the authors had chiefly in mind. They are as elusive as the gospels' authors and more difficult to define. It is once more from the gospels themselves that we will be deducing those readers' priorities and concerns. But the gospels, as we are finding, evolved over decades; a generation grew old and died, the church spread, its circumstances changed, its insights matured. Further still: At any one time the story of Jesus—its details and significance—were well known to some in the church; others, we may suspect, needed basic instruction. We do not know in what different ways our different gospels were used in the daily and weekly routine of their churches' worship and members' lives. They might well have been composed for use over and again, year by year; we ourselves know well, from revisiting a book or film, how differently we hear a story when we hear it for a second or third time. To bear the readers in mind is to bring their gospels to life. But they are shadowy, composite figures, and we speak of them with hesitation and with care.

Readers of *The Four Witnesses* will find, I hope, ever more reason to enjoy the gospels as literature and as history. Our four "clocks," however, once had a function beyond both. They were built upon a shared conviction: that our ordinary ways of seeing the world are inadequate to the Jesus we are invited to meet. The gospels are designed (in four very different ways) to make possible their readers' understanding. The disclosure made in Jesus, according to our witnesses, is difficult, opaque, and easily misunderstood: A revelation, an unveiling, is under way—the self-disclosure of God—and our writers need the subtlest, most careful strategies to bring it within the readers' reach. For such disclosure, in that place and at that time, was offered very rarely and only to a privileged few; it involved strange visions and a "journey" (whether in body or mind) to heaven. Among the forms that such an unveiling would surely never take, one would think, was the life and death of an artisan killed by the enemies of Israel. To see what was there to be seen in this life was to be pried open to new and unimaginable insight.

Some readers of *The Four Witnesses* will enjoy these foundational stories of the Western world as literature that can fire our imagination as it did our forebears'. Others will be fascinated by the guidance we offer here back to the gospels' functions: we let each text work on the reader as it was intended to work on the members of a young and fragile church all those centuries ago.

As we listen like detectives to our four witnesses, we have good reason to be intrigued; we may well, at moments, be confused. Is there a single answer, underlying all four accounts, to the question that Jesus posed: *"Who do you say I am?"* It is, as noted above, in the stories of Easter, the closing pages of the gospels—and of *The Four Witnesses*—that our final, critical clue falls into place. It lies not in what the gospels tell us, but in the way they tell it: in the *sort* of story that we have been reading all along. We are not reading just history or a set of teachings. Our writers know we need help to understand what they are disclosing, and they offer us that help as we read. We will explore their different strategies one by one. For the moment, the most dramatic may speak for them all. John seeks to bring his readers to "rebirth." This is the only language in which he can do justice to his undertaking. His readers must be brought to new life; and John himself will be their midwife.

"To describe what actually happened." This seems to be so clearly the chief claim of the gospels. Why, then, do we focus in *The Four Witnesses* on quite different themes? And how can we claim that these other themes are more fundamental for understanding the gospels than the description of the events themselves?

Each generation is driven by interests of its own. For over a hundred years enormous attention has been given to the history of Jesus himself. Historians, thinkers, and preachers have all assessed the gospels for accuracy. Many have asked, can the gospels' accounts be taken as true? The integrity of Christian faith itself is seen to be at stake in the answer.

There is a danger in such a close focus on this object of our own search. We can lose sight of the evidence as a whole, of its own character. We see only a source for the satisfaction of our own inquiry and are blind to the inquiry—perhaps quite different— in which our authors themselves were engaged.

To rediscover these authors' concerns is still to work as historians ourselves—as historians of the early church and of the texts that it created, valued, and used. In the twentieth century this study was again conducted chiefly as archaeology: beneath the present texts lay their earlier editions, waiting to be brought to light. In *The Four Witnesses*, however, we treat the texts as the finished artifacts we have before us, and we ask, how did they function in their community, what was their use and usefulness? We will discover that our authors were working as hard as any modern historian but on a quite different set of questions. They were dedicated to telling the truth about Jesus, but they were convinced that this truth was not accessible to our ordinary ways of seeing and understanding. To put it most starkly: Any truth that a modern secular historian can ascribe to the history of Jesus is by its very nature not the truth that the gospels' own editors were chiefly concerned to relay. We can—and sometimes must—discuss the gospels' truthfulness on a modern historian's terms, and we must admit as we do so that we are setting aside the gospels' own. Or we can try to understand the gospels' terms and can undertake with these texts a strange and exciting journey into the deepest questions of all: What can we ultimately know about what matters most? And how can we come to know it?

The gospels did not invite the reader to hear their evidence and assess it but to be brought to a new understanding of its content, an understanding so alien to our ordinary ways of thinking and seeing that John could describe it only as rebirth. Our writers did not think that the events spoke for themselves. To believe that Jesus had miraculous powers was not in itself to believe that he was an agent of God's will; his power could have come from the devil. More important still, the gospels do not encourage their readers to depend on the evidence of such miracles. They are clues, no more; to dwell on the clues and miss the solution is wholly and disastrously to miss the point. The readers must be helped to see the solution and interpret the clues aright. For the solution is not one, our authors believe, to which anyone would come unaided and on their own.

We do not assume in *The Four Witnesses* that our authors were right in their views of Jesus himself or of the conditions under which we might understand him. Two readers could absorb every word in this book and still read the gospels in two quite different ways at its end. One could be heartened to see how deep is the mystery of God and how extraordinary its disclosure. The second, by contrast, could be intrigued by the literary techniques with which our gospels hope to change their readers' view of the world and of Jesus.

Where, then, does this book stand to the battles still waged over the historical Jesus? Several camps are entrenched in these disputes. Readers will sometimes wonder if the protagonists have a broader, deeper agenda than any "simple" openness to the text and its evidence. There is much at stake, after all, and scholars quite rightly defend the theological positions whose importance, to themselves and to the church, they know well. New ammunition may be brought to bear by one side—new evidence uncovered, a new method of historical inquiry developed—and will be quickly deployed to contrasting effect by the others. These battles are vigorous and enthralling. I will be glad if *The Four Witnesses* can be useful to their combatants and, in particular, to the general readers who follow their progress. Such readers might well want to read *The Four Witnesses* first and so to see, at the start of their inquiry, what *sort* of books these gospels are that will be quarried for information in all their later reading.

Our chief aim, however, is not to provide more ammunition for those battles. It is to offer the reader a sight of their terrain from a quite different viewpoint, one long neglected and all the more exhilarating and fresher for that. This is not to be naive. We have set to one side the twentieth century's concern for the history of Jesus. Some readers will suspect (perhaps rightly) that we have replaced it with a concern, even more modern, for the character of knowledge and understanding. Have we discovered in the gospels (with questionable ease) just what we were looking for? Readers must decide, and after reading *The Four Witnesses* and the gospels themselves they will be well placed to do so. For this book is written to draw its readers not toward disputes discussed for decades but toward the four stories that lie at their base: the gospels themselves.

In *The Four Witnesses* the artillery of the old battles will for a while fall silent. The old slogans will be set aside, old trenches abandoned. It is time to take in some fresh vistas and fresh air. And in the quiet we will open our ears and hear the gospels speak.

Better still: We will hear them sing.

To write a book about the gospels is to be highly selective. On every page I have made claims, familiar to scholars, that other scholars would contest on grounds that students of the gospels know well. Every line of thought, in turn, could have been supported or broadened with further fascinating evidence. To do justice to these other routes is the task of a second book. More important than such details, however, is the overarching direction of *The Four Witnesses* itself: away from disputes that raged throughout the twentieth century and toward a new reading of the texts with new questions in mind. There is nothing arbitrary in this fresh approach. It grows from the gospels themselves, for it puts at the heart of our reading the questions that lay at the heart of our authors' endeavor. These questions may seem, at first sight, to be oddly distant from our own concerns. But we shall find our authors and their readers to be much like ourselves. These witnesses confront us with a strange, alien figure because they themselves found him unsettling and mysterious. Each one of the gospels, in its own distinctive way, is written to help us crack the code, to see the world in a way in which we have never seen it before and so to be able to answer for ourselves the question that Jesus posed, *"Who do you say I am?"*

I will be picking our evidence from two continents and several centuries. I do so with great caution. We certainly cannot assume that a single set of priorities, hopes, and outlooks were shared so widely or settled for so long. To take a modern comparison: It would be a bold historian who drew on Shakespeare in the sixteenth century to explain the Second World War in the twentieth. You may want to watch carefully for the quiet warnings in the following pages: that some view, for instance, is known only from later rabbis or thinkers and not from our authors' day or from Jesus' own; that it is recorded in Greece, Italy, or Egypt and not in Palestine itself. One such warning needs such frequent repetition that it is best stated here at the outset: Almost all the evidence on which we call is in writing; it relays the views of literate and literary people, passionate about these themes and committed to their own views' circulation. We cannot assume that these writers were typical of their age.

To read the gospels is to come across a world of words and phrases that we hardly encounter now outside the Bible and the church that treasures it. The gospels were written in simple Greek nearly two thousand years ago. Their early translations into English have bequeathed us distinctive words. *Disciple, spirit, testament, covenant:* these faithfully translated from their Greek originals, but they have now an archaic, churchy sound quite foreign to our authors' everyday Greek words. Wherever possible, I will use words for the central features of the story as ordinary in English now as the Greek originals were then. A *disciple* is a pupil. A *spirit* is a breath or wind. *Spirit* had been linked, by great thinkers and in popular thought alike, with the life that air makes possible and that lasts as long as breath. Long before Jesus, that "life" had come to seem as independent as the air is of ourselves, the individuals who for our brief lives have a share in it. We are mortal; not so, on such a view, the "Breath" that gives us life.

Two further examples call for explanation here. We will encounter them over and again. First: The Old Testament was the later church's name for the collection of books that formed and forms the Bible of the Jews. We will write of this collection as the Old Order, for it defined the promises of God that the church would call by the same name: the Old Order (or Old Covenant) between God and his people Israel. In Jesus his followers saw the launch of a New Covenant whose promises have reached us in the New Order (or New Testament). Within the Old Order are books of history, prophecy, and psalms. Among those on which we will most frequently draw are the Beginning (the English translation of its Greek name, Genesis), the Escape (Exodus), and the Second Law (Deuteronomy).

And second: *The Christ* (*mashiach,* Messiah in Hebrew) means "the Anointed One" or "Sprinkled"; an outsider would have found the double name "Jesus Christ" as odd a term as we would find "Jesus Anointed" today. As with these terms, so with others: The freight that a word carries today may be quite different from that borne by its Greek equivalent two thousand years ago.

Few words can be translated at every use into just one single word of another language. We will have to turn occasionally to other terms. The *faith* of which the gospels speak has nuances of belief, trust, and faithfulness. By the time the gospels were written the word was at the center of their readers' life; such readers did not need the explanation of *faith* that many of us would be glad to have today. The most elusive of such terms is a single word traditionally translated as *Lord.* It was used to speak both of God as "the Lord" and of earthly masters, and could be used in speech to address God, a master, or simply a stranger to whom the speaker was showing respect, as we might say "sir." Within the early church it was a favored title for the risen Jesus. We might wonder what nuance our authors are sounding when they use this word within their story of the Jesus who had not yet died. Luke, in particular, enjoys its resonance. The more he speaks of that Jesus as the Lord, the more clearly he forecloses any false distinction: "Jesus then" cannot be split apart from "Jesus now." The church has always wondered, how does Jesus stand now to "the Lord" of the Old Order, God himself? And how did he then, when he lived on earth? Luke's readers are already confronted with the question in this one rich, resonant term: *the Lord* (*adonai* in Hebrew).

We have already heard how little we know about these four figures, Mark, Matthew, Luke, and John, to whom our gospels are ascribed. We will be teasing out such evidence as we have about them when we tell the story of their gospels. The most basic elements of the texts themselves, meanwhile, have more to tell us of their authors than we might expect. All writers leave clues in their style to their background, education, and self-presentation. Does each of our gospels have such a voice of its own?

Indeed it does. The gospels are written in four distinct and distinctive styles of Greek. We must be wary of the standard "translationese" that we read in most modern versions; it can deny us just the evidence we need to place our writers in their social and national orbits. Some of these features are readily captured in translation; others can be reproduced only in a stilted, unnatural English that does no justice to our originals. These stylistic traits are best seen here at the outset by a straightforward comparison among the different gospels.

Some contrasts are quickly seen. In Mark's vivid narrative some readers have thought we can hear echoes of Peter's speech. The Greek is simple and direct; the range of words is narrow; the sentences and episodes follow (it seems) like the pearls of a necklace, one after another, with no more connection between them than the thread along which they are strung. The gospels are written in Greek. But two other languages are at issue: Hebrew, the language of the Old Order, and Aramaic, the Semitic language related to Hebrew that was widespread in Israel in Jesus' day. It has long been thought that Mark's Greek has traces of an Aramaic accent. This need cause no surprise. The stories of Jesus would have been told first in Aramaic; at some stage in the thirty years between Jesus' death and our gospel's completion, the stories were translated into Greek—and without the literary skill that would have spotted and smoothed out the foreign rhythms and idioms that remain.

An ancient tradition, as we shall see, claims that Matthew wrote his gospel in Aramaic. Our present text is unlikely to be a translation of that long-lost original; much of Matthew's story, after all, appears to be drawn directly from Mark's Greek. Might our present Gospel According to Matthew, then, be an expanded and revised translation of such an "Aramaic Matthew"? A copy of that Aramaic gospel is said to have survived long after our present gospel was in circulation; it was seen in the fourth century by one of the church's greatest scholars, who believed it to be a version of Matthew. His accounts of the text are muddling, but could he have mistaken its relation to the finished gospel that he knew so well?

The mystery of the Aramaic Matthew remains unsolved, and perhaps it always will. But we will refer over and again in the following pages to two great caches of ancient texts, lost in the deserts of Israel (the Dead Sea Scrolls found at Qumran) and of Egypt (the Gnostic and other texts found at Nag Hammadi) for over eighteen hundred years. Their discovery in the twentieth century changed our whole understanding of Jesus' times and of his early followers. The day may yet come when another shepherd in the desert comes across another store of jars hidden in a day of danger, hundreds of years ago, and among the treasures stored there, the most exciting of all may be a copy of this elusive, long-lost gospel.

Mark's seems such a simple narrative, written, we might think, by and for people who looked for nothing more than the bare bones of the story. But the closer we look, the richer and more subtle this story becomes. A fascinating question arises: How much sophistication can we expect to find—and how much of our supposed discovery might be illusory, a mere will-o'-the-wisp—in this blunt, basic text? The question becomes more intriguing still when we turn it around: How much depth did Mark see within his simple story? And how much was he determined to convey, accessible and unadorned, in a form that any reader could grasp who could read or listen at all? Mark does not pander to the educated elite. No salon in Rome would be proud to house this crude, rustic text. For a rebel is writing, one who will have his readers put away their airs and graces and hear a story where all readers are on one level before their enigmatic "king."

Luke speaks in quite different terms and to quite different readers. Here is an author of self-conscious stylishness. His measured prose is aimed at a man of letters. The church may already have seemed a preserve of the ill educated and naive; Luke's addressee, Theophilus, would have more time and respect for the claims of a well-turned text. We might think of Luke as a skilled mimic: He opens his gospel in gracious, complex Greek; he soon turns to poetic words and rhythms familiar from the Old Order's Greek translation; he then settles down to a simple but well-wrought story. Here, then, are Luke's opening verses. He uses them to set the tone of his whole gospel with a sophisticated flourish.

Inasmuch as many have set their hands to ordering a narrative of the matters brought to their fulfillment among us, just as those have handed them down who were from the beginning eyewitnesses and ministers of the word, so I have decided in my turn, having followed the whole story from the outset accurately and in the right order to write to you, Theophilus, so that Your Excellency may learn, of the teachings about which you have been informed, that they are well founded.

(LUKE 1.1–4)

So much for Luke's self-introduction. Now comes the story of Jesus' birth. The account includes two great songs of praise. Luke draws freely on the Old Order. We do well to hear Mary's song in the famous sixteenth-century King James Version, which rings for us today, better than any other, with the dignity and poetry of Luke's Greek:

My soul doth magnify the Lord, and my spirit hath rejoiced in God my Savior.
For he hath regarded the lowliness of his handmaiden.
For, behold, from henceforth all generations shall call me blessed.
For he that is mighty hath magnified me; and holy is his name.
And his mercy is on them that fear him throughout all generations.
He hath showed strength with his arm; he hath scattered the proud in the imagination of their hearts.
He hath put down the mighty from their seats, and hath exalted the humble and the meek.
He hath filled the hungry with good things, and the rich he hath sent empty away.
He remembering his mercy hath holpen his servant Israel, as he promised to our forefathers,
Abraham and his seed forever.

(LUKE 1.46–55)

Where Luke has Mark's own text in front of him, he works steadily to enhance the other's almost clumsy account (I use my own translation here, as throughout the rest of the book, unless otherwise indicated, in order to reveal the distinct voices of the gospels):

And getting up early, in the dark—very early—Jesus came out and came away to a lonely place and there started praying. And Simon and those with him, he hunted him out and they found him and say to him, "Everyone is looking for you." And he says to them, "Let's go elsewhere, to the towns round about, so I can preach there, too; for to this end have I come out."

(MARK 1.35–38)

Coming out when it was day, Jesus left for a lonely place. And the crowds started searching for him and came up to him and held him back from leaving them. But he said unto them, "To the other cities, too, must I proclaim the good news of the kingdom of God; because to this end have I been sent out."

(LUKE 4.42–43)

More is at stake when Luke is actively shaping his narrative. In this next passage Jesus sets out on the journey that will take him to his death. Mark is not concerned to flag its importance; on his narrative goes. Luke's language stresses—and interprets—this turning point in the drama. Again he turns to the Greek Old Order and draws on its literary language:

And moving on from there he comes to the borders of Judaea beyond the Jordan.

(MARK 10.1)

Now it happened in the fulfillment of the days for his being taken up that he set his face firmly to go to Jerusalem.

(LUKE 9.51)

We have seen how carefully Luke crafts his introduction. So do our other authors, in their typically different ways. Mark's story hits the ground running: ancient words of promise are blossoming into fulfillment here and now. To our ears, Matthew has perhaps the most striking start of all: He lists Jesus' ancestors. We do not find the dramatic sense we expect in an author. Matthew, methodical from the start, anchors Jesus in the lineage that God's Anointed needs. John draws us, as we might expect, into a different world. He opens with a hymn; poetry is needed to say what must be said, and an attitude of awe.

In each case these first lines position the reader to hear all that follows in the appropriate way. The styles of reading required are closely linked with the style of Greek that evokes them. Here is John's opening:

In the beginning was the Word,
and the Word was with God, one-to-one,
and the Word was God.
He was in the beginning with God.

(JOHN 1.1)

John's Greek, like Mark's, has a Semitic flavor; here Hebrew has been as strong an influence as Aramaic. The Greek that results is rhythmic and simple. To our surprise, perhaps, this can make John the hardest of our four witnesses to read. He often lacks the small connecting words that characterize Greek and that would guide the reader through the line of thought: *and, but, for, next, therefore*. John's Jesus speaks, to pupils and opponents alike, in long speeches of short, loosely connected sentences. He can seem rambling and repetitive. In this example, we will indent the lines into which John's words can be divided. This will clarify his Jesus' distinctively spiraling argument.

"On that day," said Jesus, "you will know that I am in my father and you in me and I in you."

Here the movement begins:

"All who hold to my commands and keep them, those are the ones who love me;
*   and the ones who love me shall be loved by my father,*
*   and I shall love them and shall show myself to them."*

Judas—not Judas Iscariot—asked him, "Lord, what has happened, that you intend to show yourself to us and not to the world?"

Jesus rephrases his promise:

"All who love me shall keep my word,
*   and my father shall love them*
*   and we shall come to them and make a home with them.*
All who do not love me do not keep my words."

He now returns to his starting point:

"And the word that you hear is not my own;
it is the word of the father who sent me."

(JOHN 14.20–24)

A good many of the differences in our authors' language, rhythm, and style can be brought out in English; we will hear them clearly in the pages to come. Our four gospels form a quartet of different instruments, each of whose characters and timbres are brought out precisely by the contrast with its neighbors'. Only when we hear all four together can we gauge the beauty and resonance of each. In this extraordinary quartet we are offered not the one but "The Four Greatest Stories Ever Told."

CHAPTER 2

Joy of Man's Desiring:
Jerusalem and Jesus

Jesus and Israel

In the chapters that follow we will be listening to four sets of variations on a single theme, in different keys with different instruments. Each is composed on a grand, orchestral scale, for the theme itself is already richer than most symphonies can claim. The history of Jesus is not the story of a single figure over his life's thirty years, surrounded by just a few friends, crowds, and enemies. His history grew from and was part of the story of his nation as a whole. To understand the terms in which this Jesus spoke is to trace the longings, hopes, and fears whose evolution spanned all Israel's history. They had found elaborate expression, in the centuries before Jesus, in the histories, prophecies, prayers, songs, and poems of the Old Order. Its motifs were treasured in his own day and developed further still. For the promises and demands of God, laid down in the Old Order, defined all that his people was and hoped to be. If we would understand the variations sounded by our witnesses, we do well first to hear their orchestra play, as clearly as possible, the exhilarating theme.

This chapter, then, offers an introductory overture that stands back from the gospels themselves and, where possible, stands behind them. We will witness three scenes and hear a final survey. In each scene we listen to the hopes that fired Jesus' life, his pupils', and our writers' too. These hopes were developed, of course, perhaps even transformed, by Jesus himself, by his first pupils, and by the churches of our own four witnesses. But here in the "musical" language that was shared by them all are the motifs beneath the dazzling variations that our four gospels play.

The Key to the Story: Jesus Confronts Jerusalem

The first scene evokes the morning sacrifice undertaken every day in the Temple in Jerusalem. Such rites are alien to us now. Before the end of the first century C.E., the Temple would be destroyed by the Roman army. It has never been rebuilt. But in this tradition of the Temple and its sacrifice lies a key to our gospels that we will finally be ready to turn in the final chapter of this book. For at issue in this sacrifice was not mere ritual. God had commanded that this offering be made, morning and evening, every single day. At stake was far more than just Israel's own concerns and hopes. On this obedience to the creator's will his whole creation's order could be thought to depend.

From the sacrifice at dawn, silent and solemn, to the noisy, crowded celebration of a festival. In the days before Passover, pilgrims flocked to Jerusalem: The city of twenty-five thousand residents might house three hundred thousand when Passover began. Here was a time of remembrance and thanksgiving, of celebration and of hope. It is no surprise that among the crowds, around 30 C.E., was the mysterious prophet Jesus with his entourage. But what role was he to play in the festival? Those around him on their pilgrimage, the authorities and the Roman garrison, and anyone who had heard of him had good reason to wonder. For Jesus spoke of God's kingdom, and Passover was the time, in popular expectation, for God's Anointed agent to appear, to rescue Israel from its enemies and to institute God's open, undisputed reign.

In our third scene we hear of the terrible end to which such hopes could be reduced. Jesus lived under the power of Rome, and there was no place in its empire for any rival to its rule. In a familiar procedure three convicts were taken out of Jerusalem to a hill used over and again for executions. They were hung up on crosses to die, as painfully, slowly, and visibly as possible. Each convict would carry a placard declaring the charge against him. Such a placard was hung up, we are told, above one convict's head to mock his claims and his followers' credulity. Here was a warning to all passersby not to defy the power of Rome: *Jesus of Nazareth, the king of the Jews.*

Surely this was the end of Jesus' movement. He was only one of several such leaders who seemed to look for Israel's future in its glorious but long-vanished past. His inspirational hopes should have been as doomed to disappointment as the others'. In an extraordinary twist, however, this one movement survived. And more than survived. Around 30 C.E. Jesus died an ignominious death; his followers had scattered in fear. By 60 C.E. those same followers had won adherents to Jesus' cause in cities throughout the eastern Mediterranean and in the empire's capital, Rome itself. Persecution, indifference, mockery—nothing, it seemed, could stop the spreading allegiance to this unlikely hero. From Jesus' crucifixion to a faith with adherents in all the major cities of the Roman Empire—and all within thirty years.

In *The Four Witnesses* our chief concern is with those later years when our gospels are coming to completion. We know far more about them (largely thanks to the evidence of the gospels themselves) than we do about the intervening decades, from Jesus' death to 60 C.E. But one narrative survives of those earliest years, in the second part of Luke's work, the Mission (Acts). To end this chapter we follow a few of the threads with which Luke links Jesus' pupils to his own generation, when Peter and Paul have been killed, the young Mark has grown old, and the moment is clearly approaching when the last of Jesus' own pupils and eyewitnesses will die. The memories of those first followers must be preserved; the church's story and teaching must be enshrined in writing. And in Luke's generation it was—in the four gospels that we can still read today after two thousand turbulent years.

Jerusalem, 30 C.E.: The Daily Offering

The Temple in Jerusalem, just days before Passover. The priests were gathering in the early morning for the daily sacrifice. It was still dark; the teeming city was not yet awake.

"Whoever swears by the temple," said Jesus, *"swears by him who lives in it"* (Matthew 23.21). The Temple was the house of God. Its buildings covered thirty-five acres on a vast plateau, largely manmade, at the eastern edge of Jerusalem. Its heart was the Holy of Holies, a chamber entered just once a year on the Day of Atonement by the high priest alone. Anteroom to the Holy of Holies, and divided from it by a veil, was the chamber in which the altar of incense was kept. This was entered by the officiating priests twice daily for the rites of the morning and evening sacrifice. As we shall see throughout *The Four Witnesses,* to approach closer to God's presence than was proper or permitted was to risk death.

Out through a farther veil, enormous and famously beautiful, woven with a panorama of the heavens in scarlet, purple, and blue, were twelve steps down to the Courtyard of the Priests. None but priests were admitted. Here was the great altar, built of stone, forty-eight feet square at its base and rising nine feet from the courtyard itself. The sacrificial animals were killed in this courtyard, to the north of the altar; a ramp on the altar's opposite side led up from the courtyard to the altar's flat top where the fire was always alight, and those parts of the animals were burned that were consigned to God himself.

Beyond a parapet, and on the same level as the Courtyard of the Priests, was the courtyard reserved for other Jewish males. This whole central area was surrounded by outbuildings and a wall. The next courtyard out and eastward from the center was for Jewish women; balconies on the wall dividing their court from the men's allowed them to watch the sacrifices from above. Gentiles were allowed only in the farther great courtyard to the south, a vast open area in which birds were sold for sacrifice, animals checked, and money changed. This lay twenty feet lower than the altar's area, down two more flights of steps and out beyond a balustrade, four feet high. It gave due warning: "No gentile is to enter within the next courtyard and the balustrade around the sanctuary. Whoever is caught will have himself to blame for his subsequent death."

The Temple was guarded overnight by young priests who slept there. At cockcrow an officer arrived to supervise their morning's work. One priest, by the light of the altar fire alone, went to the altar itself to clear the night's cinders. Half-burned limbs would be raked aside and reburned during the morning. The warm smell of wood smoke and of roasted flesh would never leave the area. The altar fire was set.

The priests kept watch for daybreak. The cry came: "The whole east is alight." A lamb was brought out from the sheds and the ninety-three sacred tools from their storeroom beside the sanctuary. The design and function of the old Temple's every room and utensil, according to the Old Order, was inherited centuries before by King Solomon from his father, David, and by David from the hand of God. The great gate of the Temple was opened; the early morning worshipers could enter. But there was nothing raucous here; we are told (by an author clearly awed at the Temple's rites) that the sacrifices were conducted in uncanny, reverential silence.

The gate's sound was the signal: the lamb was to be killed. Its throat was cut and the blood allowed to flow. *For the life of the flesh*, reads the Old Order, *is in the blood; and I have given it for you upon the altar to make reparation for yourselves; for it is the blood that makes reparation, by reason of the life* (Laws of Ritual [Leviticus] 17.11). The stain and smell of blood contrasted with the priests' linen clothes and brightly colored sashes. The lamb's carcass was divided among six priests; they took its parts, still moist, around the altar and laid them on the ramp leading up from the south. A seventh took the offering of baked cakes offered in the name of the high priest. On a feast day the high priest would carry it himself.

We have a poetic description of Simeon, the high priest, at this daily service, written around 175 B.C.E. by Jesus, the son of Eleazer, the son of Sira, known as Ben Sira or "Sira's Son." Its tone is telling: There is reverence in this account, a solemnity that we do well to hear as we encounter rites so strange to ourselves. If we are ever to capture the tone of the Temple's worship, it will be through the verses of Sira's Son. We may well wonder if all priests and all worshipers shared his sensibilities, but his is not the only account to evoke such solemnity and see such significance in the rite. As we follow the ritual's course, we will hear the lines of Sira's Son as commentary. And more: The author's own grandson translated the poem into Greek; the importance that the original saw in the service and its priest was raised to a pitch higher still in this second version.

The high priest, wrote Sira's Son, was

like a star of light from among clouds,
and like the full moon in the days of festival;
and like the sun shining resplendently on the king's temple,
and like the rainbow of God's order that appears in the cloud.

(WISDOM OF SIRA'S SON [BEN SIRA] 50.6)

The language is highly charged. The sun and moon give light to God's creation; after the Great Flood a rainbow confirmed his promise never to destroy it. In the high priest's presence and actions, God's commitment to his creation is made clear. But there was more still. Sira's Son had devoted the first part of his poem to the praise of God's own Wisdom, with which God had created and forever ordered the world. This Wisdom had described herself in some of the poem's most evocative lines:

I have grown as tall as a cypress on Mount Hermon,
as tall as the roses of Jericho;
as a fine olive tree in the plain.

(WISDOM OF SIRA'S SON [BEN SIRA] 24.10)

Here at the poem's end in this account of the morning sacrifice we shall hear the language of Wisdom afresh when the poet describes the high priest at the altar. For in the enactment of this ritual itself, the whole order of creation was made secure.

The sun was rising. The Temple's sanctuary—the Holy of Holies and the outer chamber—faced east; its façade, one hundred fifty feet high and wide, was covered with gold. Its top was already caught by the light and blazed in the early sun.

An officer gave the command: "Recite a blessing." And the priests said, in the famous words of the Old Order,

Hear, O Israel,
the Lord our God is one Lord;
and you shall love the Lord your God with your whole heart,
with your whole being, and with your whole strength.

And when the Lord has brought you into the land
which he swore to your fathers that he would give you,
then do not forget the Lord,
who brought you out of the land of Egypt, from the house of slavery.

(SECOND LAW [DEUTERONOMY] 6.4–9)

There followed the offering of incense, the most solemn moment of the service. To a small altar in the outer chamber two priests brought coals and incense. Once all was prepared, the officer would give the command. On a feast day the high priest himself was likely to officiate: "My Lord High Priest, offer the incense!"

In this offering is one source for the next description from Sira's Son: Simeon himself, the high priest, he writes,

was like the fire of incense upon the offering,
like a green olive tree full of berries,
when he covered himself with the garments of glory.

This account of the high priest is already carefully phrased. The grandson and translator of Sira's Son saw clearly what his grandfather had been sketching. He elaborates the description of the high priest himself: The high priest was like a cluster of roses (adds the grandson's Greek) on new-moon days, like a cypress exalted in the clouds. The grandson ensures that the central point is not missed: The high priest at his service represented the active, ordering Wisdom of God himself.

The sacrificed lamb was now burned. The high priest was led up the altar ramp by a prefect. The limbs were handed to him one by one; he threw them onto the fire. Says Sira's Son,

> When the high priest went up to the altar there was majesty,
> when he received the portions from the hands of his brothers,
> until [adds the grandson] the arrangement of the Lord was completed,
> and they had perfectly finished his service.
>
> (WISDOM OF BEN SIRA [SIRA'S SON] 50.19)

Yet again the poet's grandson and editor deepens the connection with God's own work at creation. He knew well the Greek translation of the Beginning (Genesis), first book of the Old Order: *And the heaven and earth were completed,* he read there, *and all their arrangement* (Beginning [Genesis] 2.1).

In the east, the morning sun; in the Courtyard of the Priests, the altar fire; its backdrop, the glittering façade of the sanctuary. As the day began, the lifeblood of a lamb was poured out on the ground; the creator of the "cosmos," of the "arrangement" of all things, was acknowledged, and the whole lamb was consigned to the fire for his praise.

The city was waking. It was time in the Temple, too, for the people's silence to be broken.

The high priest processed around the altar and prepared to pour out the drink offering of wine. Two priests blew a long blast, a quavering blast, and another long blast on the trumpets. They came and stood by the chief musician. As the high priest poured out the wine, the chief musician clashed the cymbals, the attendants broke into singing. When they reached a break in the singing they sounded the trumpets and the people bowed down in worship. At every break in the singing there was a blast of the trumpet, and at every blast the people bowed down.

> Then the priests sounded forth [writes Sira's Son,]
> on trumpets of turned metalwork.
> All the people of the land gave a ringing shout of joy
> in prayer before the Merciful One.
> Then he went down and lifted up his hands over the whole congregation of Israel:
> and the blessing of the Lord was on his lips.
>
> (WISDOM OF BEN SIRA [SIRA'S SON] 50.16–20)

The high priest gave the blessing from the Old Order:

> *The Lord bless you and keep you,*
> *the Lord make his face to shine upon you and be gracious to you;*
> *the Lord lift up his face upon you and give you peace.*
>
> *(CENSUS [NUMBERS] 6.24–26)*

The description of this service recorded by later rabbis here comes to its end: "This was the rite of the daily Sacrifice of a Whole Animal in the service of the House of our God. May it be his will that it shall be built up again, speedily, in our days. Amen."

The rabbis looked forward to seeing the Temple rebuilt and its worship restored. More than just Israel and its offering was at stake. The high priest embodied the Wisdom that had ordered the world. His service represented that whole world's order and guaranteed its stability and completion. Just as the high priest burned incense at the daily service, so, says Wisdom in the poem of Sira's Son,

I, Wisdom, have breathed out a scent like choice myrrh,
like galbanum and stacte,
like the smoke of incense in the holy Shelter.
(WISDOM OF BEN SIRA [SIRA'S SON] 24.15)

Little wonder that the daily service was believed to predate the Temple's construction. To do justice to the service, Jewish tradition turned to the beginning of all human life: to the Garden of Eden. The incense offered by the high priest had been offered, tradition would have it, from the very day that Adam was expelled from Eden. From that day, we are told, Adam offered a sweet-smelling sacrifice—frankincense, galbanum, stacte, and spices—in the morning with the rising of the sun. Here is the status of the high priest at work. Sira's Son sees in his action a shadow of that most solemn rite when humankind first sacrificed to God:

Above every living thing is the beauty of Adam;
greatest of his brothers and the beauty of his people
was Simeon the high priest.
(WISDOM OF BEN SIRA [SIRA'S SON] 49.16–50.1)

The sun is high in the sky. The bustle of the day has begun. On the day to which we now turn, that bustle and activity would have been even greater than usual, for Passover was drawing near. Pilgrims were nearing the city from far and wide. And among them, rumor had it, was the "prophet" that had caused such stir up north in Galilee. He spoke himself of the Kingdom of God. Some of his followers, we may suspect, sooner spoke of the rule to be given to their leader himself: Jesus of Nazareth.

Jerusalem, 30 C.E.: Before the Festival of Passover

There was excitement in the air. Yet another group of pilgrims—men, women, and children—surged through the gates into the city. In inns, in synagogues providing for particular groups, in homes with rooms to spare—wherever there was space, clusters gathered of pilgrim families in festive, holiday mood.

Whole neighborhoods traveled together; new friends were made and partied with old. Jerusalem was the center of the Jewish world; its Temple was the center's center. The Jews were dispersed to all corners of the Mediterranean, but here they were seen to be what they really were: a single nation united in its ancient capital by ancient laws. Celebration and solemnity were mixed together, and their high point would be the evening that started Passover itself, when the newly killed lambs would be roasted and every Jew in Jerusalem, man and woman, young and old, would have a share in the feast.

At Passover, centuries before, God had freed the Jews from slavery in Egypt; on that night began their trek to Israel, the Promised Land. As before, so again: At Passover, it was said, God would once more free his people. There was more to be celebrated than an ancient victory. "In every generation," the people were urged, "a man must think as if he came out of Egypt himself. For it is written, *You shall tell your son in that day: 'We do this because of what the Lord did for me when I came out of Egypt'*" (Escape [Exodus] 13.8).

That freedom won by Moses, the Jews' greatest general, had long since been lost. The Promised Land to which he and Joshua, his successor, had led them had seen war after war, conquest after conquest. Now the Romans held sway. Judaea was just a minor province of the largest empire the West had ever seen. Its governor's modest rank reveals its character in Rome's eyes: "Knights" such as Pontius Pilate generally ran the barbarous fringes of the Romans' rule. Tight control must be kept on such a recalcitrant region; the army staffed its garrison from Israel's neighboring enemies.

This, then, was the vaunted Peace of Rome, the empire's chief blessing on its subject peoples. It was Augustus, "To Be Worshiped," first of the emperors, who had brought this peace to a desperate world. Two generations of war had racked Rome's domains; warlord after warlord had crossed Europe and the Middle East to fight for the greatest trophy in the world: command of Rome and all its lands. Augustus's victory in 31 B.C.E. had brought the struggle to an end. He had been declared "god, son of god, savior" of his people and of all Rome's subjects, "by his benefactions outdoing even the heavenly gods."

How was the province of Asia to do justice to this "savior, whose birthday marked the beginning of a gospel for the world"? By changing the calendar, decided its government, to start the new year on that very day. Even in Jerusalem sacrifices were offered on the emperor's behalf. But "savior," "heavenly gods"? The Jews acknowledged just one God, and the savior he would send was no Roman emperor indifferent to God's people and derisive of their faith.

Just briefly, a thousand years before Jesus, the Jews had enjoyed the power promised by God: King David's reign was a golden age in the nation's history, when Israel, too, had an empire and safe borders and a land it could call its own. Who, then, would restore to Israel what was its own by right? The prophets of old had no doubt: *The days are coming, says the Lord, when I will raise up for David a righteous Branch, and he shall reign as king and deal wisely, and shall execute justice in the land* (Jeremiah 23.5).

David's descendant on David's throne in David's capital, Jerusalem. The city meant more to the Jews than we can easily imagine. *Open for me the gates of justice*, rang out one of the great songs of praise, sung each Passover in Jerusalem, *that I may go in and give thanks to God* (Psalm 118.19). The crowd knew the song well. It was sung at other festivals, too: at Shelters (Sukkoth), the autumn celebration of harvest, and at the winter Feast of Dedication (Hanukkah), known as the Feast of Lights, when the Jews recalled the Temple's return to sacred use after its desecration in 167 B.C.E. At Shelters and dedication the crowd waved palm branches in celebration: "Hosanna! Save now!" rang out the refrain.

A later generation imagined how that song or "psalm" of praise will sound when God's chosen general, his Anointed agent, has won his final victory over Israel's enemies and marches at last into Jerusalem from the Mount of Olives: *Blessed be he,* the citizens will sing, lined along the walls to greet the army, *who comes in the name of the Lord.*

Then the troops: *We have wished you prosperity, who are of the house of the Lord.*

To and fro, to and fro, until soldiers and civilians join together for the final verse: *O give thanks to the Lord, for he is good, for his mercy endures for ever.*

The victory of God's agent would be more than just a national triumph. The same psalm was invoked in the dreams of the subsequent tribunal, when God was to judge all humankind: "*Open for me,*" the suppliants will plead, "*the gates of justice in Jerusalem.*" They will be questioned: "What were your life's works?" "I fed the hungry and thirsty, I clothed the naked, I brought up the orphan and gave alms." And so to the verdict: "*This is the gate of the Lord, through which the just may enter. Come on in, you that did feed the hungry and thirsty, who clothed the naked, brought up orphans, and gave alms.*"

For Jews, Jerusalem was in every way the center of the world: in present history, in God's final victory over Israel's enemies, in his judgment on all humankind. Here is the setting of all the events that will inaugurate and mark God's undisputed rule. "*Do not fear, Jerusalem,* said an ancient prophet Zephaniah, as he thought of God's reign, *the God of Israel is in your midst; you have no more evil to fear*" (Zephaniah 3.16).

Yet more pilgrims were approaching the city. Many came, of course, from the neighboring villages. Others walked for a week to cover the eighty miles or so from Galilee. But far more flocked to the holy city than just local families. Along the great trade route from Babylonia came large caravans of pilgrims. They brought with them their contribution to the Temple's treasury, along with armed guards to protect it from the robbers who well knew those wagons' value. From Asia Minor and North Africa, by land and sea, pilgrims traveled for the great feasts, above all, for Passover. However they had traveled, their entry to the city itself would be on foot. To ride into the holy city, it was said, was to be a king—on a colt to signal peace or caparisoned on a horse for war.

Jerusalem was filling. And not just with people. Every family had brought or purchased a lamb for the festival; up to thirty thousand lambs would be killed in the Temple area on a single afternoon, in shift after shift of priests and families. The carcass was then brought back to the lodgings or camp, roasted, and eaten that night with ceremony and partying. Everyone must have a mouthful; "the Passover share may be no larger than an olive," went an old saying, "and yet the songs of praise break through the roofs." For on this night, hundreds of years ago, God had ordered the Jews in Egypt to kill and eat a lamb in haste and to sprinkle the gateposts of their houses with its blood. Vengeance had threatened the Egyptians, who would not set Israel free: In every house unmarked with blood the firstborn son would be killed that night. Even the king of Egypt would then at last let his Jewish captives go.

Every child learned that story of the first Passover and heard the prayer that God remembers his people and his promises. Every Jewish child learns and hears them still: "Our God and God of our Fathers, may you remember us and our fathers and the Anointed, son of David, your servant, and Jerusalem your holy city, and all your people, the house of Israel. May their remembrance come before you, for rescue and for goodness."

So solemn was this season that other great moments in Israel's history had been linked with it. Centuries before the first Passover, Abraham, father of the nation, had been ordered by God to sacrifice the only son borne to him by his wife Sarah. Here was his one hope for the descendants God had promised him, and it was to be taken away in the most brutal fashion that any parent could imagine. Abraham prepared to sacrifice as he had been ordered and at the last moment was held back by God from the terrible deed. Such faithful obedience had won God's further promise: *"Because you have done this, and have not withheld your son, your only son, I will multiply your descendants as the stars of heaven and as the sand on the seashore"* (Beginning [Genesis] 22.16). In Passover's drama some later teachers saw that promise fulfilled. According to this tradition, "When I see the blood of the Passover lambs," says the Lord, "I will pass over your houses; for I see there the blood of the sacrifice of Isaac."

Camps were springing up on the Mount of Olives, across the Kidron Valley from the city. Pilgrims had to spend the night of Passover in Jerusalem itself; to ensure space for all the visitors, the Mount was declared part of Greater Jerusalem for the festival. Talk would have turned to this prophet from Galilee, this Jesus, or "Godsave"; his name was a version of "Joshua," the name of Moses' successor who had finally led the Jews into their Promised Land. What was this Jesus planning? An uprising against the Romans? But he had no army, just a ramshackle gang of followers, country people like himself from the north. There were certainly firebrands among them. One had the nickname "Zealot": that was already a name to reckon with, a name that in the next generation would sum up the most dedicated, violent enemies of Rome. Another was called "Iscariot"; this might even recall the Romans' name for Zealots: *sicarii,* knifemen. But what match were these for the thousands of troops guarding every gate and vantage point the city had to offer?

There would always be hope, ready to burst into flame. Every ten years or so another leader would urge the people to defy the Romans and take the freedom that God promised. As often as not such uprisings harked back to Israel's past. The great desert, through which the Jews had trekked for forty years, never lost its power to draw the hopeful: Here God had shown his power before, and here he would again. In a strange mirror image of past wonders, one leader in the 40s C.E. even claimed that the Jordan River would part once more and let his followers out of Israel into the desert. The Red Sea had parted to let the Jews out of slavery in Egypt; the Jordan itself had given the Jews dry passage for their entry into the Promised Land. And now, claimed this would-be prophet, Theudas, he himself was to lead his followers in a new "Escape," a new Exodus. Such hope, such urgency, such certainty. Then the Roman soldiers were sent out, and a single charge swept the patriots and their fervor away.

Rome was not easily defied. The parents and grandparents in the crowd remembered the riots forty years before: The crowds of an angry Passover regathered fifty days later for the Feast of the Fiftieth Day [Pentecost]; violence broke out, and by its end two thousand culprits hung crucified around the city.

But perhaps among the ancient songs of Passover this ballad was already being sung, all those years ago, as Jerusalem was filling and the crowds were wondering and the word got around that Jesus was two days' . . . one day's . . . just an hour's journey away from the city. What had happened—and what was still to happen—on this most holy night of the year? More than just the redemption of Israel was at stake. This ballad has reached us as an insertion in the Aramaic translation of the Escape (Exodus).

The First Night: when the Lord was revealed over the world to create it.
The world was without form and void,
and darkness was spread over the face of the abyss,
and the Name of the Lord was the light, and it shone.
And he called it the First Night.

The Second Night: when the Lord was revealed to Abraham and to Sarah his wife.
And Isaac was thirty-seven when he was offered up on the altar.
The heavens were bowed down and descended, and Isaac saw their perfection,
and his eyes were dimmed because of their perfection.
And he called it the Second Night.

The Third Night: when the Lord was revealed against the Egyptians at midnight.
His hand slew the firstborn of the Egyptians
and his right hand protected the firstborn of Israel
to fulfill what the scripture says:
"Israel is my firstborn Son."
And he called it the Third Night.

The Fourth Night: when the world reaches its appointed time to be redeemed.
The iron yokes shall be broken
and the generations of wickedness shall be blotted out,

and Moses will go up from the midst of the desert
and the king the Anointed from on high.
One will lead at the head of the flock,
and the other will lead at the head of the flock,
and his Name will lead between the two of them,
and I and they will proceed together.

This is the night of the Passover to the name of the Lord:
it is a night reserved and set aside for the redemption of all Israel,
throughout their generations.

Jesus Enters Jerusalem: The Story in John

The next day a great crowd who had come to the feast heard that Jesus was coming to Jerusalem. So they took branches of palm trees and went out to meet him, crying, "Hosanna! Blessed is he who comes in the name of the Lord, yes, the King of Israel!"

And Jesus found a young ass and sat upon it; as it is written in scripture,

"Do not fear, daughter of Jerusalem.
Look, your king is coming,
sitting on an ass's colt."

His followers did not understand this at first; but when Jesus was glorified, then they remembered that this had been written, and that they had done this to him.
(JOHN 12.12–16)

All four of our witnesses tell the story of Jesus' Triumphal Entry. Their accounts have varied emphases. John's crowd pours from the city singing a royal welcome, a "greeting" such as cities gave to visiting and triumphant kings. Palm branches fill the air as they would each winter at Dedication, to celebrate the Temple's reconsecration: "May God," ran the Dedication prayer, "never deliver his people again to blasphemous and barbarous nations." The rites of Dedication were based on those of the older Festival of Shelters. At the very word *Hosanna,* said the rabbis about Shelters, pilgrims should wave palms to and fro, back and forth, for God is God of north, south, east, and west; they should wave the branches up and down, for he is God of heaven and earth. To speak of those branches of palm trees at Jesus' entry, John takes up a word that the Greek Bible used only once: in describing the origin of Dedication. Here in his story of Jesus' arrival are the national hopes of Passover and of Dedication combined.

Such fervor was dangerous. But the Roman command? It makes no move. This is strange. We might wonder if the songs of welcome and even the palms were seen only later—and only by Jesus' own followers—as pointedly relevant to Jesus himself. The great praise songs were certainly sung at some points of Passover and perhaps as a matter of course when pilgrims entered the city. The ass might have warned the soldiers that this group's leader had some special status, but John confirms that even Jesus' followers saw little significance in it at the time.

The arrival of Israel's king upon an ass is foretold in a further prophet of the Old Order: Zechariah (9.9). John highlights the link, *as it is written in scripture.*

Matthew picks up the prophet's note, left aside by John, that this arrival would be *humble.* Just how humble was it to enter the city on an ass? After all, it is in Zechariah's same prophecy the act of a *king,* but of a king who comes in peace. For such a triumphant entrance was expected to follow the general's victory, not precede his greatest battle. There is in Jesus' Triumphal Entry far more than meets the eye; the Jesus of our witnesses sets on edge every standard expectation and every hope.

The gospels invest Jesus' entrance with all possible marks of his royalty: from the songs and rites of Passover, Shelters, and Dedication. With these signs comes pathos, too. The crowd's songs were more true and their actions more apt than they had ever been. This is the arrival of their long-awaited king, whose coronation would be in a Roman prison, his crown a plait of thorns. So little, as our authors would have it, did the people of Jerusalem understand what was happening among them. John adds to the prophecy of the mounted king, *Do not fear, daughter of Jerusalem.* He is hinting at the promise now fulfilled before the city's very eyes: *Do not fear, Jerusalem,* we heard in Zephaniah's prophecy of God's coming: *the God of Israel is in your midst; you have no more evil to fear* (Zephaniah 3.16).

Zechariah's words about the ass were not forgotten. A later rabbi resolved two apparent contradictions in scripture:

It is written, *I, the Lord, will act with haste but in due time.* How can both these be true? If Israel is worthy of the Anointed, God will hasten his coming. If not, it will happen in due time.

Another contradiction: It is written, *And there before me was one like a son of man, coming with the clouds of heaven;* but it is also written, *Look, your king comes humbly, sitting on an ass.* How can both these be true? If Israel is worthy of the Anointed, he will come with haste, with clouds of heaven. If not, he will come on an ass.

A king heard this and said, "That is not worthy of the Anointed; I will give him my white horse." The rabbi replied, "You want to provide an animal worthy of the Anointed; have you then a horse of a hundred colors?"

The rabbi had been dwelling on the strange but unforgettable prophecy of Daniel: *And there before me was one like a son of man, coming with the clouds of heaven* (Daniel 7.13). We shall meet with that prophecy again; of everything in the Old Order, no text has been more important for the church's understanding of Jesus.

―――――――

If the Anointed was to be God's regent on earth, how would he act? Expectations were not uniform, but we can follow the threads we have picked up so far to their classic statement in the so-called *Psalms of Solomon*. These had been written in Jerusalem to raise Israel's hopes after the Roman army's first onslaught on the city in 63 B.C.E. It is a classic statement of prayer in the face of dereliction, pleading for God to intervene and save his people:

> See, Lord, and raise up for Israel their king,
> the son of David, to rule over your servant Israel
> in the time known to you, O God.
> Support him with the strength to destroy the unjust rulers,
> to purge Jerusalem from gentiles
> who trample her to destruction;
> in wisdom and in justice to drive out
> the sinners from the inheritance of Israel.
>
> He will gather a holy people
> whom he will lead in justice.
> He will make Jerusalem holy as it was from the beginning,
> for nations to come to from the ends of the earth
> to bring back as gifts her scattered children,
> and to see the glory of the Lord
> with which the Lord has glorified her.
> There will be no injustice among them in his days,
> for all shall be holy,
> and their king shall be the Lord Anointed.
> (PSALMS OF SOLOMON 17.21–32)

Here was the role of the Anointed: to reign in power on earth over an empire that would overturn all the empires in the world—and not least, the Empire of Rome itself. Jesus himself spoke of the Kingdom of God, and Passover was the time for God's Anointed to appear and claim his own. But who would be this agent of the kingdom and God's governor on earth? Over and over in these pages we shall catch the echo of a charge that Jesus himself aspired to be king of Israel. Luke has the Jewish leaders charge him before Pilate: *"We have found this man,"* they say, *"leading our nation astray and forbidding them to pay taxes to the emperor, and saying that he is himself the Anointed, a king"* (Luke 23.2). It was an accusation that no governor could afford to ignore. In this case the charge stuck. A condemned criminal carried a placard stating the charge on which the Roman authorities had convicted him. Jesus' placard was hung above him on the cross to mock his pretensions: *"The king of the Jews."*

These were the derisive allegations made public by his enemies and executioners. But the description was not theirs alone. Jesus' followers, too, knew of kings and kingdoms. John tells one famous story in a most striking way. When Jesus fed five thousand people in the desert John follows the miracle beyond the accounts of our other writers: *The people,* he says, *seeing the sign Jesus had done, began saying, "This really is the prophet spoken of by Moses, the one coming into the world." Jesus knew that they were going to come and take hold of him and make him king; so he headed off back to the mountain by himself* (John 6.14–15).

As we shall see in more detail later on, John knows how evocative this banquet in the desert must have been. He alone records its timing: Passover, season of Israel's liberation and of the coming king. The feeding recalls the greatest of all prophets, Moses, who fed Israel in the wilderness. Once reminded of Moses, the crowd thinks, too, of the successor that Moses had promised: *God will raise up for you a prophet like me from among your own brothers. You must listen to him* (Second Law [Deuteronomy] 18.15). It is Jesus who gives thanks on the whole people's behalf; this is the role of the priest. Prophet, priest, and now king: This, in Jewish tradition, is the threefold role of the Anointed, and here, discharging it, is Jesus. The crowds seem to have read the sign with real insight. Surely they are right? So why does John's Jesus back away?

John is not the first to see in such a call to such a kingdom a *temptation* that Jesus must resist. Matthew and Luke know of it, too. Right at their story's start, Jesus is subjected to a threefold blandishment: to take a prophet's power over food in the desert; a priest's power over the temple; and a king's power over all the kingdoms of the earth. Jesus resists the devil's invitation. For this is a reign that he is to have only at the story's end, when such power is given him by God.

A short scene in Mark's trial of Jesus before the Roman governor Pilate was taken over word for word by Matthew and Luke. *"Are you the king of the Jews?"* Pilate asked, when Jesus was arraigned before him. So much could be meant by that phrase: much that was true, much that was false. Jesus was more a king, as our writers would have it, than Pilate could possibly know, by an authority that Pilate would never acknowledge and in a sense that Pilate could not hope to understand.

Our gospels' Jesus left the question in the air. It faced their readers, too. Would they call Jesus king of the Jews? Would they understand their own claim if they did? Jesus replied: *"Those are your words"* (Mark 15.2).

In the Roman Garrison

The city's garrison had good reason to be alert. Passover was a dangerous time. From the Antonia Fort, at the northwest corner of the huge Temple complex, half of its courtyards and most of the city could be seen: Jerusalem was seething. More troops would have had been brought in, and the governor himself would have moved up from the coast, from the provincial capital at Caesarea, to take command. But with crowds so huge and so excited any trouble would spread like wildfire. There was no love lost between the garrison and the Jews. Twenty years later there would be a crisis at Passover: A soldier on the Temple ramparts turned his back on the rituals and broke wind. Stones were thrown, the troops were sent in to restore control. Perhaps twenty thousand pilgrims were killed, perhaps more. These were brutal times.

Not that anyone opposed such festivals in themselves. Temples and their gods were the pride of every pagan city and the focus of its civic life. And every temple had its festivals. Sacrifices, feasting, and drinking—such celebrations went on for days. They were the high point of a region's year. No pagan would deny the standing of another city's gods or ignore the different names under which any one of the gods might be active and revered.

But the Jews? They were so exclusive. They acknowledged one God and one only. No one would deny that he was powerful; magicians everywhere used his name in spells. But the Jews would concede no dignity to other gods. Pilate once had the regimental banners carried into Jerusalem. This was enough to stir an extraordinary protest: Jews gathered in crowds outside Pilate's palace in Caesarea and sat down. When Pilate ordered the guards to kill them, "Go ahead," they said; "better that than to go against God's laws." Pilate gave way.

There had been troublemakers from Galilee before. The most dangerous had been called Judas. He had carved out a territory for himself in a guerrilla war, attacking travelers and settlers and even a city when the army was distracted. It may have been the same Judas who came south, ten years later, trying to stir things in Judaea as well. The group founded then would become famous long after Judas's own defeat: the Zealots.

And now this Jesus. He was in the city, and no orders had come through to arrest him. In this crowd it would be hard enough to find him, let alone to corner him quietly, away from the mob. He might be just a maniac with a handful of supporters; he might be a dreamer with no plans for action of his own. But if he was preparing trouble and had the crowd behind him, the troops would have a riot on their hands. Hundreds of thousands of pilgrims could be ranged against them, and the nearest reinforcements three days' march away in Caesarea.

The soldiers as well knew of those riots forty years before. It had all started at Passover. The following Feast of the Fiftieth Day saw a pitched battle in Jerusalem itself, and for a moment the outcome was genuinely in the balance. The governor's own troops could not cope with the trouble. He had called on the imperial soldiers to help; they were crack regiments based in Syria. The city's garrison forty years on still had good reason to be alert.

The End of Hope?

Jesus had reached Jerusalem. His entry, as our witnesses record it, was a triumph; within a week he had been put to death.

Jesus of Nazareth, read the placard above his head as he died, *the king of the Jews.* So much for this "king." We will hear more from our witnesses of this last week in Jerusalem: Jesus' pupils deserted him, his supposed subjects bayed for his blood, the Roman governor sentenced him to death. We have some knowledge of crucifixion and can reconstruct the likely course of Jesus' last hours. Two further troublemakers, we are told, were also due to be killed. The three of them could be dealt with together. Whipped and beaten, already faint from loss of blood, condemned men were made to carry the wooden beams from which they would be hung. Mark tells how Jesus' cross was carried for him by Simon of Cyrene, *the father,* Mark says, *of Alexander and Rufus.* Mark expected his readers to know the family. We might wonder, when had their links with Jesus' movement begun? The victims were led to a bleak patch of rising ground outside the city's wall. Here was the regular site for executions. A series of posts stood out against the sky, eight feet high; into the top of each was cut a notch.

The routine was familiar. Nothing marked out this set of crucifixions from the last. Sometimes rope was used to fix the prisoner to the cross, sometimes nails. There is an ancient tradition that Jesus was nailed.

The beam was laid on the ground. The soldiers put Jesus onto his back across the beam and along it stretched out his arms. First one hand, then the other: a soldier would press the back of Jesus' hand against the beam, hold a nail to the wrist, and drive it home, through pulse and bone, to the wood behind. The soldiers lifted the beam's ends onto two forked poles, hoisted the beam and Jesus into the air, and slotted the beam's center into the notch at the top of the post.

Now for the feet. Each of Jesus' ankles was sandwiched between a block of wood and the side of the upright post. From each side a nail was hammered in.

And there Jesus would hang, for as long as it took him to die.

It was an infamously, spectacularly cruel form of execution. It was used for rebels and runaway slaves. The longer they lasted, the better. A stool might be attached to the post, on which the victim could rest; his circulation would revive, his suffering would be prolonged. So much the better, too, that the mob could see what became of troublemakers: Here was a warning to anyone else who might dare oppose the might of Rome.

Living in Hope

Jesus died in ignominy. His followers were scattered. The histories we have of Palestine in the thirties provide a long list of subversive, radical, or revolutionary movements crushed by Rome. Jesus earns just one short mention, which Christian editors have probably altered, to give Jesus the dignity that he called for in their eyes.

For Jesus' followers insisted that their leader, dead and buried at Passover, was alive. Nothing, it seemed, could quell their conviction or their spread. We hear of their lives from the letters of the missionary Paul and from the second part of Luke's work, the

Mission (Acts). Luke has organized his story carefully; the results are not always easy to reconcile with Paul's account. We will be looking more closely at Luke's narrative in chapters 7 and 8. For the moment, then, we just follow in the Mission's own order a few key moments and key figures in its narrative; here are the cities and crises in which our gospels' evolution is most likely to belong. Here, too, is a picture of the activists who were responsible for the gospels' spread: a small group, many of them known to one another, traveling by land and sea along the eastern coast of the Mediterranean, inland to the cities of Asia Minor, and westward to Greece. Here are some of the threads, of which so few can now be followed, that link the years of Jesus' life on earth with the generation that rounded off that life's stories as we have them now.

Chief hero of the Mission's first half is Jesus' own friend and first follower, Peter. He preaches in Jerusalem, performs miracles, leads the church. He is the natural target of the authorities' suspicion and is arrested. He escapes and heads straight for the home of Mary, "John Mark's mother." This is the Mark with whom, by an ancient tradition, our first witness is to be identified. He was Jewish, a city boy; it would be no surprise if he spoke both Greek and Aramaic. He knew Jesus' movement from its earliest days.

Mark was a cousin of one Barnabas, clearly a trusted figure in the Jerusalem church. Barnabas was sent to check the reports of strange developments in the bustling city of Antioch, five hundred miles to the north. Jewish and Gentile adherents of Jesus were worshiping together; the requirements of the Jewish Law were being ignored. Here was a real crisis in the church's life. Was the Jewish Law binding on the Israel, reformed and renewed, that Jesus' followers were coming to believe themselves to be? We shall return to Antioch; it is the likely setting for Matthew, writing forty years later. The lines of division between church and synagogue were as hotly contested in Matthew's day, as in Barnabas's before him.

By the time of Peter's escape a further figure has been introduced to Luke's drama: Paul. This scholarly, fervent Jew was born only a few years after Jesus. He became one of the fiercest opponents of the young church. But not for long. On a journey to Damascus he had a blinding vision of Jesus and became his most famous missionary. His letters to various churches, as collected in the New Order, are the earliest Christian documents we possess. The church would be unimaginable without him. In *The Four Witnesses* we will have special reason for gratitude to Paul, for in his letters lies the final, critical clue to our gospels' understanding.

From Antioch, Barnabas, Paul, and John Mark set out on a joint mission; in its middle, far from home, John Mark left them. When they made plans for a second tour, Barnabas spoke up for his cousin, but Paul was adamant: He would not rely on John Mark again. Barnabas and Mark went one way, Paul the other.

He was not, however, alone. Parts of the Mission's second half appear to be taken from a journal, kept on Paul's journeys by a companion: "We sailed to Macedonia. . . . " How did the Mission's author, identified within a hundred years as Paul's "dear friend Luke, the doctor," have access to this account? Perhaps it had been his own, as Paul's companion; the church, then, would have found a witness beyond reproach to chronicle its early years. This second half of the Mission stars Paul as he travels far and wide to spread the gospel. Opposition is never far away. Among the most dangerous incidents is at Ephesus, where a riot springs, not from the synagogue, but from the pagan silversmiths who made a living from statues of their patron goddess, Artemis. Here is a second crisis for the church: its looming conflict with the dominant pagan world.

It is with Ephesus that John, writing his gospel almost fifty years after the silversmiths' riot, has been linked since the late second century. The connection with Ephesus does not involve just our fourth gospel. A second John was writing on Patmos, an island thirty-five miles off Ephesus, around the time of the gospel's completion. This John the Seer wrote the closing book of the Bible, the Book of Unveiling (Revelation). The veil believed to lie between the daily world and the true nature of things was for the Seer and other visionaries drawn back. Here was a sight (granted only in strange, coded forms) of how things really were.

The Roman Empire had brought peace to the whole Mediterranean. People and their trade moved freely; so did their ideas. John the Seer surveys the empire and sees all the possibilities it brings; he sees, too, the power that sought for itself the worship due only to God. His image of this all-demanding beast and of its destruction has occupied the world's imagination ever since. Through the New Order runs a thread of excitement; it is nowhere more vivid than in the Book of Unveiling. The ancient poetry of Israel is alive: Images of a cosmic cataclysm stand alongside dreams of peace under God's control. "A new heaven and a new earth" are promised. What form will they take? How will the old pass away and the new come to be? There is far more disclosure in the New Order, wrought through far more strategies and styles, than a superficial reading will encourage us to see. The clue that Paul offers us is unlocked by the Seer: Here comes to light our gospels' real character and aims.

Luke ends the Mission with Paul's arrival in Rome; he may have arrived as early as 56 C.E. Paul, it seems, has been reconciled with Mark. Mark sends his regards as well, apparently from Rome, in the First Letter of Peter; here is the assistant, working on the recollections of Peter, to whom tradition will ascribe our earliest gospel. Rome: It is in the center of empire, as Luke would have it, that the church belongs; the old center of the world, Jerusalem, has given way to the new. All is going well.

Paul's journeys are nearing their end. His years of preaching could be variously assessed. He had *completed the gospel of the Anointed* (Letter to the Romans 15.16) in a whole quadrant of the empire. His preaching had been open and for all to hear; in Ephesus, Luke tells us, Paul hired a lecture hall for daily discussions, held publicly and without interruption for two years (Mission [Acts] 19.9–10). And yet the faithful were just thinly scattered along the trade routes of the empire. After the first hectic months in Jerusalem as Luke reports them, we hear little of the numbers involved in the church's life. They were probably very small; in Paul's day the whole church of Corinth could meet in a single patron's house (Romans 16.23). By the time Paul reached Rome a few thousand had heard him preach the word; some of them had been converted, more not; tens of millions remained unreached.

Paul admitted no discouragement; he insisted that he would preach on, come what may. Others were less assured; without results a mission can falter, its leaders lose heart. There is a touching pattern to the collection of short stories or "parables" with which we will see Mark introduce the teaching of Jesus. Here is Mark's chance to impress upon the readers the immediacy of Jesus' teaching and its importance to their needs. His choice of theme is striking.

Mark's Jesus gives a programmatic sermon, built around three vignettes from the farmer's year. The seed must be sown; whether it grows and when, whether its plants survive to bear fruit, or how such small beginnings become the field full of grain ready for harvest are not for the farmer to know. His task is to sow and to wait and to recognize that, however carefully planted it might be, some seed never sprouts at all. The missionaries of Mark's day were not the first or the last to wonder whether their "seed" was entirely wasted.

"Listen [said Jesus]. *A farmer went out to sow his field. Some of the seed fell on the path, and the birds came and ate it up. Some seed fell on stony ground. . . .*
(MARK 4.4–5)

To sow, to wait, to harvest: Here was a rhythm that the Old Order and Jesus both knew well. When the field is ripe, it is time for harvest. The wheat is gathered in; the weeds are consigned to fire. The image had been used for generations: Here was a way to speak of God's final judgment upon the world, the dramatic sifting of good from evil, wheat from chaff. The world is "ripe," had said one of the Old Order's starkest prophets, Joel. Let the enemies of Israel beware: They are about to be harvested—corn and grapes, body and blood—and to be swept, ground, pressed, and trampled to oblivion. The Seer knows the prophecies of Joel; both tell of a harvest to come and of the cataclysm it will bring.

Now in my vision [wrote John the Seer] *I saw a cloud and on it one like a son of man, with a gold crown on his head and a sharp scythe in his hand. Then an angel called aloud to him, "Put in your scythe and reap. Harvest time has come and the harvest of the earth is ripe." Then he set his scythe to work on the earth, and the harvest of the earth was reaped.*
(BOOK OF UNVEILING [REVELATION] 14.14–16)

The stories of Mark's Jesus also tell of harvest. His followers have dwelled upon the image ever since. For this Jesus knows of Joel and of God's impending judgment on the earth. Jesus' generation and Mark's both asked, when would they see the dramatic, final reaping of this ripe earth? When would God set up that final assize?

Deep down in Jesus' stories lurks a different sense of season and an answer. Harvest is already under way. As Jesus speaks. Here and now.

———

Paul was urban through and through; Peter was a country man. He had a lot to look back on. He had grown up among fishermen and farmers. The focus of worship was the one Temple in Jerusalem of the one God, whose image must never be drawn or carved. Talk with outsiders called for Greek, but Peter and his neighbors were united by their Aramaic mother tongue. He was growing old now in a pell-mell city where a million people spoke a babble of languages and served a hundred gods, where the emperor Augustus had repaired eighty-two temples in a single year; where every deity in every cult must have its statue. Such idolatry was a public, daily offense to the Jews in Rome who observed their faith, just as it had been to their forebears in Babylon centuries before. The ancient prophet Isaiah had declaimed,

Fallen, fallen is Babylon;
and God has shattered to the ground
all the statues of her gods.

(ISAIAH 21.9)

Jerusalem had been besieged and captured by the king of Babylon in 587 B.C.E. The inhabitants were deported to Babylon; its empire became the symbol of all that was loathed and feared in alien domination of Israel. Prophet after prophet had looked forward to Babylon's destruction. It is in just such terms that John the Seer would speak, a generation after Mark, of the angry destruction that he hoped to see let loose on Rome:

After this I saw another angel coming down from heaven with great power and the
earth was lit up by his glory. And he cried out in a great voice:

"She has fallen, Babylon the great has fallen,
and has become the dwelling place of daemons,
because from the wine of the desire of her adultery all the nations have drunk
and all the kings of the earth have committed adultery with her."

(BOOK OF UNVEILING [REVELATION] 18.1–3)

The prophet Jeremiah had lived through the capture of Jerusalem. He, too, looked forward to the vengeance on Babylon:

Flee from the midst of Babylon, do not be cut off in her punishment.
Babylon was a golden cup in God's hand, making all the earth drunken;
the nations drank of her wine, and so the nations went mad.
Suddenly Babylon has fallen and been broken. Wail for her!

(JEREMIAH 51.6–8)

This is the rich seam of threats and warnings from which the Seer will mine his imprecation as he looks on Rome and its untrammeled, overbearing power. The Seer's angel will plead,

Come out of her, my people, so that you may have no part in her wrongdoings and may suffer none of her scourge. For in her heart she says, "I sit enthroned as a queen, I am no widow and will never see grief."

(BOOK OF UNVEILING [REVELATION] 18.4, 7)

The Seer will look westward across the Aegean Sea and think bitterly of Rome. Peter, meanwhile, was living there. For however idolatrous and unyielding its rule, Rome had left in peace, for a decade or more, the Jews and Christians of the city itself. By the early 60s C.E. Peter was growing old. It was time for his recollections to be written down; tradition has it that he or his converts turned to Mark. And none too soon. A single disaster would bring the complacent, optimistic days in Rome to an end forever. On July 19, 64 C.E., a fire broke out that would blaze for a week and destroy a quarter of the city. The Seer will look forward, thirty years later, to the empire's final punishment at God's hands and still remembers that terrible warning. The Seer's angel will proclaim,

Therefore on a single day, her scourges shall come upon her,
and she shall be burned in fire,
for mighty is the Lord the God who judges her.
And the kings of the earth shall weep,
those who committed adultery with her,
when they see the smoke of her fire.
They shall stand at a distance through fear of her punishment, and will say,
"Woe, woe to the great city,
to Babylon the powerful city,
for in a single hour your judgment has come upon you."

(BOOK OF UNVEILING [REVELATION] 18.8–10)

The church, even at the time, may well have seen in the fire God's punishment on Rome. But there would be little time to gloat. For the people of Rome saw arson. The powers that be saw angry, dangerous crowds.

Someone had to be blamed.

BOOK I
Mark's Story

Introduction to Mark

The church has reached Rome. It is time to encounter our first witness: Mark, said to have worked with Peter and to have recorded his memories of Jesus. Peter and his following faced turbulent times. Mark would write in the shadow of the Romans' first great attack upon the church. There is no love in Mark's story for the powers that be, and no attempt to conciliate or attract them. Mark is driven to disclose his enigmatic Jesus not to the comfortable and gracious, but those who will suffer as had Jesus himself at the hands of the world's elite.

Paul's arrival in Rome is well attested. Early evidence of Peter's presence is famously hard to come by. We do hear of Peter and his companion Mark in the hated "Babylon," that thin disguise for Rome. *Your sister, the church in Babylon,* ends the First Letter of Peter, *sends you greetings; so does my young Mark* (1 Peter 5.13). Bishop Clement of Rome tells around 95 C.E. how both Peter and Paul were martyred; the context suggests that both died in the same onslaught and in Rome. And there the first-century evidence ends. It is in the following decades that the story emerges, with ever fuller details, of Peter's preaching, escape from Rome, return, and martyrdom; at last he takes up his cross and follows his master to death.

Our first witness tells a story of sharp contrasts. Jesus' early triumphs are relished by his pupils and stir a wild enthusiasm in the crowd. Central to his church's life were these stories, told over and over, of Jesus. Strange events are followed by stranger. The sick are healed, a storm is stilled, a family's supper is enough to feed thousands—and all without a word of explanation. There is something *uncanny* going on. How could Jesus' followers rely now on normality; how could they be sure they knew the way things really were? The surface of their humdrum world began to crack, and underneath it appeared a roiling war of good and evil, a single figure in pitched battle against untamed powers of darkness. The normal was not what it seemed to be, and in turn a "normal" vision of that battle could never hope to understand its progress, still less its overwhelming outcome.

At the very midpoint of the narrative, Mark changes key. Peter declares Jesus to be God's Anointed agent, and in the next sentence, for the first time, Jesus speaks openly of his impending rejection and death. The sound of opposition, determined and dangerous, grows closer. Jesus' chosen followers dream blindly on of privilege and power. These are both pupils and friends of their master, his companions and the missionaries that would spread his message throughout Israel. No one in Mark is closer to Jesus than they are. But they misunderstand, they get above themselves, they are ambitious and jealous of one another, and when they are put to the test, they run away.

Mark is critical of Jesus' pupils, but he looks with a far angrier eye upon the powers that be in Jesus' day and his own. His Jesus is at home in rural Galilee; the authorities in Jerusalem spy on him and test his claims, trap him, and hand him over to the power of Rome. Mark's Jesus dies in despair. He had appeared in Galilee proclaiming the Kingdom of God; he died in Jerusalem with a mocking placard over his head, *The king of the Jews.* To any normal eye, his claim is rebutted, his following scattered, his battle lost. But this gospel is not written for those who look with a normal, worldly eye. The more assured and complacent Mark's readers are, the more surely they will fail to see the real battle under way in the life of this artisan and in his "defeat." The pupils themselves fail over and again to understand, and those outside may never see into the secret at all. An unveiling is offered, and Mark works to make that unveiling possible and effective for his readers. It will never be a mere matter of reading and reflecting. Mark's Jesus lays down a stark challenge: *"All who want to follow after me must deny themselves, take up their cross, and follow me"* (Mark 8.34). For those who follow Jesus and adopt the life that he demands, persecution will never be far away.

Jesus, his pupils, and Mark himself inherited their language of hope and expectation from Israel's history and prophets: language of slavery and freedom, exile and return, sacrifice and reconciliation. Every event in Mark's story of Jesus glances back to the heroes and high points of the Old Order. We will meet its prophets in the following pages, and in the unveiling provided by the prophet Daniel we will find the single most important key to Mark's mysterious story. Daniel's story, too, was set at a time of persecution, when loyalty to Israel's God could lead to death and there was little scope for comfort or hope. Daniel is reassured through a strange knowledge to which most people had no access. Once they see how things really are in God's plan, the oppressors will seem less fearsome by far. Despite all appearances, so Daniel and Mark insist, God's plan for his people is secure and their vindication is at hand.

We will hear of Rome and its empire, of Nero himself and of his antics while his city burned, of the hideous punishment to which the Christians were then subjected. It has long been suspected that Mark's church was under an attack that had taken it by surprise, for beneath Mark's care for his frightened and persecuted people, we can still glimpse the story's response to earlier and different dangers: of complacency, ambition, disappointment. It was not long, we may suspect, since he and others in the Roman church had been preening themselves on their faith, watching things go their way, and dreaming of ever greater rewards in this world and the next. *"Some seed,"* said

Jesus, *"fell among thorns, which grew up and choked the plants"* (Mark 4.7). The thorns were the cares of this world and the love of wealth and all the desires that competed with loyalty to Jesus' demands. Such dangers face a secure and comfortable community. Mark knew them well. How hard it was—and had always been—to see how soon and how violently such triumph would end.

On the evening of Jesus' arrest, Peter denied all knowledge of his master. For the next thirty years he spread the gospel. Ancient tradition has it that he died in Rome, among those killed in the persecution that followed the fire of 64 C.E. He had taken up his cross at last and followed Jesus.

"Some seed," said Jesus, *"fell on good ground, sprouted, grew, and bore fruit: thirtyfold, sixtyfold, a hundredfold"* (Mark 4.8).

If Mark was the young man we met in Jerusalem, then we know more of him than of all our other witnesses combined. By the early second century some other clues are added: "Mark was Peter's interpreter," wrote Papias—a bishop or "over seer" of a Christian community in Asia Minor, and thus within the ambit of communities of John and Matthew—in his *Commentary on the Lord's Sayings;* "he wrote down accurately but not in order all that he remembered of the Lord's sayings and doings." This note is our first mention of Mark's gospel. Papias was writing some sixty years after its completion, and his evidence has been questioned. Perhaps he deduced Peter's influence from his importance within the gospel itself; the bishop then could have identified its author as Peter's known protégé, Mark.

For the moment, nonetheless, we are following Papias's lead. We picture a Mark who worked with Peter and who made from the mass of the apostle's stories the dramatic gospel we have today.

Papias clearly feels defensive about the order in which Mark tells of events: "Mark had not heard the Lord, nor been a follower of his, but later of Peter, who used to adapt his teaching to the needs [of the situation], but not so as to make an orderly account of the Lord's sayings. So Mark did no wrong in writing down single things just as he recalled them. For he had one purpose only: to omit nothing of what he had heard, and to state nothing falsely."

By Papias's day other gospels were available to which Mark's could be compared. Perhaps Papias had another of our own four in mind: Matthew's or John's. But we might then have expected him to defend Mark's brevity over against their fuller narratives. This is not the argument he mounts. Mark's antagonists may rather have been appealing to "protogospels"—or at least to sequences of stories—long since lost. We will find good reason to watch the shape that Mark gives to his narrative, better reason still if that shape diverged from the shape of other versions independent of his own.

We certainly should not assume that Mark was the first to tell the story of Jesus' work "from beginning to end." Mark's narrative may well have grown out of regular recitation at church gatherings. Fewer people in those days were taught to read, and far more instruction was passed on by word of mouth. As Mark's book itself may have been meant for use at services, section by section, so some stories may already have been shaped and put in order long before he wrote, in a pattern of public readings, Sunday by Sunday. We speak throughout of the gospels' "readers," but it was just as important to *hear* the story unfolding in the order in which Mark tells it. For, as we will see in our final chapter, the key to the gospel's end lies at its beginning. Here is a story that must be heard and heard again, each time with more understanding. Only then will it reveal its mystery: the true course of that battle that seemed to end in humiliation and despair when Jesus cried out on the cross, *"My God, my God, why have you deserted me?"* and died.

CHAPTER 3

Storm Warning

Mark's Context: The Church in Rome

PAUL IN ROME: JOURNEY'S GOAL

The church's early years lies largely hidden from our view. Several shadowy outlines can be seen, a very few contours are sharply (but unevenly) lit. It is time for us to fill in what details we can. We will do well to focus on a few main centers; and best of all, to focus first on Rome itself. We will be drawing bold, clear lines where our evidence offers faint and ambiguous traces. For we must bring these churches to life before our eyes. As archaeologists reconstruct from foundations the houses in which our forebears lived, so we can populate our story with such ordinary people as we are ourselves: people with hopes and worries like our own, whose lives had been unsettled or helped or even transformed by contact with this strange Jewish sect that spoke over and over of Jesus.

Rome: Paul had certainly arrived in the city by 60 C.E., perhaps as early as 56 C.E. Less than thirty years had passed since Jesus' death. His followers had already been in Rome for ten or more. One of our earliest reports of the church is from a Roman historian Suetonius: the Emperor Claudius expelled the Jews from Rome, probably in 49 C.E., after repeated riots "instigated by Chreestus." Suetonius is almost certainly referring to Jesus the "Christ," the "Anointed." The trouble may have arisen within the synagogues, between members who revered Jesus and those who did not. Or the rioters may have sought other targets: If this Anointed hero was the agent of the empire's end, then its heathen, idolatrous capital was ripe for attack at his followers' hands.

The Roman authorities were always suspicious of foreign religions. The Jews themselves had been expelled before, in 139 B.C.E. and again in 19 C.E. We cannot be sure how effectively any of these rulings were imposed or for how long. If our sources are to be trusted, that edict in 49 C.E. marked the second brush between Claudius and the Roman Jews in a decade; he had barred them from assembling—and so from attending synagogue—at the start of his reign.

The New Order may still bear a trace of that first setback for the Roman church. One of its most intriguing texts is the so-called Letter to the Hebrews. Although it was long attributed to Paul, we actually know neither who wrote it nor the whereabouts of the Jewish Christians to whom it was written. It ends with a greeting to its addressees: *Those from Italy send their regards* (Hebrews 13.24). Why should the letter's readers have valued this greeting? Perhaps because they themselves were still in Italy and in this note received a welcome word of recognition from old friends. Was it from those friends, once in Italy themselves, that the writer learned of the persecutions that his addressees had undergone? *Remember that time,* urges the writer, *when you took on such a hard struggle with suffering: you were yourselves held up to a public display of insults and attacks or you linked yourselves with their victims, you shared in the suffering of those in prison, you were glad to be stripped of your belongings—for you knew you owned something greater and more lasting* (Hebrews 10.32–34).

Insults, attacks, prison, and confiscation: Nearly two thousand years have passed since the victims packed what they could carry and left their homes behind, but we still know the names of two among the scores of exiles who left Italy for Corinth because of Claudius's edict that all the Jews should leave Rome. Those two were the Jewish Christians Aquila and his wife, Prisca (Mission [Acts] 18.2). Aquila worked in leather or linen; this was the trade also of Paul, who stayed with them in Corinth. They then traveled with him to Ephesus and hosted a Christian community (*ekklesia*, literally an "assembly," now translated as "church") in their house before returning to Rome. They head the list of allies to whom Paul's Letter to the Romans sends his greetings: They had risked their lives for him. Prisca and Aquila had come full circle, and thanks to that exile in 49 C.E. they had become Paul's closest friends.

In between such occasional repressions the Jews were well treated under the law. Both Julius Caesar and Augustus had granted them special privileges in Rome, which later emperors confirmed. By the 60s C.E. there were probably thirty to forty thousand Jews in Rome. We hear of different Roman synagogues serving different groups of Jews: those in the emperor's household or connected with the government in Israel and Syria, those speaking Greek and those speaking Aramaic, and those from southern Italy or Africa. The congregations met in the houses of wealthy members; there is still no clear evidence in first-century Rome of a purpose-built synagogue or a building converted to such "official" use.

As elsewhere, so in Rome: In these Jewish congregations lies the origin of the church. Many of its members were themselves Jewish; the synagogues were natural places in which to acknowledge allegiance to the Jewish prophet Jesus. Gentiles, too, found a home there for this new form of the ancient Jewish faith; we hear over and over of Luke's "God-fearers," gentile affiliates of the synagogues who observed parts of the Jewish Law. Throughout the following pages we will call the church's members "Christians," but this does not yet set them apart from the synagogues within which they worshiped.

A touching witness to this life together may be found in an early commentary on Paul's letters. It was written in the fourth century, long after the Roman church and synagogues had gone their separate ways, by an author we know as Ambrosiaster. He certainly knew the Jews of Italy firsthand; he himself may have been Jewish by birth and after a time in the church, returned to Judaism. "It is established," he says, "that there were Jews living in Rome in the times of the first missionaries and that those Jews who had believed in the Anointed passed on to the Romans the tradition that in revering the Anointed they ought to abide by the Jewish Law. We ought not to condemn the Romans but to praise their faith; because without seeing any miracles or any of those missionaries, they nevertheless accepted faith in the Anointed, albeit according to a Jewish rite."

We cannot now know how many of these synagogues had such members or affiliates who revered Jesus, or exactly how central he was in the faith of these different admirers. Rather than think of a single "church," we should probably imagine individuals grouped in various synagogues; they gravitated, no doubt, to synagogues whose leaders welcomed the missionaries of Jesus. And then came the edict of 49 C.E. The Jews were ordered out of Rome. Gentile affiliates, whether Christian or not, had good reason to lie low. Synagogue gatherings were suddenly few and far between.

Reverence for Jesus may already have caused friction within synagogues. We have seen as much in our first outline of the Mission (Acts) and of Paul. Jesus' adherents could readily seem like destructive parasites, disrupting the traditional orders of worship and daily life. They raised questions where no doubt had existed and sought change where none had ever been needed. Claudius's edict loosened the ties between Christians and their synagogues' well-established leadership. A new form of gathering might long have been sought; now it was needed. The church was coming to birth.

What sort of people were the Christians in Rome in the early 60s C.E.? At the end of Paul's Letter to the Romans is an extended greeting: Paul sends his best wishes to twenty-eight of his friends and associates. First on the list come Aquila and Prisca, safely back in the city after Claudius's death and the lapse of his edict. The rest of the list is as personal as its start; here lies clue after clue to the character of our small church.

Rome was a magnet. More than half Paul's list commends people likely to be immigrants; their names were popular in quite different corners of the empire. Nine of those mentioned are women. Mention of Rufus and his mother, "who has been a mother to me, too," almost certainly recalls the terrible week in Jerusalem with which our story started. Mark's readers knew the Rufus whose father, Simon of Cyrene, had carried Jesus' cross to his crucifixion (Mark 15.21); if Mark's gospel and Paul's list are both directed to the Roman church, we might well suspect that one and the same

Rufus was known to both. In the Mission we read that Cyrenean preachers made the first "gentile" conversions at Antioch; the gospel, they insisted, was for all nations. It was their activity that led to Barnabas's visit and so to Paul's. Had Rufus's family preached a Pauline gospel before Paul himself and so taken this new missionary—once the most dangerous antagonist of the church—to their heart?

Almost a third of Rome's inhabitants were present or former slaves; it is no surprise, then, that at least ten of Paul's addressees have slaves' names. Paul greets the Christian members of two households; one of the masters may have been the Narcissus, himself a former slave, who had been a close aide to the emperor Claudius and amassed a fortune of his own. His slaves would have joined the emperor's at their master's fall from favor; several names in Paul's list match those found in the vast imperial household.

Paul picks out just three of his addressees as Jewish. The church may now have been made up almost entirely of gentiles, those who had escaped banishment in 49 C.E. and those who had joined the church since. On returning to the city, the Christian Jews would have sought out "their own" synagogues and found the assemblies' character quite changed, their leaders all gentile. The church had developed a life independent of Jewish ways, its daily regulations looked less to the Old Order, its worship gave ever more prominence to Jesus. Paul's whole letter is informed by the tension to which such developments had given rise. The church's leadership was still divided over the Jewish Law; there may even have been separate congregations badly in need of reconciliation.

The troubles of 49 C.E. have made Paul wary. There is trouble brewing again: Paul has heard of grievances nursed in the church against Roman authority. The old riots may have been aimed at the imperial power, whose end the hotheads of Chreestus had seen looming. Around the time of Paul's letter, we know there were widespread protests in Rome against the unjust exacting of taxes. A regime that some Christians still reckoned illegitimate, plus gross extortion by its agents, was a volatile combination. Paul writes sharply: Nothing, he insists, must disrupt the church's standing in official eyes. He knows only too well from Prisca and Aquila how brutally the police could respond. Paul orders,

Every single person must obey the governing authorities. There is no authority that is not from God, and the powers that be were appointed by God. Anyone, then, who resists that power is in rebellion against God's decision and such rebels are bound to be punished. You want to be free from fear of the authorities? Do what is good, and you will have their praise. They are there in the service of God for the general good.
(ROMANS 13.1–4)

Rufus and his mother, Epainetus, Andronicus and Junia, Ampliatus, Urban, and Stachys: Paul's friends are just such ordinary people as crowded the tenements and made a living as artisans, small merchants, and manual or clerical staff; here were citizens and slaves, locals of Rome, a missionary from Jerusalem, and an early convert from Asia.

Within a decade they would need all the reassurance that Paul's letter could give them. And good reason to question it: *The authorities are there in the service of God for the general good* (Romans 13.4).

Paul knew that restive Christians could bring trouble on the church that it could ill afford. He trod a careful path. But such resistance to Roman rule was deeply rooted in the church's history. Jesus and Peter themselves, after all, were from Galilee, a fiercely independent area and for decades a seedbed of rebellion. We have met Peter in the great metropolis of Rome. But this is not where he belonged. It is time to hear the voices of Galilee. Beneath the choppy surface of Mark's story are flowing ocean currents that we can trace to the history of this beautiful, proud land of Jesus' birth.

Mark and Peter: From Galilee to Rome

STARTING THE STORY: GALILEE

It is no surprise that Mark's name and Peter's have so long been linked. After the gospel's prelude, Peter is the first character confronted by Jesus. He is introduced in a story pared to the bone. Here is pure drama: Peter had been a fisherman alongside his brother Andrew on the Lake of Galilee; Jesus calls them to *fish for people*. Two more fishermen join Jesus in the next scene: James and John, who had worked with their father and his hired men. Mark then presents a first healing in the synagogue, an exorcism wrought on the Sabbath: Here is a bold fanfare to Jesus' power, reverberating through this center of Jewish life and tradition. The next scene, by contrast, takes us to Peter's house: His mother-in-law is ill. Mark tells of her healing so simply and directly that scholars have found traces here of Peter's own dictation.

Mark's Peter is a touchingly human figure. He is one of the innermost few within the circle of Jesus' friends. Just these few see Jesus' dazzling transformation, hear him foretell the climax to world history, and are called to keep him company as he prays. Peter himself is the natural leader of Jesus' followers: He answers Jesus' question, *"Who do you say I am?"* On Jesus' last night with his friends, Peter is the first to promise loyalty unto death. But Peter, too, rejects the very idea of Jesus' suffering and within hours of that brave promise, while Jesus is on trial for his life, denies three times all knowledge of his master.

If Peter's reminiscences lie behind our gospel, so then do Peter's background, life, and hopes. We must trace him, our first storyteller, back to Galilee, where he and Jesus had grown up and learned the vocabulary of God's people Israel: nation, Law, and future freedom. Galilee was the first home of Jesus' movement. And so, in one thread of our traditions, it remained: Mark has Jesus' followers go back to Galilee after Easter, and in a distinctive story of those strange days (John 21, apparently an appendix to the gospel), Peter, James, and John are once more fishing on the lake. Here need be no surprise. Peter, after all, was a married man; we hear again of his wife from Paul (1 Corinthians 9.5) but of no children. Where else would Peter go but home?

What might we learn from Galilee, of Jesus and of Peter, of the crucial link (if Papias is right) in our story's preservation, who passed his recollections on to Mark? The Jewish historian Josephus knew Galilee well; he commanded the rebels against Rome there in 66 C.E. until his capture and defection to the empire. The most famous feature of the Galileans, he says, was their independence. He had good reason to speak of their hardiness; the courage of an army wins respect for its general. The Galileans, he tells his new masters, "had always resisted any hostile invasion, and were from infancy inured to war." Successive revolts in Galilee and Judaea were led by Galileans, from Judas in 4 B.C.E. to Eleazar's last stand in the war of 66–70 C.E. These leaders may even have been the generations of a single Galilean family. Within their movement sprang up the Zealots, whose fight for independence became the stuff of legend. For four years after the rest of Israel had been subdued in 70 C.E., the Zealots held out against the Romans in the desert fortress of Masada. When there was no hope of rescue or escape, their leader, Eleazar, urged the defenders to kill their children and then one another. Better this than to fall into the hands of Rome. When the Roman soldiers finally entered the fort, they found only corpses. They had come to kill, but their work had already been done.

Such war was not the only way in which Rome could be resisted. In 40 C.E. the emperor Caligula gave orders for a statue of himself to be placed in the Temple in Jerusalem. It would be a terrible desecration. The Jews protested by the thousands. The Roman general Petronius, in charge of the operation, is for our Jewish sources more than a statesman. He has become a model of the honorable, God-fearing gentile: He exposed himself to the emperor's anger—and so to mortal danger—sooner than pursue a policy that would lead to massacre.

Petronius headed for Tiberias, in the heart of Galilee, to negotiate. Roman and Jewish leaders alike saw real danger ahead—not in armed uprising against the Romans but in the weeks of inaction on the farms. The fields had not been sown; the crops were threatened. The year's taxes would be unpayable; the only harvest, Petronius was warned, would be bandits. A second source for the story places the Galilean protest at harvest time. Here Petronius saw how vulnerable were the ripe fields to fire. The emperor himself was due to sail down this coast; Galilee could confront him with scorched earth and no food. Behind these reports may well lie a deliberate strike by the Galileans and the threat of worse to come. Not even Petronius's legions could protect an entire region and a few compliant farmers from an uprising en masse. Here in the land itself was the Galileans' power and their natural weapon of resistance.

There was good reason for the authorities to take notice of their threat. Galilee was extraordinarily fertile, Josephus tells us. It sustained 204 towns and villages. Every inch of the land was under cultivation. Walnuts, palm trees, figs, and olives, needing quite different conditions, all flourished; grapes and figs were borne through ten months of the year, other fruits the whole year round. Josephus waxes poetic: "Nature seemed to have taken pride in assembling, by a tour de force, the most disparate species in a single spot, and each of the seasons, by a happy rivalry, to have claimed the region for its own."

This is the home country of Jesus and the grist to his imagination. His stories are almost always of country life. He and his friends know exactly what it was to sow and plow and wait for the crop to grow. Some seed comes to nothing, some never even start to grow, but the day will come when the field is golden and the scythe is sharp, and with the long, steady swish of the blade the wheat is cut and the ears are gathered in.

And the harvest? Patience, as we have seen, was not the only weapon in the church's armory. From the Old Order, as we have seen, Jesus' generation and Mark's had inherited the conviction that God would finally "harvest" the earth: he would assert his reign over the whole world, and Israel would be vindicated at last. God's victory would not be straightforward. The forces ranged against his kingdom, after all, were immeasurable; their defeat would involve a cataclysm beyond imagining. From the first century C.E. a Jewish poem has reached us in the so-called *Testament of Moses*. Here is the language of *God*'s kingdom, when the madness of emperors and the insolence of their armies would be ended forever:

> God's Kingdom will be revealed throughout his whole creation;
> Then the devil will have an end.
> For God will arise from his kingly throne,
> he will go forth from his holy habitation
> with indignation and wrath on behalf of his children.

> The earth will tremble and the high mountains shall be made low.
> The sun will not give light,
> and in darkness the horns of the moon shall flee.

> For the Most High God will surge forth,
> the Eternal One alone.
> In full view will he come to work vengeance on the nations.
> All their idols will he destroy.
> Then will you be happy, O Israel!
> You will mount up above the wings of an eagle.
> Yes, all things will be fulfilled.
> (TESTAMENT OF MOSES 10.1–8)

Such hope did not survive undimmed. The promise remained unfulfilled; the kingdom was still Rome's; God's power was still reined in. Paul mellowed in his expectations of Jesus' return. Peter, according to a letter that has reached us under his name, was confronted by sharp doubts among his followers. We cannot be sure that Peter himself composed this letter, but we will expect to find here the themes and doctrines remembered and revered as his. He, too, like the heirs that probably wrote this letter in his name, confronted the longing for Jesus' triumphant return. Such expectation was unyielding: such fierce hope can be brittle, its disappointment violent. Unbelievers had good reason to scoff, and the church needed all the reassurance the writer could offer. The Old Order's dreams of new heaven and new earth have become at his hands more vivid and more sweeping than ever:

> *Mockers will speak out in the last days, saying: "Where is the promise of the Lord's coming? Everything goes on as it has since the Fathers died, as it has since the start of creation."*
>
> *Remember, my beloved, that with the Lord one day is like* [or *can mean*] *a thousand years, and a thousand years is like one day. The Lord is not being slow to carry out his promise as anyone else might be called slow, but is being patient toward you, wanting nobody to be lost and everybody to change their hearts and ways. The day of the Lord will come like a thief, and then with a roar the heavens will vanish, the elements will be dissolved into fire, and the earth will be burned up and all that it contains.*
>
> *Since all around us is coming to an end like this, behave as you should in holy behavior and prayers, waiting and longing for the arrival of the Day of God, when the sky will dissolve in fire and the elements melt in the heat. What we are waiting for is what he promised: the new heavens and new earth where justice and truth will be at home.*
>
> (2 PETER 3.3–13)

Mark's Crucible: The Great Fire in Rome

Early morning, July 19, 64 C.E., in the drought of the Roman summer. All it took was a spark. From a baker's oven, perhaps, or a smithy, among the wooden workshops and stores crammed beneath the stadium's great colonnade. The first smoke rose by the Temple of Proserpina. A sirocco wind from the south was enough to fan the flames. The fire swept the full length of the stadium and headed north. First the valley: No stone mansions or open spaces stood in the way, just the colonnade packed with goods and then a warren of lanes and houses and shops—wooden buildings, every one. Then the surrounding hills: palaces and temples, the domains of the rich and shacks of the poor. Nothing could be saved.

Whole families died in the blaze trying to save the elderly or rescue belongings. The fire spread unevenly; burning debris was blown ahead and found further houses, further fuel. Large parts of Rome were built up as "islands": Their tenement blocks, rising four or five stories high around a central courtyard, housed dozens of families cheek by jowl. The danger drew near; the tenants headed for the streets. Those who ran from one outbreak were caught by another; those who made for an open square were trapped by panicking crowds and a circle of fire that brought the tall, ramshackle tenements down on them all in flames.

A baker's oven or a smithy, unguarded in the early morning? Perhaps. But who were those figures seen flitting from street to street in the light of the previous night's full moon? Who were these thugs threatening anyone who fought the flames, throwing firebrands into any house as yet untouched? What was that they shouted as they shoved aside any protesters? "It's on orders, we've got our orders."

The flames swept north. Down on the southern fringes of the city, out of danger, lived most of Rome's Jews, and among them the adherents—both Jewish and gentile—of the strange prophet Jesus. They felt the heat blaze across the river and above the city walls, watched the smoke rise from a thousand fires, heard the crash of buildings and the screams of the crowd. The center of empire was in flames. What portent did the tiny group of Jesus' followers find in this disaster? The Old Order seemed to give clues enough, to those with eyes alert to see them. These are the words of Isaiah, the ancient prophet of Israel, written down centuries before:

See, the Day of the Lord is coming, a cruel day, with wrath and fierce anger, to make the land desolate and destroy the wrongdoers within it. The stars of heaven and their constellations will not show their light. The rising sun will be darkened and the moon not give its light.
"I, the Lord, will punish the world for its wrongdoing, I will put an end to the pride of the arrogant and will humble the pride of despots. I will make the heavens tremble, and the earth will shake from its place in the day of my burning anger."
(ISAIAH 13.9–13)

The fire's victims eyed with a fierce suspicion these Christians' safety from the fire, who spoke of their enemies' destruction and who watched without despair as Rome's homes and temples burned. For after the flames came the rumors and the search for suspects on whom to pin the blame. The city's anger must be satisfied. Who had those shadowy figures been, out on the streets the night before the fire? Whose were the orders not to douse the flames?

The Christians, too, would be looking for a sign in this disaster, but of a quite different kind. Peter's church might look for hope beyond the empire's domination, but how was such unstoppable power to be defeated? What would be the sign that God was marshaling his forces and preparing the war that would inaugurate the reign of his Anointed, the untrammeled exercise of his power here on earth?

A cataclysm was needed, and in this smoldering city perhaps it was at last in view. Perhaps God was at last purging his world of the arrogance and idolatry of this new Babylon.

Therefore on a single day her scourges shall come upon her,
and she shall be burned in fire,
for mighty is the Lord the God who judges her.

And the kings of the earth shall weep,
those who committed adultery with her,
when they see the smoke of her fire.
They shall stand at a distance through fear of her punishment, and will say,
"Woe, woe to Babylon the powerful city,
for in a single hour your judgment has come upon you."

                                    (BOOK OF UNVEILING [REVELATION] 18.8)

Peter's excited band of followers would have had good reason to ask, was this mael-strom in Rome what they'd been waiting for? The start of the judgment and so of the kingdom to follow. Here and now. What the prophet Isaiah had spoken about, and what they were told, Jesus himself had foreseen also: *"The sun will be darkened,"* Jesus said, *"and the moon will not give its light; the stars will fall from the sky and the heavenly bodies be shaken"* (Mark 13.24–25).

God's Kingdom: Nero or Jesus

THE IMPERIAL COURT

The church spoke of kingship, of God's power realized on earth. Just a mile from Peter's church was another king enthroned on earth, wielding a more palpable power. One of Nero's palaces, still under construction, was threatened by the fire. At last the emperor himself had returned to Rome.

He was too late; by the end of the week that palace, too, would be in flames. But rulings were issued: to open the army's great parade ground for refugees and the emperor's own gardens, too; to provide encampments for the homeless; to bring in food from the harbor and to keep the price of bread down.

Who was this emperor, still vivid in the world's imagination as a tyrant, mad with power? His policy scarred the church with its first persecution; the rumors of his immortality fueled the Book of Unveiling (Revelation) and so have shaped the church's vision ever since of its final and most vicious enemy.

History has not been kind to Nero. He was loathed by the ruling classes in Rome, and the historians on whom we chiefly depend for evidence did nothing, sixty years after his death, to rehabilitate his name. They depended on goodwill from emperors of new and nervous dynasties. No historian could criticize the present rule, but the hor-rors of an old regime offered a mirror in which our historians could safely comment on the new. The historian Suetonius we have already met; in the following pages we shall hear the words of Tacitus, the greatest historian of his century, a man whose tight, bit-ter prose speaks volumes of the anger with which he views the empire around him.

Nero's career included actions enough to appall any historian: He had murdered his own mother, his first wife, and the chief rivals to his throne. A friend of the emperor, however, would have left a far more positive account of the fire's aftermath than the story we hear from Tacitus. Nero offered tax breaks for those who repaired the city; he regulated the new buildings' materials, spacing, and design in measures of which even his enemies approved. One of the tenement blocks built after the fire was in use for almost two thousand years; it was demolished only in 1877. Public buildings in the fire's area were once more in use within a year; if Tacitus did not overstate the damage, the fire's effects would be efficiently and quickly reversed, almost certainly through the emperor's energy.

The fire offered an opportunity dear to Nero's heart. He was disgusted, Suetonius says, by the squalor of old Rome. Here at last was a chance to build a capital worthy of his empire and himself, Greek in style and grand in execution. Such a vision comes as no surprise. This emperor, ruler of Europe and beyond, powerful beyond imagination, was—he believed—an *artist:* above all, a poet and musician such as the god Apollo, who appeared with a lyre on his coins. Early in the fateful year of 64 C.E. he had been ready to perform his own proudest composition. He may even have done so in public. Within a few months the irony of its theme would return to haunt his court. The emperor's poem concerned the destruction of another great capital, victim of the most famous war in the ancient world. Nero was emulating that world's greatest poets when he chose his poem's subject, "The Burning of Troy."

To capture some sense of life at court, let us set just one person in comparison with our witness Mark. Whose career might we follow in those vast palaces, dangerous with intrigue? As Peter had his Mark, so the emperor had a poet. In the young Lucan, Nero found a willing protégé. Feted at court and promoted beyond his years, Lucan wrote an enormous poem on the origins of Rome's Civil War. The war had ended a hundred years before—not long enough to extinguish its passions and ideals, the memory of old betrayals and the scars of power lost and won. Lucan's heroes were the old elite of Rome; Nero's dynasty was founded by the general who outmaneuvered and outfought them. The young poet had to take care to show his loyalty. Even by the standards of imperial sycophancy his praise of Nero is extravagant:

> If fate could find no other way for the advent of Nero,
> Then we complain no more against the gods.
> Rome owes much to the horrors of her civil war,
> Because what was done was done, Nero, for you. When your watch on earth is over
> And you seek the stars at last, the heavenly palace you prefer
> Will welcome you and the sky rejoice: whether to wield the scepter of Jupiter,
> Or to mount the sun's chariot and circle earth with your moving flame—
> Every god will give place to you, and nature let you decide
> What deity you wish to be, where to establish your universal throne.
> But to me you are already power divine. And if my breast receives you to inspire my verse,
> I would not trouble the gods of poetry or inspiration;
> You alone are sufficient to give strength to a Roman poem.

Such praise was born of fear. It was followed soon enough by hatred. Within a year Lucan was barred from publishing or performing poetry; the emperor was jealous of his success. A conspiracy followed in which the poet was implicated. Lucan tried to save himself, it is said, by betraying his mother. To no avail: He had his veins slashed as he lay in a warm bath, and he died reciting his own poem on Rome's Civil War.

Lucan and Mark: They were writing in the same city and in the same years. Each was responding to the mightiest power he acknowledged in the world. It would be hard to imagine two such different tributes, to two such different kings.

The emperor had returned to his capital. He had given orders for the refugees' relief. And what then? Over the years a rumor grew: Nero had sung poetry on his private stage as Rome burned. Tacitus relays it as a rumor, no more. Writing around the same time, Suetonius tells the story with more detail and with no doubt of its truth: Nero had sung from the Tower of Maecenas, one palace still safe from the blaze, "pleased by the beauty of the fire."

The story was gradually taking the form in which the Western world would evermore remember it. A hundred years later Dio completed its development. In his version, Nero is given a spectacular view of his burning capital: "Nero went to the top of the Palatine, and in the garb of a professional singer he sang of Troy's destruction—but looked on Rome's."

Here was power on earth: limitless, fearsome, and hated beyond the grave.

For six days the city burned. By the time a firebreak had been cleared, three of the city's fourteen regions, we are told, were no more; seven were ruins of their former selves.

And then the fire broke out again.

Was this God's vindication of his faithful servants? The Christians had good reason to ask. Here was punishment upon the power of Rome, sure enough. And God had taken due pity on his own people: All those across the Tiber were safe from the flames. Here the Christians could keep their homes safe from looters and their families from the panic. Here they could wait for the promised and final deliverance. Their hour was coming.

If these were the hopes of Mark's church, its members would to be cruelly disappointed. It was not God's vindication that lay ahead, but the first attack aimed specifically at Jesus' followers by Roman power. These Christians in Rome were not the first to be so mistaken. Jesus' own pupils, in Mark's story, never did see what lay ahead. We hear Jesus speak of his coming death, and the young Peter is deeply shocked. A few pages later Jesus repeats the warning and straight afterward finds his pupils squabbling: "Which of us is the greatest?" A third time the knell sounds: The Son of Man is going to be handed over to the Romans, who will mock him and spit at him and scourge him and condemn him to death. And in the very next scene James and John sidle up to Jesus and ask to sit at his right hand and his left when he is invested with his kingly power.

Had the leaders of Mark's church, ever more complacent and less alert, been congratulating themselves in turn? Here in the empire's ruined capital, livid with anger and fear, would be an end to those easy, sleepy days. Three times on the night of his arrest, Mark's Jesus tells his closest friends to stay awake: *"And what I say to you I say to everyone, Stay awake"* (Mark 13.37). But how readily we block out difficulties that we cannot solve and dare not see!

Three times those friends fall asleep while Jesus prays in agony.

The Great Fire: Finding the Culprits

That young poet Lucan, in the long run, had his revenge. When he had been banned from poetry he wrote a prose account of the fire. We are told he blamed Nero for the blaze. Another conspirator in 65 C.E., a member of the emperor's own guard, claimed the same. Their account gave weight to a dark suspicion. Who, after all, had been those figures spreading the fire and claiming to act on orders? By the time Tacitus wrote, the emperor's guilt was widely believed. Tacitus himself wondered if those shadowy figures were really just looters. Suetonius has no doubt: They were the emperor's agents. The historians' sources spoke up well after the event, but with the authority of courtiers in the know. Lucan, after all, was a figure to respect.

In the days after the fire, prayers were offered to the god of fire and to the goddess Proserpina, near whose temple the fire had broken out. Vigils were observed, banquets held. Nothing, we are told, would lay the story of imperial arson to rest. Suspicion fed suspicion: The fire had restarted on the estates of Tigellinus, Nero's own chief of police. The mood was turning ugly. The blame must be shifted and scapegoats found. There was no love in the city for the so-called Christians: They insulted the gods of Rome and even squabbled with the Jews. Tacitus gives us one of the earliest descriptions by a pagan. He encountered them firsthand when he ran the province of Asia in 112 C.E. He writes,

> There was a group, loathed for its vices, that the people called Christians. Responsible for the name was Christ; he had been put to death by Pontius Pilate when Tiberius was emperor. This checked the horrid superstition, but not for long; it burst out again, not only in Judaea where it had started, but in Rome, too, a sink into which everything vile and shameful flows and finds its vogue.

How were these "culprits" found? Some would have been easy targets. Claudius had died in 54 C.E. Even for Jews who were Christians, there had been little to fear since then and so no reason to hide; those who had gone into exile returned; those who had escaped the emperor's edict resumed the life of their synagogues. Claudius's edict had given gentiles, however committed to the church, good reason to disown any link with Chreestus and the Jews. If they had been able to meet at all, it was not as a synagogue. How things had changed: In 64 C.E. it was the Jews who must keep their distance from any incriminating "Christian" connection.

Here for the first time the distinction between Jews and Christians was becoming important in the empire's eyes. Tigellinus may have had inside information to sustain it. The empress Poppaea was said to be attracted to Judaism; in the same year of 64 C.E. our historian Josephus won access to Poppaea through a Jewish actor in Rome and so secured some relatives' release from prison. The Christian sect may have had friends in high places, too: We have just one uncertain hint of an aristocratic convert in the fifties. Valued allies in the days of Claudius, however, were by 64 the very spiders that the authorities sought at the center of the Christian web.

Was this all the information that Tigellinus's agents used? Tacitus's Latin at this point is obscure, and his text has been muddled by generations of scribes. He tells us, without making any point of his own to the Christians' discredit, that those "who confessed" were first arrested; thanks to their testimony "a huge number" was convicted in turn. What did those first "culprits" confess—their faith or their guilt? Or has Tacitus preserved for us a trace of Nero's own propaganda in a deft confusion of the two?

Once holding a few suspects in his prisons, Tigellinus had no scruples; the torture of slaves and exslaves extracted further names. Was this all he had to hand? Before we close the file on these arrests, we should listen to the faint echo that has reached us of a sadder story. More or less contemporary with Tacitus was Bishop Clement of Rome. Here a quite different voice speaks of the church and its heroes; he is devoted to the community that Tacitus so heartily despises.

In his Letter to the Corinthians, Clement recalls Peter and Paul. He writes of "jealousy" surrounding them. We might wonder how much he knew about it that he did not find in Paul's own letters; we are not the first to read a context out of these texts themselves. Clement is certainly drawing on Paul's own account. Paul had probably written his Letter to the Philippians when he was under a form of house arrest in Rome. It sounds an unexpected note: *Some here are proclaiming the Anointed through rivalry, yes, and competition; . . . they are proclaiming the Anointed through jealousy, and expect to add further weight to the chains I already bear* (Philippians 1.15–17).

But Clement may have heard more—darker details of which Paul could not have known: details of Paul's own end. Clement berates the Corinthians for the jealousy that is tearing their church apart. He reminds them of such division's terrible effects:

Because of jealousy and envy the greatest pillars of the church were persecuted and they worked on even to death. Because of wicked jealousy Peter endured a good many labors and then went to his appointed place of glory. Because of jealousy and strife Paul left a living example of what is won by patient endurance. He was exiled and stoned, he preached to the world and bore his testimony before the authorities. And so he was freed from the world and went to the holy place.

Jealousy? Envy? We know that the disagreements that had burst open in Antioch lay between the church's factions still. Were they so bitter in Rome that one group would inform on another? Jewish Christians and gentile, advocates of the Law's observance and radicals determined to ignore it, Christians from Asia and locals to Rome, slaves of the emperor's own household and independent patrons—perhaps, for all Paul's work and Peter's, too much divided the church's groups and too little held them together.

When fear was in the air, when troops were searching the streets and Tigellinus was hungry for culprits, how many Christians sought safety for their families and them-selves with the names of old opponents and long-resented "apostates"? It is no coinci-dence that Mark's Jesus warns his pupils, *"And brother will betray brother to death, and father his son, and children will rise up against their parents and kill them. And you shall be hated by all on account of my name"* (Mark 13.12–13).

THE FINAL ENEMY

A far cry, this, from the tranquillity promised by Paul: *"You want to be free,"* Paul had asked, *"from fear of the authorities? Do what is good, and you will have their praise. They are there in the service of God for the general good"* (Romans 13.3–4). Further still from the kingdom for which the church had waited with such longing was the reward that God had prepared for his saints.

Chief source for the church's comfort was the Old Order, still in our hands today. We, too, can look back to the prophets of old and hear again of the sufferings *they* had undergone: of exile and danger, of the pride of God's enemies and the humbling of his people. Mark knew these predictions well. As the Jews pored over them, so the church searched them, too, for clues to God's purpose and its fulfillment in history.

Such visions had long been familiar. In the form of a disclosure made to a privileged seer, the questions of a sad, beleaguered people could be answered and its hopes raised with the sure prospect—divinely revealed, divinely guaranteed—of its victorious future. The text of the Old Order read most avidly by those who yearned for such ful-fillment has been the Book of Daniel. God's people learned here to expect terrible per-secution and to look for God's final intervention on their behalf. *In the first year of Belshazzar king of Babylon*—that is, six hundred years before Mark wrote—*the prophet Daniel had a dream* (Daniel 7.1).

He saw a vision of terrifying animals, a sequence of the enemies that would oppress God's people. Most fearsome of all was the fourth, the last: *There before me was a beast, terrifying and frightening and very powerful. It had large iron teeth; it crushed and devoured its victims and trampled underfoot whatever was left.* The vision continued: *There before me on the beast was a little horn. This horn had eyes like the eyes of a man and a mouth that spoke boastfully* (Daniel 7.7, 8).

How was such a vision to be interpreted? Who was meant by the beast? There was clearly a consummation to be hoped for: God's final rescue of his chosen people, and until that came about, the code in which God's enemies were described could be applied over and again, generation by generation, to the particular oppressors and dangers of the day.

"You shall be hated by all," warned Jesus, *"on account of my name, but whoever stands firm to the end will be saved"* (Mark 13.13). Centuries of oppression had taught Israel to refine its hopes, to find grounds for hope in the very conditions that defied it. Their final form is deeply poignant: By the first century C.E. there was a widespread belief that before God's vindication of his heroes, their troubles would get worse—worse than they had ever been.

Our concern in *The Four Witnesses* is with one Jewish sect that outgrew its origins and became the world-wide church. But Jesus' followers were not the only Jewish group to stand in an uneasy relation with Jerusalem and its authorities. Over and over we will turn to the documents discovered in the 1940s at Qumran beside the Dead Sea. Thousands of fragmentary manuscripts, painstakingly restored, have opened before us an unimagined landscape. A sect, apparently based at Qumran, nurtured hopes that God would deliver all his people from the errors of false leaders and the oppression of its enemies. With intense, sophisticated speculation the sectaries looked forward to a final war in which their own sect, the heroes of God's cause, would have a leading part to play.

"On the day when the enemies fall," we hear in these scrolls, "there shall be a battle and terrible carnage before the Lord, for that shall be the day appointed for the destruction of the children of darkness." But not just the wicked will suffer: "It shall be a time of great tribulation for the people that God shall redeem. Of all its afflictions none shall be as this, from its sudden beginning until its end in eternal redemption."

In this specter of a final catastrophe the enemy was vividly imagined—in particular, its commander. Daniel had spoken of an evil ruler who would imagine himself greater than all the gods (Daniel 11.36). At Qumran the picture was filled out. A figure had been seen in a dream,

who will proclaim himself the Son of God, they will call him the Son of the Most High. They will reign for years on the earth and they will trample all. People will trample on people and one province on another—until the people of God arise, and all will rest from the sword. The people of God will inherit an eternal kingdom, they will judge the world in truth. The Great God is their helper.

God's greatest general, in the writings from Qumran, is Melchizedek: "My king is justice"; over against him in the final battle stands Melchiresha, "My king is wickedness." Such a mirror image was in the church's mind as well. The reverence due to Jesus stirred thoughts of its own antithesis. Most frightening of all, the church's enemies, it was said, would be a figure opposed in every detail to God and his Anointed; he will demand for himself the worship that is due to God. We read of him in another Pauline letter: *He will oppose and exalt himself over everything that is called God or is worshiped, so that he sets himself up in God's temple, proclaiming himself to be God* (2 Thessalonians 2.4).

What gave rise to this image, of a despot demanding worship for himself? Throughout the empire ritual sacrifices were offered to the gods in thanks for the emperor or on his behalf. It was a thin line between such offerings and a sacrifice *to the emperor himself*, a sacrifice such as all devotees paid to their God or gods. When a pogrom broke out against the Jews in Alexandria in 38 C.E., delegations from both sides went to Rome to plead their case. The philosopher Philo was one of five representing the Jews. His own account evokes the visceral fear that the emperor Caligula stirred. Caligula opened the interview: "Are you the god-haters who do not believe me to be a god, a god acknowledged among all other nations but not to be named by you?" The delegates insisted that they had sacrificed for the emperor's welfare with utter loyalty. "Yes," replied the emperor, "you have sacrificed, but to another god, even if it was for me. What use is that? You have not sacrificed *to* me."

At issue was not the incarnation of God or a god, such as the Christian tradition claims. That remained a notion quite foreign to pagans. Worship was a response to power, grateful worship to the benefits brought by its due exercise. "What is a god?" asked a famous maxim. "The exercise of power. What is a king? Godlike."

The cult was offered to rulers to recognize the honor they were due. It was modeled on the cults of the ancient gods. The titles and dignities proper to these could be adapted or attached to the new cult of a ruler. On various inscriptions in Greece one emperor can be called after the king of the gods, "Caesar Augustus Jupiter Savior"; another, "Trajan Hadrian New Dionysus, Olympian, God of all Greece"; Nero himself, "Jupiter Liberator Nero"—"Nero, King of the Gods, Liberator." The sobriquets were chosen for good reasons: Hadrian was famous for his love of Greece, Nero had given the Greeks their freedom. How much recognition was due to whom, for what, how soon, and then for how long after his death? These were sensible questions subtly asked in each case and answered with nuance and care.

What, then, were the limits to the emperor's authority? It was naive, perhaps, but quite consistent to link power over nations with power over nature: a temple to Augustus, and an Augusteum, built opposite the harbors at Alexandria, was described by Philo (when he had good reason to praise Augustus) as a "saving hope" for sailors. A notoriously extravagant panegyric of 143 C.E. claims that "at the very mention of the emperor's name everyone stands up and praises and worships him and utters twofold prayers: one on the emperor's behalf and one to the ruler himself about the suppliant's own matters."

The question already faced the authorities in 64 C.E.: how to distinguish between the Jews loyal just to the synagogues, on the one hand, and the church's Jews and gentiles, on the other. A wedge was steadily inserted between them: The Jews were an ancient race, loyal to their ancestral faith. Through all the uprisings in Judaea—even through a vicious war, four years long and more, for the freedom of their land—the millions of Jews spread around the empire remained, it seems, loyal to Rome's rule. The credit the Jews had won from Julius Caesar and Augustus was not forgotten, and for decades there had been sacrifices offered in Jerusalem, in the Temple itself, for the emperor's safety.

Members of the tiny Christian sect, on the other hand, had abandoned their historic beliefs, whether Jewish or pagan, in favor of conventicles said to celebrate hideous impieties. They had no present ritual with which to acknowledge the emperor's power and no history of loyalty to the empire. This was the group, as Tacitus put it, "loathed for its vices," that the people called Christians: one of the many "vile and shameful things that had flowed into the sink of Rome." They deserved whatever punishment came their way.

Jesus had spoken of persecution to come and of the danger it posed to the eager commitment of a young church. There would be good reason to remember his words. Whether with warning or encouragement, or just with the reassurance that he had anticipated all the turmoil through which his followers must go, Mark's Jesus speaks to the needs of Mark's church: "*Some seed fell on rocky ground, where it did not have much soil, and it sprung up quickly through having no depth of soil. And when the sun rose it was scorched and withered away*" (Mark 4.5–6).

REBUILDING THE CITY

We have heard much of Nero from his enemies, but even Tacitus admits a grudging respect for the emperor's reconstruction of Rome. His vision embraced the whole city, its enlargement and the supply of its food from the harbor town of Ostia. Here was a strategy worthy of the emperor and his capital.

Token of such authority and far more bitterly remembered was the palace that Nero planned for himself. The "Golden House" was to cover nearly two hundred acres in the very center of Rome—buildings, parks, and a lake filling the whole valley where the Colosseum now stands. The main front of the palace would have stretched for over four hundred meters: "One house," snarled the satirist Martial, "took up the whole of Rome." Its public function as the heart of government did nothing to appease the aristocrats whose burned-out homes were passing into the emperor's hands. Connecting this palace to the civic center of old Rome was the ancient Sacred Road. This would become in Nero's plan a colonnaded avenue flanked by bazaars. The site's archaeology suggests that Nero altered the road's course. It was to be aligned with the entrance to the Golden House and, above all, with an enormous statue of bronze, one hundred twenty feet tall. The colossus and its vestibule would command the palace entrance on the Velian Hill and so the whole skyline of Rome.

Such giant statues were not unknown. They made clear as nothing else could the protection and power of the god they showed. Whose then were the features that would look down on the new city? The statue was to show Nero himself. The emperor was later said to have planned a name for the city to match its presiding power. This venerable city, now the undisputed center of the world, was to be called City of Nero.

From Galilee to Rome: The veneration of Jesus had come a long way. Little enough in Rome's metropolis recalled the inland sea of Peter's childhood, fringed with small towns and with farmers' villages in the hills above. Still less, the unchallenged focus of worship: the one Temple of the one God, whose image must never be drawn or carved. Nero would have known something of the Jews' new "Christian" sect, if only that it was tiny, unpleasant, and easily suppressed. Of its leader, this rustic Peter, he may never have heard. But while the emperor was grooming himself and his city for the eternal memory of his reign, that small sect was dwelling on the ancient prophecies of Daniel and their promise of a king to rival even Nero's power. Daniel had written,

> *As I looked, the Ancient of Days took his seat. Thousands upon thousands attended him; ten thousand times ten thousand stood before him. The court was seated, and the books were opened.*
>
> *In my vision at night, I, Daniel, looked, and there before me was one like a son of man, coming with the clouds of heaven. He approached the Ancient of Days and was led into his presence. He was given authority, glory, and sovereign power; all people, nations, and men of every language worshiped him. His dominion is an everlasting dominion that will not pass away, and his kingdom is one that will never be destroyed.*
>
> *(DANIEL 7.10, 13–14)*

It was in this highly charged atmosphere of incipient doom and eagerly awaited glory that Mark composed his story of Jesus, who himself was ignominiously put to death and yet was due to usher in the kingdom of the one true God.

CHAPTER 4

Composing the Story

Jesus and Rival Powers: Divine and Daemonic

THE POWER OF GOD?

"Do you still not understand?" Try as they might, Jesus' friends in Mark's story get it wrong—and not just about his imminent death. The story tells of such strange happenings: A daemon is expelled, a fever cooled, and a whole crowd in consequence brings to Jesus their sick and infirm. The first half of Mark's story is one long demonstration of Jesus' power, and not just over sickness. He feeds thousands with a single armful of food, he walks on water and stills a storm, he takes to himself the prerogative of God to forgive the wrongdoing that has crippled a man.

Modern explanations of these strange stories abound. What would Mark himself have us make of them? He has a vision of his own, built into the way he tells the stories and the connections that he sees among them. Some of these emphases are no doubt Mark's; others he may have inherited with the stories themselves.

To follow these clues is to launch ourselves on just the adventure that Mark set before his addressees. Mark's clues are *designed* to be elusive, to tease his readers into a different way of thinking. Jesus' challenge to his followers becomes Mark's challenge to his own readers: *"Do you still not understand?"* The question confronts Mark's reader long before Jesus is betrayed and killed. It is in the miracles, the demonstration of his power, that Mark's Jesus baffles his own pupils right from the start—and is expected to baffle Mark's readers in their turn. Responses to the appearance of such power varied then as now. Claimants to miraculous power were familiar enough; so were the categories into which they could be fitted. They could be met with credulity, skepticism, or scornful disbelief, with sophisticated appraisal or with simple faith. We can do more justice to these responses when we have in view a fuller picture of our writers and their world; we will return to the theme when we meet Luke, the "physician" among our witnesses.

We can do justice, meanwhile, to Mark's Jesus only when we have met a few of these claimants and categories. Mark insists that Jesus is *different:* He is strange and elusive and quite beyond his own pupils' grasp and ours—until we expose ourselves to a new and different form of understanding.

Miracles, magic, domination by spirits and dominance over them—such things and the beliefs surrounding them are alien to us now. Some historians of Jesus tend to play them down, but the historian of Mark and of the church must attend to them carefully. At issue was *power:* the power of the elements and of illness, of emperors and of nations. All cultures must find ways to speak about power and understand it, to relate its different vehicles to one another and to their subjects, to acknowledge their status and secure their goodwill. We have seen as much in the worship offered to emperors. But there were further powers to which Mark's world deferred. We will understand his Jesus when we can sense the hold these "supernatural" powers had on people's hearts and minds—and then see the extraordinary power with which Jesus confronts and confounds them. In these next few pages we hear of far more than just the echoes of an ancient illusion; we meet our witnesses and their readers, flesh and blood in their most basic, natural hopes and fears.

Jesus was not the only holy man to have come from Galilee. Hanina ben Dosi, who lived just a few miles north of Jesus' hometown, Nazareth, was probably a boy when Jesus died. Various stories are told of him, not least of his healing powers. When a boy fell ill, we are told, his father, a famous teacher in Jerusalem, sent two of his pupils to Hanina. Hanina prayed, then told the pupils that the boy was healed. On returning to their master they found that the boy had recovered at the very moment Hanina declared him well. We hear that Jesus, too, healed at a distance; a similar check was made on the timing of one patient's recovery (John 4.41–54).

More than just miracles link Jesus with Hanina. Both were teachers. Hanina lived in poverty (to his wife's disgust!) and spoke out against the worldliness of others. Just a handful of sayings ascribed to him have come down to us. They are pithy reminders of life's true priorities. They may stand as examples of a teaching style that flourished for generations:

> If your fear of wrongdoing inspires your wisdom, your wisdom endures;
> if your wisdom inspires your fear of wrongdoing, your wisdom does not endure.
> If your good works exceed your wisdom, your wisdom endures;
> if your wisdom exceeds your good works, your wisdom does not endure.

Powers of healing were immensely important in the early church. Mark's Jesus gives his twelve appointed pupils the power to exorcise; Paul reminds his church in Corinth that he has worked wonders among them quite as much as his opponents have (2 Corinthians 2.12) and tells the Romans of the signs and wonders with which he has spread the gospel (Romans 15.19). Luke will tell of miracles wrought by Peter, John, and Paul: cripples and a paralytic healed, a woman and a lad raised to life, liars punished with death, a magician blinded. The later church was proud of its ongoing power: "So now we who believe in Jesus our Lord," writes Justin, a martyr in the second century, "exorcise all the daemons and evil spirits, and thus hold them subject to us." Such miracles helped secure conversions for centuries to come.

The character of this power was questioned soon enough. One of the church's earliest defenders, Quadratus, denies at the start of the second century that the sight of Jesus' healing was just of some fleeting mirage. He is clearly countering charges already being raised by skeptics. Quadratus fights back: "The works of our savior were always present for they were true; those who had been healed and those who had risen from the dead, who were not just seen being healed and raised but were constantly present too, and not just when the savior was living but also for some time after he had gone, so that some of them survived even till our own time."

The miracles were both more and less important to Mark than we might expect. We focus first on Jesus' exorcisms. This is Mark's own move: His Jesus' first healing is to cast out an evil spirit. Later, in a dramatic set piece, as Jesus turns toward Jerusalem and his death, a spirit mounts a final challenge to his power and is dramatically overcome. Mark knows how much weight these exorcisms bear.

Expelling Daemons . . .

To be an exorcist was special but far from unique. The Jews had a reputation for such gifts or skills. At Qumran there was a text that retold the story of Abraham ("Abram") and the punishment of Pharaoh for taking his wife Sarah ("Sarai"). Here on the left is the story as it is told in the Old Order; on the right is a version in which it was read at Qumran in the time of Jesus.

The Lord inflicted severe plagues on Pharaoh and his household because of Abram's wife Sarai. So Pharaoh summoned Abram and said, "Why did you not tell me she was your wife? Why did you say, She is my sister?" (BEGINNING [GENESIS] 12.17–20)	The Lord sent an evil spirit to scourge Pharaoh and all his household. And the scourges grew ever more grievous, so he sent for the sages of Egypt, all the magicians and healers, that they might heal him and his household of this scourge. But not one could stay to heal him, because the spirit scourged them and they fled. And Pharaoh called Abram and said, "What have you done to me with regard to Sarai? You said to me, She is my sister, whereas she is your wife." So I prayed for him and laid my hands on him and the scourge departed from him and the evil spirit was expelled.

In the history of Israel, David was famous for having freed King Saul from an evil spirit by his singing; the Old Order's psalms are known as the Psalms of David. A fragment from Qumran ascribes to David one such psalm, unknown from the Old Order itself, to use in opposing an evil spirit ("Belial"). This was not the last generation to fear powers that in the cold light of day could be banished as mere nothings and dreams:

> Of David. On words of incantation. Cry out all the time in the name of the Lord
>   toward heaven when Belial comes to you. And say to him:
> "Who are you? Be afraid of man and of the seed of the holy one.
> Your face is a face of nothing and your horns are horns of dream.
> You are darkness and not light; injustice and not righteousness.
> The prince of the army is against you; the Lord will cast you
>   to the nethermost hell."

Techniques to ensure the successful invocation of such power could be elaborate. Josephus describes an exorcism performed by the Jewish Eleazar in the presence of the emperor and of Josephus himself; this is presented as an eyewitness account. Eleazar used roots and incantations: "He put to the nose of the possessed man a ring which had under its seal one of the roots prescribed by Solomon, and as the man smelled it, drew out the daemon through his nostrils, and, when the man at once fell down, adjured the demon never to come back into him, speaking Solomon's name and reciting the incantations which he had composed."

A great many texts have survived with rules for such spells. Their very quantity shows how widely the hope was shared, and over how many centuries, that performing them would be beneficial. In the texts, the names of Solomon and of the Jews' God are frequently invoked. We are here in a strange land on the border (and sometimes well over any border) dividing Judaism from the pagan world; this ambiguous region was clearly exploited by gentiles who called on the Jews' God with more awe than understanding. Here is a short extract from the most famous of these texts:

> To expel a daemon make a specified mixture of herbs, hang a magic amulet on
> the sufferer, and call upon the angels' help to take the daemon captive: "I adjure
> you by the God of the Hebrews, who delivered his people from the task-work of
> the King of Egypt and brought upon Egypt the ten plagues because he would
> not hear. I call on you by the great God Sabaoth, through whom the Red Sea
> turned backwards, which Israel journeyed over. I call upon you, every daemonic
> spirit, to say who you are. I call upon you by the seal which Solomon used. . . . "

. . . AND EXPLAINING THEM

We may well feel that we are hearing in these beliefs and practices the echoes of a quite alien world. But these were solutions reached by thoughtful people who faced challenges that vitally mattered in daily life. The terms in which we discuss health, sickness, and the powers of the natural world are quite different from theirs. But the writers of Mark's day thought at least as carefully and deeply as we do. As we shall see in the following pages, they, too, knew that words can mean different things to different people, that our own interests and prejudice affect our judgment, that power can be abused or feigned, that life rarely conforms to the categories through which we try to understand it. For the moment we hear of the influence that such beliefs had on daily life; when we listen to the testimony of our "physician," Luke, we will step aside into the world of medical schools and hear the eager disputes in which rival professors sought explanations and cures for the diseases around them.

The world was believed to be full of the spirits of which we have heard: daemons. In the world of Greece a daemon could be good, bad, or neutral. To call Jesus a daemon was, for a Greek philosopher, not to charge him with malicious intent. The Greeks' language, though, became an international language, much as English is today. All countries and cultures from Rome to the Middle East shared its terms—but not the assumptions and meanings that undergirded them. The cultures of the ancient world were divided by a common language. *Daemon* was used in the Greek translation of the Bible only for agents of evil; to call Jesus a daemon was, for anyone versed in that Greek Bible, a terrible charge.

All power and life could be attributed to some living force, a deity great or small. The Jews, under the supremacy of the one true God and him alone, could ascribe to living daemons an influence over humankind that can and should be countered by the invocation of God's name. Pagans allowed their reverence freer rein: The need was not to subordinate all such powers to one but to ensure that every possible source of blessing or curse had been appeased. Some found this comically credulous. One philosopher, Carneades, asked wryly how far down the scale such divinity extended—to the nymphs who enlivened woods and fountains? And to powers more minor still, the satyrs who danced attendance on the great gods?

OF MIRACLES AND MAGIC

Exorcisms were wrought by exactly repeated rites and formulas. Their use was open to a darker interpretation: the manipulation of higher powers for human—and potentially malicious—ends. *Magic* had become a pejorative term; no clear definition set it apart from beneficent, healing power. Malicious magic was punishable by death; there was good reason to disown the title magician oneself and to pin it instead on one's enemies or competitors. A hard-headed Roman author could say in passing, "There is no one who is not afraid of becoming the object of lethal spells." Amulets and charms survive in their thousands, invoking the gods' blessings upon the writer's family and endeavors, and harm or revenge upon their enemies.

Fear, then, played its part in the assessment of wonder workers; so did the search by rivals for popular support as well as the derision of cynics and the rhetoric of rival schools, each seeking legitimacy and public support. Plato, the father of all Western philosophy, reacted angrily to magic's practitioners and their claims: "Mendicant priests and soothsayers come to the rich man's door with a story of a power they possess by the gift of heaven to atone for any offense that he and his ancestors have committed with incantations and sacrifice, pleasantly accompanied by feasting. If he wishes to injure an enemy he can, at a trifling expense, do him a hurt with equal ease, by means of invocations and spells which, they claim, prevail upon the gods to do their bidding."

Jesus himself appears in Jewish literature as a magician who incited Israel to worship false gods and who led them astray. To accuse Jesus of working by magic was not to deny that he did *something*. On the contrary. Rabbis recognized the power said to reside in Jesus' name and adamantly opposed its invocation: It was daemonic. According to one story, a snake bit Rabbi Eleazar. A certain Jacob from Galilee came to cure him in the name of Jesus; when a second rabbi protested, Eleazar replied, "I will give you proof that it is permitted for him to cure me." But before he could finish his proof—and so before he was healed—he died. "You are lucky, Eleazar," said the second rabbi, "that you departed in peace and did not break through the fence with which scholars defend the Law of Moses."

So much for the powers surrounding Mark's Jesus and the power ascribed to him by his enemies. How does Mark interpret his Jesus' power?

The Power of Jesus

"BY THE PRINCE OF DAEMONS HE CASTS OUT DAEMONS"

Mark well knew how ambiguous was Jesus' power. Its presentation is central to the gospel. Jesus' very first healing is an exorcism. He is in the synagogue on the sabbath; over and over the propriety of such "work" as healing on the sabbath, the day ordained by God as a day of rest, will be an issue. It is the possessed man who launches the incident: He comes up to Jesus unbidden and cries out, *What is up between you and me, Jesus of Nazareth? You have come to destroy us. I know you, who you are: the Holy One of God"* (Mark 1.24). To name a power is in magical technique to control it. But if the spirit expected to constrain Jesus' authority by his declaration, he was deluded; Jesus sweeps him away.

"You have come to destroy us." The battle is under way. God's Anointed is armed and in action. Mark is not just telling the story. He is confronting from the very start the questions to which the incident gives rise: the nature and extent of Jesus' authority. He frames that first exorcism with the crowd's amazement at Jesus' *teaching*. For the teaching goes beyond just words: The healing itself raises a question and provides the clue to its answer. Twice more in the following chapter Mark has Jesus exercise a strange authority: He declares the forgiveness of a man's wrongdoing and declares himself

above the sabbath law. In both cases he invokes the standing of the Son of Man, a term that Mark will use with care and deep significance. Does this series of dramatic claims and actions leave us confused? So it should. Mark sets out to unsettle our expectations and raise questions in our mind.

By the time we end this first section to Mark's narrative, the surge of Jesus' power has amazed the crowd, offended the religious leaders, and routed the powers of sickness. Mark now records the considered response of Jesus' opponents, and in doing so he throws down a gauntlet to the church's critics of his own day. The officials who had come up from Jerusalem to check out this strange new wonder worker claimed that he was in league with dark powers: *By the prince of daemons he casts out daemons* (Mark 3.22). Mark enters a stark warning. To find in Jesus' miracles the devil's work is to deny in them the work of God. This is blasphemy: to treat as evil the breath of God that enlivens his creation. *"Men shall be forgiven all wrongdoing,"* says Jesus, *"all blasphemy—except blasphemy against the Breath of God"* (Mark 3.28–29). For this there is no forgiveness.

Mark frames this scene with a pair of comments. Before it we are told that Jesus' "folks" wanted to restrain him; they thought him out of his mind. Then at its end we hear of Jesus' mother and brothers and of their attempt to see him: *"Who is my mother,"* he asks, *"who are my brothers?"* He looked about at those sitting round him: *"Here are my mother and my brothers. All who do the will of God, they are my sister and brother and mother"* (Mark 3.33–35). In his way, Mark has created a sandwich of three short scenes: Jesus' "folks" and his family are linked with each other and, in between, with the dispute over devilry. Who, then, were Jesus' "folks"? Were they his own family, frightened into a terrible error by his strange power? Not for the first time or the last, Mark leaves us with a mere hint, resonant and poignant.

Mark has cleared away the first challenge to Jesus' power. He is now free to explore the stories of Jesus' healings for the value that he himself invests in them. In chapter 5, Mark uses his sandwich style again; this time one miracle is inserted within another. The twelve-year-old daughter of a synagogue's official, Jairus, is near death. Jairus comes to Jesus in person to plead for his daughter's health. The two of them struggle through the crowd toward Jairus's house. A woman with a menstrual flow unstaunched for those same twelve years manages to touch Jesus' clothing—and is healed. She had hoped to remain undiscovered; such discharge left its victim "unclean" in the sight of the Law and called for a special ritual for cleansing both her and anyone who touched her. But Jesus stops, turns, asks who touched him, and speaks with the woman. The minutes tick by. *"Your trust,"* he tells her, *"has saved you"* (Mark 5.34). And at that very moment a message reaches Jairus that his daughter has died.

The man at the community's center and the woman on its margins; his public appeal for help and her frightened, covert touch; his urgency and her cost of crucial time: Here is a play of deep contrasts. In one way, however, Jairus and the woman are linked: As Jesus tells her that her trust has healed or "saved" her, so he tells Jairus: *"Just go on trusting"* (Mark 5.36).

That word for *saving* was used for "medical" healing: the Greek god of healing, Asclepius, could be referred to simply as "Savior." The term, though, had a far wider sense than our *curing*. "Safety" might lie in rescue from trouble or from threat to life and limb, in safe passage of a journey or war, in the maintenance of health and wealth. The Greek translation of the Bible showed a powerful sense of God's involvement in such saving; where there was no other hope or resource, *there* was God at work for his people. By Mark's time the church had enriched the word further: It was Jesus who offered the one real safety or rescue from all that threatened in this life and the next. Within the church, "trust" or "faith" no longer needed to be specified as trust or faith "in" anything; "trust in Jesus" could be taken for granted as the meaning intended. The woman hears Jesus speak; so do Mark's readers. Jesus' words are heard by the woman, the reader, and the reader watching the woman. How much do we envisage her as having heard in Jesus' simple statement? How much do we hear in it for her future and for our own? Mark leaves the possibilities open and forever sounding: *"Your trust,"* said Jesus, *"has saved you."*

An exorcism at the start of Jesus' work; also, an exorcism at the turning point in Mark's story, the start of its second half. Jesus' exorcism of the boy in chapter 9 is one of Mark's most moving episodes. He may well have fused two versions of the story together to maximize the drama. The story is now a climactic set piece. When Jesus' movement toward suffering is already under way, he expels a daemon so powerful that his pupils had been powerless against it. So furious was its attack that the boy seemed dead. This is the only story in which Jesus actually forbids the daemon to reenter its victim. Everything is told to emphasize his power. But our attention is drawn not only to Jesus. A familiar theme comes to the fore again. The father's desperation echoes down the centuries: *"Lord, I do trust, help my distrust, please!"* (Mark 9.24).

JESUS FEEDS THE PEOPLE

Jesus' power shows itself in many forms. He does not just heal the sick. We have heard already of the meals that he gives to the hungry crowds. Mark sounds chords in these stories just as rich but different in character. Jesus took pity on the people gathered to hear him, because (Mark tells us) *they were like sheep without a shepherd* (Mark 6.34). And so he feeds them, thousands of people in a desert, just as Moses had fed the Jews "from heaven" on their way through the wilderness from Egypt to Israel. After the first such feeding Jesus sends his friends on ahead across the Sea of Galilee and then walks across the sea to join them. Again we remember Moses, he had been given power to divide the water of the Red Sea when the Jews left Egypt and the whole nation walked in safety across the sea bed.

After that first feeding the leftovers had filled twelve baskets: Twelve was the number of the tribes of Israel. After the second, seven baskets had been filled: Seven had long been seen in the Middle East as a round number of fullness, and there were said to be seventy nations in the world. John the Seer, in his first vision, sees a figure holding seven stars and writes to seven churches, way beyond the borders of Israel, in Asia Minor. Does Mark see in these two miracles the satisfaction of the Jews' hunger and then of all the world's? Characteristically, Mark does not spell out these miracles' significance, but there is clearly more at issue here than a day's hunger for supper, satisfied by Jesus.

These stories look forward to the future as much as back to Israel's past. *Taking the five loaves and the two fish,* Mark writes, *and looking up to heaven, Jesus gave thanks and broke the loaves* (Mark 8.6). The motif recurs. We will see Mark's Jesus again with bread in hand at the meal with his pupils on the night before he died: *Jesus, taking bread and saying a blessing, broke it* (Mark 14.23).

The church quickly came to hear a deep resonance in that last meal, the "Last Supper" before Jesus' death. It was a hint of the banquet with which God will reward his nation when his Anointed has swept its enemies away. God's community, in harmony and entire under his regent, gathered around tables groaning with fine food. Here was a dream to stir the heart and raise the spirits of an impoverished and scattered people. At every celebration of the church's greatest ritual, the Great Thanksgiving, the church set out to follow Jesus' example and command: The minister or priest took bread, gave thanks, and broke the bread for distribution to the people.

The dream of plenty was fostered for generations. Moses had asked God for a successor to himself so that the Jews would not be like sheep without a shepherd. The theme sounds over and over through the Old Order. The prophet Ezekiel, centuries before Jesus, had imagined the nation as a flock of sheep, desperately in need of care and of good pasture in which to feed. He had seen the shepherds fail their duty and the flock scattered in exile. He imagined its rescue at God's own hands:

> *Prophesy against the shepherds of Israel* [God had ordered him]. *Say to them: Woe to the shepherds of Israel who only take care of themselves. Should not shepherds take care of the flock? You have not strengthened the weak or healed the sick or bound up the injured. You have not brought back the strays or searched for the lost. You have ruled them harshly and brutally. So they were scattered because there was no shepherd. They were scattered over the whole earth, and no one searched or looked for them.*
>
> *So I myself, says the Lord, will search for my sheep and look after them. I will bring them into their own land, I will tend them in a good pasture. They will lie down in good grazing land, and there they will feed in a rich pasture. I will search for the lost and bring back the strays, I will bind up the injured and strengthen the weak.*
> (EZEKIEL 34.1–6, 11, 14, 16)

Mark heard these echoes and sounded their notes again. In response to Moses' plea God had appointed Joshua to succeed him. "Jesus" was a variant form of that same name. It is Jesus, a second Joshua, *who took pity on the crowd* and fed them so lavishly, says Mark, *because they were like sheep without a shepherd.*

And in Mark's understanding Jesus feeds them still, in the Eucharist, the Service of Thanksgiving, which looks back past the Last Supper and past the feedings to Ezekiel's words. And so the Thanksgiving looks forward with Ezekiel, too, to the celebration with which God will restore his people's health and wealth—to the banquet of the Kingdom of God.

There is so much to be seen in such stories. We would not be the first to miss their significance. When Mark reports the response of Jesus' pupils, he has an eye too on his readers. Just after the second feeding, Jesus' pupils find themselves on a boat with only a single loaf. When he warns them about the "yeast" of their enemies their minds turn just to this shortage of food. *"Why are you talking about the lack of bread?"* asks Jesus. *"Don't you realize? Don't you understand? Are your hearts so callused? As the prophet said, 'You have eyes; can't you see? You have ears; can't you hear?'"* (Mark 8.17–18).

JESUS ON THE WATER

Moses had led his people on an exodus from slavery in Egypt to freedom in Israel; on their way he had provided food in the desert. Was Jesus a second Moses? It was certainly possible. *"God will raise up for you,"* Moses had promised long ago, *"a prophet like me from among your own brothers. You must listen to him"* (Second Law [Deuteronomy] 18.15).

There was clearly a link between Moses and Jesus. But it was not enough just to draw the comparison. Moses had led God's people to freedom and had died, after a glimpse of the Promised Land itself, on the verge of its final occupation. Jesus had been abandoned by his "nation" and had died in abject failure—and yet had been raised from the dead. Here is no duplicate of Moses or his career.

Moses had once been granted a glimpse of God himself. No more frightening privilege could be imagined; for no one could look on God and live. So on the top of Mount Sinai, with Moses hidden in a cleft of rock, God's glory had *passed by.* It is with Moses in mind again that Mark tells of Jesus stilling the storm on the Sea of Galilee and later walking across its waves. The sea was for the Old Order the element of chaos: It was way beyond human control, an image of the fierce, shapeless mass that God reduced to order in creation. To walk on the waves is to subdue them—and this is the prerogative of God: *He alone,* we read in the ancient book of Job, *stretched out the heavens and walks on the waves of the sea* (Job 9.8).

Jesus' followers had good reason to be afraid as he approached across the water. But he did not head for their boat. Mark tells us that *he made as if to pass them by* (Mark 6.48). Mark's readers should by now be as awestruck as Jesus' pupils had been on the night itself. In this story it was the pupils, not Jesus, who played Moses' role: In that uncanny figure on the lake they saw the glory of God himself *pass by.* Yet again, though, understanding eludes them.

Jesus' pupils on the boat were beside themselves. For they did not understand about the loaves, Mark tells us, *but their hearts were callused and hard* (Mark 6.52).

Opening the Eyes of the Blind

With the feeding of the second crowd, we have reached the midpoint of the gospel. Triumph has already been tinged with the premonition of danger. Jesus will now turn to Jerusalem, center of his enemies' power. Around this axis revolves Mark's whole story. Jesus has just asked his pupils, *"Do you still not understand?"* They have so far failed to grasp the nature or significance of his power; now they will be dumbfounded by his impending rejection and death.

A blind man is brought to Jesus for healing. It is worth following the story alongside the crucial episode that follows it. We will dovetail the two scenes, letting each gain from its relation to the other. Here is the start to the blind man's healing

> *They came to Bethsaida, and some people brought a blind man and begged Jesus to touch him. Jesus took the blind man by the hand and led him outside the village. When he had spat on the man's eyes and put his hands on him, Jesus asked, "Do you see anything?"*
> *(MARK 8.22–23)*

"Who," asked Jesus in the central scene that follows, *"do men say I am?"*

Jesus' contemporaries, according to Mark, had tried to find the answer, honestly enough. There had been King Herod's murder of John the Baptizer, a man so obviously just that he might well come back to haunt the oppressor and comfort God's people. More exciting was the talk of Elijah. This ancient prophet was due to return; he would prepare the world for God's final intervention in its history. If that was who Jesus was, then God's judgment was nearly under way, and all Israel's suffering was about to end.

These answers would not do. It was the right place to look, the book of the Old Order between God and Israel. But Jesus' followers were sure he was more central in God's plan—a figure that would be announced by others, perhaps, but not himself the forerunner to a yet greater agent of God. Other hopes were in the air, built around other titles familiar from prophecy, but if those were the key to understanding Jesus, the reader would need help to turn the lock. What Jesus had done and undergone in Mark's story so far—and what Mark's church knew Jesus was about to undergo—did not fit with any of the Old Order's hopes and promises so clearly that the story would speak for itself.

Mark quickly leaves the popular rumors about Jesus aside: He was neither Elijah nor John the Baptizer. It is time, then, for his followers to face the question for themselves: *"And who do you say I am?"*

There was a range of titles known from the Old Order: Son of God, the Anointed. They were grand but had been used of various heroes. Son of God? A good many kings and prophets had been given that accolade, not to mention Israel itself, God's own nation. To be a Son of God was to obey him, serve him, be chosen for special favor. Fine so far as it goes. But there was more than that to Jesus.

There had been Anointed servants of God as well, and the Old Order looked forward, as we have seen, to an Anointed yet to come. It is misleading to think of an expectation universal and uniform among all Jews. But one outline at least was common and clear: the Anointed would see all Israel's enemies scattered, its oppressors defeated once and for all. He would be a king, anointed and acknowledged as a king should be. One of the Old Order's psalms had long been read as an account of the Anointed and his standing in God's plan:

> The Lord said to my Lord,
> "Sit at my right hand
> until I make your enemies
> a footstool for your feet."
>
> (PSALM 110.1)

Jesus' question hangs in the air: "And who do you say I am?"

Peter speaks up: "God's Anointed" (Mark 8.29). It is a brave insight. Jesus has not yet done what the Anointed should do, and he has little of the majesty that the psalmist ascribes to him. Peter's declaration shows that he has hopes way beyond the successes of their present motley band. This should be a high point of the gospel, a fanfare of triumphs foreseen and understood.

But it is not; far from it. Jesus simply orders his pupils to tell no one about him. Here is a strange anticlimax. Why does Jesus not confirm that Peter is right? Would there be a danger in his proclamation as God's Anointed? Would there be something in this title that would mislead and distract those who heard it used of him? Mark is exploring with the utmost care what possibility his readers have of understanding. They need all the help he can give toward its growth and proper use.

In the story of the blind man Jesus has applied the mud to the patient's eyes. *The man looked up and said, "I see people; they look like trees walking around"* (Mark 8.24). The healing is not yet successful. There is more to be done.

Jesus starts telling his pupils that the Son of Man must be rejected by the leaders of his own people and be killed and on the third day rise again. Peter is appalled. Such talk will not do. Little enough in Jesus' life so far has matched Israel's expectations of the Anointed. To be rejected by the Jews' own leaders was enough to disqualify any claimant to the role—and enough to horrify those around Jesus who cared for him, his followers and his closest friends. *Peter took him aside, and began to tell him off* (Mark 8.32).

In his starkest words of the whole gospel Jesus turns on Peter: "Get out of my sight, Satan! You are set in men's ways, not God's" (Mark 8.33). Peter, first of Jesus' followers, is addressed as Satan, chief of evil's forces. It is a terrible moment. Jesus' next words are to the whole crowd as well as to these close friends who so persistently fail to understand him: "All who want to follow after me must deny themselves, take up their cross, and follow me. For all who want to save their life shall lose it, and all who lose their life for my sake and the gospel's shall save it" (Mark 8.34–35).

How much has Peter really grasped? How much more must he undergo before he understands even as much as he has already declared? Titles are only a beginning. The gospel now launches upon its second stage: The reader and Peter are about to learn what this agent of God has been anointed for. Now is the time for us to open our eyes and see.

Only with that blind man, among all the healings of the gospel, does it take Jesus a second movement to effect the healing. From blindness to a blur, and with a further touch from a blur to clear sight: *Once more Jesus put his hands on the man's eyes. Then the man's eyes were opened, his sight was restored, and he saw everything clearly.* (MARK 8.25)

JESUS ON THE MOUNTAIN

Moses had been given a glimpse of God; so had the ancient prophet Elijah, centuries later, on that same Mount Sinai. As both were heroes of Israel's past, so both looked forward, as well, to its future. Moses spoke of the prophet to be raised up one day in his place: *God will raise up for you a prophet like me from among your own brothers. You must listen to him* (Second Law [Deuteronomy] 18.15). And in the very last words of the Old Order God relays through the prophet Malachi his promise to Israel: *I will send you Elijah* [back on earth] *before that great and dreadful Day of the Lord,* [the day of God's judgment on the world] (Malachi 4.5).

In the most mysterious scene of Mark's gospel, placed six days after Peter's declaration, Jesus takes his three closest friends with him up a high mountain. There he is transformed before their very eyes; his clothes appear dazzling white. Peter, James, and John see two figures flanking him, Moses and Elijah, and hear from heaven a command that Moses would have recognized: *This is my beloved Son; listen to him* (Mark 9.7).

What does Mark see in this story? Jesus is surely the prophet foretold by Moses. Once Elijah is seen to have returned as the Baptizer, the stage is also set for God's final intervention on earth. So far, so good. But Moses and Elijah do not share the dazzling brightness of Jesus' figure. He has a higher dignity than theirs. We might have expected him to have been given such glory only at or after his death; we might even wonder if the six days between Peter's declaration and the mountain scene hint at Jesus' six days in Jerusalem that led up to his crucifixion. But Mark is clear: Jesus has this splendor already, half way through the story. Since when has it been his? From his baptism by John, when a voice from heaven declared, *You are my beloved Son?* From his birth? Or from the beginning of time, when God spoke over the waters of chaos and brought them to order?

Moses and Elijah had shared more than their insight into God's plan; they had seen the glory of God himself. Was this the glory that they saw again as they talked with Jesus? And so in turn: Was it *Jesus* that they had seen in their glimpse of the glory of God all those centuries before?

Mark is too discreet to spell out and so to limit the implications of this strange story. We can look too hard for precision where it is not for us to find. Some questions do not yield a crisp, clear answer. We do well, then, to introduce a series of questions and for the moment let them stand. It is hard to imagine what we could ever hope to see, in our ordinary humdrum lives, of the glory of God. Our eyes are dulled by the cares of daily life, our world is a cracked and grimy vehicle for such light. Perhaps it is as well. If we are to imagine God in terms of light at all, it will be as a brilliance that would blind us.

What form, then, would be taken by this glory, if God ever chose to reveal it, wholly and without remainder, to humankind? What would it *look like?* If it were shaded, we would not know it; if it were held out for us to see, we could not bear its sight. What would this glory *do* on earth so that humanity could know it confidently for what it was and learn safely what it was here to disclose? Mark knows the difficulty. His whole gospel is written to meet it. We must follow his gospel right through its end if we are to hear and understand his solution.

When Moses came down from Mount Sinai after his glimpse of God, his face shone; the people were afraid to go near him. When Jesus comes down the mountain the crowd is amazed and runs to do him obeisance. However little the crowd understands, there is about Jesus something that makes him awesomely special at the very moment that he is setting out for his death.

"Do You Still Not Understand?"

THE GREAT FIRE: PUNISHMENT

Mark's church faced terrible days in Rome. Where was Mark to find consolation or hope for his people? Mark knew the vision of Daniel like the back of his own hand: the threat the prophet foresaw to God's people, from beast after wild beast, grew ever worse.

> There before me, Daniel, was a fourth beast, terrifying and very powerful. It crushed and devoured its victims and trampled underfoot whatever was left. . . . There before me on the beast was a little horn. This horn had eyes like the eyes of a man and a mouth that spoke boastfully.
>
> (DANIEL 7.7, 8)

Daniel's eye was fixed on that fourth and last animal in his vision.

> I, Daniel, was troubled in spirit. I approached one of those standing there and asked him the true meaning of all this.

He gave me this explanation: Another king, the fourth and last, will arise. He will speak against the Most High and oppress his heroes [or saints, holy ones,] and try to change the set times and the laws. The heroes of God will be handed over to him for a time, times, and half a time.

(DANIEL 7.15, 16, 25)

Mark's church would be looking for a sign, any sign that the present horror was within God's plan. For Tigellinus's men did their work well: The "culprits" were found. Tacitus tells the story of the Christians' execution. The historian loathed Nero as deeply as he despised the Christians; only Nero could have been so cruel that the Christians' punishment won them sympathy.

Derision accompanied their end: they were covered with wild beasts' skins and torn to death by dogs; or they were fastened on crosses, and when daylight failed were burned to serve as lamps by night.

Nero had offered his gardens for the spectacle, and gave an exhibition in his stadium. In the dress of a charioteer he mixed with the crowd and paraded on his chariot. And so for these culprits who had earned the most severe and exemplary punishment there arose a feeling of pity: they were being sacrificed, it seemed, not for the welfare of the state but to the ferocity of a single man.

Jesus had spoken of God's imminent kingdom and of its quiet inauguration in the lives of those around him. These were the lives now being sacrificed to an emperor's madness. The church longed for more, needed more. Jesus had spoken, too, of the triumphant completion of God's reign, when the world of empires and ambitions would be swept away and God would wreak punishment on all those who had oppressed his people. Here in Rome was those oppressors' direst triumph, extinguishing God's people for a crime it had not committed. Where was the church to find hope in this? As Daniel had spoken of persecution, so had he spoken of the vindication to follow. He had seen God triumph over that fourth and final beast and invest his chosen agent with authority over all creation.

I, Daniel, looked, and there before me was one like a son of man, coming with the clouds of heaven. He approached the Ancient of Days and was led into his presence. He was given authority, glory, and sovereign power; all people, nations, and men of every language worshiped him. His dominion is an everlasting dominion that will not pass away, and his kingdom is one that will never be destroyed.

(DANIEL 7.13–14)

Daniel's angel interprets this scene with which the prophet's vision had reached its climax. That image of delegated power was one that the church, in its darkest days, would never forget:

But the court will sit [Daniel was told], *and the king* [represented by the fourth and final beast] *will be stripped of his royal power. It will be reduced to nothing. And kingship and rule and the splendors of all the kingdoms under heaven will be given to the people of God, the heroes of the Most High.*

(DANIEL 7.26–27)

THE SON OF MAN

With the figure of *one like a son of man,* we reach the heart of Mark's gospel. It offers no easy route to understanding. We tend to approach Mark's story as we might any narrative in a biography, novel, or newspaper. Shown examples of these three, we distinguish the styles and functions of each, but more unites than divides them. The character of such a story is quickly recognized, and we read what follows with the appropriate expectations: a biography will follow its subject's life, a novel will build to a final climax, a newspaper will highlight just a few details. Biographers give us all the evidence as we go, novelists enjoy twisting the last pages of their plot, journalists have readers of a certain social and political caste in mind.

What sort of story, then, is Mark writing? Is Jesus all that is hard to understand, in a narrative we can otherwise place as easily as any other? Far from it. It is the kind of story in which he appears, that is—and is meant to be—confusing.

As odd as any element of the gospel is the figure of the Son of Man. The phrase is used in Mark only by Jesus himself, who appears to speak with it only about himself—about his activity on earth or at his glorious return. This Son of Man, however, is always "he," never "I"; we might well ask if Jesus is keeping some distance between himself and this strange figure whose earthly career so exactly matches his own. This "Son of Man" holds a vital clue to the character of Mark's gospel. We must trace the term's path through two languages and two hundred years. Its twists and turns have driven scholars to despair. Its main lines on the map, however, are at last more or less clear.

In Jesus' own time and Aramaic language, *son of man* was a way of saying "I and those like me." (In English we sometimes use *one* in a similar way: What would one do if . . . ; One can only hope that . . .) The most common form of the phrase was quite definite: Our equivalent would be "*the* son of man." It was suitable, then, as a title. Whether it was already known as such—whether indeed Jesus himself was (one of) the first to use it as a title—has been disputed by historians for nearly a hundred years. It may still be in dispute a hundred years to come.

Mark had readers in mind, however, that were thinking not in Aramaic but in Greek. The phrase inherited by Mark keeps the precision of the original: "the son of the man." In Greek this gives a clear hint that we should know which "son" and which "man" are at issue. Most translations, therefore, use capitals: the Son of Man. This Son of Man is definite but obscure: The phrase in Greek has no accepted usage or obvious reference at all. Where, then, would the Greek-speaking church find a point in this portentous phrase, familiar on the lips of Jesus and nowhere else?

The term would remind Greek speakers of just that prophecy in Daniel that fueled the hopes of synagogue and church alike: of that vision of a heavenly figure, *one like a son of man* who stood for God's heroes, harassed, suffering, and eventually appointed to an everlasting power. Daniel's indefinite phrase had been translated into the Greek Old Order literally and directly: *like a son of man.* In the proclamation of Jesus, however, the Greek-speaking church was seeking—and offering—more: a precise and definite figure, the Son of Man.

Daniel's prophecy, it seemed, was transparent at last. Interpreters (the church could claim) need look no further. The prophet's phrase could now carry the weight that it deserved: reference to a single, specific figure of supreme importance in God's plan. Here, once and for all, was *the* Son of Man.

What could the church then make of Daniel's vision? God's plan was fixed: The final victory of his people was sure. This the Jews and then Christians were determined to believe. They needed to. Israel never seemed free from foreign occupation nor the church from suspicion and attack. But none of this annulled God's purpose. If God's people could only see how things really are, beneath the dangers and setbacks, they would regain their strength and confidence and trust.

The Jews had known for centuries of visions where the cosmic battle between God and evil is fought out in strange and allusive forms, and its final outcome—the victory of God—is enacted "in heaven" long before it is apparent on earth. *This* is the sight offered to a seer such as Daniel. It was the rarest of privileges. The Seer's task is then generally to reveal (part of) what he has seen to those around him.

The exotic cast of Daniel's vision was not spun from air. The battle's animals and its victorious Man, as described by Daniel, hark back once more to Eden and the beginning of all things: to Adam, surrounded by the animals and given charge of them. Things have gone terribly—cosmically—wrong, when the beasts turn on Man and attack him. What will be signified by the restoration of order, when at last the beasts are defeated and the Man is again enthroned? More than just Israel and the Middle East are at stake. The whole created order hangs upon the outcome of this battle.

Such visions and their figures are strange to us. Modern scholars have two (very different) way of explaining them.

It is natural, as one possibility, to think of the actors on Daniel's heavenly stage as symbols, standing for powers and nations on earth; as symbols they need decoding and can then be put aside. Who then are the beasts? The enemies of God's people. And who is the "one like a son of man"? The heroes of God, who will be vindicated and given the power that is their due reward. Let those heroes once see the battle's end in this vivid pictorial form, and their hearts will be steadied for the earthly struggle that is yet to be undergone.

As a second possibility, however, we can leave aside the categories with which we are familiar: the tidy distinctions between dreams on the one hand and reality on the other, between the ethereal symbols that we encounter in the first and the conflicts and dangers that confront us in the second. Once we suspend such distinctions,

Daniel's angel does not just decode each of the vision's elements into its "real" counterpart on earth, and with that, exhaust its role. He leaves both in place. The "one like a son of man" has "really" been seen receiving power in heaven; precisely this assures us that the heroes of God will finally be given power on earth. It is a vision that Daniel has been given, not a fantasy that we might discredit as a dream.

In either of these views, Daniel's "one like a son of man" belongs in visions, in the battle imagined as fought out in God's own realm beyond the skies, far from our normal sight or understanding.

In Mark's Greek narrative, however, far more looms into view. His Son of Man is both Daniel's visionary figure *and Jesus,* alive on earth as Peter's friend, healing, forgiving, suffering. But this is not where the prophet's "one like a son of man" should be at all. There is a strange confusion here: All our familiar categories and distinctions are breaking down. A warrior has walked out of a heavenly vision and is striding the earth. Strange enough, if Mark's readers would have thought the prophet's figure "just" a figment of his divinely ordered dream. Far more frightening, if Daniel had seen a "real" battle waged in heaven; for its chief agent was now revealed for all to see, mustering his—frail, human—forces for its equivalent on earth.

But a new possibility now lies open. If those around Jesus longed to see what a seer sees, to share that vision into the secrets of God's plan, they needed no dreams, no rare privilege. They needed only to open their eyes and to see what was—to their and our amazed incomprehension—taking place before their very eyes.

The sight was easily missed.

When Jesus was alone, those around him with the Twelve [the closest circle of his followers] *asked him about the riddles he used. "To you," he said, "the secret of the Kingdom of God has been given. But to those outside, everything happens in riddles, so that* [as Isaiah says]

> *'Looking with all their might they may not see,*
> *and listening with all their might they may not understand;*
> *otherwise they might change their ways and God forgive them.'"*

(MARK 4.10–12)

No wonder Jesus' pupils, in Mark's story, found it so difficult to understand. No wonder our witness works so hard to help his readers in their turn to open their eyes and *see.*

Are these actions of Jesus still signs in code? Such a sign here on earth would seem to do the very thing it points to, to win the victory that it portends. We must wonder, then, if these events disclose things to the reader, the new seer, or achieve them; if they anticipate a final battle or wage it. If Jesus fought this battle as "standing for" God's heroes, what still lies ahead for those heroes themselves to do or undergo?

And if the Son of Man is not just a token for those heroes but a figure himself that walked on earth and lived and died, then Mark's readers have good reason to wonder, what will be the form of his coming, when he comes to claim dominion over his own? The more dramatic Mark's traditional language becomes, the more actively will readers seek its explanation. Mark drives his readers on towards the climax of the gospel, where their questions will be given an answer that no reader could foresee. Of all our four gospels, Mark's supposedly simple, "basic" story has the most surprising and gripping denouement of all.

"They will see the Son of Man," said Jesus, *"coming in clouds with great power and glory. And he will send his messengers to gather his chosen ones from the four winds, from the ends of the earth to the ends of the heavens"* (Mark 13.27).

"My God, My God, Why Have You Deserted Me?"

CONDEMNED

There was so much to hope for from the story of Jesus but so little yet to be seen. So much excitement, such signs of triumph both present and to come—and all are swept away in the last pages of Mark's story. The denouement is unremittingly stark. Among Jesus' followers there is foreboding, betrayal, desertion. Witnesses are perjured, the crowd turned, the governor outmaneuvered. Brutality starts early and rises—on a chill, calculated scale—to execution. In a single night Jesus has been cornered, arrested, interrogated, and condemned. By daybreak all the pieces are in place for his death. Before the day is over he is buried.

The first hearing is before the high priest. All Jerusalem is relaxing. The Passover meal is over, the holiday is under way. But in the priest's palace is no celebration. Powerful men have gathered by night. The talk is intense, decisive. On this night's work may hang the future of the Temple, all its observances laid down by God, the whole Law entrusted to Israel.

The high priest questions Jesus. In this question and answer, all the titles of Jesus that have sounded through the story converge in one great statement of his true character. Even to speak of his claim—even to pose an incredulous question about it—is to stir a sense of God as so near, so immediately, awesomely *present* that Mark for once evokes the Jewish tradition: No one mentions God by name; the high priest speaks of the Blessed, Jesus of the Power. So terrible is Jesus' claim that he must either be believed—or condemned to death.

Again the high priest questioned him: "Are you the Anointed, the Son of the Blessed?"
"I am" said Jesus, "and you will see the Son of Man seated at the right hand of the Power and coming with the clouds of heaven."
The high priest tore his clothes.

(MARK 14.61–62)

Clothes were torn as a sign of mourning; blasphemy was worse than death.

"Why do we still need witnesses?" he said. "You have heard the blasphemy. What do you think?"
They all condemned him: he deserved to die.

(MARK 14.64)

KILLED

"My God, my God," asks one of the psalms, *"why have you deserted me?"* (Psalm 22.1).
When the execution party reached the site of execution, Mark tells us, Jesus was offered wine mixed with myrrh to deaden the pain; he refused it. Then he was stripped of his clothing; most such convicts would have been made to walk to their crucifixion already naked. Their clothes became booty for the executioners.

At nine o'clock in the morning he was crucified. The punishment was as public as possible. Passersby jeered at him and shook their heads. Over and over in the gospels we will hear of Jesus' words about the Temple and its future. The crowd knew one version of them and used them to mock the dying man. *"So, you who are going to destroy the temple and build it in three days, come down from the cross and save yourself"* (Mark 15.29–30).

Sings the poet in the same psalm,

All who see me mock me,
they hurl insults, shaking their heads:
"He trusts in the Lord, let the Lord rescue him.
Let him deliver him, since he delights in him."
A band of evil men has encircled me,
they have dug into my hands and my feet.
They divide my garments among them,
and cast lots for my clothing.

(PSALM 22.7–8, 16–18)

Scattered through the psalms are such poems of lament, accounts of the derision and attack that the just endure from their own people, among whom they live and from whom they would have expected help. But no: *They put gall in my food,* recalls one, *and gave me vinegar for my thirst* (Psalm 69.21).

At three o'clock in the afternoon, Mark writes, Jesus spoke the last words before his death: *"Eloi, eloi, lema sabachthani"* (Mark 15.34). The bystanders misheard his cry. They thought he was calling on the prophet Elijah to rescue him. One of them soaked a sponge in the soldiers' vinegary wine and held it on a stick to Jesus' face. The taste, even the smell, would revive the convict—and give time before his death for Elijah to appear: *"Come on,"* laughed the man, *"let's see if Elijah comes to take him down"* (Mark 15.36).

Jesus had not been calling on Elijah.

"Eloi, eloi," he had cried, *"lema sabachthani."* "My God, my God, why have you deserted me?"

And when Jesus died? Just for a moment Mark's testimony moves from the cross to that veil that kept the Temple's sanctuary from public gaze. It was embroidered like the sky, the barrier between God and humankind. *The veil of the temple was torn in two from top to bottom* (Mark 15.38).

The Chamber of Incense, perhaps even the Holy of Holies, lay open to view. The most numinous and precious space on earth was unveiled. Such was the disclosure so rarely afforded to the seers. It was offered to those around Jesus at his death, and it had been offered to Mark's readers, if they could only recognize it, from his story's start. *And coming up from the water,* we hear when Jesus was baptized, *he saw the heavens torn apart and the Breath as a dove coming down upon him. And there was a voice from heaven: "You are my son, the beloved; in you have I have taken delight"* (Mark 1.10).

Mark has turned our attention from the crucifixion to the Temple. But only for a moment.

And when the officer who stood there in front of Jesus, heard his cry and saw how he died, he said, "Yes, this man really was Son of God" (Mark 15.39).

By Mark's time that title has gathered weight: Jesus, for the church, is *the* Son of God, as no one else before or since could ever be. A foreign officer who acknowledged Jesus as "Son of God" had already seen more than the leaders of Jesus' own people. Christian readers who forty years later knew the title as Jesus' own and as Jesus' alone could see that the officer's claim was more profound—and more profoundly true—than he could himself have known. Son of God, Anointed: Jesus' titles have attracted all the significance that his followers saw in Jesus himself. The terms did not define Jesus; within the church their attachment to Jesus redefined the terms.

"My God, my God," started that psalm, *"why have you deserted me?"*

At its end the tone changes. Confident of rescue, the poet calls upon his audience to praise God:

He has not hidden his face from the afflicted,
but has listened to his cry for help.
All the ends of the earth will turn to the Lord,
and all the families of the nations will bow down before him.

(PSALM 22.24, 27)

As Jesus had suffered, so would his followers. Mark was not the last to look from one suffering to the other. Later generations would find closer connections still. The

Christian historian Sulpicius Severus, writing around 400 C.E., tells of Peter's and Paul's end:

Thus a beginning was made [in 64 C.E.] of violent persecution of the Christians. Afterwards also laws were enacted and the religion was forbidden. Edicts were publicly published: "No one is to profess Christianity." Then Paul and Peter were condemned to death. The former was beheaded, Peter was crucified.

He apparently believes them to have been killed after the main persecution; tradition has put their death in 67 C.E.

By the end of the second century an elaborate legend was known of Peter's death. When persecution loomed in Rome, the church persuaded Peter to flee for safety. As he crept through the gates in disguise, he had a vision of Jesus coming into the city. "Lord," he said, "where are you going?" "I am coming to Rome," replied Jesus, "to be crucified." "Lord, are you being crucified again?" "Yes, Peter, I am." With that Peter came to himself. He turned about and rejoined the church to face his arrest and death. He is said to have been crucified upside down. Peter had taken up his cross at last and followed his Lord.

He had come a long way from Galilee. *"Some seed,"* said Jesus in that story of the farming, his sowing, and the harvest, *"fell on good ground, sprouted, grew, and bore fruit: thirtyfold, sixtyfold, a hundredfold"* (Mark 4.8).

From Mark to Matthew

Nero: Dead and Alive Again?

On June 9, 68 C.E., Nero committed suicide. He was just thirty-one. Rebellion against his rule had spread: Armies had declared against him and the senate in Rome had declared him a public enemy. For the next year the empire was torn apart again by civil war. From Spain to Judaea, from Germany to Africa, Roman legions and their auxiliaries were on the move. Four generals held power in quick succession. As the troops converged on Rome the question loomed, could the empire survive this vicious implosion of rivals? The last battle was fought in the temples and streets of Rome. Smoke rose once more above the city: The shrine at its heart, the Capitol's temple of Jupiter, was in flames.

Was this, then, the end of Nero? Not quite. Strange rumors spread—that he was still alive, out on the eastern fringes of the empire, and would sweep back into power. "Everyone now wishes that he were alive," wrote an orator in Asia Minor forty years after Nero's death, "and most believe that he is." The emperor who had been so hated by the grandees of Rome and the West never lost the affection of his eastern provinces. He loved the Greeks' culture, promoted their commerce, and proclaimed their freedom. In Greece he had been acclaimed as "Jupiter Liberator Nero." From farther still had come Tiridates to be crowned king of Armenia and in turn had paid homage to Nero as the god Mithras.

The Jews had no such love of the emperor. Israel burst out into rebellion in 66 C.E.; Nero sent extra troops to restore control. When the city and Temple had been destroyed, two years after Nero's death, Jewish writers would take up the story of his return and imagine his revenge on the empire that had turned against him. Here would be the finest irony of all:

> The fugitive from Rome [we hear in one oracle] will come to the west,
> brandishing a great spear.

Great wealth will come to Asia, which Rome itself
once plundered and deposited in her house of many possessions.
She will then pay back twice as much and more
to Asia, and there will be a surfeit of war.

The New Emperor

It was not to be. Final victor of the wars and conspiracies of 69 C.E. was the very general to whom Nero had entrusted command over Judaea, Vespasian. How was this new dynasty to become legitimate? Vespasian had among his dependents a useful ally, the Jewish historian Josephus. The historian was an unlikely courtier at Rome: he had commanded the Jewish rebel forces in Galilee for over a year, was captured by the Romans, and then served in their generals' entourage for the rest of the war. He had been shown remarkable favor by Vespasian and therefore had to write with care:

> More than all else, what incited the Jews to the war was an ambiguous oracle, likewise found in their sacred scriptures, to the effect that at that time one from their country would become ruler of the world. This they understood to mean someone of their own race. The oracle, however, really signified the sovereignty of Vespasian, who was proclaimed emperor on Jewish soil.

Which is the prophecy Josephus has in mind? The best fit is offered by passages in the Book of Daniel that together identify the world ruler in that same vision that we have encountered before:

> *In my vision at night, I, Daniel, looked, and there before me was one like a son of man, coming with the clouds of heaven. He approached the Ancient of Days and was led into his presence. He was given authority, glory, and sovereign power; all people, nations, and men of every language worshiped him. His dominion is an everlasting dominion that will not pass away, and his kingdom is one that will never be destroyed.*
> *(DANIEL 7.13–14)*

Jesus, the Jewish rebels, and now Vespasian. Israel's dreams of a savior were taken over and used by the very dynasty that had ravaged its land and razed its capital to the ground.

Vespasian had his eyes on more than just the rebels. The tribute formerly paid by all Jews to the Temple in Jerusalem was now to be paid to the shrine of Jupiter on the Capitol in Rome. The Romans expected to discover in other nations' gods variant forms of their own; Vespasian would gladly have seen the Jews' God associated (by pagans, if not by the recalcitrant Jews) with Jupiter. One trace of such a strategy may have reached us in the news Vespasian spread of a particular prophecy. The prophecy's setting was well chosen.

When the empire first seemed within his reach, Vespasian had paid a visit to Mount Carmel, a famously numinous mountain between Galilee and the coast. Here Elijah had defeated the pagan gods in the name of Israel's God alone; here the philosopher-mystic Pythagoras had meditated; here in Vespasian's time was a shrine (Tacitus tells us) to the god Carmel, free from the temple and cult statue that in most pagan shrines so offended the Jews. Before long its dedication would change, to honor Jupiter of the Heavens. The predictions from the shrine were encouraging: Whatever Vespasian planned or wished, however ambitious, would succeed. How fitting that he should have consulted there a priest named Basilides, "King's Son."

Vespasian was a usurper, and not even of noble birth. "He lacked prestige," says Suetonius, "and a certain 'majesty.' These, too, were given him." The favored god of Alexandria, Serapis, helped his cause; a dramatic scene of healing helped give Vespasian the standing that he needed. It is worth envisaging the scene:

Many marvels occurred to mark the favor of heaven and a certain partiality of the gods toward Vespasian. One of the common people of Alexandria, well known for his loss of sight, threw himself before the emperor's knees, pleading with him to cure his blindness. He had been told to ask, he said, by the god Serapis; and he begged the emperor to deign to moisten his cheeks and eyes with his spittle. Another, whose hand was useless, begged the emperor to step and trample on it; he had been prompted by the same god. Vespasian at first ridiculed these appeals. When the men persisted, he wavered: he feared the discredit of failure, but was inspired with hope of success by the appeals of the men and the flattery of his courtiers. Finally he directed the physicians to give their opinion, whether such blindness and infirmity could be overcome by human aid.

The scene is now interrupted by the doctors' consultation and then is staged with due care; the political stakes were high. The doctors, in Tacitus's circumspect report, give a most nuanced prognosis; they, too, could ill afford a mistake. Our historian knows only too well the place of flattery. There is more to this story than meets the eye. We have seen Mark invoke the heroes of Israel's past as models for Jesus. The technique was not his alone. Roman emperors, too, had precedents on which to draw. Vespasian—and the crowd—knew of an earlier visit to Egypt by the most famous general of all, Alexander the Great. Alexander had come down the coast from Syria and visited, alone, the temple of Jupiter Ammon at Siwah, in Libya; he was said to have asked the god if he would become lord of all the world. A (late but) popular tradition had the god Serapis appear to him in a dream. From the time of this visit to Siwah, Alexander encouraged the rumor that he himself was the son of Jupiter. It is one of the most mysterious shifts in his extraordinary career. We will never know what he was told in the temple of Ammon or what he really came to believe about his own descent.

He may well have been greeted by the priest as son of another god Amun from neighboring Egypt: "Son of Amun" was one title of the Egyptian pharaohs whose throne he had taken. Whatever its basis, the word spread: The god Ammon had visited Alexander's mother, perhaps disguised as the last pharaoh; Alexander was the god's own son. With Alexander the world of Greece adopts a new myth. The story of direct divine sonship, once the privilege of ancient heroes sung by poets, walks out of the shadows of the epic past and becomes a possibility for heroes of the present day.

Four hundred years after Alexander, Vespasian reaches Egypt from Syria. He goes alone into the temple of the god Serapis, asks how stable is his empire, and is given a vision of a distinguished citizen whom he knew to be many miles away. Historians have long speculated what careful planning might lie behind this series of auspicious signs. For in a curious coincidence, Vespasian's vision was of another—or the same?—Basilides, "King's Son," later discovered by Vespasian's troops at a suitable distance from the city. Here in Alexander's city, Vespasian can inaugurate his role as a new Alexander.

Serapis was already associated with healing. The first miracle ascribed to his power, around 300 B.C.E., had been to restore a courtier's sight in the entourage of Ptolemy I who founded the cult. We have, too, several versions from Alexandria, in effigies and on coins, of a strange image: a foot and ankle topped by Serapis's head. They almost certainly recall Alexandria's colossal statue of the god, whose foot could be touched by suppliants for healing. From Serapis's healing foot to Vespasian's: The link was readily made. Vespasian was to tread on the crippled hand.

Vespasian was heir to a rich tradition. Here is how the story of his intervention ends. Tacitus tells us,

> The doctors distinguished between the cases: the blind man's sight had not been completely eaten away and would return if the obstacles were removed; the cripple's joints were dislocated and could be restored if a healing pressure was applied. Such might be the will of the gods, they said; and perhaps the emperor had been chosen for his divine service; in any case, the glory for any success would be the emperor's, mockery for any failure would fall on the patients themselves. So Vespasian, believing that his good fortune was capable of anything and that nothing was any longer incredible, with a smiling face and amid intense excitement in the crowd, did as he was asked. The hand was instantly restored to use and daylight shone again for the blind man. Eyewitnesses still recall both stories even now, when falsehood brings no reward.

A papyrus from Alexandria preserves part of an acclamation sung to Vespasian when he entered the city's great stadium. Many have long wondered whether his triumphant entry followed that demonstration of his godlike power:

> You are our one Savior and Benefactor,
> O Lord Augustus, to be Revered,

Benefactor, New Serapis, Son of Ammon,
we give you thanks . . .

The Jews had good reason to resent Nero, the Christians to detest him. His attack on the church in Rome was never forgotten. John the Seer presents him as the mirror opposite of Jesus: wounded to death and yet alive. The hideous beast envisaged in the Book of Unveiling stands for the power of Rome, which demanded the worship of its emperors from every nation under their control:

> *One of the beast's heads seemed to have a fatal wound, but the wound had been healed. The whole world was astonished and followed the beast. Men worshiped the beast and asked, "Who is like the beast? Who can make war against him?" The beast was given power to make war against the heroes of God and to conquer them. And he was given authority over every tribe, people, language, and nation. All inhabitants of the earth will worship the beast—all whose names have not been written in the book of life belonging to the Lamb of God.*
>
> *(BOOK OF UNVEILING [REVELATION] 13.3–5, 7–8)*

So much for the collapse with which civil war had threatened Rome's power; so much for the vindication of God's heroes. The empire after the civil war was stronger than ever. "O Rome," runs a graffito in a house of Ephesus, "ruler of all, your power will never die."

Three pretenders over the next twenty years declared themselves to be Nero. The first arose within a year of his death. Here may well be the explanation of a cryptic note in Mark's story: *When you see the abomination that causes desolation standing where it does not belong—let the reader understand!—then let those who are in Judaea flee to the mountains* (Mark 13.14). In the turmoil of 69 C.E., how easy it must have seemed for this "Nero" to sweep south from Asia Minor and to join up with the Syrian troops based in Israel. Perhaps this, then, is the period of the gospel's final revisions: When the known world was again collapsing into chaos and rumors were spreading like wildfire that the church's fiercest enemy was alive and under arms.

The Christians had seemed to Nero and Tigellinus an easy target for blame and punishment. But they had a strength of their own. We can look forward to the following centuries and wonder how this tiny movement grew as it did. Two local examples take us from one extreme to the other.

In one town, excavated in the 1930s, we follow the touchingly modest and domestic clues that ruins can offer us to a church's life. Dura-Europas was a garrison town of six thousand people on the empire's eastern frontier, 250 miles inland from Israel. A house there was converted into a church complex in the third century. Two rooms were knocked into one for the main assembly hall; a side room was converted into a baptistery; the courtyard was paved and embellished with benches and a portico. A capital cost was involved, for the latrine was covered over and the house could no longer be used as a family home. That must have been a serious decision for a church whose membership (judging from the size of the new assembly hall) numbered hardly more than sixty-five. If this building was the city's only church, those sixty-five formed the city's whole Christian presence. The Christians were not the only small caucus; the city's synagogue installed extra benches in the same decade to increase its capacity to 125. We might contrast this with the pagan shrine to Mithras, the Mithraeum, popular with the army: On its walls are scratched hundreds, perhaps thousands, of soldiers' names.

The Americans who excavated Dura asked next, was the refurbishing of the church a sign of growing numbers? They found that any such increase may have been artificial. The garrison was being strengthened to face threats from beyond the empire's border; the Mithraeum, too, was rebuilt by legionnaires around 215 C.E. and redecorated in the 240s. As the military presence grew, so did the commerce that served it. The synagogue was growing at least as fast in prosperity as in size; during these decades its walls were painted with the some of the most famous decoration that survives from the Roman world.

Sixty-five Christians in a town of six thousand: Two centuries of mission to the east seem hardly to have scratched its surface. Turn back to Rome itself, however, and we see what a future could lie in such beginnings. In the very decade of Dura's building campaigns, we hear of the church in Rome: 154 ministers of various ranks and 1,500 widows and poor people were supported there by the Christian congregations. Of the capital's million inhabitants, perhaps forty thousand swore allegiance to Jesus, perhaps more. Over the following years the church would undergo the fiercest persecution of all. Within eighty more years, however, the tables would turn: The Christians would be ready to claim the empire for their own.

At last the words of Paul, copied and preserved by the tiny church that first suffered from the wrath of Rome, could assume the role they have been asked to play in "Christian" countries ever since:

> *You want to be free from fear of the authorities? Do what is good, and you will have their praise. They are there in the service of God for the general good.*

On the Trail of Mark

How sure can we be that we have taken the right paths as we followed the trail to Mark? Is this how our first witness came to write his testimony? More is at stake, of course, than just the date of the gospel's completion and the name of its final editor. Different emphases could be discovered in the text as a whole.

Some scholars have found in Mark a sustained polemic against a group of church leaders who were claiming an unyielding power for Jesus and so for themselves; Mark is then stressing how important was Jesus' suffering and how blind were those follow-ers (in Jesus' day and Mark's) who saw for themselves a route to power and status. Other scholars have suggested that Mark is trying to make peace, to hold two quite different views of Jesus together. The differences that we see among our own four wit-nesses then become, on this view, no greater than the differences current within Mark's own community.

As we have seen, to reconstruct the church's life from the gospels is to walk through a hall of mirrors; too many possibilities offer a plausible reflection, too few solid facts can be grasped and relied on. If we are to explore these endless reflections, we do well to be clear what we hope to find in them and how. You, the reader, have now seen for yourself the aims of our historical search. It serves our chief purpose, to understand the stories themselves. This is a part of the scholarly tradition that is steadily gaining adherents: an increasing sense that the gospels should first be read and valued as the complete texts that they are. It will come as no surprise that within this movement itself the gospel has won as many different interpretations as interpreters. We make no claim to have cracked the code of the gospel once for all.

In *The Four Witnesses* we will continue to draw attention to the *disclosure* that our authors are trying to make possible. They have a difficult message to put across, not because the story is complicated or because there is a large cast of characters to intro-duce and control, but because the story can be understood only if we let our outlook and expectations be turned upside down. Mark has no separate introduction to explain what needs doing; he has just the narrative itself with which to do it.

We are reading a straightforward story, but far more than a story. And for as long as the readers look only at its surface, Mark locates them starkly among those outside the mystery. As Mark's Jesus said,

> *"To those outside, everything happens in riddles, so that* [as Isaiah says]
> *'Looking with all their might they may not see,*
> *and listening with all their might they may not understand;*
> *otherwise they might change their ways and God forgive them.'"*
>
> (MARK 4.10–12)

Mark is not a naive or unquestioning writer. He is an expert witness and must pass on, within his testimony itself, the key to understanding all that he says. His contri-bution was quickly overshadowed: Matthew and Luke both used his narrative, but the church valued their fuller versions of the story over Mark's spare, dark drama. Each had, as well, his own purpose and momentum, which would eclipse Mark's particular sense of mystery.

Matthew knows, too, how difficult it is to pin Jesus down. It is time to hear our sec-ond witness: He speaks in a different voice, from a different outlook, with a different set of needs and pressures and dangers in mind. It is these that shape his own distinctive answer to the question of Jesus that echoes through the gospels, *"Who do you say I am?"*

BOOK II
Matthew's Story

Introduction to Matthew

From Mark to Matthew: from the violent, restless story of an émigré, ill at ease in Rome's self-regarding glamour, to the architectural dignity of Matthew's gospel, the story of a leader of an ancient, settled, and distinguished community. We are in Antioch in Syria, the third largest city of the Roman Empire, due north from Jerusalem along the Levantine coast.

Mark was Jewish; so is our Matthew. In our next chapter we first hear from within Israel of the war for freedom that ended in 70 C.E. with the destruction of Jerusalem. Matthew is writing within ten years of the catastrophe, and from his contemporaries we hear plangent questions directed at God: How could he have abandoned his holy city to the gentiles? We will hear, too, of Antioch and of the Jewish community there in the aftermath of the war. We will then approach Matthew's gospel itself. To introduce our other witnesses we present what they believe and watch how they hope to bring their readers to believe the same. In Matthew we gain from a different emphasis: on the work that has brought Matthew and his community to the position that his gospel represents. The result is subtle, balanced, and in its own terms final. But long, exciting, and sometimes frightening work lies behind our gospel. To follow its course is to share—and to admire—the adventure of a whole church as it faces the question of Jesus, *"Who do you say I am?"*

We know little enough about Matthew himself. We hear in the gospel itself that Jesus, *passing by, saw a man seated at the tax desk, called Matthew, and said to him, "Follow me." And he got up and followed him* (Matthew 9.9). When the gospel then lists Jesus' twelve chosen pupils, it specifies Matthew as *the man who made his living out of tax collection* (Matthew 10.3). Matthew's story of this tax collector's call is indebted to Mark's account of a similar incident; the pupil chosen in this way, however, according to Mark (and to Luke) was called Levi. It may be that Matthew was a Levite (a member of the priestly tribe of Levi) and was known by both names.

And did this pupil write or edit the gospel that bears his name? Our earliest evidence appears in the fragments that have reached us of Papias's *Commentary on the*

Lord's Sayings, written around 125 C.E. Within fifty years of our gospel's completion, a collection of Jesus' sayings was linked with Matthew: "Matthew in the Hebrew [or Aramaic] language arranged the sayings, and each person translated them as best he could." We have heard already of the "Aramaic Matthew." Papias is the first to mention such a text, and the story of its existence (and so its identification with texts seen in later generations) may have been caused by a misunderstanding of precisely this passage in Papias's work. Papias has just been talking about Mark's disorganized record of Jesus' sayings, and the crucial sentence about Matthew could be taken to mean, "Matthew organized the sayings in the style used in Jewish writings; each of them (Mark and Matthew) transmitted them as best he could." This inference could have been drawn from comparing the two gospels themselves. Of all the hoped-for evidence for our gospel's writer, only the name Matthew would then remain, and closer comparison between these two gospels could have suggested to Papias himself or to his source that the author of "Matthew" knew more than Mark about the individual Matthew himself. The route lies open to a retrospective attribution to this Matthew. Yet again the individual to whom the gospel is ascribed is slipping through our fingers.

We have looked for evidence outside the gospel for evidence about its origin. We will find more than enough, of a quite different kind, within the text itself. For it is not the name of a single author that helps the gospel to unfold before us but a sense of the conditions and crises that the church was facing for which our "author" compiled or completed this rich, poetic text. Matthew draws on an extraordinary wealth of traditions and stories, but he wears his learning lightly. Here is a scholar and teacher at work; in later decades he would be called a rabbi. He steers his readers through a forest of meanings and allusions, and he brings them to a clearing at its heart of which they had no inkling at the journey's start.

Matthew searches the scriptures for clues to the identity and standing of this baffling Jesus. The terms in which he pursues his search are inherited from the synagogues and their vast knowledge of the Old Order. Matthew draws from deep wells of tradition unknown to most of his Christian readers today. But their streams still flow, deep beneath the ground of the church's belief. And these streams break through the surface still, running fresh and clear, in the Judaism that Matthew knew and loved well.

Matthew sifts the evidence about Jesus; he is awed by the solution to which it leads him. Here are some of the terms that we will watch him explore. Was Jesus a leader like Moses, bringing his people out of slavery into some Promised Land? We see him on a mountain, teaching obedience to the Law of Moses, and in the next breath, it seems, rewriting it.

Was Jesus a king, after all, as spoken of in ancient oracles? Was he destined, despite his disgrace and death, to bring Israel to freedom at last? We see him acknowledged by the mysterious Wise Men and hounded by the murderous Herod, but when the devil offers him all the kingdoms of the earth, he refuses them.

Was Jesus somehow a new Israel, overcoming the temptations in the desert to which the old Israel had succumbed? What exactly might such a claim mean? He is announced as God's Son; he creates around himself a "new" people, a community with new rules and rites and leaders. But where does this leave the Israel of old, declared by God's irreversible Law to be his own people, his "child"?

None of the categories available to Matthew said quite enough. Everything called for a deeper explanation. Who can Jesus have been? Who must he have been, if all the disparate pieces in Matthew's jigsaw were to fit together?

Jesus' adherents in city after city had to make a crucial decision: to be loyal to the synagogues or to establish a separate church. There were practical, day-to-day questions to answer; above all, should the Jewish Law be obeyed by Jewish and by gentile Christians? Radically different answers were being reached by different teachers. The most famous missionary of the church's first generation was Paul, and it would have been easy, at the end of the first century C.E., to believe that Matthew fiercely resisted Paul's view of the Jewish Law. In chapter 6, we hear how Paul answered the questions that Matthew would have to answer in turn, thirty years later in the church's life.

Those for whom Matthew wrote have been on the cusp. Matthew believes that the decision is now clear: They must leave the synagogues behind. We, too, know of the pain to which differences in deep belief can lead: bitterness, separation, and before long an angry misunderstanding. Matthew trod a distinctive path: His was a careful, subtle route but one that called for a brave, final decision from his readers.

And when at these chapters' end, we turn toward Luke, we will look once more and from a different angle at his supposed teacher, Paul. We can understand the situation facing Matthew only when we have been introduced to Paul. And more: To understand all four gospels—their dynamic and their function—we need Paul's help again. For in the understanding he attained of his own person and role, we will find the solution to our overarching question: What unites these four stories that tell of Jesus in such different ways?

Some of Matthew's main themes ring out loud and clear. They were all too easily learned by the church and all too often replayed: Matthew's disappointment at the synagogues fueled, for centuries, Europe's hatred of the Jews. But this was not Matthew's real music. Matthew foresaw doubts and difficulties that would face his readers, the knowledge without which they could make no responsible decision, the key recognition, as he saw it, that without his help would lie beyond their grasp. These are the themes on which Matthew plays; they were not audible for long. It is time to hear this sensitive scholar once more, whose harmonies were distorted out of all recognition in the polemics of a later age.

CHAPTER 5

The Promised Land?

Not Peace, but a Sword: Christians and Jews

ONE BATTLE LOST . . .

Haunting evidence of the Jews' revolt from Rome lies on a plateau eight miles south of Jericho, in the bleak, baking desert of the Dead Sea's western shore. In the cliffs behind the ruined settlement of Qumran are caves in which a vast cache of manuscripts was hidden two thousand years ago: texts of the Old Order and commentaries on them, rules for a community's life and discipline, psalms and calendars for its worship, and teachings on its troubled past and glorious future. The manuscripts rail against the sect's enemies and predict the final war under God's command in which they will be driven from Israel once and for all. It was in the war with Rome—the very war on which such nationalism pinned its hopes—that the settlement itself was destroyed. And there in its caves, until 1947, the manuscripts remained.

The writings from Qumran are fierce and confident, but not everyone in Israel had joined forces against Rome. "The Christians at Jerusalem," we hear from an early church historian, Eusebius, "had been given a command before the war in an oracle revealed to approved men there: to depart from Jerusalem and to inhabit a certain city, to the north and across the Jordan, called Pella." The report has been distrusted. Eusebius is almost certainly relaying the report of a historian from Pella itself. Some Christian sects that adhered more closely than the church at large to Jewish thoughts and ways later flourished there; they gained much-needed stature from claiming an "early" foundation. Better still if their founders were the church's heroes from Jerusalem itself. Pella itself was unlikely to welcome these Jewish emigrants. Just before the rebellion started in 66 C.E., a wave of pogroms swept Syria. The Jews attacked city after city in revenge. Pella, a wholly gentile city, was among them. This reopened old sores: The city had been held briefly by the Jews, 150 years before. When its gentile citizens refused to adopt Jewish ways, the captors had destroyed it. Pella had no love for the Jews.

Visible in this small story is a first strand of the theme that will weave in and out of the pages to come: the deepening rift between synagogue and church. The Christians from Jerusalem were themselves Jewish. If they went to Pella and were to be safe there, they had to make clear to their hosts that they had no part in the rebellion and no allies among those who had attacked the town. One route open to them, uncertain and unwelcome as it would have been, called for a fateful claim: that as Christians they were not "really" Jews at all.

. . . ANOTHER BATTLE BEGUN

If the church of Jerusalem had shown no loyalty to the Jewish cause, the synagogues in turn owed no allegiance to this disruptive offspring. So many links might have held the two together: links of family and history, of shared loyalties to shared hopes. But this erratic sect had left Jerusalem, its own home city and the nation's, in the lurch. Tension would grow bitter. Jesus' followers were making ever more dramatic claims for their master; the synagogue's leaders, by contrast, were drawing tighter, clearer boundaries between the ways of life their members must share and the deviant beliefs they must avoid. There was strain from both sides: the synagogues reining in, the Christians pushing out. Any uneasy, partial truce soon fell apart.

Matthew's Jesus says,

> *"Do not think that I have come to cast peace upon the world. I have not come to cast peace, but a sword. For I have come to set a man against his fathers and a daughter against her mother and a daughter-in-law against her mother-in-law, and a man's enemies will be the members of his own household."*
>
> *(MATTHEW 10.34–36)*

Mark knows of fear, Matthew of bitter division. A new community is coming to birth; the church is emerging from the synagogue. There is a fervor here, a clarity of purpose that sees a glowing future for its own adherents—and a terrible destruction threatening its opponents. The new is separated from its parent by painful decisions, divided families, and contested loyalty. Old loves and long allegiances are being sundered.

The church's leaders were growing more confident of their independence. They grew to define themselves by opposition to the synagogue leaders whose control they had left behind. But ordinary people with less power of their own were less sure of their leaders'. Some were still hedging their bets three hundred years after Matthew finished his gospel: They were going to synagogue on Saturday and on Sunday to church. No such loyalty, divided and wavering, could satisfy Matthew. Hard decisions faced his readers. A choice had to be made.

CIVIL WAR: PAST AND FUTURE

The Christians were not alone in leaving Jerusalem during the war. Josephus records the flight of aristocrats and leading citizens "as swimmers deserting a sinking ship." Wise heads could see the onslaught from Rome that would follow the insults of small rebel victories. Josephus has strong political views of his own. Right-thinking nobles in Jerusalem opposed the war, he tells us; those who stayed spoke up bravely against it and suffered torture and death for their integrity. Twelve thousand young nobles, we hear, were killed in a single purge. Josephus himself, once he became a protégé of the Romans, was used to encourage the rebels to surrender. God was now fighting for the Romans, he called out, and so persuaded a good many ordinary people, he tells us, to put themselves at the mercy of Vespasian's son and chosen general, Titus.

The war with Rome was in large measure a civil war, with all the bitterness and uncertainty that this suggests. Matthew's Jesus warned of division; Matthew's readers knew only too well what terrible forms such division could take.

The war tested every bond that held families and towns together. Short- and long-term prospects, old loyalties and scores, new dangers and advantages: All had to be weighed. At worst a city would be razed to the ground by its captor; at best its leaders might persuade a vengeful conqueror that his advantage lay in preserving it, fortified and garrisoned by his own troops. Such declarations of loyalty were of doubtful worth; once a rival army approached and threatened, its supporters would seek to hand over the city to its control—and to their own. Danger and fear, ambition and hope all worked for high stakes. Vivid examples of such division are offered by Tiberias and Sepphoris, cities that dominated Jesus' Galilee. Tiberias had once been the region's capital; the honor now belonged to Sepphoris—a city near Nazareth that was built up by the Romans in Jesus' time. Here already was cause enough for bitterness between them.

Josephus draws out these cities' ambiguous responses to the war. His account is testimony to the fearsome mix of suspicion, rivalry, and hotheaded violence to which the collapse of Roman order led. Throughout this story we will keep watch, too, on Josephus himself. Here is no impartial witness but a former general of the rebels now writing for their conquerors. In his narrative we find care for himself, sad hope for his people, and praise—fulsome, necessary praise—for the dynasty that had razed his sacred city to the ground.

Of Sepphoris, Josephus says that the majority of its inhabitants were Jewish, but it remained loyal to Rome, welcomed the Roman general in the first campaign, and by its example kept its region at peace. There is more to this than meets the eye. Josephus himself, as the rebels' commander, had let Sepphoris build fortified walls on the rebels' behalf, and in his absence the more fanatical party of rebels seized control. These dealings laid him open to a charge later made by a rival, Justus, who came from Tiberias.

Justus, too, had defected to Rome; Josephus was not the only rebel who had to defend the history of his loyalties. Justus claimed that by building Sepphoris's walls Josephus had fomented rebellion in the city. Josephus's response must be treated with caution; he was by now the emperor's protégé and could ill afford to let such charges stand. So he claims he had been fooled by the citizens into believing they were on the rebels' side; in fact they were fortifying their city on the *Romans'* behalf. Josephus is reduced to a double-edged defense: He is not guilty of stirring Sepphoris's rebellion because his efforts to do so were confounded by its citizens themselves.

And Tiberias? The city had been built on a burial ground, which would render any Jewish inhabitant permanently impure. Even to populate the new city was hard enough; Herod Antipas, it seems, had to force Jews to live there. Relations with its neighbors would forever be tense. But with a palace, stadium, and, for its Jews, "an enormous house of prayer," this was a grand city. Its loyalties were always in doubt: Faction after faction had control, general after general approached the city with his forces and looked for its support. One faction in Tiberias, it seems, tried the same ploy as the council in Sepphoris, letting the Romans know secretly of their loyalty while having the rebel Josephus build their walls. Josephus blamed the machinations of his rival Justus, commander and historian, who hoped to seize power for himself by stirring resentment against the new capital, Sepphoris. Sepphoris was loyal to Rome; the rebels were longing to attack it. Tiberias, urged Justus, should use the rebellion for its own advantage.

Throughout this account of the cities' shifting schemes—each met, as Josephus insists, with his own statesmanlike response—lurks the mass of "the Galileans": rural people under Josephus's command and supposed control who apparently would turn against a city at the first opportunity. "The Galileans," says Josephus, "seized the chance, too good to be missed, to vent their hatred on Sepphoris, one of the cities that they detested. They plunged into the town, set fire to the houses which the terrified inhabitants had abandoned in a flight to the citadel, and looted everything." Jesus' movement sprang from the febrile countryside of Galilee. It is among the most striking developments of these years that this rural sect should have found so ready a niche in the cities of Syria, Asia Minor, and Greece and, within just twenty years of Jesus' death, in the teeming capital of empire, Rome itself.

War with Rome, war with rival cities, war with one's own neighbors. Matthew's Jesus is as stern and divisive as any city's leader, but he has nothing to do with enmities such as these. He is blunt:

"You have heard that it was said: 'An eye for an eye' and 'A tooth for a tooth.' Well I, I say to you: Do not oppose the evil one. But whoever hits you on the right cheek, turn the left cheek to him, too. You have heard that it was said: 'You will love your neighbor' and will hate your enemy. Well I, I say to you: Love your enemies and pray for those who persecute you, so that you might be the children of your father in heaven."
(MATTHEW 5.38–39, 43–45)

Jesus himself had lived before the war. His followers saw in him Emmanuel, "With-Us-God," the child promised by the prophet Isaiah who would rescue the Jews from the onslaught of their enemies. The crisis that Isaiah faced seven centuries before was being faced also by the Israel of Matthew's day: a hostile empire sweeping the land, the capital under threat. Isaiah's Israel suffered war for years, but Jerusalem was saved. Where then, in Matthew's day, had his new Emmanuel been when his people were surrounded by the Roman army and desperate for rescue?

Jesus was killed by Israel's conquerors. His followers did nothing to throw off the rule of Rome, and now they claim that in him is fulfilled the Old Order's most famous promise of freedom. Set deep within Matthew's gospel is a polemical, stark claim: Isaiah's King Hezekiah had relied on God as the prophet had demanded; his Jerusalem had been spared. The Israel that Matthew knew did not, as Matthew saw it, turn to Matthew's God, and Titus had swept all before him. The ancient prophecy of Emmanuel was being fulfilled in ways that Israel, with its old hopes, could not see. For the kingdom of God is at last at hand. Here is a new "rebellion" against foreign rule; it will generate a new "civil war" as bitter as the last. Division and anger within Israel are not over yet.

Matthew's Jesus will tear families and communities apart, and all within ten years of a revolt that divided the Jews into warring factions and resulted in Jerusalem's destruction. Such antagonism had reduced Israel to a ruin, and now, says Matthew's Jesus, it must be fueled again. In the war the source of bitterness was the evil of the common enemy. In the coming strife, division is stirred by Emmanuel, the very agent who should be driving that enemy from the land. But the enemy to be expelled is not Rome's army; Israel's factions will not be warring over local advantage or Israel's independence. This Emmanuel brings a kingdom of a different kind.

Matthew's gospel was heard by a weary, war-torn, divided people. A church that shunned the one war calls for another. Who could this Jesus be—who must he be—for his demands to win adherents to his cause?

FROM TEMPLE TO SYNAGOGUES

Matthew writes perhaps fifteen years after Mark, ten years after the fall of Jerusalem in 70 C.E. Jewish writers of the time are asking why God has allowed such destruction of his chosen home on earth. Several *Books of Unveiling* have reached us from the centuries on both sides of Jesus' life. The *Book of Unveiling* that we have in the New Order itself is only one of many that have survived. Another, completed after the Romans' destruction of Jerusalem, is written as if its author were Baruch, pupil of the ancient prophet Jeremiah. The technique is familiar in writings from Jesus' time. Readers of this *Book of Unveiling,* faced with the horror of the Temple's razing, are to recall the Temple's previous destruction, lamented by Jeremiah, in 587 B.C.E. "Baruch" speaks throughout as if he is in the ruined Jerusalem known to Jeremiah; all that he says applies to the Jerusalem of the author's own day, 70–100 C.E. The author taps into the history of Israel; the destruction that confounds his readers is not the first such destruction that Jerusalem has suffered. God will be loyal to his people now as he has been in the past. Israel recovered from the defeat lamented by Baruch and will recover again. From the city's loss, "Baruch" is drawn to ask after the whole of God's plan, from Adam to God's last judgment upon the world. The author pursues a deep, sad meditation on the evil that afflicts his people but builds it upon a series of visions, probably current before he wrote, that unveil the vast, sweeping victory of God and his Anointed.

Such hope is not offered too cheaply or too soon. Jerusalem has been taken. Jeremiah has left for Babylon. "Baruch" sits in front of the Temple's doorway and raises a lament over his beloved city. We might find the poem formal and stylized. But for such a disaster, "Baruch" has chosen the systematic dirge he needs: The whole created order, element by element, should respond to the desolation of its central and most precious jewel:

> Blessed are those who were not born,
> or those who were born and died.
> But we, the living, woe to us
> because we have seen all that has befallen Jerusalem.
> You, O sun, keep the light of your rays within you,
> and you, O moon, extinguish your light.
> For why should the light ever rise where Jerusalem's light is darkened?
> You wives, do not pray to bear children,
> for the barren will rejoice more.
> For why do they bear in pain only to bury in grief?
> Why should children ever be named again,
> where this mother Jerusalem is desolate,
> and her children carried off in captivity?

The Jewish leaders, meanwhile, must hold together their confused and frightened people. They retrench. If the laws regarding the Temple and its worship can no longer be kept, all the more reason to obey those laws that can. The study of the Law in the local synagogues, reverence for the Law above all other gifts of God: These were the tasks of a Judaism that lacked the Temple, and their observance marked the boundaries of its beleaguered people. Not that even these moves were free from Roman oversight. The center of Jewish scholarship after the war was at Jamnia, just inland from the coast. From the academy established there by Johannan, son of Zakkai, grew a movement that over the following centuries would dominate and define Judaism as a whole. We might imagine the Judaism that had been based upon the Temple of Jerusalem as the mother from which were born the Christianity and Judaism that we know today; the church of Matthew and the academy of Johannan were the twin children from which almost all that has followed can claim descent.

The traditions that tell of Johannan had no wish to belittle him. We hear that he was one of those who escaped from Jerusalem during the war; he hid in a coffin. He, like the Christians' leaders, would have no part in the rebellion. He secured an interview with Vespasian and predicted that the general would become emperor. As for Josephus, so for Johannan: such a prophecy secured Vespasian's favor. He gave Johannan permission to open an academy at Jamnia. Vespasian may have taken a more active role in its placing than this story suggests. The Jewish majority at Jamnia had risen in arms to join the rebellion; Vespasian suppressed the uprising and quartered there, Josephus tells us, "a sufficient number of those who had surrendered." Control of the coastal towns was important. Vespasian settled Jews there who would keep their compatriots in order; Johannan, prophet of the general's future glory, would have been well chosen to ensure the city's calm.

"God with Us"?

Just at this fragile moment in Jewish life the question of Jesus is demanding the synagogues' attention. The synagogues, in turn, were dominating Christian thought. The Jews within the Christian community had been brought up in the synagogues and attended them still. Gentile Christians knew full well that Jesus had been Jewish and that his teaching then and his community now were both currents within the great river of Judaism. How, then, were these followers to relate to the community, leaders, and practices of their local synagogues? The first focal point was the Law of Moses. It had been entrusted to the Jews alone. It was God's greatest gift to his chosen people, and its observance set that people apart from all the other nations of the world.

What part, then, was this Law to play in the life of Jesus' followers? Those followers were divided. Some made angry claims: Jesus had wholly superseded the Law. Matthew was appalled. The Law was God's greatest gift to Israel and the world; it was the voice of God's own Wisdom made audible to humankind. If Jesus had spoken against the Law, he had spoken against God himself. Our present gospel is adamant, but it bears traces of an attitude, maintained in Matthew's own community, less clear-cut than Matthew's own. For others, too, were thinking carefully. What was Jesus' connection to the Law if he was God's Chosen One of whom the Law had spoken and yet was disowned by the people to whom God gave the Law? If he had fulfilled prophecy after prophecy from the Law and yet been killed in the Law's name? If he had been disgraced and put to death and yet brought back to life? These were the questions at which Matthew's church had chipped away. The answer to which it finally came—subtle, careful, and hard to hold to in the bitter divisions of the time—was devastating. It was almost absurd, unless it was true.

The Law was not just a theme for theory and speculation. It mattered day to day: for the present members of Matthew's church, for those who opposed it, and for those who were wondering, Jews and gentiles alike, whether to seek admittance. To be loyal to the Law was to be loyal to its interpreters within the synagogue and to the way of life that they and the Law enjoined. This had practical and public implications: what to eat and with whom; when to fast; what pagan rites to take part in, attend, or avoid; what to do and not do on the Sabbath. Most acute for gentile males was the call for circumcision. As important as the painful and irreversible operation, was the loyalty that it signaled to a community that was distinctive, self-contained, and the object, all too often, of vicious attack.

The synagogues' leaders faced a sharp question in turn: What was the proper attitude toward those who looked both ways, toward the Jewish community and the gentile? On the one hand were gentiles who respected the synagogue's Law but would not commit themselves to its entire and exclusive observance. On the other were Jews whose social and business ties immersed them deeply in gentile ways, far more deeply than a Law that defended Israel's pure and separate life, its "holiness" to God, allowed.

And now, within the synagogues' own life, was emerging a route that such people could follow. A new sect: Its Jewish members attended their local synagogues and claimed loyalty to Jewish ways, but the sect's leaders were developing its own rites of admission, its own communal celebrations, and its own structures of authority and discipline. This sect was growing within the synagogues but was taking on a life of its own. By the end of the first century C.E. it would be visible as an entity in itself: the church.

In Rome we have seen how the young church was confronted by imperial power. In Antioch we will be offered our fullest picture of the relations between Jews and gentiles in and around the church. If our second witness was indeed writing at Antioch, he was at the center of the most startling and important development that the early church would undergo. It is time to hear of this great city Antioch, its synagogues and its church.

ANTIOCH: THIRD CITY OF THE EMPIRE

The Jews of Antioch, Josephus tells us, "were constantly attracting to their ceremonies a large crowd of Greeks, and had made these in some measure a part of themselves." There may have been a Jewish presence in Antioch since its foundation in 300 B.C.E. Josephus tells of mercenaries who had fought for Seleucus I; in his new capital they had been given space and special rights. These were proclaimed on bronze tablets, since such privilege was precious and easily threatened.

Antioch, on the river Orontes, was one of the great cities of the Roman East. "As large as Antioch" became a Jewish proverb; as many as a quarter million people may have been crammed within its walls. Seleucus had chosen its site well. To the north spread a plain rich in grain, olives, and grapes, and in fish from its lake. Behind the city rose the mountains of Lebanon; through a break between two ranges ran the artery that led to the markets and goods of the east. From the south came Jericho's dates, Damascus's wool, glass from the prized works in Sidon. And from the coast on its west, purple dye, the rarest and most precious of colors. Antioch looked in all directions at once. Within fifteen miles its river reached the Mediterranean. The city lay in the crook of an elbow: Asia Minor to the northwest, Arabia to the east, the Levantine coast to the south, and the sea to the south and west. All the markets of the empire lay open to its ships.

Natural port of call on any sea voyage from Antioch was the island of Cyprus, visible on a clear day from the city itself. When Jesus' followers in Jerusalem first came under attack, they fled up the coast: to Phoenicia, Cyprus, and Antioch. With them went their message, which they preached, as we would expect, to Jews. In Jerusalem, however, this group had been suspected of disloyalty to the Temple and the Law, and among the fugitives, Luke tells us, were some Cypriots who brought to Antioch a missionary claim that would change the course of history: The gospel, they maintained, should be preached to gentiles, too. When the church in Jerusalem regathered and heard of this news, it was the Cypriot Barnabas who was sent to investigate. A wise move: Here was a man who will have known the city and been known to its radical missionaries. If any envoy from Jerusalem could be valuable at such a delicate moment, it was Barnabas. For there were sharp questions to answer: What should these gentiles be encouraged to do? To join the synagogue? To be circumcised? To observe the whole Jewish Law? The Christians in Antioch itself were faithful to Jerusalem after all; when famine struck, they sent generous aid. But seeds of tension had been sown in Antioch, and they would grow into the fiercest debate of the early church.

Antioch had been the hub of Seleucus's empire and was center of the Romans' eastern government in turn. Four legions were based here, some twenty-four thousand soldiers. Their presence was enough to keep control for hundreds of miles around. The legate Varus saw trouble coming in 4 B.C.E., when Herod died and his likely successor, Archelaus, went to Rome to have his authority confirmed. Varus sent one legion to Jerusalem. When its commander lost control, Varus swept down through Galilee and Samaria with two more. Their arrival was enough to quell the insurrection. We have heard already of the outcome. Varus rounded up two thousand ringleaders and had them crucified.

Imperial and military pride converged: The emperor Tiberius built a great temple to Jupiter and the city's public baths; when an earthquake destroyed much of the city in 37 C.E. the emperor Caligula paid for its reconstruction. King Herod also made his impact here. He was tireless in building. In Jerusalem he rebuilt the Temple to the God of the Jews. Herod himself was of mixed descent but wished to assert his Jewish identity. His wife, on the other hand, was Samaritan; Herod built a new temple to the emperor Augustus in the region's capital, Samaria, and renamed the city "Sebaste" or "Augusta" in the new emperor's honor. And here in Antioch, as Josephus recalls with a flourish, "did Herod not pave that broad street, once shunned because of its mud, with polished marble, its full length of two and a half miles, and as protection from the rain, adorn it with a colonnade as long?"

That marble road ran the length of the city, north to south. As it neared the southern gates, there on the left, nestling within the city walls, was the main Jewish quarter. Chief pride was its great synagogue. It attracted royal patronage: King Antiochus

Epiphanes, scourge of Israel, had plundered the Temple in Jerusalem in 170 B.C.E., but his successors gave the bronze from the booty to the Jews of Antioch, who used it to adorn their synagogue. The bronze was far from the spoils' most valuable part, but here was an unrivaled dignity for the building and its people. Josephus tells how the Jews of Antioch "adorned the temple with great splendor by the design and expense of their offerings." There was one Temple for Jews and one alone: in Jerusalem. Is that Josephus's reference? There is a more telling possibility: Josephus is giving us, perhaps by mistake, a glimpse of the status that Antioch's great synagogue had assumed in its people's life. The Temple in Jerusalem, after all, had been sacked by the time Josephus wrote; here in Antioch were the remnants of its ancient and precious contents. Here, too, according to some stories, were the tombs of the martyrs killed by Epiphanes in their faith's defense. This was a venerable site. If any city other than Jerusalem was going to claim such a "Temple," it would be Antioch. Its unusual dignity may then have influenced far more than just Syrian Jews. When the high priest Onias III was exiled from Jerusalem in 175 B.C.E., he took refuge in Antioch. The new and "illegit-imate" dynasty of high priests had him murdered. His son, who had a right to inherit his father's office, took the example of Antioch one extraordinary stage further: He founded a "Temple" in Egypt, a rival to Jerusalem's in a pagan land; it won sufficient resources from the authorities and from Egyptian Jews to survive until 73 C.E.

All historians have their heroes. Jonathan, fighting in the 140s B.C.E. for the free-dom of Judaea and Jerusalem, won respect and an alliance from King Demetrius II of Antioch. When Demetrius faced a revolt at home, he called on Jonathan to help. The Jewish historian of the Story of the Maccabees, Book 1, has a clear view on what fol-lows:

> Jonathan sent off 3,000 experienced soldiers to Antioch. The king was delighted at their arrival. The citizens gathered in the city's center, 120,000 of them, intending to kill the king. He took refuge in the palace, while the citizens occu-pied its streets and began to attack. The king called on the Jews for help; they ral-lied round him in a body, spread out round the city, and that day killed 100,000 of its inhabitants. They fired the city, seized a great deal of plunder, and secured the king's safety. The Jews were covered in glory, in the eyes of the king and of everyone else in the kingdom.
>
> (STORY OF THE MACCABEES, BOOK 1, 11.41)

The Jewish mercenaries were admired by everyone—except the citizens of Antioch. When Jonathan's army had returned to Jerusalem and Demetrius was once more in control, the Jews of Antioch still had to live beside the neighbors burned out and bereaved by their countrymen.

"Put away your sword," said Jesus at his arrest to his follower who had wounded the high priest's servant; *"for all who take up the sword shall die by the sword"* (Matthew 26.52).

We today have, from recent events in Bosnia and Kosovo, some sense of the vio-lence with which such generations lived. Details about Antioch's intramural battles are scarce; Josephus's figures are often questioned. But ten thousand or a hundred thou-sand: such casualties in a city of a quarter million left hardly a family untouched. The Jews of Syria suffered far more violence than they inflicted, and in the war with Rome the Jews of Israel would suffer far worse still. It is in this world that Jesus preached and Matthew wrote. Matthew warns his readers: Jesus came to cast not peace on the earth but a sword. But this sword is no weapon of war. Matthew wants us to hear as well, in the very first teaching of Jesus, his response to the public world of violence and the power of arms. This Jesus will cause division by resisting division. For the church to stand so firmly against the world's ways will trigger the world's ways into ever more vehement action around—and within—the church.

Blessed are those who mourn, for they will be comforted.
Blessed are the meek, for they will inherit the earth.
Blessed are the merciful, for they will receive mercy.
Blessed are the peacemakers, for they will be called children of God.
Blessed are those who are persecuted for the justice of God,
for theirs is the kingdom of heaven.

(MATTHEW 5.4–5, 9–10)

Suspicion simmered from generation to generation. In 39–40 C.E. there was a riot against the Jews in Antioch. Similar riots had flared in Alexandria in 38, and a wave of violence may have spread through the east. The emperor sent to Alexandria an edict confirming the Jews' rights there; an identical edict was sent to Antioch. The Jews' rights had clearly been threatened. When the rebellion was over in 70 C.E. they were in jeopardy once more. The citizens of Antioch petitioned Titus to expel the Jews from the city. Josephus, as ever, knows to speak highly of his Roman masters. He records Titus's insistence: The Jews are to be allowed to stay in Antioch, with all their rights preserved. Josephus says nothing of the victorious general's two other moves.

Just to the south of Antioch grew the groves of Daphne. Amid them were the tem-ples to Apollo and Diana; sanctuary could be taken here. Here could still be seen, it was said, the laurel tree into which the girl Daphne—"Laurel"—had been turned as she fled from Apollo's advances. Apollo's shrine was the setting for elaborate, orgiastic rites. Daphne was the favored town for summer villas, a fashionable resort for the hol-idays of the rich and the festivals of the city at large. Public buildings there would be popular. Titus pulled down the synagogue at Daphne and built a theater on the site; the cost was met, as the theater's name declared, "from the Jewish spoils."

The road to Daphne left the city at the southern gate. Here was the Jewish quar-ter and one end of Herod's marble road. Looming over the Jews was the gate itself. It was adorned by Titus, we are told, with the angels' statues he had taken from the

Temple in Jerusalem and, above them, in unmistakable victory, with statues of the conquerors' gods. Proudest of all: Here on the way to shrines of Apollo and Diana, linked throughout Greek history with the sun and moon, was Selene's statue, goddess of the moon itself, her chariot drawn by four bulls. Let the Jews in Antioch know their place: protected—as trophies in the Romans' triumph. Every day was a reminder of their subjection to imperial power as they went about their business in and out of Angels' Gate.

Jesus the Teacher

"BLESSED ARE THOSE WHO KNOW THEMSELVES TO BE POOR"

Matthew has much to say that needs a delicate, careful presentation. Every detail matters. To give his readers a clear sense of the gospel's overall direction, Matthew gives his story a bold, clearly contoured shape. Great architects can be recognized by the balance of detail and structure on their buildings' facades. Every small area attracts our eye and admiration; but we never lose sight of the building's overall coherence. Matthew is a supreme architect.

The work of Matthew's Jesus falls into five clear sections. Each starts with an account of his actions and of dialogues with inquirers and opponents, then follows a block of his own teaching. To signal the end of each such block, Matthew rings the changes on a single formula. Jesus' first talk ends: *and it happened when Jesus finished these sayings, the crowds were amazed at his teaching* (Matthew 7.28). In the next section he sends out his twelve most trusted pupils to announce the coming of the kingdom of heaven. A series of short, pithy sayings follows, with encouragement and warning together. *And it happened when Jesus had finished instructing his twelve pupils* [the closest circle of his followers], *he moved on to teach and preach in their cities* (Matthew 11.1). In shaping the story Matthew gives his readers all the guidance he can. This affects the "style" of Jesus himself. Here is not the hurtling, restless Jesus of Mark's gospel but a thinker and teacher as organized as the Matthew that is describing him.

The result is a story with a grand sweep; it has a stateliness foreign to Mark. The narrative sections show a clear progression. The first introduces us to Jesus; in the second we hear of miracles, of those who ask for Jesus' help and those who see it given; in the third the Jewish authorities resist his claims; the fourth, in response, shows Jesus founding his new community, the church, and in the fifth, Jesus reaches Jerusalem and the scene is set for the story's climax. The gospel's architecture is not merely formal, the arrangement of a tidy mind. The readers are being challenged as well as informed in an overarching, purposeful sequence of offers and demands. Each block of teaching is duly given a fitting climax, a clear warning to the audience—and the readers—to take to heart what they have just heard. The first and most famous "sermon" has an uncompromising close:

"Everyone who hears these words of mine and acts on them [says Jesus] *will be like a sensible man, who built his house on the rock. And the rain came and the rivers rose and the winds blew and fell upon that house; and it did not fall, for it was founded on the rock. And everyone who hears these words of mine and does not act on them will be like a fool, who built his house on the sand. And the rain came and the rivers rose and the winds blew and fell upon that house; and it fell. And great was its fall."*
(MATTHEW 7.24–27)

With this sermon Matthew introduces Jesus' public work. Matthew has arranged a long, beautifully balanced symphony of sayings. Theme after theme is stated, developed with examples, and then rounded off. As each such section balances its neighbors, so the whole collection comes full circle at its close. Almost everything is arranged in sets of three: Three laws from the Ten Commandments are unfolded, then three from later in the Law. Three themes of Christian life are explored: gifts to the poor, prayer, and fasting. Matthew's instinct for order is seen here at its clearest; what we find in this opening program can be found again in every section of his story and in the gospel's structure as a whole. Matthew is an architect. He takes pleasure in his text's clear, balanced shape and in the crisp instruction that it makes possible.

The opening lines of this sermon are as dramatic as any in the Bible. Here, right at the start of Jesus' work, is the most famous teaching in the Christian world, "The Sermon on the Mount."

THE SERMON ON THE MOUNT

Seeing the crowds, Jesus went up onto the mountain. He sat down [as a Jewish teacher would] *and his pupils gathered to him, and he began to teach them: "Blessed are those who know themselves poor, for theirs is the kingdom of heaven."*
(MATTHEW 5.1–3)

No preface, no explanation. Just this dramatic start to a set of claims and promises. *Those who know themselves poor* (or literally, "the poor in spirit") would be a group more easily recognized in Jesus' day than in ours. *The poor* had always been a term for those in economic need. It became as well a phrase in the Old Order for those in special need of help from God, and so it stood for God's own people, humiliated and oppressed. The church knew the term well; in the 50s C.E. the Christians in Jerusalem seem to have called themselves "the poor." Matthew's Jesus qualifies the phrase: He speaks of "the poor in spirit" or "in breath." Such self-conscious frailty is mentioned once at Qumran. At the time of the final battle against God's enemies "those who know themselves poor will have power over the hard of heart." In this invitation to the gospel, Matthew is looking for the readers to recognize themselves among those described and praised. They must acknowledge who and what they are. They can then lay claim to the blessing that is rightfully theirs, the blessing whose first benefit they receive as they hear and know themselves addressed in the gospel itself.

In the buildup to these opening words, the tone of the gospel changes: We are moving from darkness to light. Matthew has had the Baptizer use the very words we then hear as Jesus' own: *"Change your hearts and your ways: for the kingdom of heaven is at hand"* (Matthew 3.2). In the Baptizer's mouth, this is a threat: God's judgment is at hand. The wild figure of the Baptizer is at work by the Jordan, the border between the desert and the Promised Land. The setting is a limbo as strange and numinous as his proclamation, a threshold between the Jews' ordinary life and the wild, bleak desert through which, for forty years, their ancestors had trudged to get there. It is those who are prepared to listen that come out to hear him, but he offers more to fear than hope for: *"Generation of vipers, who has warned you to escape the coming wrath?"* (Matthew 3.7). John baptizes with water in the river Jordan. He imagines the baptism of the one who will follow him: in the Breath of God and in fire. The Breath will separate wheat from chaff; the fire will burn the waste. Of the two great purging elements, water and fire, the Baptizer sees only the first at work in his own cleansing, a mere prelude to the cataclysm that his successor will bring.

God had exposed the world to his anger once before, drowning all humankind except Noah and his family in their ship. The first signs for Noah of the land's recovery and of safety were three flights of a dove. Matthew shows a telling detail in the meeting of Jesus and this stern Baptizer. As Jesus comes out of the water, God's Breath comes upon him in the form of a dove.

The Baptizer's message and Jesus' are the same. Yet there is all the world between them. The first pupils are called by Jesus and follow him; crowds of the sick and infirm are healed. Here is the other side of the message that he and the Baptizer share: *"Change your hearts and your ways,"* says Jesus, *"for the kingdom of heaven is at hand"* (Matthew 4.17).

We are moving from wrath to mercy. Jesus declares that nine ways of life receive God's blessing. They are not, it seems, restricted to "religious" life. The blessings are an invitation. Those who see themselves in this way are already within the circle of the kingdom; they are welcome within the group of pupils around Jesus in which that kingdom is becoming real on earth. The first three blessings ask readers to recognize— themselves. It is readers such as these who will hear what is really to be heard in all that follows. The Matthew who has shaped his whole gospel for the readers' help has his eye on them in every detail of his composition:

> *Blessed are those who know themselves poor, for theirs is the kingdom of heaven.*
> *Blessed are those who mourn, for they will be comforted.*
> *Blessed are the meek, for they will inherit the earth.*
>
> (MATTHEW 5.3–5)

To be embraced by these first three blessings, it seems, is to be passive. But Matthew knows that some readers will be actively seeking admission to Jesus' entourage. They are looking for guidance, what to do. He gives it. They are called on to conform to the kingdom's ideals:

Blessed are those who are hungry and thirsty for justice, for they will be filled.
(MATTHEW 3.6)

One question, over and over, faces any reader encouraged by these blessings: When will they come to fruition? The Baptizer's threats seem as far from fulfillment as ever. So do Jesus' promises: The meek are no nearer their inheritance than they were in Jesus' day, the battle for justice no more nearly won. If Matthew's church was on the edge of the kingdom, we are on it still. After two thousand years we might ask, what sort of promises are these? *"Theirs is the kingdom of heaven."* The strange balance that we saw in Mark is here, too. Matthew sets us on the threshold of the kingdom; it is already ours—but not yet for us to occupy in full.

Matthew sets up in these blessings, right at his story's start, a hope and expectation whose fulfillment the story does not provide. This Jesus, like Mark's, will speak throughout of rewards and punishment yet to come. The reader has reason always to be looking forward, through the narrative and into the future. But more has been fulfilled than a quick reading of the story lets us see. For in Matthew's church, as Matthew believes, the risen Jesus is present, active, and in command. The Jesus who spoke to his audience speaks to Matthew's readers still, and he does so in and through the text of Matthew's gospel itself. The voice of a teacher in Palestine is now the voice of the church's lord. The future to which the story steers us is not yet fully unfolded, but Matthew insists it has begun—in the future in which the reader lives. From Jesus' audience to Matthew's readers: *Here* is the movement toward the kingdom that the story encourages us to look for. It is under way, for Matthew, in the very fact of his gospel's present power among his readers.

Jesus, for Matthew, is the church's present lord. But his first readers, even those who were already the church's members, might well still have asked at the story's start, where does Jesus' authority come from that he can speak like this? Who is this teacher, declaring that God blesses just such groups and have every reason to doubt his blessing? More than self-recognition is needed and more than a wish for the world to change. If these claims of Jesus are to be trusted, all that bestowed honor in his world—and still does, for the most part, in our own—stood in stark opposition to the will of God. We have heard, in every story from Rome and Antioch and beyond, of empire and wars, of dignity and self-dependence, of patronage and calculation. These were the currency of honor, of respect for oneself and deference from others. Matthew's readers are summoned, in Jesus' opening lines, to believe that these values and standards and expectations are, in God's sight, upside down. The descriptions of those who are blessed do not so far refer to God at all; it is the rewards that these attitudes bring that reveal their standing in God's plan. Nothing now visible supports Jesus' claims. Readers who align themselves with this outlook—with the plans and praise of this God—do so on the say-so of Jesus alone. But this Jesus is no seer; he does not present himself as the mouthpiece for visions or information given by God, relayed by an angel, or interpreted by a privileged prophet. Jesus appeals to no higher authority than himself. Who can he be—who must he be—to have the authority to speak in this way? Matthew is a sleuth. He knows that in this question of Jesus' authority lies the key to the whole story that he must unlock for his readers. Matthew and those around him must have lived with the question, year in year out. We have good reason to be grateful that they dug deeper and deeper until the dazzling answer was at last uncovered that Matthew puts before us.

Luke, too, knows of these blessings, but his tone is quite different. Luke makes it clear that Jesus is speaking to his pupils alone. They are already within his circle and can be directly addressed throughout: *"Yours is the kingdom of God."* Luke's Jesus encourages; he does not need to persuade. We hear of reversal throughout Luke's first chapters: The rich are to become poor, the prosperous to become hungry, the humble to be lifted on high. Luke's Jesus speaks to those who have taken on the role of the poor:

> *Blessed are the poor, for yours is the kingdom of God.*
> *Blessed are those who hunger now, for you will be filled.*
> *Blessed are those who weep now, for you will laugh.*
>
> *(LUKE 6.20–21)*

Here is Luke's earthy world of the poor and hungry: He does not write of poverty "in spirit" or of hunger for justice. He has blunter needs in mind. And so, by contrast, to his patrons and wealthy readers he has good reason to say, beware. We shall see the care, over and again, of Luke's presentation: a Jesus who speaks as vehemently as possible on behalf of the poor but presents no threat to the power and wealth of Rome. Far from playing down this dangerous side of Jesus, Luke shapes his whole gospel around its claims. Luke's Jesus continues,

> *But woe to you, you who are rich, for you have your comfort already.*
> *Woe to you, you who are full now, for you will be hungry.*
> *Woe to you who laugh now, for you shall mourn and weep.*
>
> *(LUKE 6.24–25)*

Matthew presents his blessings without those "Woes" through which Luke warns his readers, not because he sees a world without injustice and complacency, but because he has in mind his gospel as a whole and his plans for a later attack, vehement and narrowly focused, on those who would resist it. Here in the first words of Jesus' first sermon he speaks of the kingdom of heaven, of meekness, of mercy and purity, of persecution and the prophets' suffering. However, at the end of his last public teaching, in perfect symmetry in relation to the gospel's center, Jesus launches a bitter attack on the Jewish powers that be. Seven "Woes" condemn them. *Woe to you,* he says, *scribes and Pharisees, play-actors* (Matthew 23.8). Here is the mirror image of that opening praise; what was praised there is wanting here. Jesus finds these leaders proud, specious, blind. They lock people out of the kingdom of heaven. They insist on the details of the Law's observance but neglect what matters more: judgment and mercy and faith. They purify the outside of a cup or plate but leave its inside impure, full of extortion and greed. As their forebears killed the prophets of old, so they persecute the prophets sent among them in their own day. We will hear, in this attack, the last stage of Jesus' teaching; he is drawing near to death. The tone of Matthew's gospel will darken; offer and promise will give way to warnings; the community's life will be threatened from within and without. "Blessings" will give way to "Woes."

In that opening sermon, Matthew's blessings continue. We might wonder when we have ever met with all these qualities combined in a single person. Matthew himself, over the course of his gospel, opens his readers' eyes to their presence in one person, and one alone. His Jesus will say at a climax midway through the gospel,

"Come to me, all you who are weary and burdened down,
and I will give you rest.
Take my yoke and learn from me,
for I am meek and humble in heart,
and you will find rest for yourselves."

(MATTHEW 11.28–29)

Threaded through the gospel are further hints of the character Matthew believes Jesus to be. Nothing elaborate, nothing spelled out, just clues. Only Matthew records Jesus' citation from the prophet Hosea, *What I require, says God, is mercy and not sacrifice* (Hosea 6.6). His Jesus uses it twice (Matthew 9.13, 12.7); here is a motto that matters to him, and a principle that must matter to those who would be his pupils. Jesus continues in his opening sermon,

"Blessed are the merciful, for they will receive mercy.
Blessed are the pure in heart, for they will see God.
Blessed are the peacemakers, for they will be called children of God.
Blessed are those who are persecuted for the sake of justice,
for theirs is the kingdom of heaven."

(MATTHEW 5.7–10)

Not that Matthew's Jesus is a bland or easygoing figure. As we have already heard, *"I have not come to cast peace, but a sword."* Within Matthew's figure of Jesus, which his followers have so often found so gentle, lies a stern figure. Those around Jesus and Matthew must make hard and divisive decisions. Matthew does not lull his readers into soft sentiment. This Jesus stirs enmity; his opponents will secure his death. And it will be death unrelieved by any obvious hope; he dies, as Mark's Jesus had before, with apparent despair in his closing words.

For the ninth and last blessing, Jesus changes his focus: He now speaks to his audience directly. Here at last Jesus praises allegiance to himself. Matthew knows only too well what such loyalty can lead to. His church in Antioch, reviled and slandered, needs all the encouragement he can give. His Jesus puts such suffering into a striking context: to suffer calumny for Jesus is to follow in the footsteps of the prophets. For prophets did not just predict the future; they revealed what was really offered and demanded by God, if his plan for Israel was to be fulfilled:

"Blessed are you when people revile you and persecute you
and utter all kinds of evil against you falsely on my account.
Rejoice and be glad, for your reward is great in heaven,
for in the same way they persecuted the prophets who were before you."
(MATTHEW 5.11–12)

Now that his attention is on the pupils themselves, Jesus carries on with warning and encouragement together. The pupils' blessings bring duties with them:

"You are the salt of the earth. But if salt has lost its taste, how will it be seasoned?
It is now good for nothing except to be thrown out and disdained.

You are the light of the world. So let your light shine before men,
that they might see your good works and give glory to your father who is in heaven."
(MATTHEW 5.13–16)

Jesus has laid out the basis of all that follows. We have before us the fundamental outlook that will bring or keep a reader inside the group of Jesus' pupils. Here is Matthew's invitation to his gospel. It is designed in itself to bring closer what it speaks of, the kingdom.

This is as dramatic a fanfare as any of our witnesses gives to Jesus' teaching. But our other writers also know the value of a gripping start. When we read Luke's testimony, we will encounter another set-piece launch to Jesus' public role. Here are the same themes and background, differently handled. Luke describes a powerful moment. Jesus is in the synagogue in Nazareth, his hometown. He stands up to read, is given the scroll of the prophet Isaiah, and finds the right passage. Here is the version that Luke uses:

"The Breath of the Lord is upon me,
because the Lord has anointed me
to preach good news to the poor."

(LUKE 4.18, ISAIAH 61.1)

Luke's Jesus reads just the verses he needs. He then draws out the point: *"Today,"* he said, *"this text has been fulfilled in your own hearing"* (Luke 4.21). Matthew knows Isaiah's promise, too, and in this first teaching of Jesus he echoes line after line of Isaiah's prophecy. His blessings imply what Luke's narrative expounds: The Old Order's most famous promise is being fulfilled—in the presence of Jesus, here and now. Isaiah had written,

> *The Breath of the Lord is upon me,*
> *because the Lord has anointed me.*
> *He has sent me to preach good news to the poor,*
> *to heal the brokenhearted,*
> *to comfort all that mourn,*
> *to give, to all those that mourn in Jerusalem,*
> *beauty for ashes,*
> *the oil of joy for mourning.*
> *And they will called the trees of justice,*
> *planted by the Lord for glory.*
>
> *"For I the Lord love justice,*
> *and I will make an everlasting order with them;*
> *all that see them shall acknowledge,*
> *they are the nation that the Lord has blessed."*
>
> (ISAIAH 61.1–3, 8–9)

Matthew's introduction is complete. He has set up the expectation he needs: of blessings upon those loyal to Jesus' program and of persecution, too; and, of a kingdom in which old means of power will be overturned but whose approach is still hard to see. So distant can that kingdom seem, so fantastical the promises that speak of it, that Matthew's readers asked then and ask now: Who was the Jesus who had the right to speak like this?

A New Moses?

Matthew presents a series of answers. Jesus, he is clear, is not defined by any one precedent, description, or title; neither is he summarized in a collage of old figures, roles, and expectations. There were a good many roles for God's expected agents to fulfill and a range of titles to describe them. Jesus, insists Matthew, was more than any one of them or all of them together. This is no thoughtless promotion of his hero. On the contrary; at every move Matthew claims for Jesus a relation, specific and unique, to his people, the Jews, and to the Jewish Law. One theme underlies all others and provides the figured base upon which all other harmonies are woven: Jesus' similarity to Moses.

GIVING THE LAW

Seeing the crowds Jesus went up onto the mountain (Matthew 5.1). Jesus is not the first teacher whose law was issued on a mountain: *And the Lord came down upon Mount Sinai,* we are told in the book of the Escape (Exodus), *onto the mountain. And the Lord called Moses up to the top of the mountain; and Moses went up* (Escape [Exodus] 19.20). Moses, in some traditions, sat down to receive parts of his Law, as Jesus did to deliver his. Here in a dramatic start to his instruction, God laid down the Ten Commandments. This was the launch to the Old Order's long and elaborate laws:

> *And God spoke all these words:*
> *I am the Lord your God, I have brought you out of the land of Egypt, out of the house of slavery; you shall have no other gods besides me.*
> *You shall not make any images of anything in heaven, or on earth, or in the sea; you shall not bow down before them or worship them.*
> *You shall not take the name of your God in vain. . . .*
> *(ESCAPE [EXODUS] 20.2–7)*

Here began the teaching revealed to Moses and relayed by him to the people. It was said, however, that he wrote the Old Order's whole first section: from the very first words of the Bible to the story of his own death in the Second Law (Deuteronomy). We will hear more of the first book, the Beginning (Genesis), when we read John. The Escape (Exodus), the second, has already been important for the story of Passover and will be again. From the Laws of Ritual (Leviticus) and the Census (Numbers), we learn in ever greater detail of the Law. And in the Second Law we are given a variant account, from Moses' own mouth, of Israel's liberation from Egypt; of God's commands; of the years in the desert and the distant sight given Moses, just before his death; and of the Promised Land that he would never enter.

These are the five books of Moses; their narrative and commandments together form the basis of all that is to follow in Israel's history. Moses bequeathed to Israel these five books, the foundation of the Law, just as Jesus is portrayed by Matthew in five sections of action and instruction.

Moses and Jesus: Their roles are not the same but are closely linked. Moses received the Law on Mount Sinai. The Jews were not allowed to *come up onto the mountain* (Escape [Exodus] 19.12), for fear they might break through the limits set for the people, gaze on God and die. Only Aaron, Moses' colleague and spokesman, could go with him. Jesus *comes up onto the mountain* and from there issues his "law" to the pupils and crowds that have followed him. Jesus, then, has the role of a new Moses: He is the lawgiver. He also fills the role of the people, but with an important difference: He draws nearer to God than any people could have dared before. His pupils gather close to him, as Aaron had to Moses. And the crowds themselves? Taking up the role of the ancient Jews, they receive the new "law," and yet, by their presence on the mountain, far closer than the Jews had been at Sinai, they play the role of Aaron or of Moses himself. For Moses on Sinai received the Law from God and issued it on his return from the mountain. On Matthew's mountain it is the pupils and crowds that receive the "law": They have come there to receive the commandments—from Jesus.

Who, then, must this new lawgiver be? Here is a strange, enigmatic figure. He clearly recalls Moses, and yet he seems to fill the role of Israel, too, and in the most awesome of connections, the role of God himself. Jesus, Moses, the people of Israel, and God: There is more to their connections than meets the eye. They are nowhere so closely interwoven as in the first and most famous chapters of Matthew, the story of Jesus' birth.

THE BIRTH OF JESUS

The birth of Jesus the Anointed was like this (Matthew 1.18). Dreams and angels, prophecies and portents, and Wise Men—astrologers, highly educated, highly skilled—following a star from the exotic east: no wonder the story is as familiar as any from the New Order. Matthew, as we have already seen, keeps a steady eye on Moses. Matthew's contemporaries knew elaborate stories of their ancient heroes' birth. One of the fullest accounts is in Josephus. Matthew's first chapters will blossom before our eyes when we pair them with Josephus's story of Moses. We have no reason to believe that Matthew knew Josephus's version. It is far more revealing that they shared a fund of traditions on which both could draw—and that Matthew could expect his readers to recognize his portrait of Jesus.

Here is the world of stories in which Matthew and his readers lived. His gospel is a text of its time; the content, style, and significance of such stories were all familiar to his readers. He uses this shared knowledge, in his few lines of narrative, to establish a claim that he never even needs to state: that in Jesus a new Moses was born. Upon this foundation he can build further, more striking claims; it will be several pages before we have done justice to this rich and subtle story. If we want evidence of Matthew's grand, architectural achievement, we need only watch the themes of these opening pages unfold in the narrative that follows them. To understand the first chapters of Matthew is to understand the whole. Everything springs from the gospel's beginning, and everything comes full circle, in a perfect symmetry, at its end.

Josephus told of the Jews' slavery in Egypt. "One of the sacred scribes of Egypt," he wrote, "announced to the Pharaoh that one was due to be born to the Jews who would bring down the rule of the Egyptians and raise up the Jews; if he came of age he would surpass everyone in merit and be famous forever."

And Matthew? He tells of Herod and the astrologers. As we soon see, Matthew's Jesus stands squarely in the tradition of Moses and inherits his standing from the start.

When Jesus had been born in Bethlehem [writes Matthew], *in the days of King Herod, astrologers came from the east to Jerusalem. "Where is the boy," they asked, "born King of the Jews? For we have seen his star in the east and have come to do him homage." When King Herod heard this he was deeply disturbed and so was all Jerusalem with him. He summoned all the high priests and scribes of the people and asked them, "Where is the Anointed to be born?"*

"In Bethlehem of Judah," they replied. "For this is how it was written through the prophet,

And you, Bethlehem, in the land of Judah,
are by no means the least among the leaders of Judah;
For from you shall come out a leader
who will shepherd my people Israel."

Then Herod summoned the astrologers secretly. He sent them on to Bethlehem and said, "Head on, inquire about the child in every detail. And when you have found him, tell me, so that I might come and do him homage, too."

(MATTHEW 2.1–8)

Herod was not the first king to be afraid for his kingdom. Frightened by that warning from the sacred scribe, according to Josephus, "the Pharaoh ordered that every son born to the Israelites should be thrown in the river and killed. Any midwife found disobeying the order would be killed and the child with her." From one massacre to another. Herod's strange visitors head off to Bethlehem, find the child, and then return home without betraying his whereabouts to the king.

Then Herod [Matthew tells us], *seeing that he had been tricked by the astrologers, was furious: he sent orders and had all the boys killed in Bethlehem and in its region, of two years old and younger. Then was fulfilled the saying of Jeremiah the prophet:*

A voice in Ramah was heard,
a weeping and much crying:
Rachel weeping for her children;
and she would not be comforted,
because they were no more.

(MATTHEW 2.16–18)

Matthew's narrative from the start puts Jesus front and center; we have already heard of his conception. The story in Josephus started more broadly with that general threat to Jewish children; it now hones in on Moses and his father. "Amram, a well-born Israelite," said Josephus, "fearing that his whole nation would be extinguished, and anxious for himself, for his wife was pregnant, was at a loss what to do; he prayed for God's help on his people." We hear in other stories that the Jews in Egypt gave up all marital relations—anything to prevent the birth of children that Pharaoh would murder.

Mary, the mother of Jesus [Matthew has told us], *was engaged to Joseph, and was found to be pregnant before they slept together. Joseph planned to release her discreetly from the engagement. But as he was considering this, an angel of God appeared to him in a dream.*

(MATTHEW 1.18–20)

The Jews' restraint, of course, could have prevented the birth of just the one child that they needed: Moses himself. There is in one version of this story a clue that God himself ensured Moses' birth by a miraculous conception. Moses and Jesus may have even more in common than at first appears.

In Josephus's story Amram's wife was already pregnant. Might this be the child whose birth Pharaoh was resisting, with such terrible results for Amram's people?

God took pity on Amram and appeared to him in his sleep and urged him not to despair of the future. "This child, whose birth has filled the Egyptians with such fear that they have condemned the Jews' children to death, will indeed be yours; he shall escape those looking out to destroy him and shall free the Jews from their slavery in Egypt. He will be remembered for as long as time endures, not only by the Jews but by the other nations, too."

As God spoke to Amram, so as well, centuries later, he would have a message for Joseph. The angel said to him,

"Joseph, son of David, do not be afraid to take Mary as your wife. For what is conceived in her is from the Breath of God. And she will bear a son, and you shall call him Jesus; for he shall save his people from their wrongdoing."

(MATTHEW 1.20–21)

The child Jesus is safely born. But he must be rescued from Herod's soldiers; he escapes to Egypt. Here is an ancient motif in reverse: Moses, as a young man, killed an Egyptian and had to flee from Egypt. Each, in good time, would return: Moses to Egypt, Jesus to Israel.

The adult Moses, separated from his nation but safe in a foreign land and by now with a local wife and children, is ordered by God to return to Egypt to lead the Jews to freedom. It is safe for him to go back: *for all those are dead,* Moses is told, *who sought your life* (Escape [Exodus] 5.19). Moses sets out. The liberation from Egypt is about to begin. This young exile will emerge from the shadows and become the great prophet and lawgiver of Israel. When he next travels north it will be with the whole people of Israel behind him, on their long trek to the Promised Land. God would remind his people, in words recorded by the prophet Hosea, of that journey in centuries to come. God is speaking of the whole nation of Israel when he says, *"Out of Egypt have I called my son"* (Hosea 11.1).

Joseph eventually has another dream. An angel tells him to go back home, *"for those are dead who sought the child's life"* (Matthew 2.20).

Hosea's words, as Matthew believes, are now fulfilled again: *"Out of Egypt have I called my son"* (Matthew 2.15). Matthew is clear: They have unfolded into their true and final fulfillment only now, in the return home of this single child.

A mysterious star shines; foreigners come to do obeisance to the king of the Jews; the Jewish authorities and Rome's appointee conspire to have him killed; Rachel, buried near Bethlehem, is remembered weeping for her children. It is a strange start. But everything has its place. At the end of the gospel the authorities will at last succeed: They have Jesus killed by the Roman prefect. The claim is recorded on his cross, *This is Jesus, the king of the Jews;* there is darkness over the earth; the foreign officer and his attendants acknowledge Jesus as son of God; and at a distance, watching the death, are three women. One Joseph at the gospel's start, who says not a word in the story, takes on a father's role toward this child born from a virgin's womb. Another Joseph, just as silent, appears just once, at the story's end: He provides a new tomb for Jesus and buries him.

FULFILLING THE LAW? MORE THAN MOSES

Moses brought the Law to the Jews. What will this new Moses bring? *"Do not think,"* says Jesus, *"that I have come to undo the Law or the prophets; I have not come to undo but to fulfill"* (Matthew 5.17). And then come six paragraphs contrasting, one by one, six of the Old Order's laws with the instruction of Jesus. Here are the two last paragraphs, the most famous of all. We have met them already earlier in this chapter. Matthew uses these paragraphs to close off the series with a startling flourish:

> *"You have heard that it was said: 'An eye for an eye' and 'A tooth for a tooth.' Well I, I say to you: Do not oppose the evil one. But whoever hits you on the right cheek, turn the left cheek to him, too. And if anyone wants to sue you and to take your shirt, give him your coat too. And whoever makes you walk one mile, go with him for two. To those who ask of you, give; and those who want to borrow off you—do not turn them away.*
>
> *"You have heard that it was said: 'You will love your neighbor' and will hate your enemy. Well I, I say to you: Love your enemies and pray for those who persecute you, so that you might be the children of your father in heaven. For he has the sun rise on the wicked and on the good, and he has the rain fall on the just and on the unjust. If you love those who love you, what reward do you have? Do not even those who make a profit from collecting taxes do the same? So you must be perfect, just as your heavenly father is perfect."*
>
> (MATTHEW 5.38–48)

These six sayings can seem to run directly counter to the Law. Some versions may even have been spread by those who believed Jesus' teaching to undo the Law and who welcomed the revolution. It could well be Matthew who cast the sayings into such a crisp, resolute form. Jesus would have had good reason, of course, to issue such important instructions at different times in different ways; he may have made these declarations programmatically at one time, less formally at others. But it is striking that of these six commands, three are recorded in substance by Luke in less formal settings and style. If Matthew has collected and refined them into their present form, it is because he has a clear purpose in mind: He uses these sayings as examples of Jesus' opening claim, *"I have not come to undo but to fulfill."* If they had been misused by others to flout the Law, all the more reason to deploy them; here, properly understood, was what Jesus had meant by his claim to fulfill it.

It is a remarkable series. Jesus addresses three of the Ten Commandments, those on murder, theft, and divorce. He moves on to three laws laid down later in the books of Moses: on oaths, vengeance, and the hatred of enemies. Jesus identifies the trajectory on which each law lies and drives the law further along it. To fulfill his "new" demands is way beyond the reach of most of us and beyond even our ideals. At issue is not just behavior—our actions and words. Jesus is targeting the attitudes that underlie our behavior, and his teachings call for attitudes so extreme that we might wonder if they address the real world at all:

"You have heard that it was said to those of old: 'You shall not kill'; and whoever kills will be liable to judgment. Well I, I say to you: All who are angry with their brother or sister are liable to judgment; and all who insult their brother or sister will be liable to the courts; and all who say 'You fool' will be liable to the hell of fire."
(MATTHEW 5.21–22)

Jesus' first blessings spoke of the world turned upside down. Here is legislation to match. And only those embraced by the first have any hope, it seems, of obeying the second. Is Matthew's Jesus, then, changing the Law, filling it out, or revealing its true basis?

Of one thing we can be sure: Readers recognized the paragraphs' opening formulas as a device to avoid direct mention of God. The same instinct has led Matthew to call God's kingdom *the kingdom of heaven.* When Jesus starts off, *"You have heard that it was said . . . ,"* he is in effect saying, *"You have heard that God said to those of old . . . "* To contradict God would be unthinkable; Jesus could not be changing laws that he knew were laid down by God. And he is not. Anyone who fulfilled these commandments of Jesus would be fulfilling the Law's commands.

Perhaps, then, he is expounding God's Law, speaking as a teacher to pupils who have not yet understood what the Law has really meant and demanded all along. Such pupils have fulfilled the Law as it stands, yes, and must do so still. But that does not yet meet the requirements that the Law intended. Now if *this* is the status of Jesus' words, he has chosen a most misleading way to express it. Jesus launches each command, *"Well I, I say to you . . . "* He speaks on his own authority. He refers to no higher power. The power Jesus claims when he extends these laws is as great as God's power when he laid them down. God's authority then and Jesus' now: They are on a par.

Here is no mouthpiece such as Moses was, relaying the Law of a greater power; here is no lawyer such as Jesus' and Matthew's time knew well, interpreting that Law for its day-to-day observance. Here is one greater than Moses and far greater than the lawyers. Who—or what—can this Jesus possibly be? One clue lies in the words with which the Wise Men reached Jerusalem: *"Where is the boy,"* they asked, *"born king of the Jews?"* (Matthew 2.2). It is time to see what this title might reveal.

"Where Is the Boy
Born King of the Jews?"

ANOINTED TO REIGN

The prophet Isaiah wrote,

Arise, Jerusalem, for your light has come,
the glory of God has risen upon you.
The nations shall come to your light
and kings to the brightness of your dawning;
the wealth of the nations is coming to you, convoys from the East,
bringing gold and incense and singing the praise of the Lord.
(ISAIAH 60.1, 3, 5–6)

A conjunction of stars or planets, a comet, or a strange sight in the sky: These could easily portend a great event, a crisis, or a special birth. "A comet blazed into view," records Tacitus of Nero's reign. "About a comet the crowd's view is: it bodes a change of regime. So people asked who would succeed Nero, as if Nero were already dethroned." Memory of such a "portent" may well underlie Matthew's story: Halley's Comet crossed the sky in 11 B.C.E., and four years later the planets of Jupiter and Saturn, "stars" symbolic of empire and of Israel, shone three times in bright conjunction.

But as important for Matthew as the night sky itself were the Old Order's prophecies of the Jews' coming king. Famous among them was a prediction in the Census (Numbers). The prophet Balaam was hired by King Balak, an enemy of the Jews, to pronounce God's curse on them. The plan went badly awry: Time and again Balaam spoke of Israel's glorious future in terms of a king's scepter and a star. Century after century the passage echoed through Israel's hopes. When the passage was translated into Greek, three centuries before Matthew wrote, its meaning was made more direct: The "scepter" it spoke of became a single "man," a king. At Qumran the passage was taken to refer to the Anointed, the Messiah. And at the next and last revolt against the Romans, in 135 C.E., the rebels' leader was heralded as the Anointed and changed his name to show that the prophecy had been fulfilled at last: He had been simply Bar Kosiba, "Son of Kosiba"; from now on he would be known as Bar Kochba, "Son of the Star." No wonder Balaam's prediction has fired Matthew as well. Here are lines from that Greek version:

> The Lord the God of Israel is with the Jews,
> he has brought them out of Egypt;
> they shall eat up the nations of their enemies.
> Thus says Balaam, the man who sees truly,
> and knows knowledge from the Most High:
> "I give my blessing, but it is not yet near:
> A star shall rise from the Jews,
> and out of Israel shall a man—that 'scepter' of the ancient text—arise."
> (CENSUS [NUMBERS] 23.7, 24.8, 24.17)

The star was once a metaphor for the king and his splendor; it has become for our gospel a portent in the sky. Gentiles come from far afield to do obeisance to this strange new king. The king's own subjects do not join them. Far from it. King Herod in Jerusalem is frightened for his throne; he plans not homage but murder. *All Jerusalem was thrown into turmoil with him:* There is no hint that his Jewish advisers seek to protect the child (Matthew 2.3). They know the further prophecy of the place of the new king's birth, and they reveal it. Gentiles acknowledge Jesus at the story's start, and a gentile at its end. It is the Roman officer in charge of Jesus' execution whose words round off the story of his death: *"This man, he really was son of God"* (Matthew 27.54).

Jesus' future status is far more openly proclaimed in Matthew's narrative than in Mark's. This Son of Man will have angels of his own, will sit—as God should do—in judgment, and will delegate his kingly power to his pupils. Within the story, however, Jesus does not play the king. Before his public work even starts he is offered all the kingdoms of the world—by the devil. *"I will give you all these,"* said the tempter, *"if you bow down to me and worship me"* (Matthew 4.9). But these are not the terms on which Jesus will be king. He turns the offer down. Before he assumes his reign he must die. Rescue is at hand, if he only calls upon it: *"Do you not realize,"* he asks at his arrest, *"that I can call upon my father and he will give me then and there more than twelve legions of angels?"* (Matthew 26.54). Here is an army far more frightening than any legate's forces sweeping south, swords drawn, from Antioch to Jerusalem. But no. The only rule that Jesus accepts is the rule planned for him by God, in God's own time.

Jesus had gone up the mountain at the very start to unveil God's blessings and commands to his pupils and the crowds. And on the mountain, in the gospel's closing words, Jesus' inner circle of pupils will be given their last disclosure of God's plan. In

Jesus' final words we will discover the authority with which those commandments are invested from now on. Matthew's strategy is complete: All the words spoken by Jesus while on earth can at last be heard and understood for what they will always be. The voice of the earthly Jesus has become the voice of the risen Lord; they are one and the same.

> *The eleven pupils went to Galilee to the mountain at which Jesus had told them to be. And when they saw him they fell prostrate before him, but some hesitated. And Jesus came up to them and spoke to them saying, "All authority has been given to me in heaven and on earth. Go out, therefore, and make pupils of all the gentiles, baptizing them in the name of the father and of the son and of the Breath of God, teaching them to keep all the commandments that I have commanded you. And look, I am with you always, every day, until the aeon's completed end."*
> (MATTHEW 28.16–20)

A king at the last, but within the story this Jesus refuses authority, is denied by his people, and lets himself be killed by the powers that be. We still do not know, as we read the story, what right he had, in those opening words, to speak with an authority equal to God's. Jesus is from the start much more than Moses, but while on earth he makes himself far less than a king. We do not yet have the measure of this man. Jesus himself warns,

> *"The men of Ninevah will rise up at the judgment with the present generation and will condemn it, because they changed their hearts and their ways at the preaching there of* [the prophet] *Jonah—and look, there is something more than Jonah here.*
> *"The Queen of Sheba will rise up at the judgment with the present generation and will condemn it, because she came from the ends of the earth to hear the wisdom of Solomon—and look, there is something more than Solomon here"* (Matthew 12.41–42).

A New Israel?

"HEAR, O ISRAEL"

This Jesus is no ordinary king. A king needs a kingdom. Who, for Matthew, are Jesus' subjects? God had claimed dominion over Israel forever; the Jews accepted his kingship still. How will this new king relate to the old? Or those who acknowledge his reign relate to those who trust God's ancient regime and its ancient ways? We have already dug for clues to Jesus in the story of his birth. Just one remains that we have not yet assessed. A detail catches our eye because it is apparently out of place.

Jesus' return from Egypt, Matthew tells us, fulfilled Hosea's words: *"Out of Egypt have I called my son."* But the words did not need "fulfilling"; they were not a prediction at all. And more: Hosea was speaking of Israel, the nation; Matthew finds this "son" in a single child. His Jesus plays the role of a greater Moses, of a future king, and now, it seems, of Israel itself. More and more of what Jesus undergoes has been undergone before, it turns out, by the whole nation of the Jews.

We might wonder, as we hear ever richer echoes sound through Matthew's evidence, if we can ever be sure which is the single dominant chord. Even one incident can ring with the resonance of half a dozen precedents and contrasts in the Old Order's story. We can, of course, attune our ears to one such theme and deafen ourselves to the others. But that is a mistake. In this wealth of connections we are enjoying the fruit of two generations' thought and work. Jewish thinkers of Matthew's and of later generations were pleased to relish more than one significance in any single passage from the Old Order. So Matthew, too, let the accumulated insights of the church, from Jesus' earliest pupils' to his own, form a dense, rich harmony. Nothing about Jesus offered more meanings and possibilities than the title with which the voice of God himself invested him: the son of God.

Jesus had been baptized by the Baptizer. As he came out of the river Jordan *the heavens opened, and he saw the Breath of God descend in the form of a dove and rest on him, and there was a voice from heaven: "This is my beloved son; in him I take delight"* (Matthew 3.16).

As in Mark's story, so here. Jesus heads straight into the desert, where he spends forty days and where the Jews under Moses had spent forty years. *"All that I command you this day,"* said Moses to the people as they drew near at last to the Promised Land,

> *"you shall observe, that you may live, and multiply, and possess the land which the Lord swore to your forbears. And you shall remember all the way which the Lord your God led you these forty years in the desert, to humble you and to test you, to know what was in your heart, whether you would keep his commandments or not. God humbled you, and let you hunger, and fed you with manna; that he might make you know that man does not live by bread alone, but by every word that comes from the mouth of God."*
> *(SECOND LAW [DEUTERONOMY] 8.1–3)*

Matthew continues the story straight after the baptism of Jesus: *Then out Jesus goes into the desert to be tested by the devil. He fasted for forty days and forty nights* (Matthew 4.1–2).

Fasting was an appropriate and familiar preparation for moments of privileged disclosure. Seers must separate themselves from the cares and appetites of the world. To fast over a long period also has a dramatic effect on our mind's working; we become more susceptible to strange appearances and voices. In one story from Matthew's time, recorded in the so-called Unveiling (Revelation) of Abraham, an angel led Abraham to the mountain, where a series of extraordinary visions and insights began: "And we went, the angel and I alone together, forty days and nights. And I ate no bread and drank no water, because my food was to see the angel who was with me, and his talk with me was my drink." The devil in Matthew's story parodies just such a moment. Abraham, a privileged seer, would be taken on a heavenly journey to see and absorb the hidden truths of God; Jesus is whisked from place to place on earth and is tempted in each case to abandon God's plan.

For forty days and forty nights. Jesus has headed out of Israel. He has crossed the Jordan, threshold of the Promised Land where the Baptizer spoke of the "kingdom of heaven." He has moved into a far greater and more frightening place of transition: the desert. In the most famous of all journeys, Moses led the Jews through the desert for forty years. To let them out of Egypt the Red Sea's waters parted before them; to let them into Israel the Jordan parted in turn. A whole generation died in the desert; none of those corrupted by Egypt were to corrupt the Promised Land. The nation was purged in this wild, alien waste that lay between its old life and its new. It was a fearsome time. Any power at work in the desert was God's power or the devil's; it was a place that would never yield to human device or understanding.

PROPHET . . .

The devil calls upon Jesus to act as *Son of God.* That, after all, is the status given him by God, and here is a call to exercise its privilege and power. *Son of God* is a title grand but vague. It needs to be made specific, to be filled with content. The devil offers Jesus three roles in turn. For the first? Jesus could become the prophet, foretold by Moses as his own successor.

The people ran out of food and complained against Moses: *"We should have died by the hand of God in the land of Egypt, when we ate bread to the full—for you have brought us into this wilderness, to starve this whole assembly to death"* (Escape [Exodus] 16.3). God provided manna for the Jews to eat, a bread rained from heaven day by day.

The hunger that the Jews had known, Jesus now knows for himself, and as the Jews were tempted to despair and needed God's help, so the devil invites Jesus to fill God's role: to create food for himself as God had created it for the Jews of old: *Then the tempter said to Jesus, "If you are the son of God, turn these stones into bread"* (Matthew 4.3).

As Moses had fed the Jews in the desert, so let the new prophet discover his power to make food. What he can do for himself he can do for the nation; at last the banquet of God's kingdom will arrive. In a parched land, to dream of God's plan for creation is to dream of a garden, of Paradise fertile and lush; in a poor land, to dream of God's final reign is dream of a feast, of enough at last for all to eat their fill. *"Turn these stones,"* said the devil, *"into bread."* But just as Moses had said to the people, when he recalled their hunger and God's reasons for imposing it, so in the very same words Jesus replies, *"Man does not live by bread alone, but by every word that comes from the mouth of God"* (Matthew 4.4, Second Law [Deuteronomy] 8.3).

. . . PRIEST . . .

What then of the second test?

The devil took Jesus to the topmost pinnacle of the Jerusalem temple. "If you are the Son of God," he said, "jump, go on . . . " (Matthew 4.5–6).

We are at the Temple now. *This is Jerusalem, says the Lord: I have set her in the middle of the nations and of the countries that are around her* (Ezekiel 5.5). Jerusalem is the central point of the world. The great maps of Europe's Middle Ages, drawn fifteen hundred years after Jesus died, still have Jerusalem at their center. The towns in which the maps were made, the great capitals of the medieval world, all take second place to the navel of creation. And the Temple itself? Jesus is at the central point of the central point of the whole world.

We are as well at the center of priesthood. If Jesus claims any authority over Jewish ways and practices, now is the time and place to assert it. The devil offers Jesus the second of his roles. He calls on Jesus to jump, to make a move that will demand a response from God. We have heard already of enthusiasts who urged the Jews into dramatic rebellion from Rome. To expect the Jordan to be parted, the walls of Jerusalem to fall: Such enthusiasts may have had many reasons for believing God would intervene, here and now, on their behalf. But if all other hope failed, one strong sense could bear them up: Surely God would not abandon those who had committed themselves so wholly and bravely to his cause. If they had obeyed (what they believed to be) God's summons to war, then he would not stand idly by. Such movements flared in hope; the Roman army closed in; the odds were overwhelming. It was for God to bring his people the triumph he had encouraged them (as they believed) to look for.

To challenge God to act: Could such a move have been devised within Jesus' own closest circle of friends? For those who looked and longed for Israel's freedom, Jesus will enter Jerusalem in triumph, but then he makes no general's moves, and God makes no obvious moves at all. Judas Iscariot will hand over his friend and master to the enemy; God's own Anointed will be in immediate danger of death. Does Judas exactly betray his master? Or does he make a revolutionary's last, despairing attempt to force God's hand?

Surely, says the devil, Jesus can trust the promise that the psalmist recorded and the devil now quotes:

"God will put you in his angels' charge;
they will bear you up in their hands
in case you hurt your foot against a stone."

(MATTHEW 4.6, PSALM 91.11–12)

But to trust in God's defense was one thing; to create a crisis that called for it was quite another. In the desert, the Jews had first run out of food. Then they ran out of water. Again they turned on Moses. They did not trust Moses to find a source; they were ready to stone him; their threats had required God to intervene. This time God showed Moses a rock from which to strike water. The crisis was resolved. Moses named its site the "Place of Testing" (Escape [Exodus] 17.7). Moses later reminded them of the crisis in the very words that Jesus now invokes: *"But Moses said, 'You shall not put the Lord your God to the test,'"* as the Jews had put him to the test at the Place of Testing (Matthew 4.7, Second Law [Deuteronomy] 6.16). Again Jesus recalls the history of Israel to prevent its repetition. Mistakes once made will not be made again. Jesus is once more the individual, tempted to fulfill his role as son of God in ways unauthorized by the God from whom he had received it; he is also a new Israel, overcoming by and in himself the temptations that had misled the old.

Here in the desert, tested and purged, a new nation is coming to birth, born from the old, steeped in its ways, but defined by the new obedience of its "Moses" who speaks and acts for the nation as a whole. Everything is converging on this Jesus. When this Son of God recrosses the Jordan into the Promised Land, he comes as leader and nation together; those he gathers around him fill out the "kingdom" that he already has and is. *"Out of Egypt have I called my son,"* and this time the son is Jesus, at once leader of his nation and that nation itself.

Jesus as a single figure and as the new nation itself: How is such a combination possible? The prophet Hosea, as we know, was not predicting the future in that passage at all; he was recalling a great event of the past. But Matthew sees more in that event than an item, closed and docketed, in Israel's ancient chronicles. The escape from Egypt still shaped the life of the Jews; here was the defining story of the nation and its safety under God. What, then, was for Matthew the defining story of Jesus and his followers? The life and death of Jesus himself. But these followers were heirs to Israel's promises; they formed a new Israel. What defined the old must define the new. To be the new Israel the church must descend from the old—in ancestry, in history, in heroes. Everything that defined Israel must be mirrored in the church.

And everything must be exceeded. There is polemic in Matthew's narrative: Where the old Israel failed, the new Israel in the founder's person has triumphantly succeeded. Matthew would persuade his readers that the old Israel is now no place for them, for Jesus' new Israel believes God where the old Israel had distrusted him, and relies on God where the old had tested him. Matthew sets a deep gulf between the two: Moses' people on one hand, and on the other hand Jesus himself; the new Israel succeeds where the old had failed. But is the contrast artificial? Matthew's Jesus was not Matthew's church. Once we look with an unsentimental eye at Matthew's church, we will find that the two communities, of Moses and of Matthew, were not so different as Matthew has them sound. Matthew's, we soon learn, had problems enough of its own; members lost heart, energy sagged, leaders abused their power.

Matthew is neither condemning the old nation nor flattering the new. The New Order's sense of God's kingdom defied its authors' categories as oddly as it does our own. We can speak in terms of place: a kingdom on the threshold, at hand, just out of sight. Or in terms of time: a king already crowned but not yet known by all the subjects under his control. Or in terms of that king himself: here within Jesus' life on earth is God's regent, disguised, vulnerable, and owed allegiance by all he meets. Or finally in terms of those subjects: their part in a dominion greater and more final than they are themselves. Mark had worked with Daniel's son of man, a single figure who lived out the life of God's heroes in their suffering and their triumph. Matthew invokes the nation of Israel, its history, Law, and hopes. His own church, then, must resolve directly its relation to the synagogue. Here is the deepest question facing his church, and Matthew's answer gives that church its deepest self-description.

Matthew has Jesus fulfill the roles of his church not because its members are more loyal, strong, or obedient than the people of Israel, but because the Jesus who is the new Israel has overcome the temptations to which his people day by day will be exposed. Matthew invites his readers into the new Israel established by an obedience and faith that they cannot hope to match. The rule of the kingdom is here and now and obeyed and established for all to see—in Jesus. It is near and not yet and resisted and disguised—in the world around him. Matthew knows full well that his readers inhabit both realms. There is always progress to be made—by the individual and the church. Matthew's eyes are forever on that progress, on his community's birth within and from the synagogues he knew and its gradual, painful growth to independence. Here at last, he insists, is a nation that will *fulfill the law and the prophets.*

. . . AND KING?

One test is still to come. From the top of a mountain, God showed Moses, just before his death, the land that the people would inherit, the land of Israel, which Moses himself would never enter. Here is the devil's final challenge to Jesus: to take up the kingdom that is surely his. Moses had died before entering Israel; is not this greater Moses ready for his power now? When the Jews spoke of the Anointed, they came to claim for him three roles. The prophet we have already seen; he will feed the people in the desert as Moses had. The priest will control the Temple and all its ways. And here is the final offer for this Son of God: to take for himself his own, to become the Anointed that he already is—to become *king. Next, taking Jesus to the top of a mountain, the devil showed him all the kingdoms of the world. "I will give you all these," he said, "if you bow down to me and worship me"* (Matthew 4.9).

Moses had told the people of the conditions that God laid down for them to live in the Promised Land (Second Law [Deuteronomy] 6.4–15). Jesus knew these conditions well. They are the basis of all Jewish life. Every Jew was required to recite them twice a day. They have been recited, prayed, and studied ever since:

> *Hear, O Israel* [they start]: *the Lord our God is one Lord,*
> *and you shall love the Lord your God with your whole heart,*
> *with your whole being, and with your whole strength.*

> *And when the Lord has brought you into the land*
> *which he swore to your fathers that he would give you,*
> *then do not forget the Lord,*
> *who brought you out of the land of Egypt, from the house of slavery.*
> *You shall not go after other gods. . . .*

The Place of Testing is soon back in Moses' mind: The Jews, he says, are never to distrust God again as they did when they demanded water of Moses. Jesus himself has already refused to distrust or test God. Now it is enough for him to quote Moses' most trenchant clause: *Jesus replied: "Off with you, Satan! For Moses said, '. . . You will worship the Lord your God, and serve him alone' "* (Matthew 4.10).

Matthew's Jesus was born king of the Jews. He was acknowledged by the mysterious Wise Men and hounded by the murderous Herod. But when the devil offers him all the kingdoms of the earth, he refuses them. He was born to be king, but the devil's terms are not the conditions for his coronation.

THE KING AND HIS PEOPLE

This "temptation" is a strange story. It is unlike anything else in the gospels: miraculous transport, a talking devil, and set-piece challenges. The style of the dialogue would have been far more familiar to Matthew's readers. To swap quotations from the Old Order was a favored form of dispute among Jewish scholars. Every line in the Old Order was liable to throw light on every other, and there could be no better way to understand and apply a passage than to bring into the discussion all possible connections from its own and other contexts. And the devil? A story has reached us about Israel's founding father, Abraham, told in very similar vein. It fleshes out one of the Old Order's most unsettling narratives. Abraham is with his son Isaac, on their way to sacrifice. Who is the victim to be? That son himself. God is testing Abraham's obedience: Will he kill his son and heir at God's command?

Abraham was on his way to a frightening mission; so, centuries later, is Jesus. Both encounter Satan. Jesus' devil looks backward to the Jews' escape from Egypt; Abraham's looks forward to Job, an Old Order figure famous for his patience under suffering. The devil, tempting Abraham, cites the consolation offered by the first of Job's friends; Abraham will answer him straight back. Let us hear first the comfort offered to Job.

> *"Look* [says Job's comforter], *you have instructed many,*
> *and have strengthened their weak hands;*
> *but now that trouble is come upon you, you grow faint.*
> *But should not your piety be your confidence?*
> *Whoever perished, being innocent?*
> *Now news was secretly brought to me: . . .*
> *'He who wounds is he who soothes the sore.'"*
>
> (JOB 4.2, 12)

In our story of Abraham, Satan came up to him on the way to the sacrifice and said, "If I try to speak with you, will you mind? *Look, you have instructed many, and have strengthened their weak hands. But now that trouble is come upon you, you grow faint.*"

Abraham answered from the psalms, *"I will walk in my integrity." "But,"* said Satan, *"should not your piety be your confidence?"* Abraham retorted, *"Whoever perished, being innocent?"* Seeing that Abraham would not listen to him, Satan said, *"Now news was secretly brought to me.* This is what I heard: 'The lamb for a burnt offering, but not Isaac for a burnt offering.' " Abraham replied, "It is the punishment of a liar, that even should he tell the truth he is not listened to."

Short sayings quoted out of context are always open to distortion; Abraham draws on the same passage as the devil to do better justice to its tenor as a whole. At one point Abraham moves further afield. He quotes from a psalm ascribed to his own distant descendant, King David; here the speaker pleads his own integrity. Abraham's move is carefully judged, for the psalm was written precisely for use at sacrifice. The devil is playing a subtle game: If he can persuade Abraham that God has no intention of allowing Isaac's death, the testing of Abraham's faith is empty. Satan is targeting God's purpose quite as much as Abraham's. There is more at stake here—the battle is being waged on a larger field—than we would ever look for.

Discussions as between two scholars, one conducted on the road to a mountain sacrifice, the other in the most numinous settings known to Jewish tradition: the desert, the Temple, and the mountain. They seem distant to us, a dream world of citations, tit for tat. Abraham's last comment in the story is telling. He already knows that the devil is speaking the truth: The victim is to be an animal, not Isaac. So is God's test a failure? No, the story is an occasion for teaching, for understanding, for wise reflection; it is not the psychological drama that we would expect it to be. Abraham's testing and Jesus': Each is conducted at a moment of dire need or of great expectation. We look for feelings or motivation, for the whispers of love, doubt, and self-preservation, not for the staging of a professorial dispute.

Behind this intellectual dance, however, lie all the passions that we recognize within ourselves. The devil is so dangerous here precisely because he speaks the language of our deepest care for those we love and for ourselves. If Matthew evokes such passions at this "distance" it is in part to keep us from the style of reading that his readers were as fond of as we are: being interested in a human figure bound by the conditions of context and character. More, for Matthew, is at stake than the story of any such figure could embrace or express. The story must be moved into a different key. Only then can its hero's feelings and motivations be seen for what they are: part of a battle whose armies and outcome affect far more than just one human actor on a wild, empty stage. The devil has an adversary here against whom he has every reason to appear in person. To defeat Jesus is to defeat God's plan for a new Israel, and in the future of this Israel, as we shall see, lies God's plan for the whole of humankind.

Such a story as this is not spun for the sake of fantasy or decoration. Our witnesses needed to say what they believed to be nearly unsayable, and they resorted to all the categories they could. We need not be surprised that so many themes are sounded in this one short passage. Matthew saw around him people as complex as we are. As we define ourselves in various terms in order to do justice to all that we are and hope for, so did they. We live in a world of wide knowledge and limitless communication; we can draw on ever more categories and examples to say about ourselves all that we want to say. Matthew has a narrower range of stories and definitions, but he plumbs them deeper and deeper; he draws up connections that a casual thinker would never sense or see. We can skim ideals, hopes, and self-definitions from cultures of which we know only the surface that we glimpsed at school. Matthew has a concentration, a close focus, that may do more justice to individuals and their culture than a modern method of picking-and-choosing. For our deepest loyalties and dreams are still secured and fed, in a dense tangle of roots, by the long histories from which we, our families, and our communities have grown.

But could Matthew's readers feel themselves involved in such a story? Or were they just the viewers—awed, perhaps, and anxious—of a cosmic drama whose progress had been out of their hands and whose result was now secure? That great reading, the *Hear, O Israel* from the Second Law, attracted long, deep thought among Jewish scholars: *"You shall love the Lord your God with your whole heart, with your whole being, and with your whole strength."* The scholars teased out the implications of each phrase; not a word, after all, would be redundant in such a command. The passage clearly underlies our present scene. These temptations are finally over and the devil's plans defeated when Jesus quotes from this passage in the Second Law (Deuteronomy).

But far more has grown out of the reading than just the narrative's last line. In each of three temptations Jesus is tempted to disobey one part of God's great command. *With your whole heart:* That, said the scholars, means with both your good instincts and your bad. The first tends naturally toward the love of God; the second must be restrained. Jesus is hungry. He could so easily satisfy his appetite. Of course he should love God, but was God, asks the devil, really looking after his everyday needs? Again the scholars asked, Why did the *Hear, O Israel* emphasize loving God *with your whole being?* It means, they said, "even if he take your life." It is not for Jesus to demand that God save him. Here the devil is subtler still: Jesus is right to love God, of course, but on condition, hints the devil—that God save him from danger. *With your whole strength,* ended the great demand; that is, said the scholars, with your whole property. Yes, Jesus should love God, but why was God not giving this son all that he could and should? Let Jesus just take his own way, and all that he needs and wants will be his. The Jews in the desert, long ago, had good reason to complain against God's provision, but they were at least on their way to the Promised Land. Jesus, too, claims the devil, has good reason to complain, for God has done nothing to give him his promised kingdom.

And so, as Matthew knows, his readers also seem to have reason to complain for generations yet to come. Threaded through this story is the story of Jesus' new Israel, of the people that will know the same temptations that he has—and that will, thanks to him, have just as much power to resist them. Where Israel went, Jesus goes. And the triumph that Jesus won is offered to those who will go, as he did, into the desert, which will purge them of the old and prepare them for the new. Let the readers once adopt Jesus' response, and they are ready, as Matthew would have it, to cross the Jordan into Jesus' Promised Land. Jesus says for himself and his followers: *"Off with you, Satan! For it is written, '. . . You will worship the Lord your God, and serve him alone' "* (Matthew 4.10).

This brings the reader much closer to Matthew's Jesus, but has this Jesus moved any closer to the reader? Where so much is at stake, can any simple, down-to-earth humanity be found within those characters' stately dance? We must attune our ears to Matthew's storytelling style; he knows what power his story has to hearten his readers, to upset them, and to thrill.

The gospel reaches its midpoint when Matthew's Simon Peter, like Mark's, declares Jesus to be the Anointed, the son of the living God. Here is none of Mark's reticence. Jesus confirms the claim and in return declares Simon to be Peter, the rock on which he, Jesus will build his church. This is a moment of high triumph. It is then for Jesus to introduce the theme of his own suffering. Simon, as we know, is appalled. Matthew has inherited from Mark the terrible rebuke with which Jesus turns on him. But Mark had not told of that earlier temptation, with the devil's offer of all the world's kingdoms and with Jesus' reply. At the gospel's midpoint and first climax here is a most poignant moment: Jesus' closest friend wants to protect him from the consequences of his calling, and has spoken with the blandishments of the devil himself. Jesus knows what danger Simon's care for him presents:

"Off with you, Satan, get out of my sight! You would make me stumble, for you think in men's ways, not God's."

(MATTHEW 16.23)

CHAPTER 6

The Old Israel and the New

Antioch: Division in the Church

Jesus himself is the new Israel that his followers will then be. But where does that leave Israel itself, the Jews who remained faithful to Moses' Law, their synagogues, and the history and traditions of their people, and who saw them ever more dangerously undermined by the claims made for Jesus by his followers? The question mattered deeply; it underlies every page of Matthew's story.

It was in Antioch that the pupils were first called "Christians" (Mission [Acts] 11.26). Here, then, they were first a recognizable group within the synagogues or a sect distinct from the synagogues altogether. The process toward such independence was long, circuitous, and painful on both sides. But out of such turmoil as seethed in Antioch grew at last two communities, separate and self-sustaining. Judaism and Christianity grew, in Matthew's generation, into shapes we still recognize today.

At the first moves toward war in 66 C.E., a swath of violence swept Syria. Twenty thousand Jews were killed in a single hour, Josephus tells us, at Caesarea; Jewish militias spread out around the country seeking revenge; gentiles anticipated the threat by further murders.

A terrible upheaval seized the whole of Syria. Every city was divided into two camps: the safety of one was the destruction of the other. They passed their days in blood, their nights, more awful still, in fear. For though each city thought it had rid itself of the Jews, they still had under suspicion those who were drawn to Jewish ways. No one would undertake to destroy this ambiguous group among them out of hand; but everyone feared it, half-native, half-alien as it was, as much as they feared the unequivocally foreign.

Gentiles were being drawn to Jewish ways. Gentile ways affected at least some Jews, even, or perhaps especially, those powerful figures of whom our historians have most to say. Herod had a house at Daphne, but when he dreamed at Daphne that his brother had been killed, we are bound to wonder if he was in Apollo's pagan shrine, where the god gave advice and warning through dreams. For Herod to mix Jewish and pagan observance need not surprise us; after all, he had celebrated the confirmation of his Jewish kingdom by sacrificing to Jupiter in Rome. Herod was a politician; he knew what gestures would stand him in good stead. A starker pressure may have driven that high priest Onias III, deposed from office and in exile at Antioch. When he was threatened by the usurper's intrigues, he took sanctuary in Daphne; this again recalls Apollo's shrine. Was this the only site that he expected pagan soldiers to respect? Antioch's church had members that moved in high circles such as these: Among its prophets and teachers was Manaen, brought up with Herod's nephew Antipas. He would have known the pressure to mix cultures and would have had the chance.

A church of Jews, of gentiles, or both; to be free from the Law, to observe it, or to find a compromise: Thirty years before Matthew wrote, these questions flared into a crisis at Antioch that divided the young church in two. We hear of it from Paul and Luke. Its details are hard to be sure of now. Paul himself was a key figure in the drama. He had to justify, in his subsequent letter to Galatia, the new position in which the crisis had left him: Neither his mission nor his teaching was now authorized by any established leaders of the church. He had become by necessity an independent figure, preaching a gospel clearly at odds with the gospel taught from Jerusalem. He was deeply suspect, then, to any community that expected its teachers to have learned loyally from other teachers, and they from others in turn.

Paul's account must vindicate his part in the crisis at Antioch; Luke, by contrast, writing the Mission (Acts) a generation after the event, has no reason to fuel such fire as smoldered on. He portrays a church unified in the development of its mission and its teaching. The place of gentiles in the church was still fluid; Matthew's gospel bears witness to that. But Luke is writing for the gentiles themselves, and he tells of a process that secured beyond doubt such gentiles' position in the church—a heavenly vision to Simon Peter, then the controlled experiment of a new practice in Antioch that Barnabas vetted and vouched for, followed by discussion among the church's Jerusalem leaders, and finally a formal agreement declared by Jesus' own brother James. In Luke's story all the church's chief authorities were involved in the process, and all agreed on its outcome.

Here, then, is the echo, still just audible, of a crisis that pulled the church apart. The senior figure Barnabas and his assistant, the convert Paul, had endorsed the practice of the community at Antioch: Gentiles could be full members without having to observe the Jewish Law. Jewish members, meanwhile, had taken to eating together with such gentiles. They would no doubt take all the care they could to observe the Law's regulations on the food to be eaten and the company in which to eat it. But compromise was called for. The Law's breach was called for by a higher cause: the unity of their Christian group. So much, Paul seems to claim in retrospect, when he writes to the Galatians, had already been endorsed before the crisis by the church's most senior figures in Jerusalem: James the brother of Jesus and Simon Peter.

This was no matter of pure theory; such practices defined the church as a community. Week by week its members, whether Jew or gentile, must live out the decision made and must justify it to themselves, their families, and their associates in the synagogues, temples, or city square. This community's Jewish members were in synagogues on the Sabbath; so perhaps, at the back, were some of the gentiles, listening and learning. But this community had meetings of its own, too, where different rules were kept, special rites were observed, and admission, discipline, and teaching were controlled by self-styled leaders answering to their own leaders in Jerusalem if to anyone at all. These leaders were probably Jews themselves, and were prominent figures, perhaps, in synagogue. But most of the synagogues' senior figures had good reason to challenge such colleagues' role in this deviant, ever more independent church.

There was trouble in store. Worries in the synagogue were matched by worries in the church itself. The Romans' suspicions must not be raised. Anyone who claimed loyalty to Judaism must be loyal to all its ways, for the Judaism that had worked so hard to secure privileges from imperial Rome must be a Judaism whose boundaries Rome could recognize with confidence. The church did not live in a vacuum; pressure on Jerusalem's Jews in general led to pressure on Jerusalem's Jewish church. Church envoys will soon leave Jerusalem for Antioch to insist the church there, too, must take care.

Barnabas and Paul had returned to Antioch after the conference in Jerusalem, and Simon Peter joined them. Whatever had been decided on Jerusalem, it left room for dispute. Jewish Christians and gentile were again sharing meals.

> *But when Simon Peter came to Antioch* [recalls Paul], *I opposed him face-to-face, because he stood condemned. For before the arrival of some people from James, Simon Peter used to eat together with the gentiles. But when they arrived, he began to back off and to separate himself through fear of those who were circumcised. And the other Jews joined in his play acting, so that even Barnabas was led astray into sharing their act.*
>
> *But when I saw that they were not making progress toward the truth of the gospel, I said to Peter, "the Rock," in front of everyone, If you are a Jew but live like a gentile and not like a Jew, how can you force the gentiles to take up Jewish ways? We are Jews by birth and not wrongdoers from among the gentiles. We know that a person is not brought to be just in God's eyes from works of the Law, except through the faith of Jesus Anointed; so we, yes, we believed in Anointed Jesus so that we might be brought to be just from the faith of the Anointed and not from works of the Law. For from works of the Law the whole world shall not be brought, in God's eyes, to be just.*
>
> *(GALATIANS 2.11–16)*

However much of this report records Paul's words to Peter, his plea did not win the church's leaders to his cause. The argument was lost. It is likely that he left Antioch after the dispute, never to return. A new style of mission was about to begin. Paul did not work at it alone, but he was the single, indisputable center of his own converts' teaching and instruction. He could not be everywhere at once. He must write, and the letters of this renegade, beleaguered missionary, have become with our four gospels, the most important texts in the Christian world.

And in Antioch itself? An unexpected story in Josephus gives us a small clue to the church's life in the years between Paul's work there and Matthew's. Trouble flared in the city, Josephus tells us, in 67 C.E. An apostate Jew named Antiochus, whose own father had been chief magistrate of the city's Jews, stood up in the city's assembly and declared that the Jews had plotted to burn down the city. He even handed over to the authorities, there and then, some foreign Jews, accomplices to the plot. They were immediately burned to death. Antiochus then persuaded the citizens to require of the Jews that they sacrifice to the Greek gods; those who refused, he claimed, would be shown up as coconspirators. All of this secured for Antiochus official control of the city's Jewish affairs and of troops enough to enforce it. He forbade the Jews' observance of the Sabbath, and when a fire did break out he blamed the Jews again.

This is a remarkable story. Who were Antiochus's victims? All of the Jews? It is possible that Antiochus had just a small group in his sights, a group that most Jews already resented and that gentiles could soon be brought to fear. Even if Josephus was only slightly misinformed, he might well have failed to spot the group's identity. They were influenced by foreign teachers; declared one day special in the week; were unable in conscience to sacrifice to the pagans' gods; and were natural suspects, three years after the blaze in Rome itself, when any threat of fire was raised. What if Antiochus forbade in fact the observance of a different day, not of the Sabbath, but of Sunday, the day on which the Christians recalled their Jesus' rising from the dead? Was the target of Antiochus's attack the Christians?

JOSEPHUS AND JESUS

Can Josephus, greatest of the Jewish historians, really have known so little about the Christians that in Antiochus he mistook the synagogues' defender for a power-mad renegade? Josephus does know of Jesus and his followers. And to see how puny and unimportant they were in the generation after Jesus' death, we need only see how Josephus treats them—and how the later church set out to correct the impression he gave.

Josephus has described two scandalous measures of Pilate, both of them bravely resisted by Jewish uprisings. His text then tells first of Jesus (bringing this section on Pilate to a close) and, after a long diversion, then tells of "another outrage," committed by a Jewish fraud in Rome, that threw the Jews into turmoil and led to their exile from the capital. Between the stories of Jesus and this outrageous fraud he inserts a long story, set in Rome, about the priests of Isis. They connived at the plan of a seducer, Mundus. The woman in question was persuaded by her maid that the god Anubis, Isis's companion, desired her. She spent the night in Isis's temple; Mundus played the god's part. When the trick came to light, Isis's cult was suppressed and the maid and the guilty priests were crucified.

This is the context in which his testimony to Jesus is set: Pilate on the one hand; frauds, Rome, and crucifixion on the other. His paragraph about Jesus himself has been discussed for centuries. How much of this report can a Jew have written who makes no other mention of Jesus and who clearly does not see himself as following this Anointed? The present text reads,

> About this time there lived a man Jesus, a wise man, if one really ought to call him a man at all. For he was one who did extraordinary works, a teacher of such people as accept truths gladly, and he won over many Jews and many of the Greeks. He was the Anointed. On the accusation of leading men among us, Pilate condemned him to be crucified; but those who had come in the first place to love him did not cease to do so. For he appeared to them on the third day as alive again; and the prophets of God had prophesied these and countless other marvelous things about him. And the nation of the Christians has still to this day not disappeared.

The text was well known in the early church. Had Josephus himself, before any Christian editor got to work on the text, treated Jesus as the first in that series of frauds? The church, if and when it had the power, would certainly have erased such a slur. Once we look for alterations to a text we can as easily find additions, too; an English bishop back in the seventeenth century already doubted that Josephus wrote, "He was the Anointed." If Christian editors tampered with Josephus's text, we might imagine an original as follows. As readers will see, the Greek terms for Jesus' teaching are double edged. And even more intriguing: Take out one letter from the word for *truths,* add a few to *wise,* and Josephus sounds more aggressive still. Here is how the text might once have read:

> About this time there lived a man Jesus, a clever man. He was one who did strange deeds, a teacher of such people as accept novelties too readily, and he led astray many Jews and many of the Greeks. On the accusation of leading men among us Pilate condemned him to be crucified. And the tribe of the Christians has still to this day not disappeared.

Throughout *The Four Witnesses* we have been acting as detectives, sifting, checking, looking for the overall patterns to an author's work that show us what makes him tick. Here is a Josephus that we recognize: conservative, blunt, impatient. It is on new, unsettling movements of the masses that he blames the disastrous war against Rome. One more "tribe" of fantasists deserves a short paragraph, no more.

The New Israel: Fulfilling the Law

PAUL: "LEAST OF THE MISSIONARIES"

"Do not think that I have come to undo the Law or the prophets; I have not come to undo but to fulfill" (Matthew 5.17). There is a vivid concern behind this saying. Matthew's community had good reason to make its position clear. Different followers of Jesus proclaimed their beliefs in different terms. Some could certainly seem, in the name of Jesus, to be declaring the Law redundant or worse. Had this Jesus claimed that his teaching replaced the Law's? Then no one loyal to the church's Jewish history—let alone to the synagogues of Matthew's day—could be his follower. Matthew's opponents within the church were fueling the attack of his opponents outside it; to resist the second set of these antagonists, Matthew must rebut the first.

And who were those within the church who so dangerously undermined the standing of the Law? We have seen one answer within the New Order itself. The most famous figure known to us against whom this charge was raised was Paul. A latecomer, a former opponent of the church, Paul was prepared to declare himself—albeit with thinly disguised irony—as *the least of the missionaries, unworthy to be called a missionary at all,* (1 Corinthians 15.9) and yet a figure who affected the church throughout the Roman east.

Paul himself was aware of the charge. He knew how readily his gospel could be understood as the Law's denial—and so how carefully he must reassert the Law's standing. His defense has seemed (to some readers) almost strained; he interrupts an argument of a quite different thrust to avoid all danger of misunderstanding. *In our assessment,* he writes to the Romans in his discussion of the Jewish Law,

> *a person is brought to be just in God's eyes without works of Law. Or is God the God of Jews alone? And not of gentiles too? Yes, of course he is the God of gentiles too—if, that is, we agree that God is one and one alone, who will bring the Jews to be just from faith and the gentiles through this faith. So are we dismissing the Law through this faith? Certainly not! On the contrary: we are establishing the Law.*
>
> *(ROMANS 3.28–31)*

At one climax to the argument of his Letter to the Romans Paul declares the Anointed to have been the *final stage* of the Law, the *conclusion* to which it had been tending (Romans 10.4). It has been disputed ever since what he means here. Different readers, all of them working to do justice to Paul, have reached widely different conclusions. Perhaps all that the Jewish Law was working toward has now been achieved, without reliance on the Law, by Jesus. There is then no further need for the Law's observance. Worse still, to be dedicated to the Law is to be distracted into positive error, into false confidence that could breed false pride. Or perhaps the Law's proper splendor is now visible at last; the Law can be obeyed with a new and broader sense of its place in God's plan. This instruction to the Roman church shows Paul at his most delicate, resonant—and ambiguous. Paul was faced with a range of circumstance in his addressees: Jews converted to the Church, Jews whose parents had converted, gentiles who had valued the synagogues' life already, or newcomers to belief in the single God of scripture. Paul's presentation of the Law is subtle, and he may well have needed to adopt different emphases in different conditions and churches. More important for our present purpose is to recognize that Paul's position was open to genuine misunderstanding then and is no less open to dispute now.

It is worth seeing just how carefully Paul pursues this discussion of the Law. He appears to be contrasting two routes to justice in God's eyes: one, through observing the Law (which he claims has never been successful), the other, through faith in Jesus (which is offered in the church). For the first he cites Moses: *those who fulfill the Law will live.* And can it be fulfilled as it needs to be? Paul quotes a further passage, from the Second Law (Deuteronomy): Moses is making clear how "close" the Law is, sitting within reach and waiting to be fulfilled. Paul uses the passage to extol our ready access to that other justice, the justice that comes from faith. He uses the very passage that extolled the Law for being so accessible to show how accessible this new route is, of Christian "faith." It is an extraordinary passage, rich and allusive, but we can well see why church leaders looked askance at the missionary who wrote it. In this passage, as so often, he is speaking of his gospel as a disclosure. The Law and God's whole plan can now be seen for what they have been all along, and the very fact of that disclosure brings within his churches' reach the part this plan assigns them.

Once more, sharp, practical questions had to be answered. Was the Law still to be observed fully by those Jews who accepted Paul's gospel and joined his church? Was any of it binding upon such gentiles, too? On the one hand, Paul. On the other, those leaders of the church who were unambiguously clear that the Law must be observed by all its members. We can well see why they were wary of this missionary, a loose cannon who admitted no debt or allegiance to those who had been at work before him. Paul's message was subtle, careful, deep; it was soon represented wrongly or wrongly understood. It is no wonder that he was held in such suspicion: *Some things in Paul's letters,* warns the Second Letter of Peter, *are hard to understand; the ignorant and unstable twist them to their own destruction* (2 Peter 2.16).

On page after page of his own letters Paul corrects the mistakes to which this teaching had been subjected—and not just, it seems, by his antagonists. He was thought, at one point, to be giving credit to wrongdoing: If evil led to God's mercy, then evil produced a good, so what should we do? Paul follows through angrily in the same Letter to the Romans: *The point is not—as we are slandered and as some people claim we say— "We are to do evil, so that good may come." Those people deserve their condemnation* (Romans 3.8).

He returns to this theme later in the letter. We may expect such a slogan to have been spread by his enemies; they would be reducing Paul's supposed position to its scandalous conclusion. But no: Paul's long and careful explanation is aimed at those who had adopted this outlook seriously and in good faith. The authority to which they appealed was Paul's; those who spread this—radical—misunderstanding of Paul's belief did so in the confidence that they were doing him and the church a service. They were, as they thought, his allies.

"Least in the Kingdom of Heaven"

Matthew admits no such ambiguity. His Jesus says,

> *"In truth I tell you, until heaven and earth pass away, not the dot on an i or the cross on a t shall pass away from the Law, not until all things come to be. All who relax one of the least of these commandments and teach others to do the same shall be called least in the kingdom of heaven. And all who teach them and do them, they shall be called great in the kingdom of heaven."*
>
> *(MATTHEW 5.18–19)*

This principle, maintained right at the gospel's start, has shaped Matthew's telling of Mark's story. Matthew must tread with great care. It may well be that pressure had grown on his church. Where it had once been possible to leave the Law's role fluid and open to differing views, now a clear line must be drawn. In Paul's day such pressure to conform had come from the church's leaders in Jerusalem. The fate of Judaism and the fate of its young sect, the church, were bound together. The Jews' rights from the empire must not be endangered; the borders of Judaism were elastic, but anything that clearly broke them must be brought back into shape. Matthew, thirty years later, responds directly to attack from the local synagogues. Paul found himself suddenly independent of Jerusalem, with all the gains and perils that this brought; Matthew speaks for a group that is slowly and painfully working free from the synagogues' authority.

The broad structure of Matthew's story is shaped by the synagogues and their leaders; so are its smallest details. His community is to mirror—at once to copy and to invert—the synagogues in its history, heroes, and ideals. Such a mirror reflects small things and large alike. We have before us just stories on the page, while Matthew had a community, individuals, and families under pressure from all sides. At issue are their daily lives, hour by hour. Beneath these distant disputes and their overarching principles lie the decisions facing people as ordinary as we ourselves are.

On every page we can see the strategy behind Matthew's story. He treads a narrow path that will encourage the synagogues' members to transfer their loyalty, firmly and finally, to the church. In Matthew's purpose ring the echoes of a vehement struggle for the loyalty of those who read them nineteen hundred years ago. The church, the synagogues, or both at once. They had so much in common with each other, so much that marked them both off from the pagan world around; how could it be wrong to attend synagogue on Sabbath and on Sunday the church? Or more dangerous for Matthew still: How can any church that is loyal to the Law not call for loyalty to the

Law's home, too, the synagogues? Surely the church *cannot* be split off from the synagogues or the members of the first from the leaders of the second.

Matthew worked hard for his emerging church. He drew the people of the synagogue away from its leaders—and so toward his own. Here was the authority ordained
by God: The leaders, admission, discipline, and teaching of the church all were in the
hands of agents authorized by Jesus. And Jesus himself had been authorized by God.

Matthew's readers, then, could be true to the Law and its ways only by abandoning
the community to whose ancestors God had entrusted that Law, for its leaders, stew-
ards and teachers of the Law, had betrayed their commission. They resisted the
church's gospel; they would be condemned, and those who followed them would share
their condemnation. It was in the church that the Law and promises given to Israel
were now coming to fruition. To stay within the synagogue was to be in immediate
danger: God was about to reject his people's false leaders, and those who remained
with them would be rejected as well.

This is a fierce, uncompromising stand. Several engines have given it power.
Gentiles were seeking admission to the church; what were the conditions on which
they could do so? Jesus' offer, it seemed, was to all nations; who, then, or what must
he be in God's plan? His authority was supreme; why, then, should the church's leaders subject themselves to the synagogues? Lofty thoughts about Jesus as well as the
considerations of daily life; the unparalleled role of worship and the determined control of its practice; Jesus' power and the power of those who claimed to represent
him—all were at issue. None of them was obviously the most important; each affected
all the others. Their combination was enough to drive the church beyond the limits of
a synagogue that used those very same years to reestablish, define, and control its own
identity.

MARK, MATTHEW, AND THE LAW

Matthew's strategy is clear even in the smallest details. At one point Mark had stepped
into a story with a comment of his own. Jesus had been asked why his pupils, before
eating, did not wash their hands in the way tradition required. Mark extends the dispute. His Jesus introduces other cases of misused tradition and then launches an
attack on the Law itself. Now the Law clearly prohibits certain foods: They are
impure; Jews may not eat them. Mark's Jesus, however, maintains that nothing coming into people from outside can make them impure. It is what comes out of people
that makes them impure: cases of evil dispute, lust, theft, murder, adultery, greed.
Food, says Jesus, does not enter into the heart to have any such effect—*declaring*, says
Mark, *all foods clean* (Mark 7.9).

But this stands in direct opposition to the Law. Matthew would let no such statement stand. It must be toned down. But how? Matthew omits that last comment,
which Mark had added in his own voice, and to round off the scene he brings Jesus
back to the dialogue's original theme: *"To eat with unwashed hands does not make peo-*

ple impure" (Matthew 15.20). The whole argument, Matthew suggests—its start, its end, and everything in between—can now be referred solely to the problem of washing before food. The food itself is not the issue. This is a careful refinement.

But Matthew cannot leave his intervention there. Mark's Jesus had issued a trenchant, uncompromising rule. Matthew's tones it down into a riddle: *"What comes out of the mouth makes people impure, not what goes in"* (Matthew 15.11). Jesus' opponents "stumble"—are scandalized—at this cryptic saying. Matthew does not explain their confusion. Do they think Jesus really is talking about food after all? In a technique we will encounter again, Matthew is reinterpreting a saying that had been used in the polemics of his day. This ruling of Jesus will have become notorious. It will have caused scandal among the Law-observant Jews but only, Matthew claims, through their leaders' failure to understand. He does not spell out those leaders' mistake. Even in the short, riddling form in which Matthew records the saying, his own interpretation could be challenged. Matthew diverts attention. A crushing attack on the synagogues' leaders becomes as well a dire warning to their followers: *"Every plant,"* says Jesus, *"that my father in heaven has not planted will be torn up by the roots. Let them be. They are blind guides to the blind; and if the blind lead the blind, they will all fall into a pit"* (Matthew 15.13–14).

Matthew is a master of his material. He knows exactly when to deflect a charge, when to counterattack, and when, in a familiar story, to let new themes unfold. He works carefully once more on a story that he found in Mark about the Sabbath. Mark's Jesus and his pupils crossed a field on the Sabbath; the pupils plucked ears of grain for food. The Pharisees objected: *"Look, why are they doing what is not permitted on the Sabbath?"* (Matthew 12.2). Jesus replied by recalling King David's similar infringement, centuries before. He had given his soldiers the sacred bread, restricted for the priests' use. David had broken the Law because of his soldiers' need; so, by implication, could Jesus' pupils for their own. As Mark records it: *He said, "The Sabbath was made for humankind, and not humankind for the Sabbath. So the Son of Man is lord of the Sabbath, too"* (Mark 2.27–28). Matthew is not content with this response; it leaves Jesus too coolly indifferent to the Law's demands. In an extra paragraph he fleshes out Jesus' answer. It is a striking moment. Matthew has asked deeply what is really disclosed in this scene. Here is one greater than the Temple. Later his Jesus will speak of something more in his presence than the prophet Jonah, more than Solomon. For the moment his Jesus adds,

> *"Have you not read in the Law that on the Sabbath the priests in the Temple break the Sabbath and are blameless for it? I tell you, there is one greater than the Temple here. And if you had understood what it meant, that passage 'I desire mercy not sacrifice,' you would not have condemned those without blame."*
>
> *(MATTHEW 12.5–7)*

Jesus has made his point: In the presence of Jesus himself, *one greater than the Temple,* there is no blame in the Law's breach. And so Matthew can truncate Mark's closing claim. Mark's Jesus had claimed defiant rights over the Sabbath: *"The Sabbath was made for humankind, and not humankind for the Sabbath"* (Mark 2.27). Such a universal claim will do nothing to help Matthew's cause. He narrows but deepens the claim. Jesus' authority is not the consequence of any other ruling, it is their basis. It is Jesus himself who vindicates his pupils' act: *"For the Son of Man is lord of the Sabbath"* (Matthew 12.8).

What accounts of Jesus' life did Matthew's community use—and what accounts was it known to use—before his own was completed? First and foremost, the gospel of Mark. Such comments as Mark records may have sunk from sight once Matthew's was completed, but there had been time enough for the word to get around: This church and its Jesus belittle the Law. Matthew works hard to rebut the charge and to resist any of those whose life or teaching gave it currency. His text's final version may even have been reversing a trend, reasserting a loyalty that the gospel's earlier editors had not needed (or had not wanted) to stress. *I am the least of the missionaries,* wrote Paul; we can expect that the self-description was well known. Many have wondered if Matthew had a particular target in his sights as he opened Jesus' teaching on the Law: *All who relax one of the least of these commandments and teach others to do the same shall be called least in the kingdom of heaven* (Matthew 5.19).

Toward the end of that great first sermon, Matthew's Jesus sums up all that he has said: *"So then: All that you would want others to do to you, do the same yourselves to them. For this is* the real heart, the summation of *the Law and the prophets"* (Matthew 7.12). From the fulfillment of the Law and prophets at the sermon's start, to their summary at its end. We have come full circle.

The New Israel: Fulfilling the Prophets

PROPHECY AND FULFILLMENT

"Do not think that I have come to undo the law and the prophets. I have not come to undo, but to fulfill" (Matthew 5.17). Matthew has in mind the prophets as well as the Law. In a bold, clear device he weaves into his story a series of passages from the Old Order's prophets "fulfilled," as he says, by Jesus. Each is flagged with a grand formula: *All of this happened,* says Matthew prior to the first, *so that the saying from the Lord through the prophet Isaiah might be fulfilled: "Look, a virgin will conceive and will bear a son. . . . "* (Matthew 1.22–23). We have encountered several of these prophecies already: about Jesus' exile to Egypt and the massacre of Bethlehem's children. Most of the sayings are connected with Jesus' birth. They form a refrain to these opening chapters of Matthew's gospel and offer resolute confirmation that here in Jesus the Old Order comes to fruition.

Matthew alone of our four witnesses invokes these particular prophecies. To modern ears, their use is strange. We may well wonder, in some cases, if the story would run just as smoothly without them; Matthew may well have drawn connections not stressed or not made at all in earlier tellings of the story. Those famous lines from Isaiah, for instance, break abruptly into the narrative. Others among the sayings, by contrast, seem so tightly bound to their fulfillment that without the prophecy there is hardly an incident worth mentioning at all: Matthew tells of Jesus going to live in Galilee near Zaboulon and Nephtali so that (and, it may seem, only so that) the word of Isaiah might be fulfilled, *Land of Zaboulon and land of Nephtali, Galilee of the gentiles, the people sitting in darkness have seen a great light* (Isaiah 8.23–9.1). Sometimes the Old Order itself did not quite make the point that Matthew needed, so Matthew makes free with the text. In his praise of Bethlehem he redrafts one prophet's prediction about David's family and adds to it a saying from the psalms of David himself.

How did Matthew convince his readers—far better versed than we are in the Old Order and its hopes—that these sayings refer to Jesus at all? *Out of Egypt,* said Hosea's God, *have I called my son;* but as we have seen, he was speaking of Israel as a nation. This is one of several such sayings that had never been predictions at all:

A voice in Ramah was heard,
a weeping and much crying:
Rachel weeping for her children;
and she would not be comforted,
because they were no more.

(MATTHEW 2.16–18)

Jeremiah spoke of *Rachel,* said to have been buried near Bethlehem, *weeping in Ramah;* if the prophet had a particular moment in mind, it was probably the exile of "Rachel's children," the tribes of Israel's Northern Kingdom, already one hundred years in the past when Jeremiah wrote, in 722 B.C.E. (Jeremiah 31.15). Matthew is bringing to life sayings whose power, it may seem, had long since been exhausted.

"A VIRGIN WILL CONCEIVE"

Most famous of the predictions is Isaiah's: *Look, a virgin will conceive and will bear a son, and they will call his name Emmanuel,* that is, *With-Us-God* (Isaiah 7.14). Matthew uses it to refer to Jesus, born of the virgin Mary. Isaiah was addressing the crisis in Israel seven hundred years before. The prophet, with the royal family or his own in mind, uses a word for *young woman* that need not involve virginity and that spoke of virginity, if it did at all, at the time of the prophecy, not at the child's conception. More striking still: Matthew draws on various versions of the Old Order's text. Among those that he certainly knew was the standard Greek translation, made two to three hundred years before he wrote. This translates Isaiah's *young woman* with a word that is (almost) only ever used for *virgin.* Has Matthew picked just the version, late and derivative though it is, that makes his point—that Mary remained a virgin when she conceived Jesus?

Matthew's whole "discovery" of these links seems forced. But his technique is most revealing precisely when it is most alien. Everything about Jesus is to be fulfillment, and far more of the Old Order is involved than a blunt search for obvious "predictions" would reveal. Matthew's community and the synagogue's shared the Old Order. Each proclaimed its loyalty to the Old Order's commands and laid claim to its promises. But most important of all were origins. The new community must show itself more deeply rooted in God's plan than Israel was itself; the church must fulfill the prophecies that had been entrusted to Judaism as a whole.

It has always been easy to reduce fulfillment to a crude correlation of words. Matthew's strategy was readily misunderstood. By the third century, pagan and Jewish critics alike were pointing out that Isaiah himself does not use the straightforward Hebrew word for a virgin. There was even a sect of Christians, said to use a truncated version of Matthew's text as their only gospel, whose members denied that Jesus was born of a virgin at all. Such critics asked what encouraged Matthew to invoke a prophecy so ill suited to his purpose. One answer came quickly to mind: If Jesus was illegitimate, then the church had been bound to provide an explanation. No early attacks claim that he was really Joseph's son, after all. What better vindication could be found for these strange origins than a miraculous birth and a prophecy fulfilled?

Those who challenge Matthew's account and those who defend it have focused on this single story of Jesus' conception. But Matthew, as ever, is working on a larger scale; we need to stand back if we are to see and assess his construction as a whole. Our architect Matthew has in mind both the detailed carving on his building, and the grand articulated sweep of its façade.

Isaiah speaks of a series of boys, already born or about to be. Each child has a significant name: *A-Remnant-Will-Return, Speedy-Spoil-Quick-Booty,* and finally *With-Us-God.* Isaiah has just told the story of God's vineyard, Israel: It has failed to bear fruit and will be cut down. Before Jesus comes the Baptizer, warning his hearers to bear fruit worthy of a change of heart and ways; for the ax is already laid to their roots and any unfruitful tree will be cut down. Isaiah tells the children's story through a drama of five whole chapters (Isaiah 7–11); at its climax the last and greatest "son" is endowed with the Breath of God. Matthew, in turn, has this poetic narrative in mind throughout his story of Jesus' birth and first appearances; at its climax, his baptism, Jesus is declared God's son and has shed upon him the Breath of God. The geography of Galilee is to our ears a strange subject for prophecy. But Isaiah also locates the climactic moment of disclosure in Zaboulon and Nephtali; it is here that *the people that walked in darkness have seen a great light.*

Isaiah's Jerusalem, over seven centuries before Jesus was born, was under threat; the king's heart shook as the trees of the forest shudder before the wind. The prophet takes with him his son *A-Remnant-Will-Return* and tells the king that if he will rely on God, the threat will eventually be repelled. As we can see, children's significant names are part of this (as of many another) story. And here in turn is the sign that God will give to enable the king to trust in his promise:

Look, a young woman will conceive, and will bear a son,
and will call his name Emmanuel, With-Us-God.

(ISAIAH 7.14)

The way to rescue will be long and hard. Whether or not the final editor of these prophecies knew the outcome, he has constructed a drama that does justice to the fearful years ahead. In this child's boyhood shall every terror come upon the nation: Warring kings will invade and its people will be reduced to hunger. Enter, meanwhile, the prophet's second child, *Speedy-Spoil-Quick-Booty.* His name portends the great invasion and the horror that followed:

The rivers of Assyria, its king and his army, will flood over Judah,
over all its channels and banks,
and will flood right up to the neck of your land, With-Us-God.

(ISAIAH 8.8)

All the nations will conspire against God's people, but in the end nothing will come of their plans, says Isaiah: *for with us is God* (Isaiah 8.10). This final rescue, however, is not yet at hand. The people will be afraid; they will seek guidance from wizards and necromancy. They will look upward and curse their king and their God; they will look downward and see nothing but darkness and distress. But the hope remains:

In days past he humbled the land of Zaboulon and the land of Nephtali; but in the days to come he will make glorious the way of the sea, the land beyond the Jordan, Galilee of the nations.

The people that walked in darkness have seen a great light;
they that dwelt in the land of the shadow of death,
on them has the light shone.
For unto us a child is born,
unto us a son is given.
And the government will be upon his shoulder;
and his name shall be called
Wonderful, Counselor,
Mighty-God, Everlasting-Father,
Prince-of-Peace.
Of the increase of his government and of peace there will be no end,
upon the throne of David and over his kingdom,
to establish it in justice
from this time and for all aeons.

(ISAIAH 8.23–9.7)

The king of Assyria will lord it over Israel; the people will be led captive into exile. But God will exact his vengeance for the Assyrians' pride, and then at last the name of that first boy will be vindicated. A remnant of God's people will have survived; they will return to their God in regret for their wrongdoing. God's remnant will return. Here as well, the third and greatest name finds its place at last: the child whose promised coming has echoed through these chapters of disaster, invasion, exile, and despair. His will be a kingdom unlike any other. Isaiah evokes the first state of God's creation. All that is corrupt in the world and opposed to God's plan will be undone. All God's creation, human and animal alike, will be restored to the condition of the Garden of Eden.

And there shall come a shoot from the stump of David's house,
a Branch from his roots.
And the Breath of God shall rest upon him,
the Breath of wisdom and understanding,
the Breath of counsel and might,
the Breath of knowledge and of the fear of God.

He shall not judge by what his eyes see,
nor decide by what his ears hear,
But with God's justice he shall judge the poor,
and decide with equity for the meek of the earth.

The wolf shall dwell with the lamb,
and the leopard shall lie down with the kid,
and the calf and the lion together,
and a little child shall lead them.
They shall not destroy in all my holy mountain,
for the earth shall be filled with the knowledge of God,
as the waters cover the sea.

(ISAIAH 11.1–9)

Matthew has Jesus fulfill those prophecies as no child that Isaiah had in mind could ever do. Every apparent fulfillment in Isaiah's time is now outranked, and if that involves as well the child's conception, so be it.

It is extraordinary, this claim that Jesus was born to a virgin. A good many heroes from the ancient world were said to have been miraculously conceived. In each case, however, the story's point is the hero's father: a god. There is no question that the mother remained a virgin. But the claim is only a small theme in a greater movement. The quotations themselves are just a few of the bolts, left visible to catch our eye, that join two stories running parallel through two chapters of Matthew's drama and five of Isaiah's. Matthew's story and our response do not depend upon the evidence a historian might find or contest for this one miraculous event. The claim underlying Matthew's story—the claim that informs all the details of his narrative and that should be assessed alongside any single "fulfillment"—is that history is controlled by God's plan, a plan whose disclosure has been entrusted to Israel. Matthew does not make the case for such a plan; he assumes it. His text is written for those who share his assumption and his detailed knowledge of the plan's unveiling offered in the Old Order. Matthew must actively defend a far tighter claim: that the plan can be discerned in the relation of that text's prophecies to the story of this child Jesus—when the prophecies, long since fulfilled, called for no such vindication and the life of the child appeared to offer none.

"Galilee of the Nations"

"FROM EAST AND WEST": THE PEOPLE OF THE CHURCH

Jesus himself, it seems, had emphasized his own and his pupils' mission to the Jews themselves; as Jesus himself was Jewish, so were all his first followers. But gentiles were attracted to the church. Could they be "full" members? And on what conditions? In Antioch, it seems, the church had first relaxed the synagogues' own rules. The dispute that followed, as we have seen, divided the church in two. Paul lost the argument; tighter rules must be applied. It was the move toward gentiles that had caused the crisis. Those who distrusted all such expansion would have had their fears confirmed. Thirty years later they remained a force within the church. The question had still to be carefully addressed when Matthew's gospel was nearing completion. What are the church's leaders, day to day, to do?

Jesus' teaching was searched through and applied afresh. *"Do not go out into any way of the gentiles,"* says Matthew's Jesus as he sends out his pupils to preach, *"or enter any city of the Samaritans. Go rather to the lost sheep of the house of Israel"* (Matthew 10.5–6). The focus is wholly on the Jews. This is a careful move. Matthew knows well the different emphasis in Mark, whose Jesus has warned of his pupils' arrest and prosecution: They will be brought before synagogues, rulers, and kings; *and the good news must first be proclaimed to all nations* (Mark 13.10). Matthew's Jesus tones down the prospect of other nations, for he has in mind a dramatic prophecy unknown from Mark, that *"you will not have completed all the cities of Israel when the Son of Man comes"* (Matthew 10.23).

Matthew is drawing a careful, strategic contrast, gradually revealed in the course of his gospel, between the mission to Jews that Jesus commands within the story's course and the mission that he will call for at its very end, to all the nations of the world. Matthew is acutely aware of the development: His Jesus looks forward to a new regime, a community with new rituals of admission, discipline, and common life. All these lie ahead of Jesus and his pupils as these appear within the story itself, but they must all be spoken of within that story. Mark knew the value of this tactic well. He used it to encourage and warn his own church with the words Jesus spoke to his pupils thirty years before. Matthew takes Mark's method and extends it boldly. Not just general themes but details in every area of the church's life can be addressed vividly in this way. This is Matthew's outstanding achievement: His gospel addresses the needs of a community in the story of a time that preceded its foundation. And it is the closing line of the gospel that his Jesus puts the keystone in place at last: All that has been anticipated is now fulfilled. The kingdom that Jesus refused from the devil is now his by right. He has been given it by God:

> *"All authority in heaven and on earth* [said Jesus] *has been given to me. So go, make pupils of all nations, baptizing them in the name of the father and of the son and of the Breath of God. Teach them to observe all that I have commanded you. And look, I am with you always, every day until the aeon's completed end."*
> (*MATTHEW 28.18*)

Matthew sets up that narrow range within which Jesus' first pupils had to work, preaching to the Jews alone. It is precisely within this that Matthew has his Jesus, long before Easter, drop hints of different and dramatic things to come. As Mark had in outline, so Matthew allows the pupils of Jesus to represent in detail the concerns and questions of Matthew's own community and in particular of its leaders. This is no fixed and consistent program; Matthew can make better use of some moments than of others. Perhaps the most forceful revision that he ever makes to Mark's story is in his account of the woman, a gentile, who begged Jesus to heal her daughter. In most of the stories they both tell, Matthew is a narrator less ambitious than Mark; he has a good many stories to relay and spends less time on their "novelistic" details than his predecessor had. This story, however, he tells with an ear alert for every nuance. Once he sees in Jesus' circle the leaders of his own present church, he sees, too, how much the story has to teach them.

THE GENTILE WOMAN

Here is Mark's version, on the left; and on the right, Matthew's retelling of the story.

Jesus moved on from there and went off to the region of Tyre. He went indoors and wanted no one to recognize him, but he couldn't escape notice. Straight away a woman heard about him whose daughter had an unclean spirit in her.	*Jesus left there and went up to the area of Tyre and Sidon. And look, here's a Canaanite woman from those parts, she came out and started yelling out, "Have pity on me, sir, Son of David. My daughter is terribly ill with a devil." But he didn't answer her a word.*
(*MARK 7.24–25*)	(*MATTHEW 15.21–23*)

Matthew has the woman speak. There is a more vivid drama here than Mark allows: on the one hand, the woman, yelling after Jesus, and on the other, his silence. Matthew makes clear from the start that she was gentile. It is the first thing we learn of her. All the more striking that she uses a title so precious to Jews and Jews alone:

> *And his pupils came up and asked him,*
> *"Send her away, she's yelling after us."*
> *"I've been sent out," replied Jesus, "to no*
> *one except the lost sheep of the house of*
> *Israel."*
> (MATTHEW 15.23–24)

Jesus' pupils know the form: The woman has nothing to with them nor they with her. She is just an embarrassment, drawing unwelcome attention by her yells. Jesus confirms their instinct. Here is a phrase whose importance Matthew knows: Do not go to the gentiles or Samaritans, Jesus had said, *"Go rather to the lost sheep of the house of Israel."* These were the ones who must hear the message: *The kingdom of heaven is near* (Matthew 10.6). Matthew's leaders have learned this lesson well. As in Jesus' day, so in theirs: All that the good news brings, it brings only to the Jews.

She came and fell at his feet—and the woman was Greek, from Syrophoenicia—and began asking him to throw out the devil from her daughter.	*But she came and bowed down before him and said: "Sir, help me."*
And he started: "Let the children be fed first, to the full; because it's not right to take the children's food and give it to the dogs."	*But he replied: "It's not right to take the children's food and give it to the dogs."*
(MARK 7.26–27)	(MATTHEW 15.25–26)

Again the woman speaks; Matthew brings her right before us. Jesus' answer in Mark was surely as brutal as any words of his could be. But Matthew pushes them still further. At least once Mark's "children" are satisfied, there may be some remnants for the dogs; Israel may well eat its fill before the good news of the kingdom is exhausted and its healing power drained. Then is the chance for the gentile "dogs" to benefit as well. Matthew deletes all mention of the children's needing to be filled, and so all hope of leftovers. There is nothing here for gentiles. Nothing.

Gentiles surrounded Matthew's church as well, gentiles who pleaded for admission. Here, in the words of the Lord himself, was their answer. That saying was forever before the church's leaders and was, we may suspect, adduced over and over to resist the admission of gentiles to its membership: *"I've been sent out to no one except the lost sheep of the house of Israel."*

But she replied, saying:	*She said:*
"Sir, even the dogs beneath the table eat	*"That's right, sir, but the dogs do eat*
from the children's scraps."	*from the scraps that fall from the mas-*
(MARK 7.28)	*ter's table."*
	(MATTHEW 15.27)

There is a pause. The tables are turning. This woman is not just desperate; she is unflinchingly clear that there are scraps to be had, that this Jewish "Son of David" has more to offer than the Jews themselves will eat.

And he said to her:	*Then Jesus answered and said to her:*
"Because you've said that, be on your	*"Woman, you've got great faith. Be it*
way; the devil has left your daughter."	*done for you as you want." And her*
And she went home and found the little	*daughter was healed from that hour.*
child lying on her bed and the devil gone.	*(MATTHEW 15.28)*
(MARK 7.29–30)	

The point is made. The woman's faith, her trust is greater than any rules; in its effect upon Jesus it overcomes even Jesus' own command. Matthew's Jesus now returns to the Lake of Galilee. He heals the blind and deaf, the crippled and the lame. Here is rich fulfillment of the promises that the prophets issued in the name of God. Matthew rounds off this summary with a touching note: All those who saw the miracles *gave glory to the God of Israel* (Matthew 15.31). The gentile mother had broken through and secured her daughter's health. But this remains the exception. Jesus is still on earth; he has not yet been invested with all power over all creation. The God of Israel will for the moment be disclosed in Israel alone.

In Mark's story, this healing of the gentile girl could pass Jesus' pupils by. For the leaders of Matthew's church was more at issue, and the story is a critical moment in Matthew's slow, steady instruction. Even the most conservative leaders of his church, fortified as they were in their exclusion of gentiles by the words of Jesus himself, must by the gospel's end be ready to hear and accept the final commandment of their risen Lord: *"So go, make pupils of all nations, baptizing them in the name of the father and of the son and the Breath of God"* (Matthew 28.19).

THE CHILDREN OF THE KINGDOM?

The gentiles in this story have hope before them. And the Jews? The Law redisclosed, the kingdom on the doorstep, Israel redefined: Where did all this leave the majority of the Jews, the historic people of God still loyal to the synagogue and unconvinced by such claims? Here Matthew's tone changes. He warns, predicts, cajoles: The gentiles are on the point of entering the kingdom, and those who should be in it from the start are threatened with exclusion.

Matthew and Luke both know of a Roman officer who came to ask Jesus to heal his servant. He thinks like a soldier, in terms of commands given and obeyed: Jesus need only give the word, and the boy will be cured. Luke's Jesus remarks, *"I have not seen such great faith even in Israel"* (Luke 7.9). This foreigner shows *even* greater trust than the Jews themselves. Luke is less worried by such themes than Matthew; he lets them arise with less fanfare or system. And the Jews themselves? Luke knows, in a quite different context, Jesus' threat against those who feel entitled to a place in God's kingdom. His Jesus has been asked, Will only a few saved? Jesus responds with a general warning against false followers: *"You will weep and gnash your teeth, when you see Abraham and Isaac and Jacob and all the prophets in the kingdom of God, but yourselves thrown out. And they will come from east and west and from north and south and will feast in the kingdom of God"* (Luke 13.28–29).

Out of that officer's story and this saying together, almost certainly separate in origin, Matthew has created an unforgettable moment. His foreigner has faith, by contrast with the Jews, who become the object of that dire warning:

When Jesus heard this he was amazed and said to those who were following,

"In truth I tell you, in no one have I found such great faith in Israel.
I tell you: many will come from east and west
and will feast with Abraham and Isaac and Jacob in the kingdom of heaven,
but the children of the kingdom will be thrown out into the darkness, the outer darkness.
There they will weep and gnash their teeth."

(MATTHEW 8.10–12)

"MAY THE HERETICS PERISH QUICKLY"

Can those who said and heard such things on Sunday have attended synagogue the day before? The daily prayers of Judaism include "The Eighteen Blessings." One, we are told, was added at the school at Jamnia at the end of the first century C.E.: "Rabban Gamaliel said to the sages: Is there anyone among you who can formulate the blessing against the heretics? Samuel the small then rose and formulated it." It is still open to debate exactly who was the target of this blessing's curse and when and where it was regularly used.

"The Eighteen Blessings" were to be said three times daily by every Jew, male and female, adult and child. But this blessing against heretics was not, it seems, part of the Sabbath's service in synagogues; a "heretic" would not be embarrassed by any demand on the Sabbath to declaim or hear this blessing publicly. We may think of the blessings as functioning more generally in the synagogues much as sections of Matthew's text functioned in his church. The blessings made clear to the committed, to waverers and to opponents, what the synagogue stood for. Here we cite just five of the blessings. It was a core of the "gospel" that the synagogue declared and invited gentiles to share:

> Heal us, O God, of the pain of our heart; remove from us sorrow and grief and raise up healing for our wounds.
> You are blessed, O God, you who heal the sick of your people Israel.

> Proclaim our liberation with the great trumpet and raise a banner to gather together our dispersed.
> You are blessed, O God, you who gather the banished of your people Israel.

And now for the extra blessing against heretics. They were not the only objects of the curse. The synagogues had as much reason as churches to resent the rule of Rome and to pray for its dissolution. The "insolent kingdom" would outlast Matthew's generation by three centuries and more:

> And for apostates let there be no hope; and may the insolent kingdom be quickly uprooted in our days. And may the Nazoreans and the heretics perish quickly; and may they be erased from the book of life; and may they not be inscribed with the just.
> You are blessed, O God, you who humble the insolent.

The apostates, the Roman rulers, the Nazoreans and the heretics: the synagogues' enemies are briskly summarized. We may suspect these Nazoreans and heretics were promising a place in the book of life. Waverers tempted by their blandishment had to be disabused of such hope. Who exactly were these two groups whose attraction the synagogues had to resist so fiercely? It is not certain that all and only Christians were intended. But "Nazorean" recalls Jesus' own origin in Nazareth and his epithet, the "Nazarene"; and Paul recommends to the Philippians' care those who have worked with him, whose names are in the book of life (Philippians 4.3). Where the church saw heroism, the synagogues saw disloyalty and error. They were looking for converts in the other direction.

> *May your mercies be showered over converts who are just in your eyes; and give us a rich reward, together with those who do your pleasure.*
> *You are blessed, O God, the trust of those who are just in your eyes.*

> *Be merciful, O God, with your great mercies, to Israel your people and to Jerusalem your city and to your Temple and your shelter; and to the kingship of the house of David, your just Anointed.*
> *You are blessed, O God, God of David, you who build Jerusalem.*

Synagogue and Church: The Breach

In the 390s C.E. John Chrysostom was working and preaching in Antioch. Chrysostom, "Golden Tongue," is one of the most striking preachers in the church's history and among those most viciously antagonistic to the Jews. If we give space to his words in *The Four Witnesses,* it is only in order to hear the concerns of an embattled church. Chrysostom knew of those who attended both church and synagogue, just as Matthew had in the same city three centuries before. "Many even of those who are reckoned to belong to us," said Chrysostom, "and who say that they think as we do go along, some for the sake of the spectacle and others even to take part in the celebration and associate themselves with the fast" of the Jews' Day of Atonement. This, he insisted, was a "pernicious practice." It is no coincidence that Chrysostom preached such sermons—several survive—at the times of the Jews' great festivals. Chrysostom was genuinely worried. His audience is not to ask how many Christians took part in the Jewish fast; if the number is known it should not be told abroad; the news must not spread or the scandal become known.

This overlap between church and synagogue could be viewed quite differently. Christians often benefited from the kindness of Jews. Christians who were sick would go to the rabbis for help. To guarantee a solemn oath, testators would resort not to the Christian Bible but to the synagogue and its venerable Hebrew text. Daily life and daily piety had good reason to respect the faith of Judaism, its antiquity and standards of behavior. Everything proclaimed by the church grew out of the Old Order; nothing could be more natural than to acknowledge some allegiance to the Old Order's ancient people. A great teacher of the church, St. Jerome, admitted the Jews' generosity, but he urged his church to refuse their offers of help. Its recipients, he says most tellingly, might be drawn to Judaism itself. Chrysostom can mount only the feeblest of attacks on the synagogues' integrity: The Jews, he claimed, deride such Christians as seek their society and their help, "and even if they do not do so openly, they are doing so deep down in their hearts." These sermons make bitter reading. The flavor of Matthew's careful thought has long since faded. Vitriol alone remains.

And Matthew himself, three centuries before? He already knows such a fusion of loyalties and is fighting the first skirmishes of this long, sad war. The synagogues' leaders must be attacked in order to draw their people away from them. He warns their followers that in the synagogues is only error, the blind led by the blind. Matthew is working for the break that is not yet complete: to establish a church that so completely represents God's ancient will, whose Jesus so totally fulfills its Law and prophets that their old guardians are redundant or worse.

No wonder, then, that Matthew speaks of *their* synagogues and denigrates their leaders. Here is an angry standoff in which Matthew's chief targets are the synagogues' leaders. Matthew's Jesus introduces his long, ferocious attack on *the scribes and Pharisees, play actors* with a telling command to the crowds and to his pupils together:

"The scribes and Pharisees sit on the seat of Moses. So everything they tell you, you must do and observe; but do not act as they act. For they speak but do not do."
(MATTHEW 23.2–3)

The Law must be upheld; Matthew's Jesus relaxes no command that was issued with the authority of Moses. Jesus' relation to Moses and Israel matters so much because Moses and Israel matter to Matthew's readers. He is encouraging, reassuring, and persuading them that his community holds the key to God's justice, the Law, and the kingdom. All that a Jew had longed for is here. Matthew must be able to make claims that meet the objections of his Jewish opponents.

Matthew's church claims autonomy from the synagogues. His leaders are clear: Theirs is the duty and the authority to admit, teach, discipline, and if necessary exclude its members. But among its people are those who are less sure. So Matthew draws the distinction as starkly as possible: to be part of the synagogues is to incur the wrath of God that is hanging over them. It is to adhere to those whose special place is about to be given to others. There is still just time to move away, to make the break from synagogue and align one's life wholly with the church.

The church was not alone in such strategy. The synagogue was a place for gentiles to gather who were drawn to Judaism and, as we have seen, for such Christians, too. "The Eighteen Blessings" were a full, fitting summary of Jewish faith and hope and life. To include the curse of Christians was to make quite clear where the synagogues' limits lay. As Matthew sought to pry people from the synagogues, so his rivals there sought to pry them from the church. To call attention to the unity and limits of the synagogues' community was a brave and appropriate strategy. Here was an invitation and the terms on which it was extended. Potential converts, pagan and Christian alike, would know clearly what the synagogues offered and required and what loyalties—to paganism or to the church—put such a candidate beyond the pale. A tactic effective for Matthew's church could be expected to enjoy no less success in the neighboring and competing synagogues.

Matthew takes up Mark's story of a vineyard's corrupt tenants. Rather than pay the produce due as rent, they beat or kill the owner's agents; when eventually he sends his son, they see their chance to take over the inheritance for themselves and kill him. *"What,"* asks Jesus, *"will the owner do to those tenants when he comes? He will kill those tenants and will give the vineyard over to others, who will give him the produce in due season."* So far, so like Mark. But Matthew's Jesus adds, *"I tell you, the kingdom of God will be taken from them and will be given to a nation that provides the produce."* The high priests and Pharisees saw the point of Jesus' stories, that he was speaking about them (Matthew 21.33–45).

"HIS BLOOD BE ON US . . . "

Jesus has been arrested, charges laid. Pilate has heard the evidence. He wishes to release Jesus; the crowd clamors for his death. He tries again and fares no better.

Pilate saw that this was not helping; a riot was starting. He took water and washed his hands in front of the crowd and said: "I am innocent of this man's blood. You, you see to it."

And the crowd answered, "His blood be on us and on our children."

(MATTHEW 27.24–25)

These were fateful words. If the Jews claimed responsibility for Jesus' death, ran the thought of Christian Europe, then let them bear it: They were by their own confession guilty of "God's murder." By the late twentieth century the church realized at last what terrible evil this text had been used to encourage and justify.

A defensive church in Antioch, nineteen hundred years ago, drew up its borders and its battle lines. Those who could not be won from allegiance to the synagogue by Jesus' teaching or his circles could perhaps be won over by fear. Those who were wavering could be won to the church's side. Those firmly within the church who were still saddened by the rift with synagogue could see how right it was to stay away from their Jewish neighbors. And those who wondered how God's justice would resolve this vengeful fight between two gatherings that both claimed obedience to his will could see what that justice required.

Within forty years of Jesus' death the Jews of Jerusalem had seen their city and Temple destroyed, tens of thousands of their people killed. The church, itself still made up largely of Jews, came quickly to diagnose that destruction as God's punishment for Jesus' death. One generation had condemned Jesus; its children had suffered for it. Here is more leverage for Matthew. No one could wish to be linked, even hundreds of miles away in Antioch, with that second generation. *"His blood be on us and on our children."*

But move on three centuries: The emperor was Christian, the empire must follow. Matthew had written for a small, beleaguered church in the years of sharpest tension between the church and the synagogues of Syria. His text was now a gospel for the whole world and all time. Matthew had attacked his local opponents, parried their charges, cajoled their people; this Jesus' warnings had been vindicated, his death avenged, his claims upheld. But Matthew's attacks were now in the armory of an imperial church whose heirs would use these weapons, with terrible effect, for two millennia to come.

"Come unto Me"

THE PROMISE OF WISDOM

Wisdom is not apparent to many [said Sira's Son].
Put your neck under her harness,
lower your shoulder and take her weight.
Search her out and seek her, and you will come to know her,

and once you have hold of her do not let her go.
For in the end you will find rest in her,
she will turn out to be your joy.
                    (WISDOM OF SIRA'S SON [BEN SIRA] 6.22, 22–28)

We have already seen examples of an overlap between Matthew's story and Luke's. They share a large number of sayings and one or two short narratives that our other witnesses do not record: most famous of all is the "Our Father." It is likely (but not certain) that each had before him a Collection of Sayings whose only trace survives in these citations by Matthew and Luke. Our two witnesses relay the sayings in different forms and in different orders, but the overlap is almost always clear.

Wisdom was evoked over and again in the collection. This is the Wisdom of God, which was active at creation and which informs the lives of all those who seek her; the same power is at work in the world at large and in the individual. It is in the Wisdom of Sira's Son that the character and praise of Wisdom had been most fully explored. Sira's Son ends with the writer's description of himself, how he has sought Wisdom all his life. Such Wisdom was acquired by steady, sensible thought and above all by the lifestyle of decades: disciplined, ethical, prayerful. The result was not dull or mechanical. To conform to the will and ways of God was to begin to understand them. Sira's Son turns at last to the reader and ends his book,

Come close to me, you who are uninstructed,
take your places in the house of teaching.
Why do you complain you are lacking in these things
and you are so thirsty for them?
I have opened my mouth and spoken:
Buy Wisdom for yourselves without money,
put your neck under her yoke,
and let yourselves receive her burden.
Wisdom is not far to seek,
and those who give themselves to her will find her.
                    (WISDOM OF SIRA'S SON [BEN SIRA] 51.23–30)

Matthew and Luke, as we would expect, relay their collection's sayings about Wisdom in slightly different words. These differences are most revealing. We have been alert throughout for the outlook that make each of our witnesses the particular witness that he is; we have to work as detectives, prying apart each text to see what is driving it. Here in the handling of Wisdom is one of the gospels' most intriguing leads. From a handful of clues we can rediscover an assumption that sets Matthew instantly across a deep divide from Luke. Small clues to an apparently small change, just a word here and there. But in that change lies the crucial trajectory of the church: further and further from the synagogues with which it shared its birth.

Matthew knows well the power of the central moment in Mark: Peter's declaration that Jesus is the Anointed. But he has abandoned all the drama with which Mark prepares his readers for the scene. Jesus' pupils still misunderstand his warning against their opponents' leaven. But Matthew has omitted Mark's biting quotation from Jeremiah, *"You have eyes, can't you see? You have ears, can't you hear?"* (Mark 8.18, Jeremiah 5.21). He has omitted as well the pair of miracles with which Mark linked it: the cures of a deaf-mute and a blind man, which challenge the reader into the real "hearing" and "sight," the *understanding* that Peter finally shows.

THE COMING OF WISDOM

Has Matthew just lost sight of Mark's most telling, careful strategy? Not at all. He has removed all traces of it precisely because he has a strategy of his own. He knows exactly what Mark was planning, but Mark's emphases are not his. At issue is not the gospel's content but what the readers should know. It is the gospel's effectiveness—how the readers can be brought to know it. Venerable traditions are in play, and different styles of instruction offered different forms of insight. Matthew, scholar and teacher, has thought about them all. Wisdom was to be acquired through one form of training and through that training was accessible to all. The dramatic unveiling of God's plan involved quite different practices and was even then reserved for those few to whom the privilege was given. Wisdom and disclosure: These traditions shape the central section of our gospel. Matthew is not discussing them; he is *using* them. For only their fusion, the convergence of two great streams in Israel's ways of thought, can begin to do justice to the Jesus that he would have his readers understand. Matthew's readers are not to observe Wisdom but to acquire it and so to recognize its source.

We take up the gospel's story at the start of its third section. Jesus is busy with miracles and dialogues. Matthew and Luke share a group of sayings about the Baptizer. When he was in prison, the Baptizer sent his pupils to Jesus to ask, *"Are you the one who is coming, or are we still waiting for another?"* Jesus refers them to the prophecies of Isaiah that were being fulfilled before their very eyes: *"Go and tell the Baptizer what you hear and see: Blind people regain their sight, cripples walk, lepers are cleansed and deaf people hear, corpses are raised to life and to poor people the good news is preached"* (Matthew 11.2–5). Matthew has taken care to have an example of each before this point. The preceding narrative includes two stories drawn from fuller versions told later in the gospel: Two men have their sight restored, one man his hearing.

Jesus has not given a straight answer to the Baptizer's pupils; he has offered them, as Matthew offers his readers, the evidence they need if they are to find it for themselves. Matthew is teasing his readers into thinking for themselves in turn. He offers a further clue—another puzzle, this time with its answer also given. Those who went off to the desert to the Baptizer, what did they hope or expect to come across? And who or what did they really see? Matthew signals the answer implicit in the story itself: The Baptizer was the prophet Elijah, returned to earth; a return, as the prophet Malachi had warned, that portended the coming of God's Anointed and the day of God's judgment. First the Baptizer, now Jesus. This combination should be evidence enough. All that the Jews had most reason to hope for and fear was happening before their eyes.

But the Baptizer and Jesus: What a bizarre combination it was. Matthew and Luke both have Jesus comment on two such different ways of life. The Baptizer had been fiercely ascetic, so his opponents said, "He is mad." Jesus enjoyed a good party, so "Look," they said, "the man is a glutton and a drinker." Both complaints are dismissed with a crisp summary: *"Wisdom,"* says Luke's Jesus, *"is justified by all her children"* (Luke 7.35). The Baptizer and Jesus, so drastically different as they appear to be, are each "Wisdom's child." So far, so good. But that is not what Matthew wants to say. His Jesus concludes, *"Wisdom is justified by her deeds"* (Matthew 11.19). Which deeds are at issue? Those of which Jesus has just been speaking: his own. The acts of Jesus are the acts of Wisdom herself.

This is striking. We have encountered Jesus as a new Israel as well as its leader; is he now to be Wisdom itself as well as its teacher? What does such an odd claim mean? Matthew does not call attention to the quiet twist he has given these words. Nothing, it seems, is being heralded of which Matthew's readers need to be persuaded or to which they have not been introduced before. He is just saying what he knows is more apt, more precise, more deeply true than the version he inherited, and however many or few of his readers know of that earlier version, he can assume they will not mind the change. Matthew is hard at work. He has seen how the questions from and about the Baptizer can open the reader's mind to the theme that will underlie the next five chapters of his gospel. Who *are* these two contrasting figures? Who and what are we really seeing in this story?

Matthew now introduces Jesus' fierce condemnation of the towns that had rejected him. There is warning here. So many clues had been given, so much revealed, but they remain blind to the wonders before them. And so to the most dramatic of all Jesus' claims in Matthew's gospel, an unforgettable statement of Jesus' relation with the father:

> *"I praise you, father, lord of heaven and earth,*
> *that yes, you have hidden these things from the learned and clever*
> *and unveiled them to mere children—*
> *yes, father, that this was your pleasure.*
> *All things have been given over to me by my father;*
> *and no one really knows the son except the father,*
> *and no one really knows the father except the son,*
> *and anyone to whom the son chooses to unveil him."*
>
> (MATTHEW 11.25–27)

Unveiling: Everything that we have teased out of Mark's account is presented here, clearly and boldly. All the unveiling of God's plan and will is channeled through Jesus.

Such disclosure is possible only through Jesus' will. Those to whom he chooses to unveil it: Who will they be? And what will they see?

Jesus continues:

"Come to me, all you who are weary and burdened down,
and I will give you rest.
Take my yoke and learn from me,
for I am meek and humble in heart,
and you will find rest for yourselves."

(MATTHEW 11.28–29)

Here are just the motifs with which we have heard Sira's Son praise wisdom. But this time it is Wisdom itself who is speaking: "Come to me." Jesus' words are the words of Wisdom herself. We have heard that Jesus is the channel of God's unveiling. But more than that: Here he is disclosed to be its content as well. He is in his own person the Wisdom of God: God's plan in action, here on earth. *"I tell you,"* says Jesus in the very next scene, *"there is something greater than the Temple here"* (Matthew 12.6). By that chapter's end he has warned again, *"Look, there is something more than* the prophet *Jonah, something more than Solomon here"* (Matthew 12.1, 41, 42).

Traditions of wisdom and traditions of unveiling: They must join forces. Matthew is setting up the readers to discover and recognize what Jesus offers: himself. The healings and other miracles that follow, the disputes with opponents, the fulfillment of prophecy, the examples and aims of parables: In all of these the reader is directly challenged to take up Jesus' offer and so to become one of the *mere children* to whom the secrets of father and son will be revealed.

The challenge continues. Matthew's Jesus tells parables, as Mark's did. That sad prophecy of Isaiah still casts its shadow:

You will listen with all your might and shall not understand,
you will look with all your might and shall not see.
For the heart of this people has been hardened,
they have heard dully with their ears
and have closed up their eyes.
In case they should see with their eyes
and hear with their ears
and understand with their heart,
and turn, and I will heal them.

(MATTHEW 13.14–15, ISAIAH 6.9–10)

Mark's Jesus had then turned to his pupils and challenged them starkly: Were they, too, so dull-witted that they could not understand? Matthew's Jesus, by contrast, gives his pupils this ringing endorsement:

"But your eyes are blessed because they see
and your ears because they hear.
For in truth I tell you:
many prophets and just men longed to see what you see
and they did not see it,
and to hear what you hear
and they did not hear it."

(MATTHEW 13.16–17)

Matthew characteristically builds on Mark's main sequence of parables. He knows of more than Mark and is glad to add the extra material to this single block. At their close he asks his pupils, *"Have you understood all this?"* It is a telling question. Mark's series of parables, we have heard, was punctuated with the pupils' failure to understand: *"You do not understand this parable, then how will you understand any of the parables?"* (Mark 4.13).

Matthew's Jesus views these closest pupils with a kindlier eye. They are still liable to weakness and error, their faith still falters, and their leader Peter still—spectacularly—fails to see that Jesus must suffer and die. But Matthew offers his readers more encouragement than warning in his portrait of those first pupils. They offer for Matthew's own church a model of its leaders, and it is important for Matthew that these leaders are basically right, that they have such insights and understanding as will vindicate their role. There are competing leaders, eager to belittle Matthew's own. To weaken their standing and reputation is a luxury that he and they cannot afford. He can warn and advise but must not undermine.

"Have you understood all this?" The pupils answer firmly, yes. Not least, they have seen how Jesus weaves his parables out of familiar settings and the Old Order together. As Jesus draws up from the Old Order the instruction that meets his pupils' needs, so will they find in Jesus' words due guidance for the church that they will one day lead. Matthew's Jesus can now round off his teaching with as personal a note as any we find in our four witnesses. Here Jesus speaks and with him Matthew, one scribe to other scribes, a vindication of their common task in the service of their church.

"Have you understood all this?" They say to him, "Yes." And he said to them,
"Because of this every scribe who is apprenticed as a pupil to the kingdom of heaven
is like a householder who brings out from his storehouse both old things and new."

(MATTHEW 13.51–52)

Luke knows of that thanksgiving to the father that we have heard in Matthew, *"I praise you, father, lord of heaven and earth."* Luke follows it, as the collection almost certainly did that Matthew shares with Luke, by Jesus' exclamation: How blessed his pupils were to see what he was showing them. It is Matthew who has separated the sayings and put two chapters of his gospel between them. He knows the power of this climactic sequence from the collection, and he shapes this whole section of his gospel around their poetry. He has an overarching theme in mind: the possibilities, the conditions, and the actual, present effect of disclosure among his readers as they read or hear his gospel.

At last Matthew reaches Mark's central scene, Peter's declaration that Jesus is the Anointed, the son of the living God. Matthew builds on it. All the hesitation in Mark's account is drowned out in Jesus' reply. Peter has been led over the course of the story to this recognition, and Matthew has invited the readers to undertake that same progress for themselves in their reading of this text. Such understanding was once a privilege reserved for Peter and the grounds for his authority. It is now accessible to all.

Is anything still reserved, held back for those more deeply immersed in the church's life and thought? We saw how quietly Matthew transforms Jesus into Wisdom. The title is not given to Jesus, the claim is not openly made. Some of Matthew's readers clearly knew of this conviction, well enough to recognize the merest hints. Others may not have learned of it at all, and they will not hear it fanfared in the gospel. Deep-set within this text, among its open claims and the progress to which it calls its readers, is the next insight for those readers to attain: that Jesus is the Wisdom of God. Then the first challenge of the gospel will yield up its secret at last. Who was this Jesus who could speak so freely of God's commands and of his own? *"You have heard that it was said to those of old, "You shall not kill." Well I, I say to you . . . "* No Moses had such authority and no king. Only an agent of God could speak with such power, an agent who shared with God in the Law's composition and who knew for himself the will and purpose that lay behind it. There is one such agent and one alone: the Wisdom of God:

"Come to me [says Wisdom in the poem of Sira's Son], you who desire me,
and eat your fill of my produce.
Those who eat me shall hunger for more,
and those who drink me will thirst for more."
Then come the crucial explanation:
All this [Sira's Son tells us] is the book of the order of the Most High God,
the law which Moses commanded us
as an inheritance for the congregations of Israel.
(WISDOM OF SIRA'S SON [BEN SIRA] 24.19–23)

The control over disclosure is in Jesus' hands, but its vehicle is here, in the reader's. The gospel itself is the means of unveiling. We will ask in our final chapter, what extraordinary authority, in Matthew's eyes, does this give to his text? What Jesus achieves in the story, Matthew's gospel is to achieve in his church. But if this is what Matthew expects his text to do, what must he believe his text to be? How can the words on his page affect their readers as Jesus had affected the pupils that were with him day by day? The presence of this text must become the "presence" of Jesus. This is the bravest and most remarkable use to which Matthew will put his story. John, as we shall see, has seen and explored the same possibility; so (with a remarkable difference) has Paul. When we have all three strategies before us we will see at last the true grandeur and effect of each.

"*And you,*" Jesus asked his pupils at the climactic midpoint of the gospel, "*who do you say I am?*"

> Simon Peter answered, "You are the Anointed," he said, "the son of the living God."

> "Blessed are you, Simon, son of Jonah:
> for flesh and blood have not unveiled this to you,
> but my father which is in heaven."
>
> (MATTHEW 16.16–17)

THE WARNING OF WISDOM

Over and over we have seen Matthew's fine sense of drama: a striking start to teaching, a flamboyant close. No wonder, then, that he rounds off his condemnation of the scribes and Pharisees with memorable power. We hear this condemnation, the "Woes," in Matthew's story of Jesus' last week in Jerusalem. His enemies are closing in. The "Woes" are set up to match the "Blessings" with which Matthew launched the teaching of Jesus. Their climax is to mirror that last and longest blessing:

> "Blessed are you when people revile you and persecute you
> and utter all kinds of evil against you falsely on my account.
> Rejoice and be glad, for your reward is great in heaven,
> for in the same way they persecuted the prophets who were before you."
>
> (MATTHEW 5.11–12)

To close off the "Woes," Matthew brings together four sayings. Luke's Jesus also warned the Jewish lawyers. They were implicated in the murder of the prophets of old. There was a saying in the collection shared by Matthew and Luke that only too vividly summed up their role: "*Therefore the Wisdom of God has said, 'I will send them prophets and missionaries, and some they will kill, others they will drive out . . .'*" (Luke 11.49). Matthew sees how powerful this saying could be at this climax to his Jesus' teaching. Before it he places a threat steeped in the Baptizer's language. Here is an echo from the gospel's opening scenes. We are coming full circle. As "Elijah" gives way to the Anointed, those warnings from the Baptizer should now become, if anything, more frightening than ever. To round off the whole block of teaching, Matthew draws another lament from the Collection of Sayings that he shares with Luke. Here is a symphonic close.

And that saying of Wisdom itself? Unlike Luke, Matthew does not relay it as another's prophecy or as the insight of an earlier sage. When Jesus speaks, Wisdom speaks; Wisdom's target is Jesus' target. "Wisdom" speaks of the guilt to be borne by *this generation* for all the innocent blood shed throughout history. Here is a sinister prelude to the cry that will echo round Jerusalem, *"His blood be on us and on our children."* Wisdom has offered herself to all those who seek her. The unveiling once confined to the innermost circle of Jesus' pupils is now available to all. So much greater is the guilt of those who turn it down. Wisdom holds an offer in one hand but a dire warning in the other.

> *"Snakes, generation of vipers, [says Jesus] how will you escape from the judgment of hell?*
>
> *"Look, therefore, I am sending you prophets and wise men and scribes. Some of them you will kill and crucify, and some of them you will whip in your synagogues and drive from city to city. So that all the just blood shed ever upon the earth will come upon you. In truth I tell you, all this will come upon this generation.*
>
> *"Jerusalem, Jerusalem, you who killed the prophets and stoned those sent to you, how often I have wanted to gather together your children as a bird gathers her chicks beneath her wings, but you would have none of it. Look, your house is left desolate. For I tell you, you will not see me from now on until you say, 'Blessed is he who comes in the name of the Lord.'"*
>
> *(MATTHEW 23.33–39)*

Future Glory, Present Death

"Blessed Is He Who Comes in the Name of the Lord"

> *"You will not see me from now on until you say, 'Blessed is he who comes in the name of the Lord.'"*
>
> *(MATTHEW 23.39)*

Matthew's crowds have said it already, when Jesus entered the holy city in triumph. So when will Jerusalem next ring to the cry? When the Son of Man returns in glory. In the last scenes before Jesus' arrest the gospel grows dark again. The Baptizer's threats were not empty. Matthew's Jesus, like Mark's, warns of terrors to come and of destruction over the world. At their end, we are told, the victorious general will arrive in triumph, to gather around himself those who have been loyal through the war. His birth was heralded by the portent of a star; his return will be accompanied by an unnatural darkness. Matthew leaves no doubt that the triumph will be the Son of Man's.

Vespasian had delegated the war's command to his son Titus, but a greater son is about to take command from a father more powerful still.

"And straight after the affliction of those days [said Jesus],
the sun will be darkened [as Isaiah said],
and the stars will fall from heaven.
And then will appear the sign of the Son of Man in heaven,
and then the nations of the earth will see
the Son of Man coming [as Daniel said] *on the clouds of heaven*
with power and great glory.
And he will send out his angels with the great call of a trumpet,
and they will gather together his chosen ones from one end of the heavens to the other."
(MATTHEW 24.29–31)

Here is danger for those who deny Jesus' call, who are not among the chosen. But danger, too, for those within the church. Into these last days before Jesus' death, Matthew collects a series of Jesus' own stories, each of them long and dramatic, with which to warn his own community of troubles and temptations to come. There is a special grandeur to this section. Gone are the short, sharp instructions and brisk examples; here are full, spacious images of the dutiful and the delinquent, the alert and the complacent, and finally of the rewards and punishments that they face. In every story emerge Matthew's care for his own church and the dangers that threaten it.

A householder, Jesus said, must travel abroad. He leaves one servant in charge of his other servants. The master will be long gone. The chief servant starts lording it over his colleagues. He takes to drinking. And when the master returns at last, unexpected and unannounced? That servant will be cut out of the household, and *he will weep and gnash his teeth* (Matthew 24.51). The servant grew used to his master's absence and from it took evil advantage. But what of those who rely, by contrast, on their master's quick return? Will such "servants" be ready and waiting when at last their lord is announced? Matthew is alert to every nuance. Jesus' delay has unsettled some in the church and discouraged others. The story of Jesus is about to reach its climax, in his death. Here, then, is the climax of his teaching—about his absence and triumphant return.

Ten bridesmaids, said Jesus, are on duty with oil lamps to light the bridegroom's way to the marriage night. Hours pass. The bridesmaids doze. In the depth of the night a voice cries out, "Here is the groom! Come out to meet him!" Five bridesmaids find their lamps empty of oil; they can provide no light. Off they rush to find a shop still open; by the time they return the bridegroom has arrived, the party has moved into the house, the doors are locked. *"So stay awake,"* said Jesus, *"for you do not know the day or the hour"* at which the Son of Man will come (Matthew 25.13).

Matthew's church knows about delay. That kingdom of heaven, still at hand, never quite arrived. It opened the church's leaders to such temptation, its members to such sagging, dissipated energy. So when would Jesus return? *"You do not know the day or the hour."* Matthew sets out to strengthen his church and to do so admits that the lord it serves can be a frightening figure. A merchant, he says, before he travels entrusts capital to his various servants to manage and invest. One gets five talents—as much money as a manual worker would earn in a lifetime—the next gets two, the last gets one. The merchant is gone a long time. When at last he returns, the first two servants give an account of their management: each has doubled his capital. But the third? *"Sir,"* he said, *"I knew you were a hard man, reaping where you had not sown and gathering where you had not scattered the seed. So I was afraid, and went and hid your talent in the ground. Here it is, yours back again."* The master is furious: Could the servant not at least have put the money in the bank to earn interest? He is thrown out into the outer darkness, *and there he will weep and gnash his teeth* (Matthew 25.30).

To complete the series and the whole of Jesus' public teaching, Matthew gives the fullest and most famous image we have of Jesus' return: the story of the sheep and the goats. It is as grand and expansive a story as any in the gospels. Matthew will encourage, urge, and if need be frighten his readers into the way of life called for by Jesus. Matthew leaves no doubt who will sit in judgment at this court: Here is the Son of Man in his due dignity at last. And the deeds themselves, for which "the just" will be rewarded? Allegiance to Jesus himself is not mentioned; no piety is called for. It is not even clear whether those whom the just have helped are members of the church or those at large who need help; "my brothers here" could refer, it seems, to either.

"When the Son of Man comes in his glory and all the angels with him, then he will sit upon his glorious throne. And all the nations will be gathered before him, and he will separate them from each other, as a shepherd separates the sheep from the goats, and will put the sheep on his right hand, and the goats on his left. Then the king will say to those on his right, 'Come, you who have my father's praise, and inherit the kingdom which has been prepared for you ever since the world began.

For I was hungry and you gave me to eat, I was thirsty and you gave me to drink,
I was a stranger and you welcomed me, I was naked and you clothed me,
I was sick and you looked after me, I was in prison and you came to me.'

Then the just will answer him, 'Sir, when did we see you hungry and fed you, or thirsty and we gave you to drink? When did we see you a stranger and welcomed you, or naked and we clothed you? When did we see you sick or in prison and we came to you?' And the king will answer, 'In truth I tell you, to the extent that you did these things to one of the least of my brothers here, you did it to me.' Then he shall say to those on his left: 'Away from me, you who are cursed, off to the fire burning for all aeons, the fire prepared for the devil and his angels.

For I was hungry and you gave me nothing to eat, I was thirsty and you gave me nothing to drink,

*I was a stranger and you did not welcome me, I was naked and you did not clothe me,
I was sick and in prison and you did not come to me.'*

*Then they will answer him, 'Sir, when did we see you hungry or thirsty or a
stranger or naked or ill or in prison and we did not take care of you?' Then he will
answer them, 'In truth I tell you, to the extent that you did not do these things to one
of the least of these, you did not do it to me.' And they will depart to punishment for
all aeons, but the just into the new aeon's life."*

(MATTHEW 25.31–46)

•

Those who accepted Matthew's invitation at the start now have his Jesus' promise
at the end: Jews and gentiles alike, those with loyalties to the church already and those
who are still wondering, are all free to recognize themselves and their attitudes in the
"Blessings" and in this statement of rewards. For they are invited to recognize Jesus
himself in those whom they help. This is an unveiling like no other. Their own actions
are now revealed for what they really are and have been all along. Action for the hum-
blest of their neighbors is action for the king of all humanity; the world of appearances
is not the "real" world at all. Matthew interprets every act of kindness as a kindness to
Jesus and so claims that any such act draws its actor into the orbit and embrace of the
church.

Or does he? Jesus' parable makes no obvious reference to piety, to faith in Jesus or
to the community of his followers. In the same way, almost all of Jesus' opening
"Blessings" could be read without reference to himself. Only in the last had Matthew's
Jesus turned the spotlight on his cause:

*"Blessed are you when people revile you and persecute you
and utter all kinds of evil against you falsely on my account."*

(MATTHEW 5.11)

Who, then, are the *brothers* of Jesus in whose service the "sheep" will earn their
reward? Matthew's community and his perspective both may have been more closed
than we would like to imagine. But Matthew's strategy remains as careful as ever: It is
for his readers to discover what exactly are the attitudes that this Jesus demands and
the deeds for which he promises reward.

God's final judgment became a classic theme for disclosure to privileged seers. For
no one on earth could know about it; any image with any authority must be derived
from its "sight" in heaven and its interpretation by an angel guide. But Jesus needs no
special vision to know of these things; his pupils need no intermediary to understand
them. The image of the animals is quickly left behind and the course of judgment
unambiguously disclosed. The basis for God's verdict is behavior whose real character
no one before could ever have known. The subject of disclosure is the character of life
on earth, not of one last judgment alone.

Matthew knows well the place and power of such unveiling. He had asked, *"Who do you say I am?"* Only the "king" himself could speak with such knowledge of the kingdom.

"Have Nothing to Do with That Just Man"

Such glory was to come, but not yet. Arrested, tried, condemned: The landscape of Matthew's gospel grows ever darker. Mark told a bleak story of Jesus' trial and death; Matthew's is, if anything, even more stark. The blame for Jesus' death must lie with Jerusalem's high priests, elders, and crowd. Judas tries to undo his treachery; he returns to the authorities, gives back their bribe, and declares Jesus innocent. *"What is that to us?"* they reply. *"That's your business"* (Matthew 27.3–4). Judas hangs himself in despair. The authorities, unmoved, use their money to buy the Potter's Field as a burial ground and turn back to their assault on Jesus. Pilate, too, finds Jesus without guilt. His wife confirms: *"You should have nothing to do with that just man"* (Matthew 27.19). She has had nightmares warning of his innocence. The sign is enough for Pilate, but nothing he says will dissuade the crowd from their aim: *"What shall I do with Jesus, the so-called Anointed?"* *"Let him be crucified"* *"Why? What wrong has he done?"* But louder and louder comes the reply, *"Let him be crucified."* Matthew's Pilate is not to bear the blame: *Pilate saw that this was not helping; a riot was starting. He took water and washed his hands in front of the crowd and said, "I am innocent of this man's blood. You, you see to it"* (Matthew 27.22–24).

So be it. Judas could not bear the responsibility of what he had done; he is driven to suicide. Pilate shirks the responsibility; he washes his hands of the whole business and abdicates his power to the Jews. Here Matthew will have responsibility remain: *"His blood be on us and on our children."*

The Old Order is never far from Matthew's mind. The prophet Jeremiah had warned of Jerusalem's coming desolation. He used potters and their craft to illustrate how God shapes and reshapes his agents and his own people Israel. Jeremiah used to act out the horrors that he foretold: He took the elders and priests to the Potsherd Gate and broke a pot there to show how easily Jerusalem would be destroyed (Jeremiah 18.1, 19.1). Jeremiah was hounded by the authorities; they sought to have him put to death.

"Know for certain," said Jeremiah, *"that if you put me to death, you will bring innocent blood upon yourselves and upon this city and all who live here, for in truth God sent me to you to speak all these words."* Jeremiah's audience was swayed, but not Jesus'. *Then* in Jeremiah's story *the princes and all the people said to the priests, "This man does not deserve the sentence of death, for he has spoken to us in the name of God"* (Jeremiah 26.15). This "fulfillment" of an ancient act is the darkest of all. Jeremiah offered only despair for Jerusalem and was saved. Jesus is Jerusalem's long-promised hope, made real at last, and is put to death.

From noon until three o'clock there was darkness over the whole earth. Matthew's Jesus died with the same words on his lips as Mark's: *"My God, my God, why have you deserted me?"* Portents followed: *And look, the veil of the temple was torn in two from top to bottom, and the earth shook and the rocks were split. And the tombs were opened and many bodies were raised of God's heroes who slept, and coming out from the tombs after his own rising they came into the holy city and appeared to many* (Matthew 27.46, 51–52).

A star when the child is born, darkness and strange portents at the same man's death, and the sun darkened and stars falling when the Son of Man returns. There is no missing this figure. All creation testifies to his importance. And at the very moment of his death we are given a hint of things to come. The prophet Ezekiel had a vision of bones, dry bones gradually given flesh again, eventually given life. The bones were Israel, a nation that must be brought to life by God's and the prophet's word:

I will open your tombs, says the Lord,
and I will bring you up out of your tombs,
and I will lead you into the land of Israel.
And I shall put my Breath within you,
and you shall live.

(EZEKIEL 37.12, 14)

From Matthew to Luke

"How Long, O Lord, How Long?"

We have encountered "Baruch" before. He started his lament, so the story runs, just before Jerusalem was captured in 587 B.C.E. "Baruch" spoke to God of its threatened destruction:

> "If you destroy your city and deliver up your country to those who hate us, how will the name of Israel be mentioned again? Or how shall we speak again about your glorious deeds? To whom will your Law be explained? Or will the universe return to its nature and the world go back to its original silence? And will the whole company of humans be taken away and the nature of humankind never be mentioned again? Where is all that which you said to Moses about us?"

> "Do you think," replied God, "that *this* is the city of which I said, *On the palms of my hands I have carved you?* No, that is not the building which is in your midst now; it is that which will be revealed, with me, that was already prepared from the moment that I decided to create Paradise. And I showed it to Adam before he did wrong. But when he broke the commandment, it was taken away from him—as also Paradise. After this I showed it to Moses on Mount Sinai when I showed him the likeness of the Shelter and all its vessels. And look, now it is preserved with me—as also Paradise."

"Baruch" was swept up into the air above Jerusalem and saw four angels with flaming torches in their hands. And a fifth came down from heaven into the Holy of Holies and took out the sacred vessels: the veil, the tablets of the Law, the priests' vestments, and the altar of incense. And he cried out to the earth,

"Earth, earth, earth, hear the word of the mighty God,
and receive the things which I commit to you,
and guard them until the last time, so that strangers may not get possession of them.
For the time has come when Jerusalem will be delivered up for a time,
until the moment when it will be restored forever."

Here an "unveiling" takes vivid form: "Baruch" sees the walls' "real" destruction by the angels; no enemy could capture the holy city while it was under God's protection. The angel said to his four companions, "Now destroy the walls, throw them down to their foundations, so that the enemies do not boast and say, 'We have overthrown the wall of Jerusalem and have burned down the place of the mighty God.' "

Titus would find enough left in the Temple to carry in triumph through the streets of Rome: the candelabra, golden table, and copy of the Law. The Temple was famous for containing no image of God, and the tablets' disappearance may well have dated from the Babylonians' earlier capture of the city. "Baruch" could claim they had been protected by the angels in 587 B.C.E. Vespasian, by contrast, could play on this almost empty Temple: on the atheism of a cult that had no image of its own god and that denied the deity of all others. His war then became a victory on the gods' behalf against the godless. To burn down the temple of a famous cult would have been to start his reign with the worst of omens; to restore "the peace of the gods" such as Vespasian proclaimed was to do a service to the whole empire and all its peoples.

And when would the Temple's restoration come? Hopes that Vespasian or Titus might rebuild it were reasonable and slow to fade; the empire often rebuilt temples out of respect for still-powerful gods and their devotees. Josephus in the late 70s C.E. mounts a plea, only thinly disguised, for the restoration of the building and its cult. It is, at our distance, a sad tribute to his conflicting loyalties and needs. He tells at length of Titus's attempts to save the Temple and of his return to lament the city's destruction. The victor, he insists, wished the cult no harm. He tells, too, but far more briefly, of Titus's parties for another prince's birthday and the emperor's: twenty-five hundred Jews killed by animals or burned to death at the first carnival, more at the second. In his progression through Syria the victorious general, to reenact Jerusalem's fall, had his prisoners killed as their compatriots had been killed at the time.

Not all Josephus's praise could warm his benefactors to the Temple. Their pride and propaganda were too tightly bound to its destruction. Why should the Roman senate accept this upstart general as their emperor? Because he had won a great war; here was the key to power in Rome. In July 69 Vespasian had been acclaimed emperor by his troops in Egypt. He was on his way to Rome. He needed the glorious conquest of a foreign power, and he needed it soon.

Vespasian's son Titus had been left in command outside Jerusalem. He closed in. The siege would have succeeded in time, but time was not on Vespasian's side.

Thousands of Roman soldiers were killed in the assault. By late September Jerusalem had fallen, and as such a victory demanded, the enemies, their city, and their Temple were utterly destroyed.

The war in Israel was hardly the war the new dynasty needed; its generals were suppressing a revolt, not making a conquest. But with skill and an official triumph it could be shown as the defeat of a dangerous foreign power. The generals needed the victory, their coins proclaimed it, and a duly grateful Rome, ignoring the past hundred years of Roman rule, thanked them with an arch, presented "From the Senate and people of Judaea's Rome to the Emperor Titus Caesar Augustus: by the instruction and advice of his father he tamed the people of the Jews; and the city of Jerusalem, sought in vain by all rulers, kings, and people before him or left untested, he destroyed."

The Temple would not be rebuilt; God's reign would not be realized on earth. "Baruch" must wait for that Temple stored in heaven. And the most famous prayer to reach us from Matthew's church must echo, century after century, through the church to which he helped give birth. After 1,900 years the church's hopes have settled; its expectations are less febrile now. But in the "Our Father" the voice of urgency still presses on the reader. First come three pleas for God to disclose his glory on earth by entering at last into the reign that is forever at hand, never quite in place. Then four pleas for those who use the prayer, chiefly for their protection when the crises loom through which the kingdom will break in upon the world.

For the devil will be let loose to test and tempt and persecute God's people; then will come God's judgment and his reign. No one who would soon be standing before God's judgment would dare to have outstanding debts to God; no one could face with confidence the testing to which God would expose the world before taking up his reign; no one could escape the evil one without God's help. Here is a prayer for those hoping and fearing for history's final fulfillment, who know the kingdom is at hand and need the blessing of that kingdom's food to see them safely to its coming.

Our father, the father in heaven,
make known the glory of your name.
May your kingdom come.
May your will be done—as in heaven, so on earth.

Our bread, the bread of the coming aeon, give us today.
And remit us our debts,
as we ourselves have remitted the debts owed to us.
And do not bring us into the time of testing;
but rescue us from the evil one.

(MATTHEW 6.9–13)

Paul: "Least of the Missionaries"?

We are about to turn from Matthew, apparent opponent of Paul, to Luke, said to be Paul's pupil. Both are writing some decades after Paul, and it is no longer clear how closely their thought can be linked to his. But the divisions with which they must live are divisions that Paul knew well and that his preaching had helped to bring about. In Paul's teaching on the Law we find some of the most careful, delicate instruction that the New Order has to offer on a theme that dominated the young church throughout its crucial, formative years. But in *The Four Witnesses* we owe Paul more than his insights into the Law. We owe him the clue that in our closing pages will unlock the gospels' mystery. For Paul came to an understanding of his own work and person that illumines the function that our witnesses intended for their work in turn. Paul was to function in his churches as the representation of the Jesus he proclaims; the gospels were to function in their churches as the presence of Jesus had functioned within their stories.

The Anointed, writes Paul, *is the conclusion of the Law* (Romans 10.4). Does Paul, then, believe the Law to have been superseded? In this case his adherents indeed are among those whom Matthew so carefully and steadily opposes. Or has the Law, for Paul, been brought at last, active and in force, to the fruition for which God had always intended it?

On the road to Damascus the glorified Jesus appeared to Paul in a dazzling vision. We will hear more of this event and its aftermath. The Paul that had been the church's fiercest enemy became as a result its most famous missionary. The vision's inner light was as important as the outer. In a letter to the church in Corinth Paul himself interprets what he really saw. He thinks back to the first words of the Old Order, to the light that shone when God spoke the words with which he launched creation: *In the beginning,* we read in the Old Order,

> *God created the heavens and the earth. And the earth was wildness and waste, and darkness was over the deep. And an almighty wind moved over the waters. And God said, "Let there be light."*
>
> *(BEGINNING [GENESIS] 1.1)*

Paul echoes those numinous words. He writes to the Corinthians, *The God who said "Light shall shine out of darkness" is the one who shone in our hearts, to bring about enlightenment, the knowledge of the glory of God in the face of Jesus Anointed* (2 Corinthians 4.6). To have seen Jesus on the way to Damascus is to have had the heart illumined by the light that blazed at creation. This Jesus who shone with that blaze must in turn have authority over all that has been created ever since. Anything, then, that restricted the gospel's offer, in particular to the Jews alone, could no longer be sustained in its old form. In Jesus not just the Jews but all nations, all *creation* was at stake.

Creation's eager longing, writes Paul to the Romans, *is looking out for the children of God to be disclosed. . . . Up until now the whole of creation has been groaning together in one great act of giving birth—and still is* (Romans 8.19). All creation is yearning; all the gentiles must hear the gospel. Here is the scope of Paul's mission in Luke's panorama of the early church.

As for Paul, so for his converts: Words must give way to dazzled contemplation. The missionary himself has an extraordinary role to fulfill. Paul writes of his conversion in terms that recall God's summons to his prophets in the Old Order. God told Jeremiah, *"Before I formed you in the womb I knew you, and before you were born I made you holy, I appointed you a prophet to the gentiles"* (Jeremiah 1.5). Isaiah told of a Servant of God who could say,

> *"Listen to me, coastlands,*
> *pay attention, you gentiles.*
> *God called me from the womb,*
> *from my mother's body he named my name.*
> *And now God says, who formed me from the womb to be his witness,*
> *to bring Israel back to him:*
> *"It is too light a task that you should be my servant*
> *to raise up the tribes of Israel.*
> *I will give you as a light to the nations,*
> *that my salvation may reach to the end of the earth."*
>
> *(ISAIAH 49.1, 5, 6)*

When we ask after Paul's understanding of his own conversion, we should think of a prophetic call from the same God who called the prophets of old and to the same mission. *The God who had set me apart,* writes Paul, *from my mother's womb and had called me through his free love, he was pleased to unveil his son in me, so that I might preach him among the gentiles* (Galatians 1.15). A striking turn of phrase lurks here. Almost all translations render the crucial phrase, "to unveil his son *to me.* "Paul, then, speaks of his experience on the road to Damascus. The terms that Paul uses can (just) bear this meaning, but they are, for any normal reader, the natural and simple Greek with which to say, "to unveil his son *in me.* "But what, then, is Paul claiming?

We must return to the letter at which we have already glanced, known to us as his Second Letter to the Corinthians. The Corinthians are disappointed and confused. Paul has promised over and over to revisit them and never reappears. Even this letter, delivered by his helpers, is only a substitute for his own expected presence. The church—his own foundation—suspects that he is easily swayed. He is said to trim his sails; is he really as devoted to the Corinthians as he has claimed? Confidence in Paul, we shall find, is confidence in his gospel, in a connection far more direct than at our distance we can easily see. And in turn, distrust of Paul soon leads to distrust of the gospel he proclaims.

Paul compares himself with Moses, greatest prophet of God's Old Order. Moses had pleaded with God not to commission him for his task: *"Lord, I am not adequate, neither of old nor since you have started to speak to [me] your servant. For I stutter and am slow of speech"* (Escape [Exodus] 4.10). Paul describes his own commission; *and for this,* he comments, *who is adequate?* (2 Corinthians 2.17). The comparison is threaded through Paul's letters. Moses was commissioned by God; so, Paul insists, was he. Moses was later said to have suffered from leprosy; Paul, too, is weak and has borne a "scourge" in his flesh. Moses offered to bear the whole punishment that the Jews deserved; Paul offers to be accursed if it will bring his compatriots to faith in Jesus (Escape [Exodus] 32.32, Romans 9.3).

All the more striking, then, is the contrast that Paul draws between himself and Moses in this letter to Corinth. That Old Order, says Paul, was written on Moses' tablets of stone; the New Order is written on the hearts of believers:

Look, the days are coming [said God through the prophet Jeremiah],
when I will make a New Order with Israel,
not like the Order which I made with their forebears,
when I took them out of Egypt, my Order which they broke.
But this is the Order which I will make with Israel after those days, says the Lord:
I will put my Law within them,
and I will write it on their hearts;
and I will be their God, and they shall be my people.

(*JEREMIAH 31.31–33*)

When Moses came down from Mount Sinai, we are told in the Escape (Exodus), his face shone. So, too, for the rest of the Jews' journey in the desert; whenever Moses came out of the Shelter of Meeting built for his continued encounters with God, his face shone. The people's other leaders would turn to Moses. With his face exposed he would relay the commands he had been given and would then veil it until he went once more into this special shelter that only he and Joshua could enter.

Such imagery is strange to us now. But we do well to bear with this language. It was centrally important to Paul, to his experience on the way to Damascus and to the understanding he reached of that awesome drama. It underlies much that he wrote to the Corinthians. And if we are to speak at all of our openness to "heavenly" truths and of the different access that different people might have to them, then we will want some language in which to speak of their reception, effect, and transmission to others. The language of light may seem crude to us. But generations have found it a valuable vehicle for saying what they feel impelled to say, and it is not clear that any more powerful or more appropriate imagery is to be found.

Let us follow Paul along his line of thought in this letter to the Corinthians. He takes up the theme of that veil that covered the face of Moses. The glory of Moses' Order, Paul claims, was fading; so in turn was the glory on Moses' face. Moses, then, veiled his face to hide not the glory itself, but the fact of its fading away. But the Order served by Paul is eternal; its glory is unfading, and any glory that it gives to its prophet or people will be unfading as well. Paul uses the veil's motif in many ways: of the veil on Moses' face and a veil on the Jews' hearts; of the veil removed when Moses turned to the Lord and a veil removed from the face of Paul's own people. Here is a paraphrase of the dense, crucial passage:

> *Right up to the present day, when the Law of Moses is read, a veil lies on their hearts. "But when he turns to the Lord* [Paul is here paraphrasing the Escape], *the veil is removed." Now "the Lord" here is the Breath of God; and where there is the Breath of the Lord, there is freedom. And we—all of us—with unveiled face gaze on and reflect the glory of the Lord and so are being transformed into the likeness we gaze on, from glory into glory, just as from "the Lord" we turn to, the Breath of God.*
> (2 CORINTHIANS 3.14–18)

But what is the role of Paul himself? He is the Moses of this New Order. His is the face, first and foremost, that should shine. (The oldest of our manuscripts omits the words *all of us* in that last sentence. In one tradition it may well have been thought that Paul alone gazed on the glory and Paul's transformation alone is that being described.) Now Paul recalls Moses: *"When he turns to the Lord, the veil is removed."* We have heard in the Escape how Moses went into the shelter and spoke with the Lord. But Paul's paraphrase speaks of *turning to the Lord.* It is the leaders of the people, in the Escape (Exodus), who *turned to Moses* and saw his face aglow. There is room for the most solemn ambiguity here. The comparison's start is striking but easily envisaged: It was upon Moses that the people of the Old Order gazed and upon Paul that the Corinthians can gaze now; the glory on Moses' face faded, the glory that the New Order gives Paul is unfading. So far, so good. But when the Corinthians are to turn to the Lord as Paul's Moses had done, where should they look? As the Corinthians now take on the role of Moses, so Paul takes on the role of the Lord. What the Corinthians need for their own transformation from glory to glory is before them in Paul himself; here in his own person, illumined by the glory seen on the way to Damascus, is the representation of the glory of "the Lord."

There is a terrible danger here, that of idolatry. Unless care is taken, the Corinthians could come to worship Paul himself. Paul knows the danger well. He rounds off the section with a most emphatic warning: *If our gospel is veiled at all, it is veiled among those on their way to destruction, among whom the god of this aeon has blinded the thoughts of the faithless, to prevent them seeing the light of the gospel of the glory of the Anointed, who is the likeness of God.* Paul has said enough for his argument but now sounds a variation on the same theme, this time with an eye on the danger to which that argument has given room: *For we do not proclaim ourselves but Jesus Anointed as Lord, and ourselves as your servants on Jesus' account. For the God who said "Light shall shine out of darkness" is the one who shone in our hearts, to bring about enlightenment, the*

knowledge of the glory of God in the face of Jesus Anointed (2 Corinthians 4.5–6).
Idolatry must be prevented, but the conditions cannot be avoided that could—by
error—give it rise. *God was pleased to unveil his son in me, so that I might preach him
among the gentiles.*

In Paul's self-understanding lies a central clue to the puzzle that confronts us: why
we have four such different accounts of Jesus' life. It was crucial for our witnesses, as
for Paul, to re-present the person of Jesus. Paul had himself to offer; our writers had
their texts. The solution to our quest lies not in the stories that our evangelists tell but
in the functions that the stories are intended to perform.

We have watched Matthew tread with great care through the conflicts that afflicted his
community. Chief among his concerns was Jesus' authority: What gave Jesus the right
to speak as he did? In what relation did his teaching stand to the Jewish Law? And how
in turn did his community stand to the ancestral faith of Judaism? Lineage is important
for Matthew. The gospel starts with Jesus' family tree; he must be firmly placed in
descent from Abraham and David. But it is not upon lineage that those should rely who
hear the Baptizer or Jesus himself and who wonder how to respond. *"Do not expect to
say among yourselves,"* says Matthew's Baptizer, *"that we have Abraham as our father. For
I tell you, God can raise up children for Abraham from these stones"* (Matthew 3.8).

Paul had already confronted such questions in terms and with a solution all his own
but with an effect far closer to Matthew's than we might expect. *I would have you
know,* he writes to the Galatians, *of the gospel that I preach, that it is not a gospel defined
by human standards: for I did not receive it from any human nor was I taught it, but
through the unveiling of Jesus Anointed* (Galatians 1.11–12). Paul reminds them how he
had been zealous beyond all his contemporaries in defense of their ancestral traditions.
But God was pleased to unveil his son in Paul—and all was changed.

Why is Paul so insistent here that he received his gospel directly from God? His
opponents are encouraging his converts to take up or return to obedience of the Law.
Have these adversaries accused Paul of peddling a gospel based on human values and
drawn from merely human sources? Far from it. Paul's opponents expect him to base
his claims on just such a foundation as they claim for their own: loyalty to and
endorsement from a self-legitimating tradition. Such a missionary should not be rely-
ing on a direct disclosure from God but on his training and validation by the
guardians of ancestral tradition. That Paul should have been a missionary through
human instruction is not a charge against him, it is the condition upon which his
preaching, for his opponents, is legitimated or authorized at all.

Paul's opponents claim him as one of their own. And so they deny him his independence; if he deviates from Jerusalem's gospel, the authority of the Jerusalem church
will override his own. But that is precisely because, in the opposition's understanding,
those leaders in Jerusalem are the source of Paul's gospel and of his authority to preach
it. They do not bring this dependence against Paul as a weakness. On the contrary, his
preaching is legitimated only and precisely by his and his teaching's place in the tradi-

tion. But Paul responds: Neither he nor his church is bound by the conditions of transmission and allegiance on which the opponents rely.

For Paul, as we have seen, has broken with the Jerusalem church. The dispute in Antioch has left him on his own. He must define himself and his authority anew and with it must define afresh the standing of the churches that he has founded and over which he claims authority still. Paul is not introducing his church into a clear ancestral community, defined for generations; neither is he himself an authorized teacher of that community. His relation to Jerusalem is transformed; so in turn is his relation to his churches. He is now a prophet in the tradition of Isaiah and Jeremiah, the prophet of God's new disclosure, not a teacher of the old. Paul is redefining the lineage of proclamation and by doing so is rewriting as well the lineage of God's people. He now claims that his church's members are the direct children of God, adopted by God himself, unmediated by tradition or law or human agency. He does not let this claim foreclose the claim that they are Abraham's children, too; it interprets that old claim and fulfills it. The parallelism between Paul and his churches is crucial: If he is bound to the authorized tradition, then he cannot preach freedom from it to them, and if they are bound to it, how can he be free?

Paul is not defending his legitimacy or authority as his detractors would have expected. He is changing the paradigm. His opponents are challenging his institutional standing; he is denying that he has one. They want to know his place in a familiar and tested structure of legitimation; he grounds his gospel in a disclosure direct from God. Paul drives his claim further: He is in immediate relation to God and is independent of human authority, so the Galatians will be as well. Paul was made a missionary directly by God; they in turn will inherit the promise made to Abraham's offspring directly from God. They will then be under no human authority but his own; his opponents will have no hold over them.

Paul must separate himself from the forms of authority familiar to Judaism. But he must also give his church an identity that will offer his own converts an adoption into the valued lineage that his opponents offer, into the lineage of Abraham. Family descent, then, dominates the Letter to the Galatians. Now Paul insists that as a missionary he is not the latecomer that his biography might suggest. For him, as for God's plan of salvation as a whole and for the Galatians themselves, there is a due time. As Paul had been formed in the womb into his mother's son, so, too, had he been formed into the likeness of God's. Gestation and birth into his own life and into Jesus' are presented in parallel.

Paul was prepared from his mother's womb to be the disclosure of God's son. And in turn, the birth of that son makes possible the "sonship" of all Paul's readers. A climactic passage sounds the refrain:

When there came the fullness of time, God sent out his son,
born from a woman,
born under the Law,
so that he might buy the freedom

of those under the Law,
so that we might receive adoption as his sons:
for inasmuch as you are sons, God sent out the Breath of his son into our hearts.
(GALATIANS 4.4–6)

The birth from a woman of God's son; the preparation of that son's disclosure in the womb that was carrying Paul; and finally, in the most striking image of all, Paul himself as the Galatians' own mother: *My children, whom I am bearing still until the Anointed is formed in you* (Galatians 4.19). In terms of pregnancy and parturition together, he suffers the pangs of rebearing those, already born into their Christian life, whose gestation is not yet complete. As he was molded in his mother's womb to disclose Christ, so in turn the Galatians are formed in his "womb" into the likeness of Christ. There is, then, no mediating tradition to which he or they are accountable. Their call was as unmediated as Paul's own. His gestation into the disclosure of Christ was in his mother's womb; so is their gestation in the "womb" of Paul. The Galatians' adoption, then, as children of God is as direct as Paul's physical sonship of his mother and as Jesus' sonship of his mother in turn. This gestation allows no room for tradition or its teachers. It admits only the shortest lineage: God's promise for the offspring of Abraham is fulfilled in the person of Jesus and in those who are growing into his likeness. Paul himself is not the mediator of a faith brought to the Galatians from without; he is the mother of their new life.

Galatia was perhaps a special case. Paul's opponents appealed to lineage and to tradition; Paul responded by redefining both. But it is not to the Galatians alone that Paul speaks in these terms. *We were as gentle as children in the midst of you,* he writes to the Thessalonians, *as a nurse might cherish her own children* (1 Thessalonians 2.7).

We have heard how Paul understands himself; now we see how he understands his converts. He has made clear what they must undergo and what they need from their missionary if they are to undergo it successfully. We shall encounter similar language once more, when we survey the gospel of John. There, too, a birth must be undergone, and John knows as well as Paul that its process is not always so straightforward or its effect so complete as a missionary or writer might want to believe.

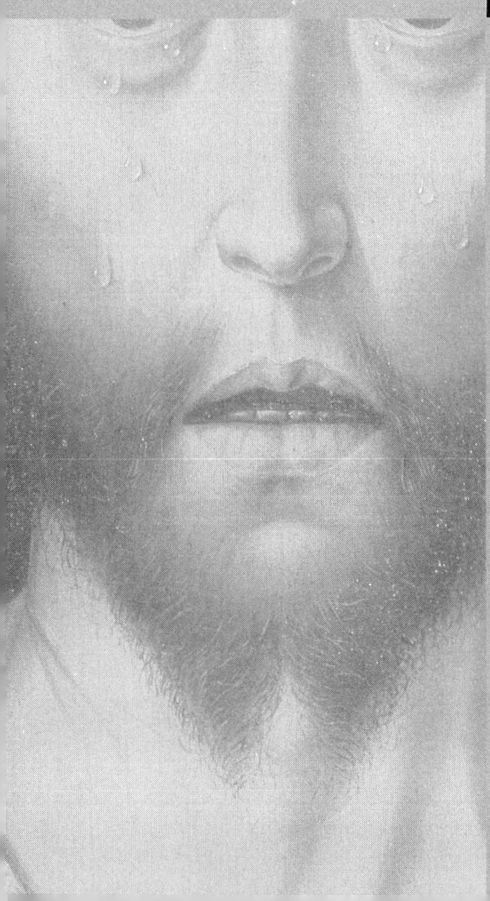

BOOK III

Luke's Story

Introduction to Luke

Mark looked to Jesus for victory, Matthew for instruction. Luke sees in Jesus an insuperable and infinitely attractive example. It can hardly be coincidence that in Luke's testimony, above all, the character of our witness and his subject coincide. Over and over the words and actions that Luke records of Jesus are matched by Luke's own comments, by his take on the story. Has Luke molded his Jesus to match his own ideals, which he longed for Jesus to have had? A good many people, after all, have done as much. Or had Luke's own ideals long since grown to match those of a Jesus already portrayed, perhaps, in this way in the stories to which Luke alone of our four writers had access? We can never know. But Luke himself is a warmhearted observer, always alert to those around Jesus; so is that Jesus himself. The convergence of such a chronicler and his hero makes Luke's account our most appealing gospel. Luke's Jesus can be frightening and uncompromising, but always he is a figure that we would want to meet and hear and get to know.

Luke, we read in the messages at the end of one Pauline letter, *the much-loved physician, sends his greetings* (Colossians 4.14). We cannot now know whether our gospel and the Mission (Acts) were written by this Luke. We hear of him again as Paul's companion: *Luke alone is with me* (2 Timothy 4.10). There are passages in the Mission that are written in the first person plural, as if by someone who had shared Paul's journeys: *On the first day of the week,* for example, *we met for the breaking of bread together. . .* (Mission [Acts] 20.7). It would be easy to think of these as entries in a diary incorporated, perhaps many years later, into the same writer's chronicle. Of course, we could just as easily turn the evidence around and ask if the later church linked these diary entries with Paul's sole companion, ascribed to him this two-part work, and so won for this whole history of the church the authority of Paul. Behind Mark's gospel, Peter; behind Luke's, Paul. Here is just such standing as the church sought for its most important texts.

This does not quite exhaust the clues, faint though they are, that might fill out our knowledge of the gospel's origin. The Mission shows striking knowledge of the church in Antioch. As we have seen, Matthew probably wrote there, for those in turmoil at the deepening gulf between church and synagogues. Did Luke, in this same great city, write for those who knew of the split, who wondered how it had been possible and why it had been necessary? Luke is writing for gentiles, and for important figures among them. *Your Excellency Theophilus,* he writes; here is a title that his Paul will use in the Mission itself to address the Roman governor before whom he is on trial.

It is not surprising, then, that *Luke* is a Greek version of a Latin name. Luke may still have been Jewish himself, of course; a former slave, who could have been his master's highly educated secretary, might well have adopted his gentile master's name. But whether Jewish himself or gentile, Luke inhabits the gentile world and knows it well. He is attuned to its culture, sensibilities, and expectations and is perhaps the New Order's most accessible and gracious envoy to those, nowadays the vast majority of its readers, who are heirs of that gentile world and its values.

Luke's story spans sixty tumultuous years, and he has a cast to match. Of all our gospels, Luke's reads most like a chronicle, a straightforward narrative whose stories construct a historical world such as we ourselves inhabit. There is, as we shall see, more to this narrative than meets the eye, but Luke clearly wants to set his story, and so its church, within the respected mainstream of Greek culture. So he wrote in stylish Greek, under His Excellency's patronage, a sustained and enthralling narrative such as graced the libraries of the empire's elite. We shall stand back at moments in the following chapters and look around at the world for which Luke wrote. Thoughtful, educated people had sharp questions to ask. "New" religions were deeply suspect; the church had abandoned its roots in that ancient Judaism of which the whole empire knew; Jesus' followers were known for their fierce language of freedom and a world turned upside down. Here, it might seem, was a new sect to be ignored if it was bound to wither away and to be suppressed if it was not. Beneath Luke's gracious writing lies an urgent need: to reassure readers such as Theophilus that this Jesus and his followers were no threat to Rome. In this text lies an invitation as well—for Theophilus to start for himself the never-ending journey of which the story tells.

At the end of these chapters we will look back on Theophilus and his world. We will see how Roman power responded to the church's claims, how easily its authorities could sweep the church's adherents away, and how angry those remained who saw in Jesus' promised reign the end of this arrogant, idolatrous empire.

Our Luke sounds by contrast so complaisant, so urbane. Has he lost the hard edge of Mark and Matthew's resolute vision? Far from it. Luke calls attention to the most inflammatory language of the early church—and transforms it. His Jesus is no threat to Rome but brings a revolution nonetheless. Using terms and style and structure molded to his readers' sensibilities, Luke undertakes the central task that he has inherited from Mark: to unveil the truth about their enigmatic Jesus. The result is extraordinary. Luke's reader is not invited to observe this story, to sit back and enjoy its adventure as a novel's. Journeys are under way: Jesus' journey from Galilee to Jerusalem; Paul's from Jerusalem to city after city of the eastern empire; and finally, the reader's own. Here for the reader is a journey into understanding, commitment—and the strange "revolution" that Luke's Jesus brings.

CHAPTER 7

The Birth of the Church

Telling the Story

"Your Excellency Theophilus"

Luke opens his gospel, as we have noted, with the most elegant sentence in the New Order: *Inasmuch as many have set their hands to ordering a narrative of the matters brought to their fulfillment among us, just as those have handed them down who were from the beginning eyewitnesses and ministers of the word, so I have decided in my turn, having followed the whole story from the outset accurately and in the right order to write to you, Theophilus, so that Your Excellency may learn, of the teachings about which you have been informed, that they are well founded* (Luke 1.1–4).

From Matthew to Luke, we have moved to a different world. This gracious sentence is carefully suited to readers of a particular taste and dignity. In *Your Excellency Theophilus* Luke may have addressed an individual, perhaps even his own patron; or he may have evoked, in a single term, the sort of addressee that Luke would like all his readers, whether so important themselves or not, to think he had in mind. Here is a text apparently addressed in person to a high official and suited to his rank; such a recipient entitled the gospel to the respectful attention of all who read or heard it, high or low.

As Luke opens the gospel with one such preface, so he launches the Mission (Acts) with another. This time he lets his opening sentence merge into the story itself:

The first book, Theophilus, I wrote about everything that Jesus began to do and to teach, up to the day on which, when he had given his instruction to the missionaries through the Breath of God whom he had chosen, he was taken up. Missionaries, that is, to whom he actually showed himself alive after his suffering in many forms of evidence: he was seen by them for forty days and told them the things about the kingdom of God. And as he was at table together with them he ordered them not to leave Jerusalem but to wait for the promised gift of the father "which you have heard me speak of, that the Baptizer baptized with water, but you will be baptized in the Breath, the Breath of God, and not many days from now."

(MISSION [ACTS] 1.1–5)

Did Luke always intend to compose this two-tier work? Its two halves, as they now stand, can seem oddly distinct from each other. They have different styles and themes; these match, as we shall see, their different functions. But they certainly share a structure. Luke's first plan may have been to write (a version of) just one of these two halves that we have now. If so, he kept its structure carefully before him when he turned to the work's expansion. He has not just bolted two separable books together; we shall see how he omits some details from the gospel that he then uses—to dramatic effect—in the Mission. We shall keep our eye, then, on the work's two halves together; their sum is greater than their parts.

So what clues does Luke give us to the circumstances of his Theophilus as "God-loving"? In these chapters we will treat this addressee as an individual, as the particular reader that Luke has in mind. This Theophilus has certainly heard of Jesus and his followers; he may even have had formal instruction in the church's faith. Is he already a committed member of the church? Or is he still an inquirer, looking as much for reassurance as for information? For he must be shown how safe or well grounded the gospel is that he has heard. He might have asked the same of a philosophical argument or a calculation in math.

We have already heard, in our introduction to Matthew, of gentiles who were attracted to Judaism but did not convert: men who were not circumcised, families that did not observe the whole Law. Josephus refers to "Jews and those who revere God" as if they formed two categories; Luke has Paul, speaking in a synagogue, address "Israelites and those who fear God" and in the same speech "Children of the race of Abraham and those among you who fear God" (Mission [Acts] 13.16, 26). There may well have been a category of such sympathizers, whose allegiance was public and valued: "God-fearers." An inscription has recently been discovered in Aphrodisias, a city of Asia Minor, revealing that here, at least, such a group was clearly identified in the third century C.E. The inscription is little more than a list of names and abbreviations, but from such spare information we can conjure up the dignity and alliances of a whole community.

The marble block is inscribed on two sides, in different hands and perhaps at different times. One side commemorates those who had given to a charitable cause, probably to the costs of a center for the distribution of food. The names are chiefly Jewish. The names of several donors are followed with further brief details: One was an elder and priest; another was a senior official; this man's mother was the building's patroness. And in the same style, three of the names are followed by the description "convert"; two by "God-fearer." The inscription's second side has been damaged at its top. It now starts in the middle of a list of names: Fifty-four survive, many of them Jewish. Next comes a gap; then a heading, "And such as are God-fearers." Beneath this is a second list of fifty names. By each of the first nine is the word "town councilor." Only one name in this second list is even partly Jewish: "Eusabbathios," a hybrid that had appeared several times in the list inscribed above.

Here is a charitable cause run by the Jewish community with which leading gentiles—including town councilors—wanted publicly to be linked as "God-fearers." It is likely, then to have been a term of honor within the Jewish community and in the city as a whole. We cannot read back, with any assurance, the conditions of one city into the life of another over 150 years before. But we will keep in our mind's eye these "God-fearers" of the third century. And we will ask, how might the Christians' claims and life and forms of worship have looked to any equivalent, in Luke's world, of those distinguished men of Aphrodisias?

Theophilus in the first century, town councilors in the third: These were people of means. We already hear from Paul of the churches' wealthier members. To frame his closing greetings in the Letter to the Romans are some references to the church from which he is writing, in Corinth (Romans 16.1, 23). Here are valuable clues to the patronage upon which such a church relied and so to the resources from which churches were able, in the decades of our writers' work, to pay for the research, composition, and copying involved in producing the gospels themselves. Paul's letter reached Rome with Phoebe. She is one of the first church officials of whom we ever hear, a "deacon" in the church of Corinth's harbor town of Cenchreae. She had been a patron to Paul "and many others"; she may well have been responsible for hospitality to Christians passing through the busy, cosmopolitan Corinth. She was clearly a woman of some wealth, with the reason and wherewithal to visit Rome. Gaius was another key figure; he is described as host to the whole Corinthian church. It is a telling description: When the whole congregation gathered (perhaps only occasionally) it was in the house of a single prosperous member. Numbers were still small. Greetings came to Rome, too, from Erastus, "the city treasurer"; a famous inscription from Corinth records that a pavement was laid by a certain Erastus, "commissioner for public works," at his own expense. In Rome itself we hear less of the church's patrons, more of the members likely to depend upon their support. Historians have long thought that the church followed the synagogues' practice and met in such patrons' private houses, without any official buildings of their own. We may even have traces in Paul's greetings of five or more "churches," meeting in different houses, all of which he regards as his letter's addressees.

We have heard of Christians among the emperor's slaves and retinue, but when were Christians first found among the generals and governors of Rome's elite? Tacitus gives us an intriguing clue: Pomponia Graecina, wife of a general who helped conquer Britain, was accused in 57 C.E. of "foreign superstition"; she was tried by a type of family tribunal, chaired by the head of the family, that handled domestic misdemeanors. This already suggests the charge to which the Christians would later be subjected: of holding orgies with secret and hideous ceremonies. Had Pomponia, then, become a member of the church? In the heyday of Roman excavation, in the nineteenth century, it was hoped that archaeology might confirm Pomponia's link with the church. The crypts in the catacombs outside Rome were found filled with broken inscriptions, piled into the passageways among rubbish and soil. In one crypt, dating from the first century C.E., were inscriptions recording various members of the Pomponian family; one was even named Pomponius Graecinus. The same crypt had clearly been used at some time for Christian burials. Was this then the family crypt of our Pomponia's family, built in the first century C.E. by Pomponia herself and a burial place for Christians from the start? The crypt's entrance was built in a gracious style and above ground. Pomponia had been acquitted by her husband's tribunal; she had no need to hide her allegiance. This was a time, then, when loyalty to the strange Jew Jesus could, despite dark rumors, be safely and publicly maintained.

The archaeologist (a brilliant Italian scholar, who devoted his life to the catacombs' excavation) offered a compelling picture of the early church's life in Rome. But his wish, it turns out, was father of the thought. It is fascinating to see the connections he made in the evidence—and the gaps that he leaped—to establish his claim. These crypts were often filled with "rubbish," including old inscriptions, when their passages were no longer in use. Exactly where the Pomponian inscriptions and the Christian symbols had first belonged we cannot know. Tacitus's story, the crypt, the crosses in the stone, and the broken inscriptions: These are loose pieces in a jigsaw puzzle whose completion will never now be possible.

We might wonder what Luke thinks he has to offer Theophilus over and above the information that his addressee can gain from the other accounts already in circulation. Luke himself, after all, claims that these had been written in direct dependence on eyewitnesses, a claim he does not make for his own account. Their authors had undertaken a sustained account, such as an educated reader might be expected to look for. Luke is offering reassurance: The claims of this church are coherent; they hang together with one another and with the ancient Jewish faith on which they are based and to which, despite all appearances, they are loyal. We might expect Theophilus to have some knowledge of the Old Order; he certainly would have seen more in Luke's story with such knowledge than without. It is into the mold of the Old Order's heroes and prophets that Jesus is cast; this is a category with which Theophilus feels comfortable. For a man brought up in Greek and Roman culture, such heroes had at least a chance of being credible.

We might wonder if Luke has lost sight of some insights already familiar to Mark— and of the style and strategy of disclosure that Mark believed necessary if those insights were to be duly grasped. But we may need to cast our eye as well on those for whom Luke was writing. They could certainly read in the Book of Daniel of heavenly journeys and of divine dramas unveiled. But the tradition in which these motifs were set was a tradition alien to Luke's readers. Mark and Matthew could draw on these themes, confident that their readers had some understanding of their background and claims, styles and images. In such a context, a writer could hope to reactivate Judaism's tradition of disclosure. This is not the world, however, in which Luke lives or for which he writes.

Luke will not put weight on material that his own readers are likely to find fantastical. Far more congenial to his Theophilus—and so more helpful to Luke's cause—is the history of Israel and its role as the history of God's chosen people. Here is the type of evidence with which Theophilus feels at home, evidence on whose basis, if at all, he will believe that the gospel is well grounded. The Old Order itself presented the fullest picture of Israel's role, a picture that Luke must show was misread by Jews of past and present. For only so Luke can ground this gospel, which divides its adherents ever more starkly from the Jews whose scriptures they invoke and inheritance they claim. The history recorded in the Old Order must be viewed afresh, and the Old Order itself provides, as Luke would have it, the basis for this radical review. What Jesus declares, the Mission expounds. The speeches of Luke's second book will interpret all Israel's history in a new and perhaps frighteningly unfamiliar way. Here is the New Order that Luke's Jesus brings.

Luke is a chameleon author. His elegant introduction is suited to the salons of Rome. But he moves on, into a story resonant with themes from the Old Order and with language to match: the prelude to Jesus' birth.

TELLING THE STORY: THE BIRTH

Our four witnesses open their gospels in very different ways. Mark launched his story with the preaching of the Baptizer and of the adult Jesus. Mark's concern was with the disclosure of the Son of Man. The battle was waged and won by this heavenly figure here on earth; in such an unveiling Jesus' ancestry and birth are not important. John, by contrast, will describe Jesus in terms that take us back to the start of all things, to the very dawn of creation. Faced with John's unimaginable claim, the details of Jesus' birth can be left aside; in such a context, these are not the claims over which an inquirer or cynic will stumble.

Matthew, like Luke, headed back to Jesus' ancestry and birth. Matthew's opening chapters place Jesus just where he needs to be: in the lineage of King David and of Abraham. The details of this lineage are not easily explained. Some are due to the pattern that Matthew is working to create: Three groups of fourteen generations lead from Abraham to Jesus. But Matthew's emphasis is clear from his very first words: *The book of the Beginning of Jesus Anointed, son of David, son of Abraham* (Matthew 1.1). Jesus is descended from Abraham and is sent in the first place to Abraham's descendants.

Matthew's Jesus is conceived and born as no other child. This origin may have assumed a steadily increasing importance in the church. An argument is readily mounted that makes it central to any understanding of Jesus. To have done what the church came to think he had done, he must have been set apart from other humans from the start. But it may have taken some years or decades for this need to become clear, and the church may well have grown, through its earliest years, without any reliance on such stories of his birth. For in the first lines of Paul's Letter to the Romans, written some twenty years after Jesus' death, Paul appears to quote a creed already familiar to his addressees. It is certainly compatible with a belief that Jesus was declared Son of God only after his rising from the dead.

> *Paul, servant of Jesus Anointed, a missionary called and set apart for the gospel of God, which he had proclaimed in advance through his prophets in sacred texts:*
>
> *About his son, who was born from the seed of David*
> *according to the flesh,*
> *designated Son of God in power*
> *according to the Breath of Holiness*
> *from his rising from the dead,*
> *Jesus Anointed our Lord.*
>
> (ROMANS 1.1–4)

Perhaps, then, it was only well into the 50s and 60s C.E. that the church's vision broadened. How could the death of a mere man have achieved so much? An upward spiral is under way. The further question was almost certainly in the air: Just how much had Jesus achieved? The greater the value that the church saw in Jesus' achievement, the more closely it would have looked at the Jesus who wrought it, and vice versa. What status, then, had Jesus enjoyed during his life on earth? The distinction between human and divine, as we have seen, was not understood then as it is now. It may well have taken a generation of thought before a close relation was seen between Jesus' status, achievement, and origins. But there is an internal logic to such claims for salvation. It became clear that a mere humanity was not basis enough for the effect that the church was coming to see in Jesus. And so the question required an answer: Who or what must this Jesus have been from the start to have achieved, at the end, the salvation of which the church was speaking?

Matthew and Luke, each in his own distinctive way, want to set this Jesus on the cusp: as human as those with whom he lives and dies, yet set apart by his "nature." They may seem to be addressing a blunt, almost clumsy question: When did such a Jesus start to be so special?

Matthew and Luke both look to Jesus' origins, but not necessarily with the same needs and queries in mind. Matthew's book opens with his family tree; here is the first and most important placing of Jesus. Luke rounds off his stories of the infant Jesus with a family tree different in detail and longer in perspective. The lineage of his Jesus is traced back to Adam, for all of Adam's descendants will be offered his gospel's blessing. Luke writes, too, as we have seen, for a gentile steeped in the stories of Greek and Roman demigods. Several such heroes were said to have been conceived by a god; there is no suggestion, however, that their mothers remained virgins. It is striking but perhaps unsurprising how little weight Luke lays on Jesus' "virginal" conception. It is declared by Luke, but carefully and quietly. Luke's readers could have found it fantastical, and this is not the point at which he wants those readers to stumble. He is going to challenge their readers' values and credulity starkly enough in the chapters to follow.

Out of these stories the church would develop an immensely subtle teaching on Jesus' being God and human together. But within the narrative there is already deep thought at work: Matthew and Luke explore as narrative the claims that the later church will develop as formal teaching. That later teaching has not squeezed elevated thoughts from simple rustic stories. Our witnesses have a delicate sense of the questions that their narratives address and of those questions among them that no narrative can answer.

TELLING THE STORY: THE COURSE OF HISTORY

Each of our witnesses, as we have seen, sets the tone of his testimony at its very start. Luke's is the longest and most elaborate introduction of all. He launches his story with an extended prelude to the theme that shapes his whole work: The Old Order, ordained by God, has itself given birth to the New. The center of God's plan and worship has always been Jerusalem, but Jerusalem has failed to see God's new work launched within its walls and its own place within his plan. As a result, Jerusalem is marked for destruction. So complete and coherent is God's design that before Jerusalem is even destroyed the new center for his mission has already been reached and established: the center of the world's great empire, Rome itself.

The random, unexpected, and frightening turn out in Luke's eyes to be part of a single, all-embracing plan. Everything and everyone is taken up by the ever-broadening ripples of the gospels' expansion. From the old to the new: By the time Luke writes, Jerusalem, hub of God's Old Order, lies in ruins. Crucial for the gospel is that it reach the world's new center, Rome. This whole movement revolves around the single story of Jesus. Seen in its light, everything falls into place; even at its darkest, history is in safe hands. From Jerusalem to Rome: Jesus had traveled to Jerusalem and been killed. Thereafter Jerusalem was just a husk; the missionary Paul would travel to Rome. The world was turning on its hinges.

Luke's story starts in Jerusalem, in the Temple itself. The Baptizer's arrival is announced in the Temple to his father. Jesus is brought to the Temple as an infant; his parents do for him exactly as the Law commands, and Jesus is recognized by the Temple's loyal servants. At the age of twelve he is in the Temple again, "in his father's house," discussing the Law with its elders. Luke's Jesus will spend a third of the gospel on his last journey to Jerusalem and to his death. On Easter Day he appears to his pupils there, and after receiving his final instruction, to wait there for the father's promised gift, *these worshiped him and returned to Jerusalem with great joy and were continually in the Temple praising God* (Luke 24.52).

As the gospel, then, opens in Jerusalem, so does the Mission. The promised gift of the Breath of God is duly given there. It is Jerusalem that sees the church's key decision made: Those conditions and rules of Judaism, for which Jerusalem has always stood, are not to be imposed on gentiles. As the Mission builds to its climax, Paul warns his friends and followers that he must return to Jerusalem, where he will suffer in his turn. Jesus had died there; Paul will be tried there and from there will be sent to the new capital of empire and of the world. He is duly arrested, and the events are set in motion that will take him finally to Rome.

Matthew was so concerned to warn and threaten that he had little time to lament the destruction of the ancient city. Luke, as we shall see, makes dramatic use of the lament that his Jesus shares with Matthew's:

> *"Jerusalem, Jerusalem, you who kill the prophets and stone those sent to you,*
> *how often have I longed to gather together your children,*
> *as a bird gathers her chicks beneath her wings,*
> *—and you would have none of it."*
>
> *(LUKE 13.34)*

Luke makes this the first in a series of such laments. Whatever Theophilus may have heard of the Jews' opposition to the church, Luke insists that this church is living out the plan of God. It is the opponents of Jesus who have resisted that plan all along, and the consequences are for them to bear. *"The Pharisees and the lawyers set aside God's plan for themselves,"* says Luke's Jesus, *"by refusing baptism from the Baptizer"* (Luke 7.30). Luke leaves no doubt what those consequences were. Jesus' triumphant entry to Jerusalem is punctuated with his plangent words:

> *As Jesus drew near and he saw the city, he wept over it, saying, "If only you, you too, had recognized on this day all that is working for your peace. But now it has been hidden from your eyes. The days will come upon you when your enemies will throw up a rampart around you, and will encircle you, and will hem you in on every side; and they will cast you to the ground, you and your children within you, and they will not leave in you one stone upon another, because you have not recognized the time of this gracious visitation."*
>
> *(LUKE 19.41–44)*

Prelude

TWO MOTHERS AND TWO CHILDREN

In the center of Israel's ancient worship, at the daily sacrifice, an elderly priest, Zechariah, is hidden from the people as he works at the altar of incense. He has a vision. An angel tells him that his wife, Elizabeth, also of the priestly caste and years past childbearing, is to have a son: the Baptizer. The movement from the Old Order to the New is under way in the last great figure of the Old. Luke does not wish to belittle this ancient faith; it is from here that the New Order grows. It is in this ancestry, too, that his church will overcome the distaste, widespread in the ancient world, for new rites and religions and for shallow, disloyal desertion of the old. This Christian faith, Luke insists, is not new; it is the new form, ordained by God, of the oldest faith of all. Everything that had brought it into being, right through to Jesus' rejection by his own people, was within God's plan.

Luke tells of the Baptizer's coming and of Jesus' in a series of matching scenes: Their families, conception, and birth run on parallel tracks, divided just by the six months between the Baptizer's conception and Jesus'. It is fitting that their mothers should be related. Here in the Baptizer and Jesus are two cousins, the last representative of the Old Order and the trigger of the New. Jesus is the Baptizer's mirror image, exactly the same as his older cousin except in the particular ways that make him his cousin's perfect opposite. Luke is at his most delicate as he holds this balance through his gospel's opening chapters.

Old Zechariah is told by the angel Gabriel that his son will fulfill all that was prophesied of the prophet Elijah at his return:

He will turn many of the children of Israel to the Lord their God,
and he will go before his face in the breath and power of Elijah,
to turn the hearts of fathers to their children
to turn the disobedient to the understanding of the just
to make ready for the Lord a people well prepared.

(LUKE 1.16–17)

Zechariah asks how he is to believe the promise and is struck dumb until the promise is fulfilled and the child born. When Elizabeth is six months pregnant, Gabriel visits Mary. She was engaged to Joseph, a descendant of King David; Joseph and Mary had not slept together. Gabriel has a second announcement to make, just like the first. Mary is to bear a son:

"He will be great [says the angel] *and will be called son of the Most High,*
and God will give him the throne of his father David,
and he will reign over the house of Israel for all aeons
and of his kingdom there will be no end."

(LUKE 1.32–33)

Here, as in Matthew, are echoes of Isaiah's great prophecies, but where Matthew spelled them out, Luke lets them sound without comment. Their roots in the past were well known; at issue for Luke were their implications for the present. Mary is as incredulous as Zechariah, but whether because of her youth or the different cast of her question, she is answered, not punished. *"How will this be?" she asks; "I have slept with no man."*

"The Breath of God will come upon you [answers the angel]
and the power of the Most High will overshadow you;
therefore that which is born shall be called holy, the Son of God."

(*LUKE 1.34–35*)

Mary believes but may be looking for reassurance still. The angel had told her that Elizabeth was already pregnant, and to Elizabeth she goes. At the very arrival of Mary, Elizabeth's child *leaps in the womb.* Only when the older woman tells of her baby's movement does Mary break into her own great song of triumph. We have met this hymn already in chapter 1, and here, as there, we keep here to the famous sixteenth-century translation, which captures, better than any other, the rhythm and language of the original:

"My soul doth magnify the Lord, and my spirit hath rejoiced in God my Savior.
For he hath regarded the lowliness of his handmaiden.
For behold from henceforth all generations shall call me blessed.
For he that is mighty hath magnified me, and holy is his name.
And his mercy is on them that fear him throughout all generations.
He hath showed strength with his arm; he hath scattered the proud
*   in the imagination of their hearts.*
He hath put down the mighty from their seat, and hath exalted the humble and meek.
He hath filled the hungry with good things, and the rich he hath sent empty away.
He remembering his mercy hath holpen his servant Israel, as he promised to our
*   forefathers,*
Abraham and his seed for ever."

(*LUKE 1.46–55*)

A virgin, unsettled and scared, is told she is to have a child; she goes to see her older relative, who has been promised a birth no less extraordinary than her own. Mary has believed the angel but has the confidence to speak of her child and his future only when reassured by Elizabeth's confirmation. One-half of the angel's promise is on its way to fulfillment; Mary is now confident of the other. Here in the very opening pages of the gospel we have a hint of Luke's insight into character and impulse. Luke is a perceptive, warmhearted observer of his story and its characters. He has more interest than Mark or Matthew in the figures that encounter Jesus, and a wider circle attracts his acuity and his care than just Jesus and the pupils themselves. He keeps an eye, in particular, on the women in Jesus' entourage. Luke alone dwells on Elizabeth and Mary. It is Luke, too, who records the story of another Mary and her sister Martha:

On their journey he went into a certain village and a woman called Martha welcomed him into her home. She had a sister called Mary who just sat at the feet of the Lord and listened to his words. Now Martha was distracted with all the serving. She went up to Jesus and said, "Sir, does it not concern you that my sister has left me alone to serve? Tell her, then, to help me." But the Lord said to her, "Martha, Martha, you are anxious and troubled about many things. Just one thing is needful. For Mary has chosen the good portion, which shall not be taken away from her."

(LUKE 10.38–42)

This is a domestic scene. It gives us a glimpse into such normal friendships as the gospels rarely show us. Martha's invitation has brought Jesus to the house. She is unsurprisingly disappointed; her own hospitality is keeping her from hearing what he has to say.

Luke's Jesus broadens the repertoire of his stories to include such settings. Matthew's Jesus already told of a lost sheep, just one in the flock of a hundred: The shepherd shares with his neighbors his pleasure at its finding. Luke's Jesus adds a second story to form from the two a natural pair. A coin is lost, the housewife searches high and low, she has her neighbors join her to celebrate its recovery. Yet again Luke has set in balance a man and a woman. It is, then, unsurprising that Luke records more details than our other witnesses of the women who supported Jesus: *Various women were with him, who had been healed from possession and from illnesses: Mary called Magdalen from whom seven daemons had gone out, and Joanna the wife of Chuza, Herod's steward, and Susanna, and many others who provided for Jesus and his pupils out of their own means* (Luke 8.2–3). Mary Magdalen: We shall hear of her again. In the last scene of our final witness the two pupils who come to Jesus' tomb find it empty and leave. It is only Mary who remains outside the tomb, inconsolable with grief. The Jesus who had shown her care and whom she had followed ever since has been killed; even his body has been removed. As the light rises on that Easter morning, it is not to those pupils that Jesus will first appear.

We have heard already from Luke's Jesus two laments for the holy city. As Jesus carries his cross to the place of execution, the women of Jerusalem weep for him. But Jesus turns to them and says,

"Daughters of Jerusalem, do not weep for me, but weep for yourselves and for your children. For look, the days are coming in which they will say, 'Blessed are the wombs that have not given birth, and the breasts that have not given suck.'

Then they shall begin [and here Jesus evokes words once more from the prophet Hosea] *to say to the mountains, 'Fall upon us,' and to the hills, 'Cover us.' For if they do this when the wood is green what will happen when it is dry?"*

(LUKE 23.27–31)

SCATTERING THE PROUD

This Jesus is apparently so gentle and yet can be fiercer, in Luke's portrayal, than in any of the other three. The tone is set from the very beginning. Here are lines from the Song of Mary in a modern translation, without any of the archaic beauty, which can disguise the force of her words:

> *"God has exercised strength with his arm:*
> *he has put to rout those who are arrogant in the planning of their hearts.*
> *He has put down mighty rulers from their thrones;*
> *and has exalted the lowly.*
> *He has filled the hungry with good things*
> *and has sent the rich empty away."*
>
> *(LUKE 1.51–53)*

These are powerful, threatening words. No official of Roman power will welcome them. Luke writes to *Your Excellency Theophilus;* we hear such a title again in Paul's mouth when he speaks to the governors Felix and Festus. We are to imagine a Theophilus of similar standing. Such an addressee invested Luke's text with more than dignity. His two volumes must confront the questions to which this Christian sect gave rise in the eyes of powerful men with government and security on their minds.

> *"A blessing on the Lord the God of Israel* [said old Zechariah],
> *for he has visited and brought ransom for his people,*
> *and has raised up for us a horn of salvation in the house of his servant David,*
> *just as he said through the mouth of his holy prophets of old:*
> *salvation from our enemies and from the hands of all that hate us;*
> *to deal mercifully with our ancestors and to remember his holy order,*
> *the oath which he swore to Abraham our father,*
> *to grant us rescue from the hands of our enemies*
> *that we might worship in his presence in holiness and justice all our days."*
>
> *(LUKE 1.68–75)*

How will such a promise sound to people dependent for their living on the empire's order? Or to those, in turn, charged with its maintenance? We have no right to be cynical. The century of Rome's civil war had ravaged its whole empire. There was good reason to be thankful for Augustus's final victory and for the peace that he imposed. "The whole human race," wrote Philo, "exhausted by mutual slaughter, was on the verge of utter destruction, had it not been for one man and leader, Augustus, whom men fitly call the Averter of Evil." Philo was speaking—in mortal fear—to a later and erratic emperor. He had good reason to flatter Augustus, founder of their dynasty, but his words were plausible enough. "Augustus was the first and greatest and most universal benefactor: He displaced the rule of many and committed the ship of commonwealth to be steered by a single pilot."

There was to be no doubt who was in control: Augustus struck coins depicting either Victory standing on the world or Augustus atop the globe himself. We have heard already of the decree issued by the provincial Council of Asia in 9 B.C.E. It was carved in stone and set up in public throughout the province. One copy has survived, at Priene, near Ephesus: "Providence created the most perfect good for our lives, filling Augustus with virtue for the benefit of mankind, sending us and those after us a savior who put an end to war and established all things. The birthday of the god Augustus marked through his coming the beginning of a gospel for the world."

The promises made by Luke's angel come in due time to their fulfillment. The birth of Luke's Jesus is first announced to shepherds at night.

> *And an angel of the Lord came to them, and the glory of the Lord shone around them, and they were struck with a terrible fear. And the angel said to them: "Do not be afraid. Look, I am bringing you good news of a great joy, which will be shared by the whole people: Today a savior has been born to you, who is the Anointed, the Lord, in the city of David."*
>
> (LUKE 2.8–11)

The Romans could well claim that their empire benefited those they ruled; travel was safe by land and by sea, civil order was maintained, trade and prosperity increased. An inscription from Halicarnassus, issued by the city's council, celebrates Augustus as "savior of the whole human race. Land and sea have peace, the cities flourish under a good legal system, in harmony and with an abundance of food. There is an abundance of all good things, people are filled with happy hopes for the future and with delight at the present." After 70 C.E. such blessings were hard to recognize in Israel itself: the temple destroyed, the city in ruins, its people killed or scattered. But the Roman Empire was used to defining peace by its own victory: Once the enemy was destroyed, the war was over. Tacitus tells of one campaign against the German tribes: "Prisoners were needless," he has the Roman general say; "nothing but the extermination of the race would end the war."

"And this," said the angel to the shepherds, *"shall be a sign for you* that confirms this proclamation: *you will find the child wrapped up in bands of cloth and lying in a trough for the animals"* (Luke 2.12). Here is a strange setting for God's promised king.

> *And suddenly there was with the angel a mass of the heavenly army praising God and saying:*
>
> *"Glory in the highest to God,*
> *and on the earth peace*
> *among those on whom God's favor rests."*
>
> (LUKE 2.13–14)

"Peace on earth": but imposed by whose power and under whose control? The army of angels may announce peace from heaven; it may be a peace to wait and hope for. But the Peace of Rome, established by its armies throughout their domain, was already Augustus's and the empire's proudest claim. Augustus wrote a summary of his own career:

> Our ancestors wished that the temple of Janus was to be closed when throughout the whole empire of the Roman people, on land and sea, peace had been won by victories. Before my birth it is recorded that from the foundation of the city it had been closed only twice; the senate ordered it closed three times while I was First Citizen.

Augustus himself confirmed that such peace was secured through conquest. He built an altar to peace on Rome's Field of Mars, mustering ground for the army and duly dedicated to the god of war. The emperor Trajan would later issue a coin that showed the goddess Peace with her right foot on the neck of a conquered enemy. Pride in their armies' achievement did not blind all Rome's authors to the ambition that had led to empire or the force that maintained it. Tacitus wrote of his own father-in-law's conquest of Britain: This Agricola is presented as a hero. We would expect no less. But Tacitus gives space as well to the Romans' enemy, the British prince who was stirring the resistance to Rome:

> Robbers of the world, now that earth fails their all-devastating hands, they probe even the sea: if their enemy has wealth, the Romans have greed; if he is poor, they are ambitious. Neither East nor West has glutted them. Alone of mankind, with the same passion they covet want as much as wealth. To plunder, butcher, steal—these things they misname empire. They make a desolation and they call it peace.

What sort of king will Jesus be, born to counter such power—but born in a stable and first announced to shepherds? King David himself, ancestor of Jesus and greatest of the Jewish kings, had been taken from guarding his father's sheep to be anointed king. It was this David, still just a youth, who defeated and killed the giant Goliath single-handedly. To be his successor was to be a shepherd, too; to be recognized by shepherds, however humble, was to stand within the succession of Israel's deepest longings.

David's own son, as famous as himself, was King Solomon. He described his own infancy. Here we learn why Luke stressed the bands of cloth, familiar clothing for an infant.

> *"I, too, when I was born, drew in the common air*
> *and fell upon the earth that suffers the same fate as ourselves.*

I bawled my first sound just as all others do,
I was cared for with bands of cloth and with concern.
Such is the start to life for every king."

(WISDOM OF SOLOMON 7.3)

The shepherds acknowledged the new shepherd of Israel, but few others would do as much in his lifetime on earth, whether among his own people or the foreign powers that ruled them. Not only a king could be denied. God himself, as Luke would have it, is about to be rejected by his chosen people. The stable and manger as well have their place in Luke's drama. The Greek version of Isaiah's prophecies begins,

"Hear, O heaven, and give ear, O earth,
For the Lord has spoken:
'I have begotten children and raised them up,
and they have set me at naught.
An ox knows its owner, and an ass the manger of its lord;
but Israel has not recognized me, the people have not known me.'"

(ISAIAH 1.2–3, GREEK VERSION)

A LIGHT TO THE GENTILES

When Mary and Joseph took the baby Jesus to the Temple they encountered two elderly figures. As Zechariah and Elizabeth had heralded Jesus' birth, so these two, Simeon and Anna, recognize him once born. Simeon was a just and pious man who was waiting for the comforting of Israel. The Breath of God that will be given to Jesus' pupils at the start of the Mission is already present and at work in at least one chosen servant of the Temple. It had been revealed to Simeon in advance that he would not die before he saw God's Anointed. He came into the Temple when Mary and Joseph were there. He took the child into his arms and said,

Now, Master, you are letting your servant go in peace,
according to your promise.
For my eyes have seen your salvation,
which you have prepared in the sight of all the peoples:
a light for unveiling to the gentiles
and the glory of your people Israel.

(LUKE 2.29–32)

The births are announced to the father Zechariah and to the mother Mary; Jesus is acknowledged first by Simeon and next by the prophetess Anna. Luke values, as ever, the balance of man and woman. Simeon was waiting for the comforting of Israel; Anna speaks out to all those *waiting for the ransom of Jerusalem* (Luke 2.38).

Over against the Romans' peace, the peace declared by the armies of heaven; over against the Temple's destruction, the promise of Israel's glory and light for the gentiles who by Luke's day had destroyed it. The contrast was acute. What would inaugurate the new "peace"? What destruction would be needed first? Such power as Rome's would not yield easily. Violence must be met with violence. Roman practice was fierce enough but no more extreme than the prospect held out by the Old Order against God's enemies.

The prophet Ezekiel relays God's warnings to the city of Tyre. There is no mercy in sight. We hear these motifs again in the Seer's song of triumph over Rome:

Thus says the Lord God to Tyre: Will not the coastlands shake at the sound of your fall, when the wounded groan, when slaughter is made in the midst of you? Then all the princes of the sea will step down from their thrones, and remove their robes, and strip off their embroidered garments. They will clothe themselves with trembling; they will sit upon the ground and tremble every moment, and be appalled at you. And they will raise a lamentation over you:

"*How you have vanished from the seas,*
O city renowned, you that were mighty on the sea,
you and your inhabitants.
Now the isles tremble on the day of your fall,
and are dismayed at your passing."

(EZEKIEL 26.15–18)

To declare a savior and a peace apart from Rome's was to rival the emperor and his proudest boast. This was subversion: dangerous for those who fostered it, dangerous, too, for those in power who gave it space within the realm of their authority. The more Theophilus knows of the Old Order, the more worrying should these opening pages of Luke's gospel sound. Our witness has drawn on the richest seams of ancient Israel's hope. As Mary sings, so had Hannah sung, the mother of another hero, centuries before. Hannah had been barren. Year after year she had pleaded with God for a child. Her prayer was eventually granted. She gave birth to a son, Samuel, the judge over Israel who launched the long, slow liberation of the Jews from foreign rule. Mary's song draws, line by line, on the thanksgiving that Hannah sang when she had given birth at last. These are not themes that any Roman official will have wanted to hear reecho round a new and fervent sect. We see Mary's song on the left, and Hannah's on the right:

My soul proclaims the greatness of the Lord
and my spirit has found gladness in God my Savior.
Because he has regarded the low estate of his handmaid.
God has exercised strength with his arm
He has put to rout those who are arrogant
in the planning of their hearts.
He has put down mighty rulers from their thrones; and has exalted the lowly.
He has filled the hungry with good things and has sent the rich empty away.
(LUKE 1.46–53, EXCERPTS)

My heart is strengthened in the Lord;
I delight in your salvation.

. . . O Lord, if you will look on the low estate of your handmaid . . .

The Lord makes poor and makes rich;
He lifts the needy from the earth, and from the dung heap he raises up the poor.
(1 SAMUEL 1.11 AND 2.1–8, EXCERPTS)

The church left no doubt that a kingdom was at issue. But what sort of king? How would his reign relate to the more immediate, palpable dominion of the emperor? The whole of Luke's work in both its halves might be seen as a vast exposition of the angel's opening promise to Mary:

"This child will be great [said the angel]
and will be called son of the Most High,
and God will give him the throne of David his father,
and he will reign over the house of Israel for all aeons
and of his kingdom there will be no end."

(LUKE 1.32–33)

Restoring the Kingdom

Luke writes as if to a senior official in the imperial service. Ten years after the end of the Jewish revolt he writes of a savior, of redemption, of God's promises to Israel. Such inflammatory words would revive all the suspicions to which any Theophilus would be prone. Far from dampening his readers' fears, Luke will record charges of which Mark and Matthew tell us nothing. When, in Luke's story, the Jewish council have examined Jesus they take him to Pilate: *"We have found this man,"* they say, *"leading our nation astray and forbidding them to pay taxes to the emperor, and saying that he is himself the Anointed, a king"* (Luke 23.2).

There lies the charge. Pilate finds no grounds for conviction. The council presses on: *"He is stirring up the people, teaching all the length of Judaea, starting from Galilee right down here to Jerusalem"* (Luke 23.5). So Jesus, Pilate discovers, is a Galilean. He sends the suspect to Herod Antipas, in charge of Galilee but visiting Jerusalem. Jesus said little enough in front of Pilate, in front of Herod nothing at all. He is returned to Pilate, who announces three times to the people and their leaders that he does not find Jesus guilty. But to no avail. They ask for the release of Barabbas; Luke emphasizes Barabbas's character when the demand is made and again when Pilate grants it: Barabbas *has been put in prison for some revolt there had been in the city and for murder;* this is the man Pilate releases, *put in prison for revolt and for murder* (Luke 23.19). If there was a rebel in view, dangerous to Rome, it was not Jesus.

The Roman authorities declare Jesus, over and over, innocent of the charge laid against him: He is not a subversive. The pattern will be repeated at the end of the Mission: Paul is charged before the governors Felix and Festus; he is eventually tried before Festus and Herod Agrippa. One governor and one Herod had examined Jesus; two governors, another Herod, and that Herod's queen all examine Paul. None finds him guilty of any charge. Only Paul's own appeal to the emperor prevents his immediate release; this explains his journey under military guard to Rome. And Theophilus can rest assured.

Luke's is a brave strategy. The Christians are under suspicion: Paul has been under house arrest in Rome, Jesus himself was suspected of subversion, and the sect's language of hope is notorious for its revolutionary tone. Instead of playing such charges down, Luke gives them all the space he can, for they are false. And under Roman law it was as dangerous to accuse the innocent as to be accused when guilty. Suspicion should not be directed at the Christians but at those who laid false charges at their door.

Luke does more than defuse the rumors of revolutionary danger. He redefines the language that gave them rise. At his hands the hope for God's kingdom is not dead; it is transformed. We shall watch Luke describe the kingdom afresh, and as the kingdom's character is shifted, so the language that describes its coming can be safely used. Talk of God's kingdom no longer sounds revolutionary, for "the kingdom of God" no longer describes a reign that must overwhelm all others in order to be realized on Earth. What, then, is the kingdom that can be looked for now? A kingdom, Luke's Jesus says, that is *"among you"* (Luke 17.21).

Such a kingdom is easily misunderstood. As moving a story as any in the gospels is told by Luke of Easter Day. Two of Jesus' pupils are walking from Jerusalem to Emmaus. A third traveler joins them. They do not recognize him: It is Jesus. He asks what they are talking about. Dejected and quite without hope, they tell him. They are talking about *"Jesus, the prophet mighty in deed and word, handed over by the chief priests and leaders and crucified; and we,"* they continue, *"we were hoping that this was the one who was to ransom Israel"* (Luke 24.19–20). Jesus hears them out as they tell of the reports filtering through: that women had found the tomb empty that morning and had seen a vision of angels, and that further pupils had gone to the tomb, too, and found it, just as the women had said, empty. We will return to this story. For the moment we ask only, why were those pupils, all their hopes dashed, walking to Emmaus?

In 169 B.C.E. Antiochus Epiphanes of Syria besieged and captured Jerusalem. It was three years before the Jews could regroup, but under Judas Maccabaeus they launched their fight for freedom. In the Story of the Maccabees: Book 1 we hear of both sides' preparations for the war. The Syrian army camped south of Jerusalem. Their commander detached five thousand foot soldiers and one thousand of his finest cavalry and moved off at night to ambush the Jews. Judas was alerted to the plan and made a brilliant countermarch: He ranged his men against the Syrian camp, bereft of its best troops. His army won a great victory. Here was the war's first set-piece battle and the Maccabees' first triumph. The battle was fought at Emmaus.

Judas encouraged his troops before the battle: "Now let us call upon heaven to help us and to remember the Order set up with our fathers and to destroy this army in front of us; and then all the gentiles will know that there is one who ransoms and saves Israel" (Story of the Maccabees: Book 1, 4.10). The author looks back at the end of his account on the battle's whole drama. On that day, he comments, there was a great salvation in Israel.

All those years later, two figures trudge along the road to Emmaus. All that they had hoped for had crumbled away. And yet there are reports of an empty tomb, of strange visions, of Jesus alive. Where should they go when so much was in turmoil, so much uncertain? To the site of the old victory, where Israel had once been saved and ransomed. Here, if anywhere, they would find the grounds for their hopes' revival. And when Jesus himself appears before them? They do not recognize him. They know what their savior and redeemer is to do: He is to be another Judas Maccabaeus, leading his people to a victorious battle against the invaders.

And Jesus said to them: "You do not understand at all, in your hearts you are so slow to trust in all that the prophets said. Didn't the Anointed have to suffer like this and enter into his glory?" And beginning from Moses and from all the prophets he explained to them, in all the scriptures, the passages about himself.

(LUKE 24.25–27)

We will return to this walk, to the gathering dusk and the hearts that burned as Jesus spoke. Luke's whole gospel reads, far more than Mark's or Matthew's, like history as we know it, a narrative of events that lead to more such events. Did Luke know that the Emmaus of this old battle was too far distant from Jerusalem for such a walk as he describes? Historians have quite rightly looked for another town of the same name closer to Jerusalem. But geography was not Luke's concern.

The one who was to ransom Israel. Over and over Luke has sounded variations on this theme: the pupils' hope for Israel and that hope's transformation. Luke's Jesus must address the pupils' same confusion in the very last words he speaks to them:

So as they were walking with him the pupils asked him, "Sir, is this the time at which you are to restore the kingdom to Israel?" He said to them, "It is not for you to know the times or occasions which the father has set by his own authority. But you will receive the power of the Breath of God coming upon you and you will be my witnesses in Jerusalem and in all Judaea and in Samaria and to the ends of the earth."

(MISSION [ACTS] 1.6–8)

Jesus' pupils must be weaned from their long-nurtured hopes for Israel and its kingdom. Luke's Theophilus, in turn, must be reassured beyond doubt that the Christians are no threat. There may have been those, too, in Luke's own day, who hankered still for Israel's restoration. These as well are to see the spread of God's kingdom in the work of his missionaries and the life of his church. To secure this change in perspective, Luke develops a strategy embracing all his gospel and the Mission's start. He frames the entire story of Jesus, from the promise of his birth to his own last words on earth, with this theme. Luke knows that there are deep suspicions to be expunged and deep-set hopes to be reformed.

Luke's perspective would prevail, if only by default. God's kingdom was not imposed upon the world; Rome reigned on, supreme. It took a distinctive insight or distinctive faith to see the dominion under which, claimed the church, all creation lay. We shall hear later of St. Polycarp, a bishop killed for his faith in the middle of the second century C.E. The story has survived of his death. At the story's end some manuscripts record the date of Polycarp's death in the most appropriate way their copyists know. Empire was in the hands, not of those who killed him, but of the Jesus whom he served. "The official responsible for his arrest was Herod; the High Priest was Philip of Tralles; and the proconsul was Statius Quadratus—but the ruling monarch was Jesus Christ, who reigns for ever and ever."

Modern readers might wonder, what was the cost Luke paid for this translation of the gospel into terms acceptable to Rome? The fiercest language of hope and upheaval, the clearest promise that this world's order is to be overturned—these have been so effectively defused that we can hear them, in a proud, affluent West, without a quiver of concern. If the glint of their protest is almost lost to our view, it is in good measure thanks to the frame in which Luke set these precious stones and the angles at which he cut them. For Luke's first concern was to ensure the survival of his gospel and church. It is easy for us to regret his complaisance, far harder to be sure that in such a context we would have stood up more bravely than he did or that anyone who did would have served the church better then Luke. Luke's gospel, after all, has survived. It was by reinterpreting this ancient language of liberation that Luke preserved it. It is here alone, after all, that we can read those extraordinary words of Mary:

God has exercised strength with his arm;
he has put to rout those who are arrogant in the planning of their hearts.
He has put down mighty rulers from their thrones.

Luke, in his cautious, conformist way, may have been in the long run the most subversive and revolutionary witness of all. *"The gentiles of the world,"* says Jesus in the collection of sayings shared by Matthew and Luke, *"pursue all the basic worldly things; but your father knows you need them. So you by contrast, you are to look for his kingdom, and these things will be given you as well."* Luke's Jesus then adds, *"Do not be afraid, little flock, for your father has been pleased to give you the kingdom"* (Luke 12.30–32).

Blessed Are the Poor

Luke's Jesus will never compromise:

"Blessed are the poor, for yours is the kingdom of God.
Blessed are those who hunger now, for you will be filled.
Blessed are those who weep now, for you will laugh.

But woe to you, you who are rich, for you have your comfort already.
Woe to you, you who are full now, for you will be hungry.
Woe to you who laugh now, for you shall mourn and weep."

(*LUKE 6.20–21, 24–25*)

No compromise; no interpretation, such as we saw in Matthew, to make the promise or the threat more spiritual. Luke draws a clear, stark contrast: The present order will be overturned. But the Roman Empire is not threatened, and neither, then, are its rich and powerful functionaries. So when will the order of this present world be undone? Luke's story carries on, in the Mission, to tell of the years and decades following Jesus' death. Jesus' return may be expected still, but any such hope is defused. The sting is drawn. History now opens out before the reader, not as a vast circle about to be closed, but as a single track that in the life and death of Jesus has wheeled around an axis to carry on, apparently in the same direction still. What, then, is there really to hope for or to fear?

The judgment to be visited upon Jews and gentiles alike; the vindication of God's people and the punishment of their enemies; the arrival of the kingdom of God, that elusive triumph on whose threshold Mark's and Matthew's readers stand—where are they on Luke's horizon? And where, in turn, is the hope which that kingdom held out to the poor and dispossessed? *"The kingdom of God,"* proclaimed Mark's Jesus on his first appearance, *"is at hand."* But Luke's Jesus, as we have seen, speaks at his mission's start not of the kingdom but of Isaiah's prophecies fulfilled: *"The Breath of God is upon me."* Mark rounded off the dramatic scene of Peter's recognition, at his gospel's midway climax, with that striking promise, *"In truth I tell you, there are some of those standing here who shall not taste of death before they see the kingdom of God arrived in power"* (Mark 9.1). Luke turns expectation away from such display. He will address such hopes under different categories; the kingdom's arrival is not to be heralded in any such way as this. *"I tell you truly, there are some of those standing here who shall not taste of death before they see*—very simply—*the kingdom of God"* (Luke 9.27).

Luke rewrites the expectations of the kingdom with all the skill at his command. He punctuates his gospel with warnings: The kingdom was not going to appear with all its glory in the days of Jesus, and neither will it in his readers'. Jesus' pupils are warned against expecting the kingdom's appearance; Luke's readers, against seeing in the crises of their time the portents of the Son of Man. No coming kingdom on Jesus' horizon, no Son of Man on Luke's: What, then, are Luke's readers to hope for, day by day? Luke confronts head-on the themes of the kingdom and of the Son of Man. He arranges a striking sequence of sayings near the end of Jesus' journey to Jerusalem. Its placing is important. Here is a first warning: Much that his pupils long for from the coming climax, they will not see.

Luke's Jesus links two subjects of hope in order to distinguish between them: the kingdom of God and *the days of the Son of Man.* The Pharisees in the story are looking for the kingdom; Jesus' own followers, for both. And Luke's readers? They, too, are wondering what prospect the gospel holds out for God's further and dramatic intervention. Luke insists that such searches are misguided.

Asked by the Pharisees when the kingdom of God was coming, he answered them and said: "The kingdom of God does not come with watching; nor will they say, "Look, here it is," or "Look, there." For look, the kingdom of God is among you."
                                                                        (LUKE 17.20–21)

The kingdom of God is among you. Or—the Greek could mean this as well—it is *within you.* Here is a striking but ambiguous claim. Is the kingdom "among" them in the person and presence of Jesus? Then there is no need to look further afield. Or is the kingdom "within" each person? In this case, to keep watch for some political upsurge is to miss the point. Both readings of Jesus' words bring the kingdom across the threshold: It is no longer at hand; it is here, arrived. The kingdom may still be a focus of hope—for its own extension to embrace more people; for its perfection within each. But upheaval in the world's imperial order is not this kingdom's work. No wonder Luke's Jesus promises only that *"there are some of those standing here who shall not taste of death before they see the kingdom of God"* (Luke 9.27).

Quite different are the days of the Son of Man. Here is the hope of Jesus' pupils, of those who know him to be the Son of Man and who look forward to his triumph. But if the shared hope for the kingdom must be transformed, so must the hopes, specific to Jesus' circle, for its master's vindication: *And he said to his pupils: "Days will come when you will long to see one of the days of the Son of Man, and you will not see it"* (Luke 17.22).

These lines, about the kingdom and this disappointed longing, are recorded by Luke alone. They introduce a series of strange predictions. Several of these next sayings are shared with Matthew. In the Collection of Sayings on which he and Luke both drew, they had functioned in part to exhilarate and warn, in part to arm readers against false claimants to the role of Jesus. The collection had worked to strengthen its readers with the prospect of this universal and imminent judgment: Only those would be safe who had followed the collection's own teaching. Luke turns this function around: Such a crisis is not here and now, nor will it be for those within his generation too easily misled by their hopes into following false claims. Disclosure is under way but not in the manner spoken of in this dramatic language. Hopes for the kingdom's arrival were backed and defined by traditional expectations; Luke undermines them all. Expectation of the Son of Man's arrival was fostering new and dangerous hopes of its own. They must be reshaped and redirected. When the Son of Man returns, it will be a sudden appearance that no one can miss. To predict it, look out for it, set out to encounter it—all these are futile and will distract Luke's readers from the disclosures he would lay before them.

Here is an excerpt of these dark sayings about the coming of the Son of Man:

And they will say to you, "Look, there it is," or "Look, here." Do not go out after it, do not pursue it. For just as the lightening lightens up the sky from one end to the other, so will the Son of Man be in his day. But first he must suffer much and be rejected by this generation. . . . On the day when Lot left Sodom [warned as he was by God that the city was about to be destroyed], *fire and brimstone came down from heaven and destroyed them all. Just the same will it be on the day when the Son of Man is unveiled.*

On that day, whoever is on his housetop and his belongings are indoors, he must not go down into the house to get them. And whoever is in the fields, he must not turn back; remember Lot's wife [who turned back to look at the destruction of Sodom and was turned to a pillar of salt]. *All those who seek to save their life will lose it; and all those who lose their life will preserve it."*

(LUKE 17.23–33)

Two chapters later Jesus' journey comes finally to its end, and Luke returns us to the theme of the kingdom. We have already heard from Matthew one story of Jesus about his delayed return: A man heading off on a journey entrusts his capital to his servants, giving five great units of gold to the first, two to the second, one to the third. The first two trade successfully with the money; the third is scared, buries his gold, and returns it to his master, intact and without gain, on the latter's return. Luke records a story told by Jesus of a similar theme but quite different in detail: The master is now a nobleman; he must travel to a far country—as any claimant to a throne might travel to Rome—to be invested with a kingdom. We are to imagine the journey that Jesus must make to be invested by God with the kingdom that is God's alone to give. Luke's nobleman is hated by his fellow citizens; they send an embassy after him—again a scenario well known to the Roman east—opposing his enthronement. His servants, meanwhile, have been entrusted with capital. They handle it as differently as the servants did in Matthew's version and will be as differently rewarded. But this side of the story is now just a part of the larger drama: The new king returns and punishes his enemies. Luke has placed his version as Jesus' very last words before his triumphant entry into Jerusalem. And he has prefaced it with his own interpretation: *Jesus told them a parable, because he was near Jerusalem and they thought the kingdom of God was about to appear there and then* (Luke 19.11). Jesus must leave if the kingdom is to come and his servants are to be rewarded with command of its cities. It is *to a far country* that the nobleman must go; none is further distant than the land to which Jesus' last days in Jerusalem will take him.

Luke makes it clear: Hopes for the kingdom had been misplaced at that crisis in Jerusalem. Jesus' pupils had longer to wait. But by the time Luke is writing, another and later catastrophe has set Luke's readers asking, is it now? With the innermost group of his pupils, Jesus had looked over the city and its Temple. Mark's Jesus spoke darkly of the Temple's destruction, when not one of its huge stones would be left standing on another. The three pupils with him asked, when would this happen? What would be the sign that this was due to be fulfilled? Mark had Jesus answer in terms of the signs, of the whole extended crisis that will culminate in the Son of Man's arrival. But what of the Temple's destruction itself? Mark's Jesus warned them cryptically that *the abomination of desolation* [of which Daniel had warned] *will stand where it should not* (Mark 13:14).

Mark's readers, prior to the crisis of 70 C.E., had experienced at least one incident to which these words could be referred: the attempt by the emperor Caligula in 40 C.E. to have his own statue mounted in the Temple. But in the aftermath of 70 C.E., Mark's readers would have seen here an unambiguous prediction of the Temple's destruction and the Roman standards raised in its ruins.

Luke has worked carefully on this passage. The portent of which Daniel warned is linked in turn, as Mark's text stands, with the cataclysm that is to break upon the world and with the Son of Man's appearance in glory. Luke must avoid misunderstanding. He breaks any connection between the Temple's destruction and the portents of Daniel. He will not have the horrors of 70 C.E. stir further horrors still. The Temple has been destroyed, but this is not the start of God's final, sweeping intervention in the history of his world. Luke will be loyal to the sayings he has inherited from Mark and loyal as well to the readers who must not be misled. Here is how he renders the dark warnings of Mark's Jesus. We see Mark's words on the left, Luke's on the right:

"When you see 'the abomination of desolation' standing where it should not"— let the reader understand—"	*"When you see Jerusalem surrounded by armies, then know that her desolation is at hand;"*

Luke is making quite clear that Jerusalem's fall is the theme of these lines. He omits all that is obscure. Mark's last comment reveals in itself how uncertain his readers would have been to grasp the prophecy aright.

". . . then let those in Judaea flee to the mountains. . .	*". . . then let those in Judaea flee to the mountains. . .*
Those in the field must not turn back to pick up their cloak.	*Those in the country round about must not reenter it, for these are the 'days of punishment,' for the fulfilment of all that has been written.*
Woe to those who have children in the womb or are giving suck in those days."	*Woe to those who have children in the womb or are giving suck in those days."*

Mark's next line is about a disaster in winter. Its inclusion would only confuse Luke's presentation: Jerusalem fell to Titus's army in August-September. Luke omits it.

"Pray that it does not happen in winter."

Luke then narrows the significance of what follows: No more is portended by the city's destruction than the exile of its citizens and the occupation, here clearly stated, of its ruins. It is upon this people that punishment has fallen; the "days of punishment" proclaimed by the prophet Hosea were to fall specifically upon the people of Israel itself. The city's fall is one thing; quite separate is the worldwide disorder due to culminate in the triumph of the Son of Man. Mark could let the two merge; Luke has good reason to prize them apart.

"For those days will be a tribulation such as has not been since the beginning of God's creation until now, and such as shall not be again. And if God had not cut short those days, no flesh would have been saved."	*"For there shall come dire need upon the land and wrath upon this people. And they shall fall by the mouth of the sword and they shall be taken into captivity into all countries and Jerusalem shall be trampled by the gentiles, until the time of the gentiles is fulfilled."*
(MARK 13.14–20)	*(LUKE 21.20–24)*

Luke has now drawn the distinction beyond all misunderstanding. The destruction of Jerusalem did not mark the Son of Man's return. It can stir no such hopes now. He can now mention the Son of Man's return without fear of misunderstanding. The days of the Son of Man and the kingdom of God can be brought together at last:

"And there will be signs in sun and moon and stars, and upon the earth distress of nations in perplexity at the roaring of the sea and the waves, men fainting with fear and with foreboding of what is coming on the world; for the powers of the heavens will be shaken. And then they will see the Son of Man coming in a cloud with power and great glory. Now when these things begin to take place, look up and raise your heads, because your total ransom is drawing near."

(LUKE 21.25–28)

Luke draws next on a saying recorded by Mark and in a deft touch introduces the theme of the kingdom: *And he told them a parable: "Look at the fig tree, and all the trees; as soon as they come out in leaf, you see for yourselves and know that the summer is already near. So also, when you see these things taking place, know that the kingdom of God is near"* (Luke 21.29–32).

"Just the same," says Jesus of the destruction of Sodom, *"will it be on the day when the Son of Man is unveiled"* (Luke 17.30).

The language of cataclysm has merged with the language of disclosure, and Luke distances his readers from both alike. It is no surprise, then, that he isolates as well the most famous moment of Jesus' unveiling: his appearance on the mountain with Moses and Elijah. With a motif characteristic of Luke, Jesus is said to have been praying; the appearance of the prophets is primarily for Jesus' benefit and not for his pupils'. Luke's account makes clear that the three pupils who witnessed this meeting had there an experience unlike anything else involved in their understanding of Jesus and his message. There must be no confusion between this once-only privilege and the general evidence upon which the gospel's credibility depends. Luke tells his story as acutely as ever, evoking the pupil's trance-like state: *The three pupils were weighed down with sleep, but staying awake they saw his glory and the two men, the ones standing with him* (Luke 9.32). Mark's Peter talks of putting up three shelters, *for he did not know what to say* (Mark 9.6). Luke's makes the same proposal, *not knowing what he was saying* (Luke 9.33). A cloud overshadows them. Luke's pupils are frightened, with good reason. The cloud surrounds them, and out of it they hear the voice, *"This is my son, the Chosen One; hear him"* (Luke 9.35). Mark has Jesus instruct his pupils to tell no one what they had seen. In Luke the pupils need no instruction. The scene has been too awesome to speak of.

THE EYE OF A NEEDLE

Luke's Jesus ends his predictions with a stern warning:

"Take care that your hearts do not grow heavy in carousing and in drinking and in worldly care, and that day then comes upon you suddenly, like a snare. For it shall come upon all those on the face of the earth. But stay awake at all times, praying that you might have strength to escape all these things that are going to happen, and to stand before the Son of Man."

(LUKE 21.34–36)

So much is under threat in Luke, but how much is actually overturned? The prospect of future reversal is distant now, almost beyond the reader's horizon. The reader's search for hope, then, will be centered on the change that Jesus effects in his lifetime and in the church. As we would expect, a measure of this change is offered by the Baptizer. Luke's Baptizer launches his preaching with the dire warning that we heard from Matthew's: *"Generation of vipers, who has warned you to escape from the wrath to come?"* Luke then expands on its content:

> The crowds asked the Baptizer, "What then shall we do?" And he answered, "All who have two coats, let them share with those who have none; and all who have food, let them do the same." And even those who made a profit from collecting taxes came to be baptized and said to him, "Teacher, what shall we do?" And he said to them, "Collect no more than is appointed for you." And those serving as soldiers asked him, "And us, what shall we do too?" And he said to them, "Extort no money from anyone by intimidation or extortion; and be content with your wages."
>
> (LUKE 3.10–14)

This is radical enough, but it is the teaching of stability. More dramatic changes are to come. It will be the church in Jerusalem, at the beginning of the Mission, that will live out to the full the ideals that Jesus proclaimed. *And all who believed,* records Luke, *were together and had all things in common; and they sold their posses- sions and goods and distributed them all, as any had need* (Mission [Acts] 2.44). It is not clear whether it was demanded of would-be converts, as Luke understood it, that they pool their resources. But we hear of one couple that claimed a greater gen- erosity than they had in fact shown; they suffered a terrifying punishment for their deception:

> But a man named Ananias, with his wife, Sapphira, sold a piece of property and with his wife's knowledge he kept back some of the proceeds, and brought only a part and laid it at the missionaries' feet. But Peter said, "Ananias, why has Satan filled your heart to lie to the Breath of God and to keep back part of the proceeds of the land? While it remained unsold, did it not remain your own? And after it was sold, was it not at your disposal? How is it that you have contrived this deed in your heart? You have not lied to men but to God." When Ananias heard these words, he fell down and died. And great fear came upon all who heard of it.
>
> (MISSION [ACTS] 5.1–5)

These are powerful moments: the Baptizer's instruction at the gospel's start, the church's leaders and lifestyle at the Mission's. First moderation, then an extreme renunciation. And in between, the gospel is shot through with Jesus' demands. *"Sell what you own,"* he says, *"and give to those in need"* (Luke 12.33). Matthew's Jesus had said, *"Whoever loves his father or mother more than he loves me is not worthy of me, and whoever loves his son or daughter more than me is not worthy of me"* (Matthew 10.37).

Luke's has a starker message by far: *"Anyone who comes to me and does not hate his father and mother and wife and children and brothers and sisters and yes, his own life, he cannot be my pupil. . . . None of you, unless he renounces all that is his, can be my pupil"* (Luke 14.25, 33).

And yet in the Mission, in his story of the church's growth, Luke lets such radical teaching fade from sight. It is enough for him, it seems, to punctuate his story with parallels between the Baptizer, Jesus, and Jerusalem's first church—and then to move on. Is he embarrassed by these demands and this history that his own church cannot hope to match?

As ever, Luke embraces the full range of the gospel's demands, possibilities, and results. He builds into his story a movement that he may well have been seeing in communities and individuals around him. The course of a convert's life is often enough tumultuous now and may well have been so then, too; an inquirer first puts such questions as were put to the trenchant Baptizer. Those questions are given answers, practical but firm. But the instructor points onward, to the more radical answers of Jesus. An early faith is fired, fueled by the highest ideals. But perspectives broaden and ideals find their place within the ongoing demands of daily life—and faith comes in time to live more comfortably with the ways of the world around. Those demands of Jesus, radical and stark, are never denied in Luke's work and are never quite forgotten. They are lodged as an irritant within the story of a church that is ever more settled, ever more attractive to our distinguished and affluent Theophilus. Luke has a deep understanding of conversion. He tells three times of Paul's dramatic encounter on the road to Damascus, but he offers his readers, as well, far more nuanced and sensitive guidance than could be gleaned by such ordinary people as our-selves from the story of Paul's experience alone.

"It is easier for a camel to pass through the eye of a needle than for a rich person to enter the kingdom of heaven" (Luke 18.25). Luke has inherited Jesus' saying from Mark. But real danger comes to the wealthy, as Luke sees it, not from their wealth itself but from the arrogance to which it gives rise. His Jesus tells of the Rich Man who was clothed in purple and fine linen and who feasted every day. Luke's vivid details con-trast his luxurious living with the misery of Lazarus, the beggar at his gates: Lazarus longed to eat his fill from the Rich Man's scraps, while the dogs licked his sores. When both died, their roles were reversed: Lazarus was now *in the embrace of Abraham;* the Rich Man was tormented by fire. Abraham allowed no comfort to be given to the Rich Man:

> *"Son, remember that you received your good things in your lifetime, and Lazarus, in the same way, evil things. But now he is comforted here, and you are in anguish. And beside all this: between us and you a great gulf is fixed, so that those who wish to pass over from here to you cannot, nor can any pass over from you to us."*
>
> *(LUKE 16.25–26)*

The Rich Man has a request: *"Send Lazarus back to my father's house to warn my five brothers what lies ahead."* Here Luke turns his story to typically powerful effect. The dialogue is still between "Father Abraham" and his "son," the Rich Man; even when the punishment is fixed and there is no hope for the Rich Man's rescue, Luke's Jesus is alert to the relationship that he and Abraham should have had. Why, we might wonder, does Abraham mention that none can cross the gulf from his side to the Rich Man's? The description's symmetry suits the solemn moment well. But why should anyone wish to visit such torment if not to offer its victims the solace for which the Rich Man asks? It is forbidden. Father Abraham cannot show pity to his delinquent children, even if he would.

"Your brothers have Moses and the prophets," said Abraham. "Let them listen to them." But the Rich Man said, "No, Father Abraham, but even if someone came back to them from the dead, they will turn their hearts and ways." "If they will not listen to Moses and the prophets [said Abraham], *they will not be persuaded even if someone were to rise from the dead."*

(LUKE 16.29–31)

"Today You Will Be with Me in Paradise"

Luke has countered the danger seen by any Theophilus among his readers. The Christian sect is not subverting the empire's order. This is not where its promised upheaval lies. Luke defuses as well, it seems, the stark sense of his Jesus' blessings and woes: The poor remain the poor in this kingdom that is present "among us," and the rich the rich. But there is a mercy at work in Luke's Jesus, an openness and humanity, by which our ordinary categories of rich and poor, full and hungry, happy and mournful are taken up and enlarged out of all recognition. Yet again Luke stresses the most inflammatory reading he can devise of Jesus' words and then devotes his story to their reinterpretation. He redefines the politics of Christian hope; he redefines its social implications as well.

No Theophilus, it seems, has anything to fear from this gospel. The empire he serves is reasserted, and the privileges that define him are left for him to enjoy. But within this stability, everything is fluid. Any challenge to his emperor or his standing Theophilus could dismiss or prosecute. The challenge mounted by the gospel is far more invasive, far more personal: *The kingdom of God is within you.*

Luke's most famous stories tell of mercy, the mercy that God has for his people and that they should have for one another. As we have seen, the boundaries of God's people are broadening. And not just to embrace the most dignified of gentiles.

A lawyer stood up and tested Jesus: "Teacher, what shall I do to inherit life for all aeons?" "What is written," said Jesus, "in the Law?" "'You shall love the Lord your

God with your whole heart and with your whole being and with your whole strength and with your whole mind, and you shall love your neighbor as yourself."' Jesus said: "You are right. Do this, and you shall live." And the lawyer wanted to vindicate himself, and so asked: "And who is my neighbor?"

(LUKE 10.25–29)

With this preface Luke launches one of Jesus' most famous stories. A man, said Jesus, was on the road from Jerusalem to Jericho. He was set upon by robbers, beaten up, and left for dead. Three people then pass along the same road: one man from the caste of priests, one from the caste of the Temple's attendants, and one Samaritan. The first two see the man lying there but pass on. They had good reason to be afraid of pollution if they came into contact with a corpse. And the third, from the despised race of Samaritans? He bandages the man's wounds, puts him on his own animal, takes him to the next inn, and pays for his keep there.

"Which of these three," asked Jesus, "do you think was a neighbor to the man who fell among robbers?" "The one [replied the lawyer] *who showed mercy on him." Jesus said: "Go and behave the same way yourself."*

(LUKE 10.30–37)

The stories of Luke's Jesus are rarely as straightforward as they seem. The lawyer had asked, "Who is my neighbor?" He sought to define the object and extent of his duty. Jesus confronts him with the question, "To whom will you be a neighbor?" At issue is now the lawyer's own neighborliness. The spotlight has moved: from the person to whom care is shown onto the person who is showing care. From that first figure the lawyer—and readers—can stand back. From this second, the lawyer and readers can take no such distance, for this figure, challenged by Jesus' question, is themselves.

PRIDE AND PENITENCE

Jesus also told this parable to some who trusted in themselves that they were righteous and despised others: "Two men went up into the temple to pray, one a Pharisee and the other a man who made a profit from collecting taxes. The Pharisee stood and prayed: "God, I thank you that I am not like other men, extortioners, the unjust, adulterers, or even like this tax collector. I fast twice a week, I give tithes of all that I get." But the tax collector, standing far off, would not even lift up his eyes to heaven, but beat his breast, saying, "God, be merciful to me, a wrong-doer!" I tell you, this man went down to his house more just in God's sight than the other; for every one who exalts himself will be humbled, but he who humbles himself will be exalted."

(LUKE 18.9–14)

The Rich Man had seen Lazarus every day and had not been a neighbor to the emaciated, scabrous beggar at his gate. No sign of regret or of change from the Rich Man in his life; no remission of punishment after his death. Luke's Jesus is looking throughout for the change of heart that will reconcile those around him and those in his parables to God and to one another. We hear that the Pharisees and scribes resented his eating with those who "farmed" taxes for profit. He tells these critics three stories of loss and rescue. The first of the series is shared with Matthew; the other two are Luke's alone.

One sheep is lost; the shepherd leaves ninety-nine to head off and search it out. He invites his neighbors to share his delight when the sheep is found: *"Just so,"* Luke's Jesus tells the Pharisees, in a more vivid summary than Matthew's, *"there will be more delight in heaven over one wrongdoer who changes his heart and his ways than over ninety-nine just people who need no such change"* (Luke 15.3–7). A woman loses one of ten valuable coins. She, too, hunts high and low and asks her neighbors to celebrate its discovery. *"Just so, I tell you, there is delight before the angels of God over one wrongdoer who changes his heart and ways"* (Luke 15.8–10).

And so to the story of the Profligate Son. Here again Luke's Jesus tells a story finely tuned to its characters and carefully worded to surprise the reader. Luke the narrator and his Jesus: Yet again, in this third witness, we are offered a Jesus whose style of teaching matches the style of the author's teaching who records it. We are seeing Jesus through a distinctive author's lens; the stories told by Jesus and the stories told about him are written in the same key. Here is the story.

The younger of two sons asks their father for his share of the family inheritance. With it he sets off for a far country and a life of dissipation. The money runs out, the economy turns sour, he begs for work and is set to tending pigs, animals unclean and avoided by any Jew. So desperate is he that he longs to eat his fill from the husks given to the pigs; as Lazarus is hungry, so is the young man. Lazarus finds no comfort on earth; the young man has a chance for rescue. He returns home. He has prepared a speech—almost self-consciously abject—asking to be employed among his father's hired hands: *"I have done wrong before heaven and before you and no longer deserve to be called your son."* His father sees him at a distance; we might wonder if he has kept his eyes more often on the horizon than he would admit out loud. He runs out to meet the boy, embraces him, interrupts his well-crafted speech, and calls for the finest clothes and a feast: *"For this son of mine was dead and has come back to life, he was lost and has been found."* The older brother, who has worked steadily throughout, complains. His father replies, *"Son, you are always with me, and everything that is mine is yours. But it was right to celebrate; for this brother of yours was dead and is alive, he was lost and has been found"* (Luke 15.11–32).

This brother was dead and has come back to life. Twice Luke has the father sound this strange, dramatic note. Who is the son of whom it can be said, *He was dead and is alive?* Where the Profligate Son went, Jesus himself is going, too. Luke leaves the claim to echo, a chord all the more resonant for being played without comment or explanation: to rescue such vagabonds as the boy, this Jesus will himself undergo all the boy's degradation for himself.

Humans reconciled to God and reconciled with one another: In the very last scenes of the gospel, Jesus' influence continues. Luke extends the dialogue between Jesus and his pupils at the last supper they share before his death. Where Mark's Jesus had predicted Peter's desertion, simply and bleakly, Luke shows us an example of the master's care. Peter's failure is now no more than a moment within Jesus' protection of Peter himself and of those around him:

> *"Simon, Simon, look, Satan has asked for you all, to sift you like wheat. But I have prayed for you yourself, that your faith may not fail. And you, when you have turned again, strengthen your brothers." He said to him, "Sir, with you I am ready to go even to prison and to death." But he said: "I tell you, you "the Rock," the cock will not crow today until you have denied me three times."*
>
> *(LUKE 22.31–33)*

In the last words of this supper, Jesus warns his pupils to sell their coats to buy swords, and they show him the two they have already. One is quickly used. When the posse arrives to arrest Jesus, one of his entourage cuts off the ear of the high priest's servant. *"That is quite enough,"* says Jesus and heals the ear (Luke 22.51).

Luke has an unfailing sense of the pupils' frail humanity. He knows that they fell asleep after that last supper while Jesus prayed. Mark has their failure echo and reecho: Three times the chosen three with Jesus doze. Luke mentions their sleep just once. With the very touch we would expect of him, he explains—he almost excuses—their weakness: *Jesus found them asleep for grief* (Luke 22.45). Luke feels the sorrow of Jesus' loyal friends and the poignancy of Judas's betrayal: *"Judas,"* says his Jesus in the melee, *"do you betray the Son of Man with a kiss?"* (Luke 22.48). There is treachery, and there is simple frailty. In Luke we do not hear of the pupils running away; our attention is kept on Jesus himself and on his solemn words to the posse, *"This is your hour and the power of darkness"* (Luke 22.53). Luke and his Jesus are both gentle, both understanding. When Luke tells of Peter's denials he adds a sad note at their end:

> *And immediately, even as he spoke, the cock crowed. And the Lord turned and looked at Peter, and Peter remembered the Lord's words, when he said that "Before the cock crows you will deny me three times." And Peter went out and wept bitterly.*
>
> *(LUKE 22.60–62)*

Mark's Jesus was surrounded at the end by untrammeled derision or worse. Luke sees more nuance in these dark, tumultuous scenes: among those in judgment over Jesus, those who look on, and those who share his fate. Where the slightest scope is given, Jesus' healing power is at work, to the very end.

Pilate declares Jesus innocent. He sends the prisoner to Herod Antipas, who had long wanted to meet Jesus and who hoped to see him perform some miracle. Jesus does not oblige. Herod has him mocked, beaten, and dressed *in a shining cloak.* The last time Jesus appeared in such a glorious garment he was between two quite different figures: Moses and Elijah. Herod has Jesus beaten; Pilate has him handed over to death. But thanks to this consultation, their long-standing enmity is resolved: *on that very day they became friends* (Luke 23.12).

Jesus reaches the place of his death and is crucified. Luke's Jesus dies a tranquil death, trusting in his God. Here is no room for torment and despair. Some of the manuscripts recording the story include Jesus' famous words as he is raised on the cross, "*Father forgive them; for they do not know what they are doing*" (Luke 23.34).

Of the two thieves crucified with Jesus, one takes up the leaders' and soldiers' mocking cry: "*Aren't you the Anointed?*" says the thief: "*save yourself—and us.*" But the other shows more understanding: "*Don't you even fear God, when you are under the same punishment* as Jesus is? *We are quite rightly here, for we have the punishment our crimes deserve; but this man has done nothing wrong.*" And he turns to Jesus: "*Jesus, remember me when you come into your kingdom*" (Luke 23.39–42).

Here in the very last minutes of his life, Luke's Jesus exerts his healing influence—and corrects any false reliance on the coming of his kingdom. It is not in this that the thief should put his hope. No more should Luke's readers in their turn. *And Jesus says to him, "In truth I tell you, today you shall be with me in Paradise"* (Luke 23.43).

We have heard how many of the crowd and of the women followed Jesus to the place of execution, lamenting the death to come. Luke recalls them after Jesus has died. In Mark's story the onlookers had merely mocked. Luke, as we might expect of him, finds sympathy among them: *All those who had gathered there, the crowds who had come to watch, when they saw what had happened, went home beating their breasts. And all those known to him stood by at a distance, including the women who followed him from Galilee, to see it* (Luke 23.48–49).

At the end Luke's focus narrows again: upon these loyal, ever-present figures. A note shared with his fellow writers becomes in Luke the close to his gospel's most touching refrain. *And the women followed after, who were the ones who had come with him down from Galilee, and they saw the tomb and how the body was laid* (Luke 23.55).

Gods on Earth?

We have heard much of the links that the New Order makes with figures from the Old. Our witnesses are sure: Jesus can be identified and understood only by comparison and contrast with the heroes of Israel's past. A rich seam of connections is quarried. To look to such heroes was a method widely shared. The New Order offered its readers a Jesus deeply grounded in his nation's past and in its longest-standing hopes. This was necessary to make his claims credible at all; it did not set him, in itself, apart from the heroes and half-gods of the ancient world. Since power was interpreted as the gift or working of a god, so power's display suggested a god's presence. So at least the people of Lystra thought when Paul and Barnabas appeared among them.

> *Now at Lystra there was a man sitting who could not use his feet; he had been a cripple from birth. He listened to Paul speaking; and Paul looking intently at him and seeing that he had faith to be made well, said in a loud voice, "Stand up on your feet." And he sprang up and walked. And when the crowds saw what Paul had done, they lifted up their voices, saying in their own language, "The gods have come down to us in the likeness of men!" Barnabas they called Zeus [that is Jupiter, the king of the gods], and Paul, because he was the chief speaker, they called Hermes [or Mercury, the god of eloquence]. And the priest of Zeus, whose temple was at the city gates, brought oxen and garlands to the gates and wanted to offer sacrifice with the people. But when Barnabas and Paul heard of it, they tore their garments and rushed out among the crowd, crying, "Men, why are you doing this? We also are men, just like you, and bring you a gospel, that you should turn from these vain things to the living God who made the heaven and the earth and the sea and all that is in them. In past generations he allowed all the nations to walk in their own ways; yet he did not leave himself without witness, for he did good and gave you from heaven rains and fruitful seasons, satisfying your hearts with food and gladness." Even with these words they scarcely restrained the people from offering sacrifice to them.*
>
> (MISSION [ACTS] *14.8–18*)

Is such a welcome really credible? Or is Luke offering a mere parody of pagan error? We do well to stand back to see more broadly what was credible in the Greek world. To gain some sense of the possibilities that were known in Paul's day, we might turn to an extraordinary hymn sung upon the arrival of Demetrius the Besieger in Athens in 304 B.C.E. The reception he was given was remembered for centuries. The fervor represented here is striking enough; so is the sophistication of the poem itself—its themes, allusions, imaginative connections. As we have seen in the history of Vespasian, when our writers describe Jesus in terms of Israel's ancient heroes they are deploying a technique familiar throughout the ancient world. This technique had most value, in paganism, when it provided the hints and echoes to link the most powerful men with the gods whose power they seemed to share.

Demetrius the Besieger was an outstanding general. His father, Antigonus, had claims to a vast area of Alexander's empire. Demetrius's victories maintained his father's position; his impetuous tactics led at last to Antigonus's defeat and death. In 304 B.C.E. Demetrius entered Athens in triumph. The song that survives was carefully composed to greet him. This was no spontaneous adulation; it put into words what the Athenians needed—and perhaps wanted—to say. Every line alludes to the gods of Greece, the history of Athens, or the rituals that accompanied Demetrius's arrival. It is the language of a god's appearance on earth. A historian writing in the early second century C.E. records signs of displeasure from heaven that a human was being treated so unambiguously as divine. This historian's biographies were immensely popular; Demetrius was a famous figure in the circles in which our Theophilus moved.

The present verse translation was made in the 1930s, to capture its tone as a hymn of welcome. We now need some help to recognize its puns and references: Demeter was the grain goddess and wife of the god Poseidon. Her chief shrine was near Athens at Eleusis, where famous mysteries were celebrated; on her wandering to Eleusis she had come to the help of Athens. Now Demeter returns with Demetrius: She brings the mysteries, he brings freedom. He is handsome as a god should be; he arrives at due time. He wears a robe embroidered with stars and suns and with himself seated on a globe; the Athenians also wove pictures of Demetrius, alongside those of Zeus, into the robe that draped the great statue of the goddess Athene herself. An altar was set up and sacrifices offered at the spot where he dismounted in the city. The hymn begs for peace. The plea was tellingly chosen; Demetrius was a soldier to the core.

This hymn shows vividly how power was linked with divinity and how the recognition of the link was best expressed:

> See how the mightiest gods and best beloved
> towards our town are winging:
> for see, Demeter and Demetrius
> this glad day is bringing.
> She to perform her daughter's solemn rites,
> mystic pomp attends her;
> he, joyous as a god should be,
> comes with laughing splendor.
> Show forth your triumph! Friends, all troop round:
> let him shine above you!
> Be you the stars to circle him with love;
> he is the sun to love you.
> Hail, offspring of Poseidon, powerful god,
> child of Aphrodite!
> The other gods keep far from earth;
> they have no ears though mighty.
> They are not, or they will not hear us wail,
> but our own eyes behold you;
> not wood, not stone, but living, breathing, real—
> our own prayers enfold you.
> First give us peace, beloved, for you can;
> you are Lord and Master.

Luke has a rich, coherent story to tell, fueled on every page by the language and characters of the Old Order. But the privilege of having such a deep well on which to draw does not belong to Luke or the church alone. As this poem makes clear, pagans as well had stories to tell of gods' activity in their own presence and in their heroes'.

Demetrius was no threat to the church. But a younger contemporary of Jesus, the wandering philosopher Apollonius of Tyana, attracted devotion for two centuries or more. Here was a serious rival to Jesus. A long account of Apollonius's life was written by Philostratus; so influential had his hero's memory become that the church historian Eusebius, writing soon after 300 C.E., composed a virulent attack on Apollonius's reputation. The cult of Apollonius attracted the hostility of the first Christians who had power to attack it. It was the temple of Asclepius at Aegae, linked with Apollonius's memory, that the Christian emperor Constantine was quick to suppress.

Apollonius was believed to have healed the sick, foretold the future, and raised the dead. And he was said by his devotees to be alive beyond his death. His biographer wrote in the terms and, where appropriate, with the judicious caution that his educated readers would value. Most of Apollonius's healings are recorded in a single section of this biography; some have wondered if these stories evolved in response to the miracles recorded of Jesus. Philostratus's biography was written in the late second century C.E., a hundred years or more after its subject's death, time enough for history to become romance. But this is not ground enough to be cynical. Luke's gospel itself, after all, reached its final form more than fifty years after Jesus had died, and Paul's story in Luke is also told in a style that Philostratus's readers would relish. Adventure, biography, the teaching of a sage: The combination was as popular in the first century as in the second.

Apollonius, it seems, was at one point active in Rome. It was a dangerous time. He incurred the suspicion of Tigellinus, Nero's most hated agent. Apollonius was said to have foreseen the emperor's narrow escape from death by a thunderbolt. Tigellinus quizzed and tested him. This "prophet," after all, could become a center of power, all too willing and able to criticize the emperor's; it might be politic to silence him.

What, then, was the source of Apollonius's abilities? Jesus' opponents had sought to trap Jesus; Apollonius's dangerous adversary, too, laid snares. "Why," asked Tigellinus, "are you not afraid of Nero?" "The same God," answered Apollonius, "who lets him seem fearsome has made me fearless." "And what do you think about Nero?" Here was the time for such flattery as those around Nero had learned well. What would Apollonius praise? The emperor's rule? His poetry? His displays of singing on the public stage? Apollonius was more subtle than Tigellinus had expected. "Much better," answered Apollonius, "than you do, for you think he deserves to sing; I think he deserves to keep silent."

Here is a miracle of Apollonius, recorded in the "Roman" section of the story and not with Apollonius's other healings. We keep the tone of Philostratus's report: admiring but cautious. He has edited his sources carefully. He wants to win respect for his story. Mere credulity will not help his cause:

A girl seemed to have died at the hour of her marriage. The groom was following the bier, lamenting his marriage left unfulfilled. Rome was mourning with him for the girl was of an aristocratic family. Apollonius came upon their mourning. "Put down the bier," he said, "for I will stop you from weeping for this girl." He asked what was her name. The crowds thought that he was going to deliver an oration, but he did nothing else than touch her and whisper something over her. He woke up the girl from her apparent death, and the child spoke out loud and returned to her father's house just as Alcestis when raised to life by Hercules. Now whether Apollonius had detected a spark of life in her which had escaped her nurses, for it is said that it was raining at the time and a vapor rose from her face, or whether he restored her life that was really extinct, by the warmth of his touch—the answer to this question could not be decided either by myself or by those who were actually present at the time.

How might such a sage as Apollonius have seen his own relation with the gods? If we can judge such a belief by the commitment to which it leads, one of the most remarkable acts of faith of which we know from the Greek world was the suicide of the philosopher and former Christian Peregrinus. We know of the event chiefly from the satirist Lucian; to him Peregrinus was an outright fraud, but of the manner of his death itself Lucian has no doubt. He claims to have been present himself. Peregrinus declared, well in advance, that he would throw himself on a burning pyre at the Olympic Games in 165 C.E. And so he did. This was his route to divinity. An act of faith? Of theater? Great importance was attached to the immortality one could earn by a famous life—and by a famous death. A "martyr" is a "witness." Martyrs might be Christian, pagan, or philosophical alike. They all bore witness—very public, memorable witness—to their faith and the loyalty they bore it.

Peregrinus's was not the only such death. The philosopher Empedocles was said to have thrown himself, around 433 B.C.E., into the volcano on Mount Etna in Sicily. We hear the story from a philosopher of the following century. Empedocles wanted, it seems, to confirm the report that he had changed into a god. For he had (apparently) raised a woman from the dead. He had then woken up one night to see a light in heaven and to hear a loud voice calling his name. He had fallen into a sleepwalking trance. When found the next day, he had told his followers not to worry but to pay him divine honors, for he was now a god. This may sound to us too odd to take seriously at all. But these narratives were recorded by a most distinguished thinker; Empedocles' philosophy was influential for generations, and anyone who respected his story would not think strange the story of our missionary Paul.

Rather different motives were declared by the Indian philosopher of Alexander the Great, Calanus, who preferred death to an impending senility. Calanus was escorted to his own pyre by Alexander's troops, garlanded himself with flowers "in the Indian style," and lay down on the pyre surrounded by the treasures that his general had given him for the occasion. Alexander ensured that Calanus's memory would be immortal. When, generations later, another Indian threw himself on a fire in Athens in 20 B.C.E., the chronicler Dio accorded him less respect. "He wished to die," writes Dio, "either because he was of the caste of sophists"—that is, in this case, of Brahmins—"and was therefore moved by ambition or because of old age in accordance with ancestral custom, or because he wished to make a display for the benefit of the emperor Augustus, who was present, and of the Athenians. He was initiated into the mysteries and cast himself alive into the fire."

Peregrinus, we know, had been influenced by the Brahmins. Dio remembers Calanus and wonders if his Indian did also. There is a tradition here: of a spectacular, voluntary death. We know a certain amount about Peregrinus; we can try to diagnose his state of mind; we can locate the traditions in which he hoped or believed he stood. But we do best to read his story and those like it as a warning against any easy expectation that we can understand those who lived, believed, and died two thousand years ago.

CHAPTER 8

The Old Order
and the New

God of Our Ancestors

"Ancient Times Were Closest to the Gods"

"The greatest fruit of piety," wrote a pagan philosopher and fierce opponent of Christianity, "is to worship God according to the tradition of one's fathers." The instinct ran deep in the ancient world: Ancestral rites and beliefs were justified by their age. Those born into them had good reason—they had a duty—to maintain them: "It is impious," wrote the pagan philosopher Celsus at the end of the second century C.E., "to abandon the customs which have existed in each locality from the beginning." New rites, by the same token, were suspect by their very nature. We will hear more of Celsus's objections to the Christian faith. He says,

> I will ask the Christians where they have come from, or who is the author of their traditional laws. "Nobody," they will say. In fact, they themselves originated from Judaism, and they cannot name any other source for their teacher and chorus leader. Nevertheless they rebelled against the Jews.

The principle was applied in practice. Following a crime wave linked with Bacchanalian rites in 186 B.C.E., the great historian Livy tells us, the Roman senate eventually banned them all except "where an ancient altar or image had been consecrated."

"The preservation," wrote the Roman statesman Cicero, "of the rites of the family and of our ancestors means preserving the religious rites which, we can almost say, were handed down to us by the gods themselves, since ancient times were closest to the gods." We have seen what close relation with the gods might be claimed by or for the heroes of philosophy and war. But what of ordinary individuals? What connection might they have felt with the gods feted and invoked in a city's public prayers, rites, and celebrations? For the moment we need not ask what personal relation such people as these—that is, people such as ourselves—would expect to have with their gods. Such a relation would not ensure for a region its fields' fertility, victory at war, or cohesion in city and state unless that individual was the king, in which case his role was not that of an "individual" at all. Worship was a response to perceived power; and the social order that its rites and convictions reinforced was already their sufficient vindication.

We live in cultures so stable that we can look to religion for the support and guidance of our private lives alone. But where a community is in thrall to the unpredictable powers of nature, great empires, and its own divisions, the gods are needed first to provide food, defend the land, and prevent civil war. The shared rites fortify the cohesion they are performed to secure: "In all probability, disappearance of piety toward the gods will entail the disappearance of loyalty and social union among men as well, and of justice itself, the queen of all the virtues." The public rites mattered; their supervision was a civic duty. "If these idols are nothing," asked Celsus, "why is it terrible to take part in the high festival?" Everyone of due standing should "accept public office in our country if it is necessary for the preservation of the laws and of piety."

Now the Jews, as Celsus conceded, "made laws"—quite rightly—"according to the custom of their country; and they maintain these laws among themselves to the present day and observe a worship which may be very particular, but at least it is traditional. In this respect they behave like the rest of mankind, because each nation follows its traditional customs, whatever kind may happen to be established." Even Tacitus, vehement antagonist though he was of the Jews, acknowledged as much: "Jewish worship is vindicated by its antiquity." This theme is most fully explored by Josephus in an addition to his main work on *The Antiquities of the Jews*. The supplement is written in two books; to each of them Josephus writes a formal introduction. We will recognize their style from Luke's own introductions. We will recognize their theme as well. Josephus defends the standing of Judaism; it is the ancient faith of an ancient community. Luke, as we have seen, must defend the church, the heir, as he would have it, to precisely this community.

Josephus, too, is writing to a powerful gentile. Here is his preface to Book 1: "Through my book on our *Antiquities*, Your Excellency Epaphroditus, I have made things sufficiently clear, I think, to those who peruse it, about our nation of the Jews: that this nation is immensely ancient; that it had its own pure origin; and how it occupied the land that we now have. A book, covering the history of 5,000 years, that I wrote in Greek on the basis of the sacred books among us." And here in turn is

Josephus's introduction to his work's second half. Josephus wins credibility for his book by citing Greek historians; Luke, by contrast, works throughout at the internal coherence of the Old Order and the New, fortified only by reference to imperial dates and official trials. "Through the first volume of this book, my most esteemed Epaphroditus, I demonstrated the antiquity of our race, corroborating its truth from the writings of the Phoenicians, Chaldaeans, and Egyptians and citing as witnesses many historians of the Greeks. . . . "

Luke insists that the Christians are the heirs to Judaism appointed by God. Celsus will have none of it. "They rebelled against the Jews in their communal life and in their beliefs." The result is absurdity: Why did God "give contradictory laws to this man from Nazareth, his son? Who is wrong: Moses or Jesus? Or when the father sent Jesus, had he forgotten what commands he gave to Moses? Or did he condemn his own laws and change his mind?" Celsus is writing a century or more after Luke. But the challenge that he raised had been raised from the start, and Luke's whole work is one long, sustained response to such attack.

TELLING THE STORY

Luke's Christianity is to be the heir to Judaism, not by excluding the Jews, but by extending God's New Order to embrace the gentiles, too. The tensions that dominated Matthew are seen by Luke from the outside in. Matthew's readers, predominantly Jewish, must recognize their independence from the synagogues to which they feel deep and ancestral loyalty. Luke's gentile readers are to absorb, believe, and benefit from the change wrought in the most exclusive, self-contained of ancient religions. Matthew looks outward to a gentile world; Luke looks inward from that world. Matthew must persuade Jews that their true community has changed to embrace gentiles. Luke must persuade gentiles that his church is indeed this community, which in its new form embraces themselves.

At issue is not simply the extension of boundaries. The character of this new community is changed, too: what makes it distinctive, what wins praise, and what its members are to hope for. A journey is to be undertaken: by the pupils of Jesus to Jerusalem; by the readers to a new understanding; and by those readers again as they follow up on their new insights in their own lives. The balance between Jesus' journeys and Paul's is well kept; both involve for the pupils, for Paul, and for the readers, a deepening perspective that comes not just from reading but from the road that their reading encourages them to follow. The stories of those journeys, Jesus' and Paul's, fuel the readers' own dual journey of understanding and of commitment. It is a journey at once triumphant and tragic, for the journey that brings the readers to Jerusalem takes them ever further from the ways, rites, and restrictions observed there. And more: The course of the text, as we shall see, brings the reader fully to see what Paul's adventures bring him ever more fully to declare.

Luke sets up small, teasing oddities from the very start. His first chapter draws deeply on the Old Order and its hopes for Israel. The angel's two promises and the subsequent poems of Mary and of Zechariah are all directed to the hopes of the Jews themselves. These children, the Baptizer, and Jesus, are going to meet all the expectations of their own people. The Baptizer, promises the angel,

will turn many of the children of Israel to the Lord their God,
and he will go before his face in the breath and power of Elijah,
to turn the hearts of fathers to their children
to turn the disobedient to the understanding of the just
to make ready for the Lord a people well prepared.

(LUKE 1.16–17)

With chapter 2 the setting changes. We are on the Roman stage: *It happened in those days that a decree went out from the emperor Augustus that all the inhabitants of the world should be registered* (Luke 2.1). And on this stage we will stay: The angels take up the empire's proudest claim of "peace on earth"; Jesus, says Simeon, will be God's salvation in the face of all peoples, a light for disclosure to the gentiles. Whatever form this peace and salvation take, they will be offered to gentiles also. To inherit the throne of David is to rival the powers that occupy his country. Jesus, as we have seen, competes in the language of those powers' propaganda. But his peace and salvation are not freedom from gentile power; they are offered to those gentiles to share.

Luke is tapping a rich seam of connections. It was a census that had sparked rebellion against Rome in 6 C.E.; the Old Order forbade any such new census of Jews, and such a registration would be the prelude to further taxation. But in Luke's story the census brings the Davidic savior to David's city of Bethlehem. The orders of Rome's emperor put in place the due conditions for the true emperor's birth; the enemy of God's people is agent of his will. From the first pages of the gospel, God is harnessing the empire to his purpose, an empire, by the same token, that this purpose does not undermine.

The birth of Jesus is clearly set in the reign of Augustus, his public appearance, just as formally, in the reign of the next emperor, Tiberias: *In the fifteenth year of the reign of the emperor Tiberius, when Pontius Pilate was governor of Judaea, Herod was in command of Galilee, when Annas and Caiaphas were high priests, there came the word of God to the son of Zechariah in the desert* (Luke 3.1–2). The Baptizer is a figure so steeped in Jewish tradition that it is already striking to find him set within this international context. Luke pursues the theme. He relishes the prediction of Isaiah that the Baptizer would fulfill. A royal road is being built that will outrank all the grand achievements of Rome's famously effective engineers. Once these lines are read as poetry—as the next of the gospel's songs, following Mary's prediction and Zechariah's—then the promise of this great avenue becomes as well a stark warning. The high and mighty should beware:

The voice of one crying in the desert [said Isaiah],
"Make ready the way of God,

make his paths straight."
Every valley shall be filled
and every mountain shall be brought low;
and the crooked routes shall be made straight
and the rough places shall be made smooth.

(ISAIAH 40.3–4)

Luke, alone of our witnesses, includes the prophet's next and most stirring line:

And all flesh shall see the salvation of God.

(ISAIAH 40.5; LUKE 3.4–6)

The first fanfare of Jesus' preaching is in the synagogue of his hometown, Nazareth. We have already heard the story's triumphant start. Jesus is given the scroll of the prophet Isaiah; he finds the passage he wants, and he reads from the prophet:

The Breath of the Lord is upon me,
because the Lord has anointed me
to preach good news to the poor;
he has sent me
to announce freedom for the prisoners
and sight for the blind,
to send out the oppressed in liberty,
to proclaim the year of God's favor.

(LUKE 4.18–19)

Luke continues in the grand style that he reserves for his story's most significant scenes:

And rolling up the scroll he gave it back to the attendant and sat down. And the eyes of everyone in the synagogue were fixed on him. And he began to say to them: "Today this writing is fulfilled in your ears." And everyone was testifying and was amazed at the words of grace that came out from his mouth, and was saying, "Is this not the son of Joseph?"

Jesus does not bask in this admiration. He already knows the pressures that will lead to his rejection here in Nazareth. His task is not to be a local hero; he must work on a larger stage.

And Jesus said to them: "You will all quote the saying to me, 'Physician, heal yourself. Everything that we have heard happening at Capernaum, do the same here in your own homeland.'" And he said: "In truth I tell you, no prophet is acceptable in his own homeland."

(LUKE 4.20–24)

Jesus carries on his challenge. Both Elijah and Elisha, two great prophets of Israel, lived at times when there was dire need in their own country. But God sent both to help gentiles: Elijah fed a gentile widow when a famine was sweeping Israel; Elisha healed the gentile Naaman of his leprosy when there were more than enough Jews who needed such help. Jesus is stirring the antagonism that his words anticipate. He has raised the stakes.

And they were all filled with anger in the synagogue when they heard this. They rose up and threw him out of the city, and took him up to the top of the cliff on which their city was built so that they might throw him down. But he walked through the midst of them and went on his way.

(*LUKE 4.28–30*)

Jews and gentiles: The limits of Jesus' mission and of God's blessing are unsettled. What was once expected is no longer assured. What to expect in its place is not yet clear. But a warning is at hand, sad and final. Jesus is on his way. And those who resist him must beware, for he may just pass through their midst and walk away.

The New Escape

JESUS: THE JOURNEY TO JERUSALEM

From the flicker of details to the gospel's broadest structure, Luke has introduced strange possibilities; he now gives his readers the space to absorb them. Almost a third of Luke's gospel is devoted to Jesus' journey to Jerusalem. We hear little of the route or of Jesus' progress along it. On its course we are once told *he went through cities and villages teaching and making his way to Jerusalem* (Luke 13.22). It is slightly more surprising, when the journey's narrative is nearing its close, to hear that *it happened in his travel to Jerusalem that he himself passed between Samaria and Galilee,* well to the north (Luke 17.11). We would have expected to hear of this far sooner, but Luke is about to tell of a Samaritan leper in a story that he has good reason to put at the journey's end; that detail of Jesus' movements may well have been shaped or placed to meet this story's needs.

There is even less in Jesus' words and actions specific to such travel. It has long been wondered whether Luke has collected here, within the loosely constructed framework of this journey, a large number of stories for which he had no more obviously suitable context. A good many sayings from the collection that he shares with Matthew, a series of important parables, a handful of healings—here, it seems, is a hodgepodge, important but disconnected, that Luke has strung together by the journey's theme and rounded off before his Jesus comes finally to Jerusalem.

We need to look more closely at this journey and at the role its story plays, for there is more to it than meets the eye. Its structure is quietly marked, but is important. Those hints that we heard right at the gospel's start are opening out: Jewish hopes embracing gentiles, too; an old order giving birth to a new; and Jerusalem and its Temple cut off from God's plan at the very moment and through the very act that brings God's plan to its intended triumph. The pendulum of this change is ever longer, the swing of its arc is ever deeper and broader. But Luke is still not ready to mount strong, programmatic claims; he is still preparing the ground. There will be space enough for open, forthright challenge: in the Mission (Acts).

THE NEW ESCAPE

When Jesus appeared on the mountain in glory to Peter, John, and James, he was flanked as in Mark's version by Moses and Elijah. Luke gives us more detail of their conversation: *They were discussing his Escape*—the very word used in the Old Order to describe Israel's liberation from Egypt—*that he was going to fulfill in Jerusalem* (Luke 9.31). Moses was the person with whom to discuss it: Here is the leader of the second Escape conferring with the prophet of the first. The veil was not drawn back just for the pupils' sake, for them to see and acknowledge Jesus' glory. Luke gives the moment a function in Jesus' progress rather than theirs. Jesus is praying at the time of the apparition; he is setting out on a lonely Escape; he is fortified by great figures of the past who have trodden such paths before.

Luke starts Jesus' long journey to Jerusalem with a signpost of grand style. A general in the Old Order had led his troops by keeping his face toward their destination; Jesus is unmistakably headed for the Jerusalem so resented by Samaria:

> Now it happened in the fulfillment of the days for his being taken up that he set his face firmly for going to Jerusalem. And he sent messengers before his face. And on their way they came to a village of the Samaritans to make ready for him; and the Samaritans did not receive him, because his face was directed toward Jerusalem.
>
> (LUKE 9.51–53)

James and John, well named the "sons of thunder," want to bring down upon the village the punishment that Elijah had invoked on his enemies' army: *"Sir, do you want us to call*—as Elijah had—*for 'fire to come down from heaven and destroy them'?"* (Luke 9.54) This was not the way of Luke's Jesus; he told the two off and went on to another village.

At the journey's start the Samaritans reject Jesus. At its end ten lepers ask for his help. He tells them to go show themselves to the priests; it was the priests' job to check on such illness and its apparent cure. As they go, they are healed. Just one of the ten turns back to thank him: a Samaritan.

And Jesus said, "Were not ten healed? Where are the nine? Were none of them found
to turn back and give glory to God except this one foreigner?" And he said: "Get up,
and be on your way. Your faith has saved you."

                                                                    (LUKE 17.17–19)

From the Samaritans' rejection of Jesus to the thanks of the Samaritan alone. As
Jesus moves slowly toward Jerusalem, he moves steadily further from the leaders that
represent it. The crowds around Jesus become ever larger and more excited. He
teaches, warns, corrects; there is scope for so much error in the crowds then and in the
readers now. The people's leaders, meanwhile, grow ever fiercer in their opposition.
For them Jesus has nothing but steady, forthright condemnation.

Some in the crowds were testing him, looking for a sign from heaven with which
he would vindicate his claims. When *the crowds were gathering, more and more,* Jesus
spoke up to warn, *"This generation is an evil generation: it seeks a sign, and no sign will
be given it"* (Luke 11.29). While he was still speaking, a Pharisee asked him to a meal.
The host was then surprised that Jesus did not wash before eating, and Jesus launched
into the series of "Woes," aimed at the Pharisees, that we have already encountered at
the end of Matthew's gospel. To make quite sure that his Jesus covered all the targets,
Luke has had a lawyer interject, *"Teacher, when you say these things you insult us, too"*
(Luke 11.45). Jesus duly turned his fire on lawyers. This was enough to launch a conspiracy against Jesus between Pharisees and scribes. A division was opening between
those who would hear Jesus' warnings and those—identified chiefly as the Pharisees—
who would not. The Pharisees started their plotting; *the thousands in the crowd were so
tightly packed that they were falling over one another,* and Jesus started telling his pupils:
*"First and foremost: keep clear of the leaven of the Pharisees, which is play acting and
hypocrisy"* (Luke 12.1). The momentum continues throughout the journey: On the
one hand, *great crowds were congregating* (Luke 14.25); on the other, the Pharisees find
him deeply suspect and turn up their noses at him (Luke 15.1). Luke inserts the characteristic note: The Pharisees loved money and so derided him (Luke 16.14).

Luke is building a vast double movement: at the same time toward Jerusalem and
away from its priorities and standards. The Samaritans reject him at the journey's start;
the Samaritan is the only leper who returns to thank him at its end. The Pharisees
invite him to meals in its first half and conspire to have him killed in its second. The
hub around which this narrative turns is, as we might expect, at the very center of the
journey, which is as well the center of the gospel as a whole.

This central point is framed by two healings. Jesus is teaching in a synagogue on
the Sabbath. A woman is there who has been crippled for eighteen years. Jesus heals
her. The synagogue's superintendent is indignant; there are six days, he tells the
crowd, on which one should work. *"Come on those and be healed and not on the
Sabbath."* Jesus himself retorts, *"Play actors, doesn't each one of you untie his ox or his
ass from the stall on the Sabbath and take it out for watering?"* (Luke 13.10). In the
following chapter we hear of another healing, once more on a Sabbath. This time

Jesus is at a meal with a Pharisee. *"Is it permitted,"* he asks, *"to heal on the Sabbath or not? Which of you has a son or an ox and would not instantly pull it out if it fell into a well on the Sabbath?"* (Luke 14.1).

Luke has clearly placed these stories to balance each other. And in between them, at the journey's central point, Jesus gives the warning that we have heard in Matthew: He proclaims the first of his laments over the doomed Jerusalem. Matthew's Jesus had already entered Jerusalem when he looked forward to these words of welcome; his prophecy will be fulfilled only at Jesus' final return in judgment. Luke's readers will hear within the story itself of the prophecy's fulfillment, when Jesus enters the city in triumph at the end of his present journey. Yet again Luke defuses any hopes, to which the words of Jesus might give rise, that the present order of society and the world is about to be undone.

He went on his way through towns and villages, teaching, and journeying toward Jerusalem. And someone said to him, "Sir, will those who are saved be few?" And he said to them, "Strive to enter by the narrow door: for many, I tell you, will seek to enter and will not be able. When once the householder has risen and shut the door, you will begin to stand outside and knock at the door and say, "Lord, open to us." He will answer you, "I do not know where you came from." Then you will begin to say, "We ate and drank in your presence, and you taught in our streets." But he will say, "I tell you, I do not know where you come from; depart from me, all you workers of injustice."

There you will weep and grind your teeth, when you see Abraham and Isaac and Jacob and all the prophets in the kingdom of God, and you yourselves thrust out. And men will come from east and west, and from north and south, and sit at the table in the kingdom of God. And look, some are last who will be first, and some are first who will be last.

"I must go on my way today and tomorrow and the day following; for it cannot be that a prophet should die away from Jerusalem. O Jerusalem, Jerusalem, killing the prophets and stoning those who are sent to you: how often would I have gathered your children together as a hen gathers her brood under her wings, and you would have none of it. Look, your house is forsaken. I tell you, you will not see me until you say, 'Blessed is he who comes in the name of the Lord.' "

(LUKE 13.22–35)

SHAPING THE STORY

We have seen Luke's use of recurring themes, the signposts that steer the reader through his story. We might wonder, of course, just how significant such repetitions are. Here is one, for instance, that surely betrays Luke as a clumsy editor. At the end of Jesus' journey Luke takes over a story that Mark had recorded at the same stage in the gospel: A rich man comes up to Jesus and asks, *"Good teacher, what shall I do to inherit life for all aeons?"* Jesus takes him through the Ten Commandments. When he insists that he has kept all these from his youth onward, Jesus warns him, *"Sell all that you have and give it to the poor, and you will have treasure in heaven"* (Luke 18.18–22).

"Teacher, what shall I do to inherit life for all aeons?" Oddly, we have heard this question in Luke's story already, several chapters earlier: in the short dialogue, between Jesus and a lawyer, that leads into the story of the Good Samaritan and his care for the wounded man. *"What is written in the Law?"* Jesus asked the lawyer; *"What do you read there?" And he said, "'You will love the Lord your God with all your heart and with all your strength and with all your mind; and your neighbor as yourself'"* (Luke 10.25–27). Luke has inherited this little exchange from Mark. Mark's version is placed far later in his story, when Jesus is already in Jerusalem and is being quizzed and tested by every faction that opposes him. In his version a scribe came up with the slightly different question, *"Which is the most important Law of all?"* (Mark 12.28). Luke, then, has moved the short dialogue and changed the opening question. But why?

Luke's questioner now asks at the start of Jesus' journey exactly what the rich man will ask at its end: *"Teacher, what shall I do to inherit life for all aeons?"* This one question now frames the journey as a whole; here is its overarching theme. Luke's readers are to notice the shape of Jesus' journey. Such signposts are not mere decoration. They help the narrative perform its function, that of steering the readers along their double arc, at once toward and away from Jerusalem, through the journey of the new Escape.

These two short stories give us, too, a touching glimpse of Luke's own handiwork. This most skillful craftsman must tidy up the hole he has left in his own later narrative. Mark rounded off that second dialogue, on the most important law, with a flourish of his own: *And no one any longer dared to question him.* Luke has removed the dialogue from its place in Mark; he does not repeat it when Jesus is there in Jerusalem, answering his opponents' questions. But in its new place he did not need this closing sentence. His version of the dialogue, after all, was the start of a scene, not its end. So he left Mark's conclusion behind. And there it still is: rounding off the story that Luke had found in Mark's narrative just before the dialogue he has moved. Luke leaves that previous story exactly as it was—with this one addition: *They no longer dared to question him on anything.*

Mark offered a dramatic prelude to Jesus' arrival in Jerusalem. When he left Jericho, last city on the road south before Jerusalem itself, the blind beggar Bartimaeus cried out to *the son of David* for help—just as the son of David was preparing to enter David's own city, Jerusalem. Luke adds an incident to the journey's end. As Jesus went through Jericho,

Look, there was a man called Zacchaeus: he was in charge of those who made their profit from the collection of taxes, and he was rich. And he was looking for a way to see Jesus, to see who he was, and he could not because of the crowd, for he was too

short. And running on ahead he climbed a fig tree so as to see him, because he was due to pass that way. And when Jesus came to the spot, he looked up and said to him, "Zacchaeus, hurry on down, for today I must stay at your house." And everyone saw it and grumbled: "He has gone in to relax with a wrongdoer."

(LUKE 19.2–7)

This story is already, after just its introduction, wholly typical of Luke. Zacchaeus is introduced with personal—almost comic—detail: He cranes to see above those taller than himself. Jesus' attention will as ever be on those that others despise. He addresses Zacchaeus by name: a name that within the story he has no reason to know. Such tax collectors as Zacchaeus were among those who came to the Baptizer to be baptized. He had ordered them, *"Do not take more than is appointed you"* (Luke 3.13). Such figures as Zacchaeus had ignored the instruction then, but he is ready to make reparation now. The requirements made at the gospel's start are echoed and met at its end. The Baptizer had told those with two coats to give one to the poor; Zacchaeus is about to give half his possessions away. Yet again, Luke's patterning marks a progress: not in any one individual, but in the sequence of figures that encounter Jesus, and so in the response that the readers can make as they encounter more and more of the gospel itself.

So for the story's conclusion? Jesus makes no demand for the reparation that Zacchaeus offers. Salvation is offered in the presence of Jesus, then and there. Jesus offers friendship; it is for Zacchaeus to respond as he will. The Baptizer had warned the crowds coming to him: *"Do not start saying to yourselves, 'We have Abraham for our father.' For I tell you: God can raise up children for Abraham from these stones"* (Luke 3.8). Abraham, in Jesus' story of Lazarus, had rejected the Rich Man's plea for help; but a man such as Zacchaeus who shows regret for his wrongdoings is back within the shepherd's fold. One profligate son, at least, has been found and rescued.

But Zacchaeus stood up and said to the Lord, "Look, half of my goods, sir, I give to the poor, and if I have extorted anything from anyone, I restore it fourfold." And Jesus said to him, "Today salvation is upon this house, for this man too is a child of Abraham. For the Son of Man came to seek and to save what was lost."

(LUKE 19.8–10)

THE READER: JOURNEY TO UNDERSTANDING

Jesus' journey is at an end. But the reader's journey is only just beginning. Luke has invited them to join his Jesus on a journey designed to last their whole lives through. We are following the thread of a single story. But the thread of Luke's narrative is woven from at least three strands. We will tease them apart for a closer look at each, then reweave them to form and follow once more their single thread.

First, then: Luke, as we have seen, is informing and reassuring his readers. He offers them insights one by one, and, more important, he offers them a progressive journey into understanding. He has shaped and punctuated his story to give them the impetus to set out on that pilgrimage and the guidance to follow it through. He lets the same themes reemerge over and over to tease, prompt questions, and challenge assumptions. Fears are raised and then laid to rest. Expectations are excited and then translated into new forms and unforeseeable fulfillment.

And second: Part of that understanding is of the nature of history itself, of God's working in the world. The Old Order has been taken up into the New; the leader of the New is followed by his pupils and missionaries in turn. As Jesus echoed Moses, Elijah, and Elisha, so Paul echoes Jesus himself. There is a shape, an order to the history of which each of us is part. We are invited to do more than assess claims; we are to recognize the single, unified pattern within which the Old Order, the Baptizer, Jesus, Paul, and we ourselves all live and work. The move toward the New Order is not random. Every element of this history has its place in the pendulum's widening arc on its ever longer swing. From the prophets to Jesus, from Jesus back to Paul; from Jerusalem and the Jewish people, over and over, to gentiles and to Rome.

And third: The readers grow in understanding by following the story of Jesus and his pupils. But the text invites the readers to do more: to enter the movement of repetition for themselves, and to become in their own lives and own way the next echo in this unceasing round. Jesus, Paul—and the reader. Jesus' journey ended in Jerusalem; that same journey took his missionary Paul to Rome. Now we as readers can enter the journey as well, seeing its rhythm and joining in that rhythm in our turn.

Luke does not expect his readers to be missionaries, any more than he expects them to be Jesus. But those who have read of Jesus' journey are now to keep their eyes on Paul. Jesus journeyed to Jerusalem; the reader was invited to follow. Paul journeyed the eastern empire and finally reached Rome. Where in turn, asks Luke, will the readers' journey take them?

> As they were journeying along the road someone said to Jesus, "I will follow you wherever you go." And Jesus said to him: "The foxes have holes and the birds of the heaven have nests, but the Son of Man has nowhere to lay his head."
>
> He said to another: "Follow me." And he said: "Sir, let me go first to bury my father." "Let the dead bury their dead; but you, go and proclaim the kingdom of God."
>
> And another said: "I will follow you, sir; but let me first say good-bye to those at home." Jesus said: "No one who puts his hand to the plow and looks back is worthy of the kingdom of God."
>
> (LUKE 9.57–62)

Here is the consequence of this third strand in Luke's strategy. It is by following that the readers can find what they seek by reading. They will learn more by living in the gospel's journey than by charting its course on a map. Luke offers his readers, as we see next, a powerful precedent: Paul himself. Luke does not claim that Paul knew or understood more at the end of *The Mission* than at his conversion near its start. Luke's narrative is far more delicate than that. He lets us say only this: In the first account of Paul's conversion Paul's helper is told only the merest outline of the future missionary's work. Paul then becomes the hero of the Mission's second half. He travels, preaches, faces opposition, battles through, and at the Mission's end he himself states fully and clearly what Luke's first account of his conversion only sketches. It is not for us to ask how much this Paul's understanding of his mission and role developed. Their ever-fuller statement is enough to make Luke's point.

As for Paul, so for readers: If they would understand those journeys of Jesus and Paul, they must undertake their own "journey" to Jerusalem and to Rome. And to undertake that journey is ever more fully to understand the destination and the role to which they themselves, the readers, are being called.

"Saul, Saul, Why Are You Persecuting Me?"

FROM THE DEATH OF STEPHEN . . .

Old Simeon gave us an early clue what to expect of this Jesus:

A light for unveiling to the gentiles,
and the glory of your people Israel.

(LUKE 2.29)

The gospel has started in Jerusalem; so does the Mission (Acts). Continuity is maintained: The missionary who is to replace Judas must be one of those who had been with the pupils themselves *throughout the time that Jesus went in and out among us* (Mission [Acts] 1.21). Zechariah had been filled with the Breath of God when his son the Baptizer was born (Luke 1.67); Simeon was prompted by the same Breath to come to the Temple when the baby Jesus was brought in (Luke 2.26). As at the gospel's start, so at the Mission's: The pupils of Jesus, gathered in Jerusalem, are filled with the Breath of God (Mission [Acts] 2.1).

Jesus' journey to Jerusalem occupied one-third of his gospel. At its end, Jerusalem and all it stands for are on the cusp: central to God's plan, scene of the crisis that must come, and yet consigned through that very process to a place in the past alone. The destruction of Jerusalem is foretold, and by Luke's day, the city is in ruins. But the scenario for God's plan started its long, slow movement from Jerusalem long before: when Jesus' journey toward the city distanced him and his pupils—and Luke's own readers—from the city's leaders. Luke's concern is not with the details of Jesus' opponents then or of the church's now. He must create a drama in which his readers can share and a cast that they can recognize of peers, allies, and antagonists.

Luke knows how gradually to present and prompt this move to independence. Theophilus must be brought to accept that the church did everything it could to stay within the synagogues' ancestral fold. And if the synagogues' resistance was stirred by the gentiles' place and standing in the church, then Theophilus must be shown as well that this place was ordained by God.

Luke works in just the manner we expect of him. Jesus' pupils have stayed in Jerusalem as Jesus had commanded them. Seven weeks after Passover the next great festival, the Feast of the Fiftieth Days (Pentecost), comes round. Peter and the other pupils are still in Jerusalem. They are surrounded by the babble of languages into which God split up human speech to counter the concerted arrogance of early humankind; for humans, the Beginning (Genesis) tells us, had once set out to reach heaven's ramparts with their Tower of Babel. They had sought a knowledge and stature that was not theirs to have. If humankind was ever to know heaven's secrets, it would not be through such an enterprise as this.

Suddenly upon those pupils came tongues of flame and a rushing wind. Their speech could be understood by all the nations in Jerusalem. The nation's punishment was over, and in its place was a gift greater than they could ever have foreseen. All that they wanted to know from heaven had now come down to earth. The curse of Babel had been undone; the wonders foreseen by the prophet Joel were being fulfilled there and then:

"And in the last days it shall be," God declares,
"that I will pour out my Breath upon all flesh,
and your sons and your daughters shall prophesy,
and your young men shall see visions,
and your old men shall dream dreams."

(MISSION [ACTS] 2.17)

The series of speeches is under way that vindicate the faith of Jesus' pupils. Here is Luke's commentary on the narrative of his gospel. At Easter Luke's Jesus opened the minds of his pupils to understand the Old Order and all that it foresaw for God's Anointed. Here in the Mission Luke does the same for his readers. Jesus' pupils explain what has happened and its significance to the crowds, to the Jewish authorities, to the leaders of the Roman east, and not least to Luke's Theophilus, looking for reassurance that the claims he had heard were well grounded.

Luke's Peter chooses his arguments with care. First he addresses the crowds. He makes clear that Jesus' death, in Jerusalem and at the crowd's instigation, was part of God's plan; they remain the heirs of God's promise to Abraham, that *in your descendants all the families of the world shall be blessed.* Over and over Peter will make clear: The blame for Jesus' death does not lie with the crowd but with its leaders. Then Peter must defend himself against the council. Here his tone hardens: The councilors are opposing the gospel as they once opposed Jesus. Peter offers no excuse on their behalf. The council becomes more hostile; the church attacks more vehemently in return.

The antagonism comes to a head in the prosecution and death of the first martyr, Stephen. He is introduced only a few paragraphs before we hear of his arrest:

> *Stephen's opponents suborned people to say, "We have heard this man talking blasphemy against Moses and against God." And they stirred up the people and the elders and the scribes and came upon Stephen and seized him and led him to the Council, and they set up false witnesses to say, "This man does not stop speaking against this holy place and the Law. For we have heard him saying that this Jesus of Nazareth will destroy this place and will change the ways that Moses has handed down to us." And as they looked at him all those sitting there in the Council saw his face looking like the face of an angel.*
> (MISSION [ACTS] 6.11–15)

We will hear more of this threat against the Temple. In the story of Jesus' own trial Luke has omitted all mention of it. His Jesus warns the city and bewails its fate, but not even a false suggestion must be given that he threatened the Temple and the Law. Such a charge could only harm Luke's cause. It is mentioned only at two removes, as a claim raised by Stephen and reported by bribed witnesses.

Luke has more in mind, however, than the tactics with which to acknowledge and rebut a dangerous charge. Some questions need more space than the gospel's narrative had allowed; some again need more evidence to be marshaled and more time to be given if a reader is to recognize their import and their answer. We have seen the bitterness with which Matthew views the leaders of his local synagogues. Luke, too, knows that he can only vindicate his church if he can prize the promises of God from Judaism and its leaders. A pattern is under way that shapes the Mission from beginning to end: The church is the heir to promises whose fulfillment, Luke maintains, the Jews have failed to see.

Luke dwells on the Temple and the Law only when his readers have heard of Jesus' death, of its place in God's plan, and of the council's response to the Feast of Fiftieth Days. In the light of these, Luke's Stephen can leave aside the witnesses' false claims. There is more pressing business to address: the obstinacy of his listeners. Stephen says they had failed to hear God's word; so, for generation after generation, had their forebears. Those ancestors had rejected Moses, who had relayed to *"the church"* of the Jews the words of life on Sinai; now they have rejected his successor and oppose his church.

Stephen's words are endorsed at the beginning of his speech and again at its end. At its start his face is like the face of an angel as he speaks of the angels who relayed the Law to Israel. At its end he is given a sight of the Son of Man in glory. Mark tells us that Jesus promised—or threatened—such a sight to the council that tried him. The council in Luke has no such privilege. It is this first martyr to die in Jesus' cause who is given, before his death, the martyr's reward. There could be no more compelling vindication of his words.

"You stiff-necked people, uncircumcised in heart and ears, you always resist the Breath of God; as your ancestors did, so do you. Which of the prophets did your forebears not persecute? And they killed those who announced in advance the coming of the Just One, whose betrayers and murderers you have now become, you who received the Law as delivered by angels and did not keep it."

When they heard this they were enraged and ground their teeth at him. But he, filled with the Breath of God, gazed into heaven and saw the glory of God and Jesus standing at the right hand of God, and he said, "Look, I see the heavens opened and the Son of Man standing at the right hand of God." But they cried out in a loud voice and stopped their ears and rushed together upon him. And throwing him out of the city, they stoned him to death. And the witnesses put down their garments at the feet of a young man named Saul. And they stoned Stephen as he called out and said, "Lord Jesus, receive my life [or breath]." And he knelt down and cried out with a great voice, "Lord, do not hold this crime against them." And when he had said this, he fell asleep.

(MISSION [ACTS] 7.51–60)

Stephen dies as his master had, with trust in God and forgiveness for his enemies. Here is the model for martyrdom. Stephen is the only person in our first three gospels other than Jesus himself who speaks of the Son of Man and the only one who identifies him unambiguously with Jesus. To follow Jesus as Stephen has is to be privileged with the direct unveiling of truths such as Israel had learned only through prophets and most Christians learned only through texts and teaching.

This moment seems complete in itself. But in one of his quietest and most compelling notes, Luke introduces here the hero of his story's second half: Saul, to be known after his conversion and ever since as Paul. Nothing is said of this Saul's feelings at the sight of Stephen's death, then or later. When his conversion comes, it will be sudden, complete, and controlled directly by God. For the moment he is wholly implicated but on the sideline, a silent and sinister figure: *And Saul was consenting to his death* (Mission [Acts] 8.1).

. . . TO THE CONVERSION OF PAUL

The leaders of Judaism, as Luke would have it, stand condemned. Far from being stung to regret by Stephen's speech, they lynch him. The gospel must break out from the opposition that hems it in, but in what direction and what form? The scene is set for the next move, the conversion of Saul. Luke's readers know well who and what he became: Paul, tireless missionary to the gentiles. We hear of his conversion three times, once in Luke's narrative and twice in Paul's own words. In Luke's story, the event shapes the whole future of the church. Now Luke presents the gospel's spread with great care. Stephen's words have been endorsed, but no move to the gentiles is yet justified. This development is spread over six chapters of Luke's story. All the church's major character will be involved and will approve; all forms of disclosure, practice, and consultation will be involved.

Saul's conversion is vividly narrated, but in this first account Luke gives few details of the duties to which it will lead his hero. Paul is on a journey to Damascus with authority to arrest the followers of this crucified Jesus. A light blazes all around him, and he hears a voice:

"Saul, Saul, why are you persecuting me?" "Who are you, sir?" "I am Jesus, and you are persecuting me. But get up and go into the city, and it shall be told you what you must do."

(MISSION [ACTS] 9.4–6)

In Damascus is a member of the church, Ananias. He, too, has a vision.

God said to Ananias: "On your way; for this man is a vessel of my choice to take my name before gentiles and kings and the children of Israel. For I will show him how much he must suffer for my name."

(MISSION [ACTS] 9.15)

This is a dramatic scene, but Luke soon turns our attention back from Saul to Peter. An elaborate story follows: Peter has a vision that he is to eat impure food; at its end comes a message from the gentile officer Cornelius inviting Peter to a meal. Paul had a vision; so does Peter. What Paul's vision would imply was left unstated; Peter's has an immediate effect on the church's life—just the effect, it will turn out, that Paul's is destined to have, and far more dramatically, in its turn. Peter and Paul are kept in parallel throughout these middle chapters: two great leaders, one of them Jesus' closest confidant and a natural bastion of the church; the other the church's most violent enemy, now converted and about to lead the church's expansion through the Roman east and to Rome itself.

Peter must overcome all his scruples, but the order to accept the invitation comes from heaven and brooks no contradiction. Peter joins Cornelius's household for the meal and speaks to them of Jesus. The Breath of God comes upon them and Peter has them baptized. This first move to the gentiles is met with a first discussion before the missionaries in Jerusalem. Peter tells of his vision again in full and vivid detail; his conduct is endorsed. Luke's most effective form of emphasis may seem to us almost blunt. As with Paul, so with Peter: Luke repeats the story. Peter had obeyed the command from heaven; the church's leaders in Jerusalem accept its implications, too: *"If God has given the gentiles the same gift* [says Peter] *as he has given us who believe in the Lord Jesus Anointed, who was I that I should be able to hinder God?"* (Mission [Acts] 11.17).

Peter and Paul: Luke keeps the balance carefully between them. Just as the Baptizer and Jesus are paired at the gospel's start, so, over far more pages, Luke alternates his stories in this part of the Mission: first one missionary, then the other. He returns now to Paul. *"Before gentiles and kings and the children of Israel"*: it is time for Paul to move onto the gentile stage. He has been known so far as Saul, his Jewish name; it is by that name that Jesus addresses him from heaven. First stop, however, on his first mission, to which Barnabas and he were commissioned by the church at Antioch, is Cyprus. There Saul encounters a Jewish magician, "Jesus' Son." He attended the Roman commander of the island whose own name was Paulus. Barnabas and Saul appear before the commander. Jesus' Son sees the danger of Paulus's conversion to the faith that these missionaries proclaim, and before the commander's very eyes *Saul whose other name is Paul* struck Jesus' Son blind. On the one hand the missionaries of Jesus; on the other a Jewish magician bearing Jesus' name; and in between them the representative of imperial power. *The commander became a believer and he was astonished at this teaching of the Lord.* From now on Saul will be known in the Mission by only the gentile name that he shared with his first gentile convert: Paul (Mission [Acts] 13.4).

And so to the story's next stage. Some who had fled Jerusalem after Stephen's death went to Antioch. We have seen in our story of Matthew how they preached to gentiles there. At issue now is not one vision to one prestigious missionary, but the growing practice of a whole church. Yet again Luke interweaves one theme with another. We hear of Antioch, are taken back to Peter in Jerusalem, and then meet with a full-scale scene of Paul's preaching at another city of Antioch, many miles from the Antioch that we already know. Here is a set-piece dispute. Paul preaches first to the Jews in the synagogue. At first they are impressed and ask to hear more; when they see how many gentiles are attracted to Paul's message they turn against it. Paul ends with this declaration: *"Since you have rejected the words of God, and do not judge yourselves worthy of the life of the new aeon, look, we are turning to the gentiles. For that is what God has commanded us"* (Mission [Acts] 13.46–47).

These encounters with gentiles will transform the young church. But any development must be careful and well considered; it must be backed by all the church's leaders. First Peter had encountered Cornelius, and Cornelius was baptized. This was intended as no threat to the Jews' place in the church, but it was enough to stir opposition. So Peter went to Jerusalem to explain his action to the rest of the church's leaders. The momentum is now gathering: One Antioch is a center of mission to the gentiles, and Paul is at work among them in the other. It is time for further consultation in Jerusalem. The church's chief authorities must be seen to endorse this steadily shifting emphasis, for a further and deeper crisis is now looming: the effective change of the church into a gentile movement. Luke takes his story forward slowly. Every church leader must approve the stages of this move, in particular, to confirm that gentiles need not observe the whole Law.

Theophilus had good reason to know of the Christians' subversive language; Luke used it to the full within his gospel and tamed it. Theophilus knows, too, that the church has left its Jewish home behind; here again, in the Mission, Luke lets both the difficulty be seen and the progress that has led to the position that he and Theophilus know well. We have reached its climax, right at the Mission's central point. A conference is held in Jerusalem, and Peter speaks up for the gentile mission. James, most conservative leader of all and natural head of the mother church, confirms a new ruling: Gentile converts are welcome and need not observe the whole Law. Everything is at last in place. Paul is free to undertake his independent missions, and their conditions are clear. Luke has no wish to rake over the embers of old disputes. If he even knew how vehement had been the disagreement at Antioch, he has no reason to air it again. The road to the gentiles is open.

Why, then, does Luke turn twice more to Paul's conversion near the end of the Mission? Both times Paul tells its story, once to the Jews in Jerusalem and once to the gentile governor Festus and King Herod Agrippa, Jewish by background, and his wife, Queen Berenice. The versions are well suited to his different audiences. To the Jews he describes Ananias as a devout follower of the Law to whom all the inhabitants of Jerusalem could bear witness. Ananias had addressed Paul as "brother," told him that he, Paul, has been chosen by the God of their fathers, and referred to Jesus as "the Just One." Paul is alert here to the sensibilities of his Jewish audience. Before the imperial authorities, by contrast, he omits all mention of Ananias and credits Jesus with a Greek proverb, *"It is hard for you to kick against the goad"* (Mission [Acts] 26.14).

At the first telling of the story, the Jews respond to Paul as we would expect in Luke: they are furious and declare Paul unworthy to live. At its second, the governor and king take far more care. Festus is bemused: *"You are raving, Paul. All your learning is turning you to madness."* The king, who knows far more about Judaism than Festus, is more circumspect: *"Soon you will persuade me to play the Christian"* (Mission [Acts] 26.24, 28). This pair of assessments is carefully nuanced. Festus is an outsider who wants to keep in favor with the Jews, but he admits he has no viable charge to lay against Paul. Agrippa is better informed and keeps an open mind. The reader has ever stronger reason to take this gospel seriously: Paul's first convert was the official in charge of Cyprus; the leaders of Asia intervened in Ephesus on his behalf; a dream will confirm that he is to stand before the emperor himself. Luke claims quite enough to ensure Theophilus's serious attention.

Paul's accounts of his conversion are well suited to their listeners. But their repetition demonstrates more than Paul's—and Luke's—rhetorical skill. We have seen how Luke values repetition; it is, perhaps, as effective a form of emphasis as any. And the emphasis is clear: Paul's commission came direct from Jesus. No intermediary is involved and no possibility of mistake. It was from heaven that Peter received that first command to eat with the gentile Cornelius and from heaven that Paul's full-scale mission to the gentiles was ordained. The response of the Jews, of Festus and of Agrippa, is their response to God's direct disclosure of his will. The Roman Festus may fail to understand; Agrippa may waver; but the Jews' violent opposition, as Luke presents it, is open opposition to God himself. Here is the assurance that Theophilus needs, that the form that the church and its gospel have taken is in precise accordance with God's will. It is the Jews' own resistance, Luke insists, that has led to their alienation from the church, which claims to have inherited the Jews' standing before God and the promises he made them. *"I would pray God,"* says Paul to Agrippa, *"that sooner or later not only you but all who hear me might become just such as I am myself—except for these chains"* (Mission [Acts] 26.29).

PAUL: JOURNEY TO ROME

Three accounts of Paul's conversion, three differing emphases and sets of details. We might expect nothing less, and we can be pleased to see Paul tailor his account to fit his different listeners' instincts and needs. But one more feature of these stories calls for our attention: the extent of the vision itself and of the instruction its Jesus gave.

Luke's own account, as we have seen, is a full and dramatic narrative. Paul himself is told little enough, and Ananias knows only that Paul will confront *gentiles and kings and the children of Israel.* Luke then gives us, near the Mission's end, the two accounts from Paul's own mouth.

In the first, Paul says nothing of his having heard in detail of his future. This time Ananias knows far more than Paul: *"The God of our ancestors,"* says Ananias, *"has chosen you for himself to know his will and to see the Just One and to hear the voice from his mouth, that you are to be witness to him before all mankind, of the things you have seen and heard."* Paul himself learns more in a later experience. *And when I had returned to Jerusalem and was praying in the Temple, I fell into a trance, and I saw Jesus talking to me: "Hurry and leave Jerusalem quickly, for they will not receive your testimony about me."* Paul protests: The testimony of such a convert as himself should surely impress them deeply. But not so: *"On your way. For I am sending you to gentiles far away"* (Mission [Acts] 22.14–21).

And in the Mission's third and final account of the conversion? Before Festus and Agrippa, Paul speaks of all that he has learned as learned at that very first experience itself. We might at first suspect that Luke's Paul is just tidying the story, distilling into one dramatic event the words of Ananias and of the later trance, or that he is just trimming his words to his different listeners. But we should look more carefully. For Luke has taken real care: His Paul now presents these further instructions as intrinsic to that first vision on the road to Damascus. They may have been implications hidden for days or years, but, as Luke would have it, they have been brought out in the end, and by the force of Paul's mission, achievements, and opponents, they can be recognized at last for what they have been all along.

It is for his readers' benefit that Luke takes such trouble. Luke's Paul is a model, distant and elevated though it may be, for Christian life: Here is the journey that one man took in his adherence to Jesus. The readers are confronted with the invitation and the challenge to take up such a journey for themselves. The shape of Paul's journey is familiar from Jesus' own: at once toward Jerusalem and from its hold. The implications of that first call are clear to Paul by the time he speaks before Festus and Agrippa. Paul may have known from the start, in Luke's view, what he speaks of only at the end. We cannot know. But for Luke's readers, his reticence is enough, for these readers may need years to discover what was implicit in the first summons to faith: a summons that has already brought them to read his book.

> *"But get up* [Jesus says to Paul] *onto your feet. For I have been seen by you for this end, to choose you as servant and witness of what you have seen of me and of what you shall yet see, delivering you from the people and from the gentiles to whom I am sending you to open their eyes,*
>
>> *for them to turn from darkness to light*
>> *and from the power of Satan to God,*
>> *for them to receive forgiveness of wrong-doings*
>> *and an inheritance among those made holy by their faith in me."*
>
> *(MISSION [ACTS] 26.16–18)*

Jesus: Innocent Martyr?

RANSOM

Jesus has come to Jerusalem and his death.

> *And it was already around noon and there was darkness over the whole earth until three o'clock and the sunlight failed, and the veil of the Temple was torn in half. And calling out with a loud voice Jesus said, "Father, into your hands I commend my life* [or *breath*]. *" And after these words he breathed out his life. The officer in charge, when he saw what had happened, gave glory to God and said, "This man really was just."*
>
> *(LUKE 23.44–47)*

A just man, whose death is preceded by the portents that for our other witnesses the death itself had caused. Faced with any of our four gospels, a reader might well have asked, what does this Jesus actually achieve? And, how? Luke's readers might have posed the question most trenchantly of all. A prophet dies in Jerusalem. Yes, but prophets had died there before; their followers had not claimed that Judaism was thereby transformed.

We need to stand back for a few pages from Luke's account and compare his account of Jesus' death with the stories of our other witnesses. We turn first to two of Jesus' most famous sayings. One is recorded by Luke himself:

> *There arose a dispute* [among Jesus' pupils at their last supper together]: *Which of them should be reckoned to be the greatest? Jesus said to them: "The kings of the gen-*

tiles lord it over them and those who hold power are called 'Benefactors.' But you, you
are not like this. On the contrary: let the one who is most senior among you become
as the most junior, and the leader as the servant. For which is greater? The one who
sits at table, or the one who serves? It's the one sitting and eating. But I am in the
midst of you as the servant."

(LUKE 22.24–27)

Here is wise and forthright instruction. But with what significance does it invest
the one who gives it? Luke's Jesus can be seen again as an example for his pupils to follow. Mark, too, knows a version of this saying, but in his hands the role of Jesus takes
definite shape and a stature without parallel.

Mark's Jesus said to his closest followers:

"You know that the supposed rulers of the gentiles lord it mightily over them and
their great make them feel the weight of their authority. But it is not like this
among you. On the contrary: whoever wants to become great among you will be
your servant; and who ever wants to be first among you will be the slave of all. For
even the Son of Man did not come to be served but to serve, and to give up his life
as a ransom for many."

(MARK 10.42–45)

Such ransom is familiar in the Old Order: money might be paid to "ransom"
slaves—that is, to buy their freedom (Laws of Ritual [Leviticus] 25.47); a sacrifice was
offered to "ransom" the Jews' firstborn children from the punishment due to strike
Egypt (Escape [Exodus] 13.13). Here is the term's most important use. Isaiah
describes the new Escape from Babylon, when God will bring his people back from
exile, back to their old Promised Land, as "ransom." This is the support that in ordinary life Jews owed their family's closest members who had fallen into debt or slavery;
this is the support that God would give his people.

Fear not, Israel. I will help you, says the Lord,
he who ransoms you is the holy one of Israel.
Thus says the Lord, he who created you, Israel:
Do not be afraid for I have ransomed you;
I have called you by name. You are mine.

(ISAIAH 41.14, 43.1)

Mark's Jesus clearly expects his last sentence to be a surprise: *"For even the Son of*
Man did not come to be served but to serve, and to give up his life as a ransom for many"
(Mark 10.45). The one like a son of man, of whom the prophet Daniel spoke, was a
figure of power. If anyone should be served, it should be he himself; for *to him was*

given dominion and glory and kingdom, that all peoples, nations and languages should serve him (Daniel 7.14). And further still: Daniel's *one like a son of man* suffered but did not die. Others were killed; he is given the victory.

Yet again Mark is turning expectations upside down. The overturn becomes ever more striking. The one like a son of man had represented for Daniel the loyal remnant of Israel, "the heroes of the Most High," and in the Old Order God ransoms this Israel at the expense of whole nations that he consigns to conquest by other empires, other kings. That promise made through the prophet Isaiah continues:

> *For I am the Lord your God,*
> *the Holy One of Israel, your Savior.*
> *I give Egypt as your ransom,*
> *Ethiopia in exchange for you.*
> *Because you are precious in my eyes*
> *and honored, and I love you,*
> *I give men in return for you,*
> *nations in return for your life.*
>
> *(ISAIAH 43.3–4)*

But in Mark? Here the Son of Man himself is to be the ransom. This figure has not just appeared on earth as a superior being, a heavenly figure unveiled in his heavenly role. Everything that the figure should control, he is undergoing for himself; everything he should be given, he is himself the payment for. It is no surprise that Mark's readers needed help to understand.

A nation's ransom, paid by an individual's death: This was a notion under development at the time of Jesus. We have already heard of the wars for freedom fought by the Maccabees in the second century B.C.E. We have two versions of their story. The second was probably written in Matthew's Antioch toward the end of the first century C.E. A high point in the drama is the ordeal to which the enemy king Antiochus Epiphanes subjected a priest, Eleazar, a mother, and her seven sons. He offered them their lives if they would break the Law. They refused, one by one, and died horribly. Their tombs were said to be in Antioch; we might imagine this narrative and Matthew's circulating at the same place and same time, each offering a proud statement of its own community's claims. The author of this second version has the hero Eleazar say these last words as he dies:

> "You know, O God, that though I could have saved myself I am dying in these fiery torments for the sake of the Law. Be merciful to your people and let our punishment be a satisfaction on their behalf. Make my blood their purification and take my life as a ransom for theirs."
>
> (STORY OF THE MACCABEES, BOOK 4, 6.28)

The author adds his own comment. His whole account is an expansion of the earlier version, which had hardly a trace of such thoughts as these. We see the exploratory care with which he is defining the effect of these martyrs' deaths:

> The tyrant himself and all his council were astonished at the endurance of Eleazar, the mother, and her seven sons, on account of which they now stand beside the divine throne and live the life of the age of blessing. For Moses says, *All the holy ones are under your hands.* These, then, having consecrated themselves for the sake of God, are now honored not only with this distinction but also by the fact that through them our enemies did not prevail against our nation, and the tyrant was punished and our land purified, since they became, as it were, a ransom for the wrongdoing of our nation. Through the blood of these righteous ones and through the propitiation of their death, the divine providence rescued Israel.
>
> (Story of the Maccabees, Book 4, 17.21)

The author knows well that God must be appeased for the wrongdoings of his people. This had once been achieved by the Temple's sacrifices. The Temple was defiled in Antiochus's day and had been destroyed before this author wrote the Story of the Maccabees, Book 4. The question was acute: How was reparation to be made for the nation's wrongdoings, when the route laid down by God himself was closed?

After Antiochus's oppression a hymn was inserted into the Greek version of the book of Daniel (Daniel 3.23–90, Greek version only). It is sung by a young man, Azariah, one of four who have refused to worship false gods and are now to be burned to death. It is a touching prayer, a plea for God's mercy that accepts that this mercy may not be working to save himself and his companions from the flames. If the hymn was in general use among the Jews, the "sacrifice" it offered to God was the Jews' own prayer as they said it. In the setting of Azariah's torture, the sacrifice is the death facing himself and his friends. The hymn hangs in the balance between the two meanings. The belief is in gestation: that the death of faithful martyrs might be as powerful as the sacrifice of fattened lambs. Azariah speaks of the Temple, defiled by Antiochus and unusable.

> There is not at this time any leader or prophet or prince,
> no burned sacrifice, no offering, no oblation, no incense,
> no place for offering firstfruits before you or for finding mercy.
> But worn down as we are and knowing our own degradation,
> may we be as acceptable to you
> as in holocausts of rams and of bulls,
> as in thousands of fattened lambs.
> So may our sacrifice be before you today,
> to bring about reparation before you.
>
> (Daniel 3.38–40, Greek version only)

"Into Your Hands I Commit My Life"

How vivid a sense does Luke have of Jesus' achievement? Or more precisely, how clear a sense does he have of the means by which Jesus achieved it? Luke's Jesus died with the words of a psalm on his lips—not the cry of despair that we heard in Mark and Matthew but a song of trust. Mark's Jesus gave up his life as a ransom for others. Luke's Jesus commits his life into God's hands, and the psalmist who had done the same and whose words Jesus quotes was himself ransomed by God. Jesus will not be rescued as Azariah, his companions, and the psalmist were. But his vindication comes in time.

In you, O God, do I seek refuge,
let me never be put to shame.
Into your hands I commit my life;
you have ransomed me, Lord God of truth.
Love God, all you his heroes;
God preserves the faithful,
but severely punishes the haughty;
Be strong, let your hearts take courage,
all you who hope in God.

(PSALM 31.1, 5, 23)

Reparation must be made to God for wrongdoing, and the death of an individual could have an effect on the whole nation's standing before God. But at issue was not just forgiveness of past wrongs; such forgiveness restored as well the order established by God between his people and himself. The Old Order was restored over and again by the sacrifices that secured forgiveness. What sort of order, then, might be served by such a sacrifice as Jesus' death had been? The words of the prophet Jeremiah echoed through the centuries:

"Look, the days are coming," says the Lord, "when I will make a New Order with Israel, not like the Order which I made with their forebears when I took them by the hand to bring them out of the land of Egypt, my Order which they broke," says the Lord. "But this is the Order which I will make with the house of Israel after those days, says the Lord: I will put my law within them, and I will write it on their hearts; and I will be their God, and they shall be my people."

(JEREMIAH 31.31–34)

God took the Jews by the hand and led them out of Egypt. Here is the model to which the prophets, the synagogue, and the church all looked as they imagined God's future action. By comparison, by contrast, or by both combined, the New Order must be described in terms of the Old. The future could be seen in the past: the Escape from Egypt.

The Escape from Egypt

THE ESCAPE: PASSOVER

Above all else, Jesus' death was linked from the first with that Escape from Egypt: with Passover. Passover was a festival like no other. At all other times the priests in the Temple stayed behind the low wall that separated the Courtyard of the Israelites from the Courtyard of the Priests. At Passover the priests stood around the Courtyard of the Israelites and perhaps beyond, in the Courtyard of the Women, too. Three kinds of sacrifice were made through the rest of the year: an animal wholly burned as a sacrifice to God; an animal divided between the fire and the priests; and an animal shared among the fire, the priest, and the family offering the sacrifice. The first had once been ordained for reparation, but it appears to have lost that sense and was offered as a thanksgiving to God. The second was to make reparation for wrongdoings and for breaches of purity. The third was a peace offering, to celebrate communion with God and with one another. It was clearly laid down by later teachers, long after the Temple had been destroyed and the sacrifices stopped, which portions of the second and third were for the priest to eat or use.

But at Passover? The whole animal was the family's. It was to be kept entire without a bone of its body broken, to be eaten within Jerusalem and with rituals unmatched throughout the year. If Philo is right, then one other distinction set Passover apart: All other animals brought to the Temple for sacrifice were killed (according to Philo) by a priest; Passover was the one occasion on which the father of the household "acted as priest": the priest held back the lamb's head, the father wielded the knife.

Passover recalled the final plague that God sent upon the Egyptians and the Jews' safety from its scourge: The firstborn sons of all Egypt's families were killed in one night; all the Jews' houses, whose doorposts were smeared with the blood of lambs, were "passed over" and their families left untouched. These were the lambs that the Jews were eating that evening at God's command, before they set out for the Red Sea and the desert beyond. This was the meal in turn that every family recalled at Passover in Jesus' time and that every Jewish family recalls at Passover to this day.

Once Jesus' death was linked with that of the Passover lamb, it could be seen as turning away God's anger. Thanks to Jesus' blood, all those who "share" in him are protected from the avenging wrath that threatens their oppressors. God's anger will "pass over" Jesus' adherents. Such wrath was never far from the church's mind. Paul speaks of the reputation enjoyed by the Thessalonian church: *How you turned to God from idols to serve the living and true God, and to wait for his son from heaven, whom he raised from the dead, Jesus who is rescuing us from the coming wrath* (1 Thessalonians 1.10). This does not yet explain why such a death might be so effective; neither (for instance) does the Old Order explain why God's angel must see blood on the Jews' doors to know that they were there. A command was given; it was obeyed; and those who obeyed were safe from the most frightening plague of all.

God had acted against the Egyptians and might act in such a way again. His people needed protection. God could well be thought angry with this delinquent, disobedient world. The Thessalonians, we hear from Paul, were *waiting for Jesus who was rescuing* Paul and them *from the coming wrath* (1 Thessalonians 1.10). The New Order is steeped in the threat of this wrath. Within the gospels we hear of it first from the Baptizer: *"Generation of vipers, who has warned you to escape from the coming wrath?"* (Luke 3.7). The Baptizer certainly had followers of his own; their descendants still survive today, a small group of Mandaeans. We know that Jesus went to the Baptizer for baptism in the river Jordan, and he may well have spent more time with the older teacher than the gospels report. In Matthew the Baptizer's opening message is repeated by Jesus word for word (Matthew 3.2, 4.17); such a close connection suggests a master's influence upon his pupil. Some of the Baptizer's followers clearly transferred their allegiance when Jesus set out on his own mission or when the Baptizer was killed by Herod. From the Baptizer's movement to Jesus' was no great move.

Much in our gospels, we might suspect, was driven by the thought of wrath threatened and forestalled. Protection was needed from God's punishments, and a New Order to ensure it. God's avenging angel threatened the Baptizer's generation as vividly as it had the Jews who spattered their doorposts with the blood of a lamb and so protected their firstborn from death. Paul's First Letter to the Thessalonians may well be the earliest document of the New Order. We might give it less weight than Paul's later writings. The rest of the Thessalonian correspondence evokes a church badly unsettled; Paul may have needed to write them in this distinctive way. But when, far more mature and experienced, Paul wrote the most famous of his letters, he launches an opening attack on the evil he sees around him: *For the wrath of God is being unveiled from heaven against every impiety and injustice of those who hem in the truth with their injustice* (Romans 1.18).

THE ESCAPE: GOD'S ORDER

Those Passover lambs, however, were not the only sacrifice, according to the Old Order, to which the Jews' escape gave rise. When the Jews were at Mount Sinai in the desert, three months after leaving Egypt, Moses received the Law from God. To accept this Law was to accept God's "Order" for Israel: to promise obedience and to be promised God's care.

Moses came and told the people all the words of God and all the commands. And the people answered with one voice and said, "All the words which God has spoken we will do." And Moses wrote all the words of God. And he rose early in the morning and built an altar at the foot of the mountain, and twelve pillars, according to the twelve

*tribes of Israel. And he sent twelve young men of the people of Israel, who offered
burned offerings and sacrificed peace offerings of oxen to God.*
(ESCAPE [EXODUS] 24.3–5)

Two forms of sacrifice have been offered: offerings wholly burned and peace offerings to be shared out and eaten. Moses' next move is to be expected: He throws blood
against the altar. But once the people have confirmed the Order's acceptance, he
throws blood again, this time over the people. This is the only time in the Old Order
that such a ritual is recorded:

*And Moses took half of the blood and put it in basins, and half of the blood he threw
against the altar. Then he took the book of the Order of God, and read it in the hearing of the people. And they said, "All that God has spoken we will do, and we will be
obedient." And Moses took the blood and threw it upon the people and said, "Look, the
blood of the Order which God has made with you in accordance with all these words."*
(ESCAPE [EXODUS] 24.6–8)

These sacrifices were naturally linked with the Passover that had made them possible. But what sort of sacrifices were they? How did this strange ritual fit into the familiar categories of worship? The question mattered enough to affect the translation of
scripture heard week by week in the synagogues. We have already met with the
Aramaic versions of the Old Order, used in synagogues in Jesus' day to ensure that the
scriptures could be understood where their original Hebrew could not. These versions
translate those last sentences with great care. To make quite clear that the sacrifices
were in reparation for wrongdoing, the versions read: "Moses took the blood and
sprinkled it on the altar to expiate for the people." This interpretation is resolutely carried through. In the next lines of the Hebrew story we hear of a meal eaten in the presence of God himself. Here is the original, remarkable narrative:

*Then Moses and his companions and seventy of the elders of Israel went up and they
saw the God of Israel; and there was under his feet as it were a pavement of sapphire
stone, like the heaven itself for clearness. And God did not lay his hand on the leaders of Israel; they saw God, and ate and drank.*
(EXODUS 24.9–11)

The Aramaic versions see here the danger of misunderstanding. The Old Order's
own regulations made clear: At every major feast a sacrifice of reparation must be
made (Census [Numbers] 28.16). This crucial sacrifice must not be shared with the
people: It was for reparation, not a peace offering to establish or strengthen community. The translators, then, were making an important point. There had been no real
meal on Sinai, just a celebration as real as if there had. "They rejoiced over their sacrifices," read these versions, "which were received as if they ate and drank."

The Order with God was established at Sinai. So far, it seems, so good. But when the church seeks to understand the New Order it proclaims, it will be faced with just the ambiguity that those Aramaic translators saw. They were concerned with the sacrifice that established the Old Order; the church was concerned with the parallel sacrifice that established the New. What sort of sacrifice was the death of Jesus, which secured his people's safety and ratified the New Order offered them by God? The church believed that its effect was greater even than the effect of those ancient rituals in Egypt and at Sinai. Their working, however, was not clear; how was the church to find clarity in its own successor to them both?

At issue were four sacrifices: the two ancient rituals recorded in the Old Order and the two rites of a festival current in Jesus' day and still vividly remembered in Luke's. There were the Passover lambs of the final night in Egypt and the sacrifices of the Order at Sinai; and the Temple's Passover, marked with an offering for wrongdoing and again with the thousands of lambs. The ancient rites were ambiguous; the modern festival was like no other. The church has thought long and hard about Jesus' new Passover, about what it achieved, and how. It is no surprise that over centuries different churches have explained this strange successor to strange rites in very different ways.

The church was already taking great care with its terms when our witnesses wrote. Jesus himself, we are told, offered one further account of his coming death. On the last night of his life, with words of deep significance, he enacted a ritual that he commanded his pupils to continue. Three of our witnesses and Paul have all recorded versions of the words that Jesus used. We have already heard echoes of the rite in the stories of huge crowds and Jesus' provision of food for them all. The accounts of that Last Supper itself display our witnesses at their most delicate and loyal.

THE LAST SUPPER

Testimony to this meal has reached us in two traditions. One is preserved by Mark and Matthew, the other by Paul and Luke. Here is Mark's version:

> And while they were eating, Jesus, taking bread and saying a blessing, broke it and gave it to them and said: "Take, this is my body." And taking a cup and saying a thanksgiving he gave it to them, and they all drank from it. And he said to them, "This is my blood of the Order, my blood which is being poured out on behalf of many. In truth I tell you, that I shall really not drink from the fruit of the vine until that day when I drink it new in the kingdom of God."
>
> (MARK 14.22–25)

Matthew smooths out the account, probably to match the words used in his church's worship. He has made Jesus' two commands quite parallel: Over the bread, Jesus gives the command "Eat"; over the wine, "Drink." The emphasis on the wine has shifted. Mark's Jesus explained after its consumption what was at stake; Matthew's beforehand. So Matthew draws wine and blood more closely together. Both writers look back to the sacrifices at Sinai, *to the blood of the Order* that God made with Israel *in accordance with all these words.* Matthew's Jesus makes clear the function of this new sacrifice: His Jesus describes the blood as *"my blood of the Order, my blood which is being poured out for many for the forgiveness of wrongdoings"* (Matthew 26.28).

That saying over the cup could be thought abhorrent. It does not appear in Paul or Luke. They know of a different formulation: *"This cup,"* says Luke's Jesus, *"is the new Order in my blood, the cup being poured out on your behalf"* (Luke 22.20). This tradition knows as well of further explanation: Over the bread (and in Paul over the cup, too), Jesus commands that his pupils continue the rite *"for my memory"* (Luke 20.19). Whether in the pupils' remembrance or in God's, we cannot now be sure.

Scholars continue to debate the nature and timing of any such Last Supper shared by Jesus and his pupils. Our concern is rather different: How did our witnesses understand the meal of which they had been told and the consequent rite that they knew for themselves? All our witnesses place the meal close to or at the time of the Passover meal. Luke describes an otherwise unrecorded order of events at the supper. It conforms closely to later Passover practice. *"I have greatly longed,"* says his Jesus, *"to eat this Passover with you before I suffer"* (Luke 20.15). If Jesus had been sharing a Passover meal with his pupils, there would have been a range of small rituals enacted through its course. Scholars have long asked how many such details would our witnesses or their readers (Jewish and gentile) have recognized or thought important.

It is within the texts themselves that we find the clues to these stories that we need. Our authors have a landscape before them through which runs a network of interconnected routes. They can move freely from one to another: from the first Passover itself to the sacrifice at Sinai; from peace offering to reparation for wrongdoing; from a particular memory of Jesus with his pupils to the weekly needs of the church's worship; and so finally from that worship to the long-promised Kingdom of God. In this short scene our witnesses are no doubt recalling Jesus' own interpretation of his death, drawn from the Old Order which he knew so well. They are themselves working intensively as well. For they must be both loyal to the words of Jesus and instructive to his church.

The Suffering Servant

"The Son of Man," Mark's Jesus said, *"came not to be served but to serve, and to give up his life as a ransom for many"* (Mark 10.45).

The church scoured the Old Order for the terms in which it could understand and describe the achievement of Jesus. Thinkers looked for figures with whom he could be linked and compared, figures whose achievement he could have matched, built on, or surpassed. We have watched Mark explore the Son of Man, Matthew explore Moses. One motif remains still to be assessed.

Luke tells how the missionary Philip was ordered by God to set out along the road westward to Gaza from Jerusalem. He comes upon the chamberlain of Ethiopia, returning from pilgrimage to Jerusalem. The chamberlain is reading from the Greek translation of the prophet Isaiah:

Like a lamb he was led to the slaughter;
and like a sheep silent before its shearer,
so he opens not his mouth.
In his humility his judgment was taken away.
Who will tell of his descendants?
For his life is taken from the earth.

(ISAIAH 53.7–8; MISSION [ACTS] 8.32–33)

Philip asks whether the chamberlain understands what he is reading. *"How can I,"* the chamberlain answers, *"unless I have someone to guide me? Who is the prophet speaking about here? About himself, or somebody else?"* (Mission [Acts] 8.34) The chamberlain asked a question that has been at issue ever since.

In the second section of Isaiah's prophecies is a series of passages that can readily be isolated from their context. They then read like a set of four songs, "Songs of the Servant of God," addressed to the Servant or describing him.

Look, here is my servant, whom I uphold,
my chosen, in whom my soul delights;
I have put my Breath upon him;
he will bring forth justice to the nations.

(ISAIAH 42.1)

Matthew will see the next lines as fulfilled in Jesus (Matthew 12.18):

He will not cry or lift up his voice,
or make it heard in the street;
he will not fail or be discouraged
till he has established justice in the earth.

(ISAIAH 42.2–4)

Then follow lines that Paul invokes for Jesus' mission and his own:

"I am the Lord, I have called you in justice;
I have given you as an Order to the people,
a light to the gentiles,
to open the eyes that are blind,

to bring out the prisoners from the dungeon,
from the prison those who sit in darkness."

(ISAIAH 42.6–7)

Who, then, are we to understand this Servant to be? He can clearly be linked with Israel itself:

The Lord said to me, "You are my servant,
Israel, in whom I will be glorified."

(ISAIAH 49.2)

By Luke's day the church was clear: Isaiah's descriptions had been fulfilled in Jesus. Here was the Servant, and here in turn was Jesus' role and achievement explained. The suffering of the Servant becomes the suffering of Jesus.

"I gave my back to the smiters,
and my cheeks to those who pulled out the beard;
I hid not my face
from shame and spitting.
For the Lord God helps me;
therefore I have not been confounded."

(ISAIAH 50.6–7)

We might well expect Jesus himself to have made this connection as he looked forward to his own rejection and death. And if he had not done so himself, surely the early church would have seen and used the link soon after the crisis. The assumption is natural but is oddly hard to back with evidence from the gospels themselves. It has for many years been wondered, why do the gospels quote these songs so rarely? The gospels' readers are faced with an intriguing puzzle. Either the "Songs of the Servant" are just a few of many Old Order passages on which our witnesses drew for occasional insights, unpursued and unelaborated, or these songs were so important that they hardly needed a mention at all: The merest allusion was enough to remind readers of the themes and precedent they knew so well. A solution may lie in the songs' setting. It is the readers of the last hundred years, after all, that have looked so intently at these four passages alone; it is time to recover the broader perspective of the prophet himself.

We started this section with that saying recorded by Mark: *"The Son of Man came to give up his life as a ransom for many"* (Mark 10.45). It appears to refer to the songs, but it does so, if at all, only indirectly. We have seen how evocative was the word *ransom.* All Israel's history and hopes are at issue: its ransom from captivity in Egypt, from exile in Babylon, and from the domination, in Jesus' day, of evil and of Rome. Jesus, then, can be seen as the Servant who dies as his people's ransom. But we meet here with a strange silence. The one song that speaks of the Servant's death speaks neither of such escape nor of ransom. To find the links we might expect our writers to have made, we must look beyond the so-called songs to the long sequence of prophecies of which they are part.

For I am the Lord your God,
the Holy One of Israel, your Savior.
I give Egypt as your ransom,
because you are precious in my eyes.
I give men in return for you,
nations in return for your life.
I am God, and there is none other that saves besides me.
I am He—am He who wipes out your wrongdoings,
and will not bring them to mind.

(ISAIAH 43.3–4, 25)

The church has thought long and hard about the Servant in the centuries since the gospels' completion. It has become used to the idea of God's Anointed agent who was to suffer and die. We can forget what a bold conception this was. God's agent was surely appointed for victory; a hard-won war against the forces of God's enemies could certainly lead to a famous victory. But in this suffering of God's own principal agent, there lay, it might seem, only defeat. The Aramaic translation of Isaiah could see, as could the church, God's Anointed foretold in the fourth and final song. But the translators insist that the degradation of which Isaiah speaks would be inflicted on the Servant's enemies; the Servant's role, by contrast, will be to intercede, to heal, and to lead his people.

In the following extract, we have put on the left the lines from Isaiah's fourth song. On the right is the Aramaic translation that became familiar in the synagogues. We might find it odd that the sense of the original has been so drastically changed. But the church as well has worked hard to interpret this song. The Hebrew original of this song does not mention the Anointed, but synagogue and church alike saw his description in the Servant. Now nothing else in the Old Order predicted such suffering for the Anointed. The Aramaic translators, therefore, conformed this song to the other prophecies that they treasured, for scripture must be consistent. The church, by contrast, saw in Jesus the suffering Anointed and thus radically redefined the hopes to which any normal reading of the Old Order would give rise. Each tradition, in its own terms, has seen how precious is this poem:

Look, my servant shall prosper,	Look, my servant the Anointed shall prosper,
he shall be exalted and lifted up.	he shall be exalted and increase.
As many were astonished at him—	Just as Israel hoped for him for many days –
his appearance was so marred	their appearances were so dark among the
and his form beyond that of the	peoples
sons of men—	and their aspect beyond that of the sons of
so he shall scatter many peoples;	men—
	so shall he startle many nations.

He had no loveliness that we should look at him,
His appearance is not a common appearance,

and no beauty that we should desire him.
and his fearfulness is not an ordinary fearfulness,

and his brilliance will be holy brilliance,
that everyone who looks at him will consider him.

Then the glory of all the kingdoms will cease,
He was despised and rejected by men; they will be faint and mournful,

a man of sorrows and acquainted with grief.
as a man of sorrows and appointed for griefs.

And as one from whom men hide their faces,
And as when the face of the God's presence was taken up,

he was despised and we did not esteem him.
they are despised and not esteemed.

Surely he has borne our griefs
Then he will beseech concerning our wrongdoings

and carried our sorrows;
and our iniquities for his sake will be forgiven;

yet we esteemed him stricken smitten by God and afflicted.
yet we were esteemed wounded, smitten before God and afflicted.

But he was wounded for our transgressions,
Then he will build the sanctuary which was profaned for our wrongdoings,

he was bruised for our iniquities;
handed over for our iniquities;

upon him was the chastisement
and by his teaching his peace will increase upon us,

that made us whole,
and in that we attach ourselves to his words

and with his stripes we are healed.
our wrongdoings will be forgiven.

Like a lamb that is led to the slaughter
like a lamb to the sacrifice,

and like a sheep
and like a ewe

that before its shearers is dumb,
that before its shearers is dumb,

so he opened not his mouth.
so there is not before him one who opens his mouth.

(ISAIAH 52.13–15, 53.2–5, 7)

Did the Aramaic translators, then, abandon all sign of the Servant's having suffered? Not quite. In the section's next lines the prophet's own dominant theme is heard. It has long been wondered, were the translators reacting throughout their version to the Servant's use in the church? If the Christians saw in the Servant a prophecy of their Jesus Anointed, then the Servant must lose all those traits on which the church's claim was based. But the translators let the Servant's death remain. The church, then, is unlikely to be in their mind. This Aramaic translation may well have been made before the church was a threat to the synagogues in which the translation was used; it would then have been completed in the very first decades of the church's life. The church's reading of this poem and the synagogues': for those who encountered them both, no contrast between the two movements could have been more powerfully drawn.

Therefore I will divide him a portion with the great	Then I will divide him the plunder of many peoples,
he shall divide the spoil with the strong,	he shall divide the spoil, the strong fortresses;
because he poured out his soul to death,	because he handed over his soul to the death,
and was numbered with the transgressors.	and subjected the rebels to the law;
Yet he bore the wrongdoing of many,	yet he will beseech concerning the sins of many,
and made intercession for the transgressors.	and to the rebels it shall be forgiven for him.

(ISAIAH 53.12)

The End

The Mission ends quietly. It has long been wondered why Luke does not give us a close to his work as stylish as its start. Did Theophilus know what had befallen Paul in the years to come and so needed no further information about Paul's future missions to the gentiles or his death in Rome? Now Theophilus, we know, had already been informed, perhaps even instructed, in these *matters brought to their fulfillment among us.* He has had good reason to ask, throughout his reading of Luke's work, why, if the church was the heir of God's promises to Israel, had Israel itself not accepted the gospel and kept its title to the promises still? As Theophilus had good reason to ask, so, too, had any Jews who were inclined to join the church. A stark, threatening text from the Old Order was soon brought to bear. Isaiah had been ordered by God,

"Go and say to this people:
'Hear with all your might but do not understand,
look with all your might but do not perceive.'
Make the heart of this people fat,
and their ears heavy, and shut their eyes;
lest they see with their eyes and hear with their ears,
and understand with their hearts,
and turn and be healed."

(ISAIAH 6.9–10)

This fierce command became well known in the church. Mark and Matthew record its use by Jesus himself; John invokes it in his own voice as author; and Luke has it used by Paul, in the very last lines of the Mission. The placing is important. Mark's Jesus calls upon it at the start of his work, after a handful of miracles, the first disputes, and one parable. Enough has been said to show what resistance the gospel will encounter, and Mark allows Isaiah's text to cast a long shadow over the story still to come. Here in a stark translation is the sense that Mark lets the prophecy bear:

> *When Jesus was alone* [Mark tells us], *those around him with the Twelve* [his closest friends] *asked him about the riddles he used. "To you,"* he said, *"the secret of the Kingdom of God has been given. But to those outside, everything happens in riddles, so that*
>
> *'Looking with all their might they may not see,*
> *and listening with all their might they may not understand;*
> *lest they change their ways and God forgive them.'"*

(MARK 4.10–12)

Those "outside" are excluded, it seems, from the start and by God's own plan. This Jesus does not seek to persuade his audience. On the contrary, he makes his teaching obscure to ensure that they remain in darkness, *"lest they change their ways and God forgive them."*

So uncompromising are these words in Jesus' mouth that scholars have asked, can he really have meant them in the sense of our present Greek text? In the Aramaic versions of Isaiah the prophecy of Isaiah itself is softened. This is the version that Jesus would have known; this, then, is it argued, is the sense in which he spoke. Isaiah is indeed to preach to the blind and deaf, "Unless they see with their eyes . . . and turn and be healed" (Isaiah 6.10, Aramaic version).

This is not, however, the sense in which Mark recorded Jesus' words. We might well ask, then, of Mark: How could he believe that Jesus sought the condemnation of his audience? We have noticed already that the parables Mark records are well suited to a church that was beleaguered and opposed, whose mission had met with scant success, whose "farmers" had sown seed far and wide with little sign of "harvest." The words of Isaiah would have been a comfort and encouragement. The great prophet had faced the same resistance, which God had anticipated in just the uncompromising words that we find so hard to hear from the mouth of Jesus. It was not for the church to ask why God had set the hearts of so many against it; the church was just to take courage from recognizing that he had.

So much for Mark's church in general; what of his text itself? Mark's Jesus divides his audience into two: *those around him with the Twelve,* to whom the secret of the kingdom of God has been given; and *those outside.* The readers in turn are likely to ask, in which group do they themselves belong? To be concerned by such a division is already to seek admission to the group *around him with the Twelve.* Even to speak of contrasting destinies, far more tightly fixed than those Mark's Jesus speaks of here, can spur readers who do not know for sure whether they are saved or damned to live lives befitting those inside and chosen for salvation. Such a stimulus is most effective precisely near the story's start: here is the hope—and fear—in which the narrative should be read.

Ours is not the first generation, however, to have found the warnings of Mark's Jesus hard to bear. Matthew made clearer still the division between Jesus' pupils and the rest. But Matthew ensured that Jesus was not himself consigning those others to their fate. He was recording a fact, that in their response they are fulfilling Isaiah's sad prophecy. He then turned quickly, as we have seen, to emphasize his pupils' privilege: *"Your eyes are blessed because they see and your ears because they hear"* (Matthew 13.16).

Matthew's Jesus explained his use of parables near the middle of his teaching. John, too, will turn to Isaiah's warning. But he will place it right at the end of Jesus' public teaching, in his own reflection on the resistance that met Jesus despite all he had done. John will acknowledge the full force of the prophecy: those of whom it spoke could not believe. He will not dwell on this exclusion, and it remains unclear how free he thought individuals were to acknowledge Jesus or not. He will turn, instead, to launch an attack on those who could and did believe but who did not dare speak up for their faith. Here are themes with which John's gospel is shot through.

So many signs had Jesus wrought but they did not believe in him, so that the word of Isaiah the prophet might be fulfilled which he spoke:

> *Lord who has believed our report?*
> *And to whom has the arm of God been revealed?*

For this reason they were not able to believe, as Isaiah said:
He has blinded their eyes and he has hardened their heart,
so that they might not see with their eyes
and understand in their heart and turn, and I heal them.

(JOHN 12.37–43)

Isaiah said these things because he saw his glory and spoke about him. Nonetheless many even of the leaders believed in him, but on account of the Pharisees did not admit it, so that they might not be thrown out of the synagogue. For they loved the glory of humankind more than the glory of God.

And Luke? He, like John, addresses Isaiah's prophecy right at the end of his book, in the closing lines of the Mission. It is Paul who expounds it, as a prophecy now fulfilled. Paul looks back over the whole course of his mission and sees how he has been the Isaiah of this later age, preaching to Israel as Isaiah had so many centuries before:

Go to this people and say:
"You will listen with all your might and you shall not understand,
you will look with all your might and you shall not see."

(MISSION [ACTS] 28.26)

There is a sad finality here. This is the third time Paul has declared that from now on he will preach to the gentiles. And this time the die is cast, not by the Jews' outright rejection of the gospel, but by their inability to agree on their response. Here, we may suspect, is Luke's final glance at the setting that Theophilus knew well. The Jews were not universally rejecting the gospel any more than gentiles were accepting it. Least of all, perhaps, in Rome; we might well suspect, from Paul's Letter to the Romans, that the church or churches there included a good many Jews. It must be enough, for Paul's final move, that the Jews of Rome are divided, and if Theophilus knew a mission that neglected the Jews themselves, here, claims Paul, is ground enough for its origin.

Luke, like John, prefers to present Isaiah's dark words in retrospect. This is not Jesus' condemnation of those who turned him down; it is the final unfolding of sad prophecy. All those in or around the church would have wondered why so few accepted its gospel, and Isaiah's words, as we have seen, were common currency. Here at the close is Luke's answer to this enigma and his last reassurance to Theophilus about *those matters which have been brought to fulfillment among us.* Luke says,

Setting up a day with Paul at his lodgings, a good many [of the Jews in Rome] *came to him, to whom he expounded and testified to the kingdom of God, seeking to persuade them about Jesus from both the Law of Moses and the prophets, from dawn to dusk. And some of them were persuaded by what was said, and others did not believe. They were in disharmony with one another, and disbanded. Paul said just one thing:*
"The Breath of God spoke well, when it spoke though the prophet Isaiah to your ancestors, saying,

'Go to this people and say:
"You will listen with all your might and you shall not understand,
you will look with all your might and you shall not see."
For the heart of this people has been hardened
and they have heard dully with their ears
and have closed up their eyes,
in case they should see with their eyes
and hear with their ears
and understand with their heart
and turn, and I should heal them.'

So know this: to the gentiles has this salvation been sent. They will hear it, yes, they will."
(MISSION [ACTS] 28.23–28)

From Luke to John

Luke worked hard to persuade Theophilus that the church was Judaism's legitimate heir and that its fierce language represented no threat to Rome. Over the decades to come, such pleas fell on deaf ears. Luke would have his addressees see, too, that the church was a natural home for educated and thoughtful people; those who quite rightly looked for a well-grounded teaching would find it here. It would take more decades still for this to become credible to the empire's elite.

We are about to leave this gentile world behind. John will have quite other concerns. This, then, is the time to look back at the gospels' place in the world of their time and at the response they won. We will follow just two threads from our earlier chapters. We have seen how important miracles were in the early church and how carefully they were appraised by pagans. At issue are not just the strategies and understanding familiar within the church but also the quite different outlooks—some of them bizarre to our ears, some of them immensely impressive—against which the church was competing. Emperors, gods, and daemons: All were centers of power. Now is our chance to set the church's claims within this context, and so to do justice both to those claims and their opponent's objections.

We take our leave of Luke several pages hence with an extraordinary document: the letter of the Roman governor Pliny, written around 112 C.E., that speaks more fully of the church than any other pagan document of its age. We can hear in this letter how the church could look from the other side, and we can imagine in its light how "His Excellency" the governor might have responded to Luke's defense.

Luke claimed that the church accepted Roman rule. He transformed the sense of its fiercest language. Not all the New Order's authors would have accepted the change. As we turn to John, we turn, too, to his namesake and neighbor, John the Seer, author of the Book of Unveiling (Revelation). The Seer foresees transformation of a quite different kind: the empire with which Luke colludes is the Empire of Satan, bitterest enemy of the church. The Seer looks out from the island of Patmos: eastward to his churches he loves in Asia Minor, westward toward the center, far from his sight, of the empire for whose end he longs.

Powers and Power

First, then: the place of "miraculous" healing in the early church, and the responses that it evoked from those outside. How did the church look to the waverers, skeptics, and potential allies who scrutinized its faith and ways from within the paganism all around? Let us return for a moment to the first point of conflict of which we heard in Mark: the miracles of Jesus. How would such an educated gentile as Theophilus read and assess the stories of these extraordinary deeds? Such questions echoed through the church for centuries.

Miraculous power would be discussed by the greatest of all Greek Christian thinkers, Origen. Around 250 C.E. Origen wrote to rebut a book written around 180 C.E. by the pagan thinker Celsus. The book had included an attack on the miracles of Jesus and his followers. Celsus's attack was well aimed: These miracles, he claimed, were wrought by magic; they could be performed by evil men, even false claimants to Jesus' own status, who used the right spells; and they depended on the presence and power of "daemons," which then required just the reverence that was paid them (to the church's disgust) throughout the pagan world.

Origen had to work hard to turn the argument in his favor. He must maintain distinctions that pagans (on the sound basis of observation) saw no reason to draw. In his voice and Celsus's we can hear the questions, fiercely argued, in which the church's credibility was at stake.

Yes, agreed Origen, Jesus' followers—right through to his own day—worked miracles by invoking his name, and yes, this invocation can be effective even when pronounced by wicked men apparently without sincerity or belief. But none of this should be counted as working a spell; the miracles were wrought just by the name of Jesus and his history. But how, Celsus's followers might have asked, was this technique to be distinguished from the use of spells and incantations? The holy names, claims Origen, have been handed down with great reverence and are concerned with a certain mysterious divine science related to the creator of the universe. This might sound even more like magic. So Origen resorts to a rhetorical question: How can it be suggested that Jesus' followers were magicians when they risked their lives for a teaching which forbids magic?

Celsus turns to the status of the daemons themselves. If they have such power over human affairs, the pagans are right to revere them. Celsus describes Jesus himself as just such a daemon—and one with too little power to protect his devotees from persecution and death. Origen draws a distinction between good influence and bad: He keeps the daemons on the side of evil. He remodels into Christian form the ageless forces of natural life, a population that inhabited, unseen and all-seeing, every corner of the ancient world. It is a classic statement of the view whose variants inform every page of our gospels:

The earth bears the things that are said to be under the control of nature because of the appointment of invisible husbandmen, so to speak, and other governors who control not only the produce of the earth but also all flowing water and air. What, then, are the works of daemons? They are responsible for famines, barren vines and fruit trees, droughts and the pollution of the air, sometimes causing even plague among men.

That grim disasters are, by a divine appointment, directly caused by certain wicked angels is testified by the psalmist in the words, *He sent forth the wrath of his anger against them by means of wicked angels.* These spirits exist and have power among bad men on account of these men's wickedness. They have no power against those who have put on the whole armor of God and have received strength to withstand the wiles of the devil, because they know that *our wrestling is not with flesh and blood but against principalities, against powers, against the rulers of this darkness, against spiritual wickedness in heavenly places.*

Origen has broadened his canvas to embrace all moral and social ills in the single divine order. Even wicked angels serve God's purpose. Origen defends himself on one flank by opening a second and far broader front. The justice and reason in this wider purpose of God have called for explanation from theologians ever since.

For the thinker Origen the solution was vast, systematic, and clear. Physicians confronted a different order of needs: What were they, day by day, to *do?* What techniques could they properly and effectively use? The Latin word for *poison* is also the word for *drug* or *potion*—whether good or bad. It is a telling ambiguity: Poison was as far beyond diagnosis and discovery as a magic potion, and one secret power was feared as deeply as the other. What, then, of beneficent, medicinal potions? Roman law trod carefully through their ambivalence for centuries.

Much medicine was steeped in the influence of the zodiac, phases of the moon, and due incantations. There was a felt coherence among all parts of the world—animal, vegetable, celestial, and human—that we might admire. And in the knowledge of these parts' mutual influence, it was believed, lay enormous power. When one Apuleius was accused of magic he replied that he was a philosopher, an inquirer into experimental and theoretical knowledge alike; surely this was the highest calling of all?

Magic was an art, drawn from secret books. At its crudest we might think of it as mechanical: The gods must obey where the rites are duly performed. But connected with the knowledge to which its practitioners aspired was a sense of intimacy with the divine. To know the connections uniting all creation was already to transcend the limits by which creatures were normally bound.

The story of Thessalus, to which we turn, is in itself minor enough; for that very reason it is a most revealing vignette of the ambiguities faced by an alert and thoughtful practitioner. How much his story is fictional need not concern us here. His story was plausible, and everything in this narrative about consultation with a god could be echoed from a dozen other stories that have come down to us from Egypt, Greece, and the Middle East. It can stand here as token of a worldview into which Christianity was born and against which it fought for centuries—in a battle that it finally won so completely in the Western world that we now read of the combat as we might of fairyland.

At the time of Nero a young doctor, Thessalus, tried out on his patients the Egyptian book of spells and prescriptions, the Book of Nechepso, with disastrous results. He left Alexandria in shame to find out what had gone wrong. He had a sense, throughout his search, that he was on his way to an encounter with the divine; more than a prescription was at stake. He finally came to Hieropolis in Egypt, got to know the temple's priests there, and finally asked them whether there was any power left in magic. This dangerous question upset them. Magic was forbidden; were they being tricked into admitting a capital offense?

Eventually he persuaded an elderly priest that his life depended on an answer. The priest offered him the sight either of a spirit from the dead or of a god. Thessalus asked for the god of healing, Asclepius, face-to-face and by himself. After three days' purification he had his sight of the god, who told him that Nechepso had known all about plants' healing power but not about the times and places at which they must be picked. There follows a long account of the influence of the planets and zodiac on such healing properties. Thessalus had taken in pen and paper without telling the priest; he had to avoid all suspicion of error. He returned to Alexandria, followed the god's instructions, and the recipes worked.

We may think of Thessalus as bizarrely gullible and (in writing up his account) naive. But he has an agenda: His text is "addressed" to the emperor himself. Now "Thessalus" may never have existed; the author may have hoped to link his book with the famous doctor Thessalus of Tralles. The emperor is most unlikely to have seen the text. But our author knows how delicate—and dangerous—is the borderline between healing powers and magic. He uses this story of a successful consultation to vindicate the priest's art and his own search; this is a beneficent result so dramatic that "Thessalus" would not be afraid for the emperor himself to hear of the techniques that made it possible.

Nero would have been an emperor with an interest in such rites. Thessalus had turned down the offer of necromancy and pleaded to see a god. Nero, by contrast, claimed to "command the gods"; here is just the ritual control of power that was so feared. And more: After the murder of his mother, the emperor is said to have used magicians and a dark sacrifice to exorcise her ghost.

We might wonder at this alien world. It was inhabited, with different nuances, by Greeks and Romans, by Jews and Egyptians alike. When occasionally we hear from ancient doctors a voice more like our own it is as far removed from Jesus' setting in Galilee as from Thessalus's in Egypt. Among the illnesses furthest from explanation and cure—and so most frightening to patients and doctors alike—was the "sacred disease" ascribed to demonic possession. We might know it as epilepsy, but the identification is not clear. The "sacred disease" would have been a doctor's natural diagnosis if he was confronted by the possessions cured by Jesus.

A pupil of the great doctor Hippocrates wrote in the fifth century B.C.E. a treatise on the disease to rebut all such special pleading. To our author the disease was as "sacred" as any other, no more or less; all life was due to god, and all illness was physiologically based. "Possession" was a fraudulent diagnosis. So were the remedies that went with it: a mix of incantations and diet. "The men who first 'sanctified' this disease must, I think, have been of the type of our present-day magicians and purifiers and mendicants and humbugs, who pretend to be very pious and to have special knowledge."

Hippocrates' pupil wrote eloquently of the illness and the principles to which it conformed, but he offers in his treatise no cure. The disease continued to frighten. We can sense the grip that it held on people's minds from a strange story of the doctor Menecrates. He claimed to have power over the spirits of desperate illnesses, of which the "sacred disease" was one. The story does not dispute that he had success, and such was the aura surrounding this power that he aped Jupiter, king of the gods, and could insist on his former patients' attendance as courtiers in his heaven.

Menecrates met his match when he praised his own power above the king's. The king invited the doctor and his entourage to dinner. The king was more sophisticated than he seemed. He offered a banquet to the rest of his guests but to Menecrates and his followers just the incense and offerings befitting such "gods." Eventually Menecrates up and left, humiliated and still hungry.

This is the world in and for which our witnesses were writing. The distinctions and categories within which that world assessed diseases and their cures were inescapably untidy. But a range of possibilities was clear. We should not do the church's opponents an injustice. Where credulity and fear were so widespread, there was a long battle to be fought for empirical testing and reasoned practice. The church's claims and attraction made the battle no easier to win. "If one offers no reasons for one's views," remarks the greatest of all ancient doctors, Galen, "it is as if one had come into the school of Moses and Jesus and heard talk of undemonstrated laws. If I had in mind people who taught their pupils in the way that their followers teach theirs, I should not have given you a definition; for they order them to accept everything on faith." For "some do not even want to give or receive a reason for what they believe. They just use such expressions as, 'Do not ask questions; just have trust.'"

The Verdict of Empire

Luke worked hard to reassure Theophilus, but his defense was not enough. The Christians attracted the authorities' attention only too often. The accusations may have been anonymous and stemmed from personal vendettas; the crime involved may have been unclear. But the Christians suffered nonetheless.

In one case we have the authorities' full version of the procedures followed: from Pliny, governor of Bithynia in 110 to 112 C.E. He wrote a long letter to the emperor Trajan to seek advice on how to deal with these Christians. It is worth following his account and his questions with care; this is not a letter from which we should expect to read off the details of a practice already standardized. Pliny was always a nervous man and had more reason than usual to be anxious now. What was simple had become complicated. He had handled a few cases with no doubt that gross crimes underlay the mere charge of being Christian: These Christians met at night; they formed a secret society of the kind banned by imperial decree; and at their meals (so people said) they ate human flesh. The words of Jesus used at the Thanksgiving Service were readily misunderstood: *"Take, eat: this is my body. Drink from this, all of you; for this is my blood."* So Pliny had dealt with them, briskly and brutally, but he had certainly not crossed beyond the bounds of his authority.

An anonymous pamphlet had been put out and was reaching more people, to judge from Pliny's wording, than his officials alone. Here was an attempt to stir up public feeling, a danger to public order worse than the Christians were themselves. More and more people, men and women, young and old, citizens, provincials, and slaves, were being accused. From the torture of two slaves, meanwhile, and the examination of several defendants, Pliny had learned that those rumors of foul crimes were false. This new evidence could be trusted: The slaves held office in the church and were tortured to death; the defendants had already renounced the faith and had no reason to disguise any of the sect's crimes.

Whatever he had suspected of those first Christians to be tried, Pliny cannot let the emperor think he has executed subjects by mistake. Why exactly is Pliny worried? If there were Christians in high places at Rome, they could have caused him trouble, even if the emperor were his friend. The crimes associated with the "name" of the sect he now believes to be imagined; "the name" itself and its obstinate maintenance must be presented as reasons enough for the executions that have taken place so far. The emperor's endorsement of future prosecutions on these grounds will validate those already pursued whose original basis has collapsed. Pliny had good reason to write up his measures' effect. His past procedure might be questioned in theory, but, he claims, it had revived an important part of Bithynia's economy and civic life. Trajan knew well what was required, and he provides Pliny—and future governors who will hear of this correspondence and read its published form—with the due mixture of endorsement and freedom.

Here is Pliny's letter, a vivid description of the church as it looked from the outside:

I have never been present at a formal examination of Christians. So I know neither what should be punished and investigated, nor how far. I am also very unclear on the following: Should there be any distinction made on grounds of age, or should even the youngest be treated no differently from the older and stronger? Should retraction be given a pardon; or to anyone who has ever been a Christian, does it not do any good to have stopped? Is the name itself to be punished if no crimes are attached; or the crimes associated with the name?

For the moment, for all those brought before me on the charge of being Christians, I have followed the following course: I have asked them in person, Are they Christians? Those who admit it, I ask a second and third time, warning them of the punishment ahead. If they persist, I order them taken away for execution. For I had no doubt, whatever it was that they were confessing, that their stubbornness and inflexible obstinacy should be punished. There have been others of similar folly whom I have put on the list, since they were Roman citizens, for sending to Rome.

Pliny's procedure, then, is about to be assessed at Rome. It could come to the emperor's ears. Here, perhaps, are the grounds for Pliny's concern.

Soon enough, thanks to this procedure itself, the charges are spreading, as so often happens, and more varieties have cropped up. An anonymous pamphlet has been circulated containing many names. Those who denied they were Christians or ever had been, when they had invoked the gods at my dictation and had made offerings of wine and incense to your statue (which I had ordered to be brought into court for this, together with the statues of the gods) and when furthermore they had reviled the name of the anointed "Christ"—none of which, it is said, can anyone be compelled to do who is really a Christian—these I have thought should be let go.

Others, named by an informer, said that they were Christians and then denied it. They had been, they said, but had stopped: some of them two years ago, some longer still, one or two as many as twenty years back. These, too, all did reverence to your own and the gods' statues, and reviled the anointed "Christ."

Next we are offered a fascinating glimpse of the suspicions to which this new sect was giving rise and of the sect's conformity to Roman rule; even its meetings, it seems, had stopped on the governor's orders.

They also declared that this was the sum total of their guilt or crime: they had regularly met before dawn on a fixed day, sung a chant in alternate verses to Christ as if to a god, and bound themselves by an oath—not to any crime, but not to commit theft, robbery, or adultery, not to break any bond, and not to deny a deposit when called on to restore it. After this it had been their custom to disperse and later to reassemble to take food together, but food of an ordinary, harmless kind; this they had in fact stopped doing after my edict in which, as you instructed, I had forbidden all political societies.

This made me think it all the more necessary to extract the truth from two slave women, who were called deaconesses, and by torture. I found nothing other than a degenerate and extravagant superstition.

I have therefore postponed all future examination and hurried to consult you. The matter seemed worth your consideration, especially in view of the number of people being brought to trial. For many of every age, every class, and both sexes are being brought into the danger of trial and will be in the future. And the contagion of this wretched superstition has infected not just towns, but villages and rural areas, too.

Pliny finally plays his own hand: He is looking for an opportunity to let the suspects go.

I think it can still be checked and directed to better ends. It is certainly true that temples are beginning to be thronged again that were almost deserted, and that the sacred rites that had for a long time lapsed are being performed once more, and that the flesh of sacrificial victims is everywhere on sale, for which recently hardly a buyer could be found. From this it is easy to infer what a vast number of people could be reformed if there were opportunity to retract.

And here in turn is the emperor's brisk reply. Pliny has raised a procedural question about a minor sect. The matter is quickly settled. Trajan did not expect these Christians ever to come to an emperor's notice again.

You have followed the course of action that you should have, my dear Pliny, in pursuing the cases of those charged before you with being Christian. For no general rule can be laid down to meet every case as if by a fixed formula. These people are not to be hunted out. If they are brought before you and the charge is proved, they must be punished; in such a way, however, that whoever denies that he is a Christian and makes it clear by his actions, that is by offering prayers to our gods, then however suspect his past conduct might be, he is to obtain pardon thanks to his retraction. But anonymous pamphlets must play a part in no accusation. They belong among the worst precedents and not in our age at all.

The Dragon's Defeat

Rome's empire was unshaken by the followers of Jesus. Rome's leaders hardly noticed them. Luke followed one strategy toward the empire; the Seer adopted quite another. If we want a glimpse of the dangerous fervor that Luke disowns, we might look at the Book of Unveiling (Revelation). The Seer leads us away from Luke toward the dramatic unveiling of which we have already heard. This is not just destruction foretold;

this is the disclosure of a destruction already settled and visible in heaven. The battle is over and won; it is the Romans who cannot see what the Seer encourages his churches to recognize: The power of Rome is already over. The new *Babylon has fallen.* The psalmist's king is king already:

> *The Lord has said to me, "You are my son, today I have begotten you.*
> *Ask of me, and I will make the nations your inheritance;*
> *you shall break them with a rod of iron."*

(PSALM 2.7)

The Seer has given us an invaluable clue to the character of our four testimonies: to their character as unveilings. Mark's, we have discovered, is closely modeled on the form that such unveiling was expected to take. But he has turned it upside down: What should be happening in heaven and be available only to a privileged seer is instead happening here on earth and is available for all to grasp—if only they would open their eyes and see.

Our fourth witness, John, works in much the same way. We need not be surprised. John, after all, since the second century has been linked with the great city of Ephesus; the Seer was writing within ten years of our gospel's completion, and on Patmos, just thirty-five miles off the Ephesian coast. But our witness does not just invert the form that an unveiling was expected to take; he abandons the themes for which they were best known. Here in John's gospel is no clash of heavenly forces, no balanced struggle fiercely fought. Mark's Jesus can be seen to wage war against the great enemy and, despite all appearances, to be victorious. John, by contrast, is expounding the victory. For his chief concern is shared with Mark but has been raised to a new intensity; what matters to John is the process and effect of unveiling itself.

As we turn our attention to this fourth witness, let us acknowledge our debt to the Seer and bid him farewell. This is almost his last appearance in our court. He can attune us to the sense of mystery with which John's Jesus is invested and can remind us—as we have already learned from Mark's evidence and Matthew's—that our normal distinctions are (for such a seer) inadequate to the truths that he must reveal.

Among the Seer's visions in the Book of Unveiling is a *sign* in heaven: *There was seen a woman clothed with the sun, and the moon was beneath her feet, and on her head was a crown of twelve stars. And she had a child in her womb, and she cried out in her pangs and strained to give birth* (Book of Unveiling [Revelation] 12.1–2).

The Jesus of our fourth witness will speak of his followers' future in terms of such pangs and their triumphant aftermath:

> *"When a woman is in labor* [John's Jesus says], *she is in distress,*
> *because her hour has come;*
> *but when the child is born, she no longer remembers the agony,*
> *because a person has been born into the world."*

(JOHN 16.21)

Now enters, in the Seer's vision, the great enemy, the serpent of Eden transformed into a terrifying image of the serpents seen everywhere in the pagan cults of Asia Minor:

> *And there was seen another sign in heaven, look, a great fire-red dragon with seven heads and ten horns and on its heads seven crowns, and its tail swept away a third of the stars of heaven and hurled them to the earth. And the dragon stood opposite the woman about to give birth, that when she gave birth he might eat the child. And the woman bore a son, who is to shepherd all the nations "with a rod of iron"; and the child was snatched away to God and to his throne.*
> (BOOK OF UNVEILING [REVELATION] 12.3–5)

The dragon's attack recalls the Greek story of the god Apollo's birth: His mother, Leto, before she gave birth, was pursued by the Python, a dragon that Apollo later killed.

> *And there was war in heaven, Michael and his angels fighting against the dragon, and the dragon and his angels fought, and he was defeated and there was no longer any place for them in heaven. And the great dragon was cast out, the ancient snake, called Devil and Satan, the Accuser, the deceiver of the whole earth—he was cast down to earth and his angels were cast down with him. And I heard a great voice in heaven saying,*
>
> > "Now has come salvation and the power
> > and the kingdom of our God
> > and the power of his Anointed.
> > For our companions' Accuser has been cast down,
> > who accused them before God day and night,
> > and they have conquered him through the blood of the lamb
> > and through the word of their testimony,
> > and they did not love their lives more than death.
> > Therefore rejoice, O heavens and you who live in them.
> > Woe to the earth and the sea,
> > because the devil has come down to you in great wrath,
> > knowing he has little time."
>
> *And the dragon pursued the woman who had borne the son, and the dragon was angry with the woman and went out and waged war against the rest of her children, those keeping the commands of God and bearing the testimony of Jesus.*
> (BOOK OF UNVEILING [REVELATION] 12.7–13, 17)

The Seer weaves a tapestry of connections. The woman's first son is clearly Jesus; the church had long seen in that great royal psalm a song in which Jesus speaks:

"The Lord has said to me, 'You are my son, today I have begotten you'" (Psalm 2.7). The woman, then, is an image of Mary. The woman also recalls Eve: The snake in Eden had deceived her; God had in consequence declared the snake to be Eve's enemy, the snake's offspring the enemy of hers. It is no surprise that the great dragon—the ancient snake—pursues the woman's further children. But who are these children? Such a mother once was Israel, "mother" of the people of God. The Seer has a different people in view: The followers of Jesus are now *those that keep the commands of God* (Book of Unveiling [Revelation] 12.7). The woman is thus also the church.

The seer does not spell out these connections. Still less does he explain their combination. The woman is an image of Mary, Israel, and the church. Once more the sequence of events in heaven anticipates that on earth. But their order confounds all our expectations. Satan's forces have been thrown down to the world, and heaven's song of celebration announces the victory of those who died for their faith in Jesus. But his later followers are still under siege from the dragon at the section's end—under siege, what is more, precisely because of the dragon's expulsion, celebrated in that heavenly song. For in such an unveiling, the plan of God is secure. The dragon has been expelled from heaven; he has little time; his final defeat is sure.

There is poetry here, a multiple reflection on the links between history and God's will. John, as we shall see, has a sense of God's plan as rich as the Seer's—of the parallels, echoes, contrasts, and fulfillments that shape God's overall design. But our evangelist transforms the formulae for such unveiling. The Woman is as vivid an example of his strategy as any could be. For such a Woman will appear in our fourth gospel, too. And all that the Seer reports, John inverts: Where she appears (on earth), what form she takes (so ordinary), and how she is recognized (in this apparently straightforward story). As everything else in John's unveiling is on earth, so she is on earth, too. All the importance that the Seer ascribes to the Woman in heaven, our fourth witness gives the Woman here on earth.

The snake of Eden becomes in the Book of Unveiling a dragon whose tail could sweep away a third of the stars of heaven; the snake of which we shall hear in John's garden has been occupied by Satan but has a wholly human form. The Woman of the Book of Unveiling bears other children who will face the dragon's wrath; at the gospel's end, John's Woman will be a mourning mother in need of protection.

"Woman," Jesus will say moments before his death, *"look: there is your son"* (John 19.26). Here is the first of the Woman's other children: the follower that Jesus loved, who sat beside him at his last evening's meal, who has stayed beside the cross while he is dying. In this figure is a model for Jesus' later followers. Jesus commends to each other's care his mother and his closest friend. He commends to each other as well the church and all her children.

But this is not the end of John's story. His Jesus has already told us to expect more. He spoke to his pupils on their last evening together:

"When a woman is in labor she is in distress,
because her hour has come;
but when the child is born, she no longer remembers the agony,
because a person has been born into the world.
So you, too, have distress now;
but I will see you again, and your hearts will rejoice,
and no one will take your joy away from you."

(JOHN 16.21–22)

BOOK IV
John's Story

Introduction to John

One witness remains to be heard, the most distinctive of all. In the first three gospels we clearly have been offered views of the same landscape—from different viewpoints, with different interests in mind, and in different terms, but with landmarks and contours recognizably in common. At first sight John's gospel seems to depict a different continent, photographed through a quite different lens. We will look once more for details of this "John" himself that might explain these contrasts, but yet again will find almost all we need within the texture of the book itself.

Mark, Matthew, and Luke presented a rapid succession of incidents, of disputes, and of short, sharp sayings by Jesus; in John we move to a stately series of set-piece miracles and long, spiraling discussions. Just five obvious miracles are described by John; only one of them, the feeding of five thousand people in the desert, is clearly known to our other witnesses. John's Jesus concludes his public teaching with a climactic miracle: He raises his friend Lazarus from death. The crowd is enthusiastic, the authorities are frightened, and they initiate maneuvers that will lead to Jesus' death. This account is John's alone. Where did such a story come from, that our first three witnesses knew nothing of the event or of its place in the climax to their story?

John's story moves at a quite different pace and has different scenes to put before us. We might well wonder if the Jesus of our first three witnesses is recognizably the same as John's at all. In our first chapter on John we will briefly compare our gospels' two extremes: Mark's portrayal of Jesus and John's. In John's we discover motifs of which Mark has made no use. John, like Mark, sees in Jesus a "heavenly" figure present—incomprehensibly—on earth. Mark was gripped by the battle fought out in the presence of Jesus; John looks for this figure's origin. We must follow John's lead back to the very start of things and to the eternal character and plan of God: to the "Word" with which he designed and triggered all creation. We let the questions echo that John's community knew well, about the power of speech, about its limits, and about the deepest aspiration of all: to express to another, to one that we love, all that we think and believe and long for and are. And so our first chapter in this story of John will come to its end.

In the next chapter we trace the intriguing strategy that shapes the first half of John's testimony. Readers may have wondered why we have drawn in *The Four Witnesses* on the language of a courtroom: witnesses, testimony, and cross-examination. The idea is not my own. The account of Jesus' trial before the local authorities is in John's gospel briskly told. For Jesus has been "on trial" from the story's start. He has been quizzed, witnesses have been examined, charges tested and refined. The whole gospel is one long, overarching trial. And the judges? We, the readers, are invited to assess this Jesus, to hear his opponents' claims and his own, to make up our own minds on this defendant. It is in the last scenes of the gospel, as the wheels of Roman justice turn slowly but inexorably toward his execution, that the truth will become painfully clear: Of all the people in this court, one and one only is the real Judge. He is standing in the dock, the "defendant," mocked and belittled. And his verdict upon all those ranged around him hangs on just one decision of their own: their verdict on this Judge himself. In chapter 11 we follow the story of this trial through to the end of Jesus' public work.

Mark knew that his gospel could be misunderstood. John has in view a function for his gospel so remarkable that modern readers can miss all sight of it. We can read his gospel scene by scene, savor John's more elaborate dialogues and fuller telling of the miracles but fail to see the movement into which he is inviting us and through which he offers, step by step, to lead us. Each of our four witnesses believes his gospel's truths to be elusive and his readers to need sustained and careful help if these truths are to be grasped. John's strategy is the bravest of all. He sees the majesty and depth of his task with a poet's eye: If his readers are to see what is there to be seen, they must be "reborn," and once they are reborn, they will see with all clarity what has made possible their rebirth. Here is the only language to do justice to the process through which the readers must go—and through which John will steer them. John, poet and mystic, is the midwife of this extraordinary new birth.

Such language had been used already in the church to speak of baptism, the rite of admission to this new community. John is not the first to ask: How might baptism's role be related to a book's? A transformation is invoked at baptism; a transformation is made possible by the sustained, ordered reading of such a text as his. Paul, too, that "fifth witness" to whom we owe so much throughout *The Four Witnesses*, had seen the power that a text could have. In his Letter to the Romans he sets out to heal his readers' delinquency through and during the letter's reception. The world is caught (as Paul presents it) in a desperate spiral of wrongdoing at its start; the readers are to be healed of their ill judgment by its end. We will hear of this letter in our last chapter of all. For in this aim, so close to John's, Paul provides the final key to our whole inquiry.

As Paul by his instruction, so John, in his different terms, by the telling of his story: The reader is to be transformed. A cripple is healed; a blind man regains his sight; Jesus' own friend Lazarus is raised from the dead. Each of these stories tells of a single figure; each tells, too, of the reader. For it is the readers who are drawn through healing and sight to new life and who hear the climactic command of Jesus echoing in their tomb, *"Lazarus, come on out."* Only now are the readers ready to hear the dialogue of Jesus and his closest friends, the long farewell on the night of his betrayal.

What will John's readers see on their way to this rebirth and as its consequence? We have found in Mark the strange inversion of a well-known formula: events that belong in a vision of heaven acted out on earth. John pursues this possibility further still. The dreams of a world renewed are being fulfilled before our very eyes. All that Israel's worship hoped for—everything anticipated in its rites and festivals—find their fulfillment in the person and mission of Jesus. The true Temple was not a building in Jerusalem; it was Jesus himself.

We have already seen how closely linked were the Temple and the Garden of Eden. To do justice to his Jesus, John starts his gospel before the dawn of time, in the deepest counsels of God. *Let there be light,* said the God of the Beginning (Genesis), and creation was under way—of day and night, land and sea, vegetation, animals, and humankind. Adam was entrusted with the Garden of Eden, to tend it, to name its creatures, and so to complete their creation. But a serpent spoiled the Garden of Eden, and into the garden where Jesus was, came the traitor, a tool of Satan.

Everything, in John's mystical vision, comes full circle. On Easter Day his Mary Magdalen weeps outside the empty tomb. She turns and sees the "gardener." He calls her by her name. "Adam" and "Eve" are once more in Eden. No serpent lurks. All creation is restored.

CHAPTER 9

From the Beginning to the End

A New Voice

JOHN: "THE PUPIL THAT JESUS LOVED"

None of the gospels is signed; none declares clearly who wrote it. But the last scenes of John's gospel give us the nearest we have to a signature.

> *And there stood by Jesus' cross,* [writes our fourth witness,] *his mother and his mother's sister. So Jesus, seeing his mother and the pupil standing by whom he loved, says, "Woman, look: there is your son." Then he says to the pupil: "Look, there is your mother." And from that hour the pupil took her into his own home.*
>
> *(JOHN 19.25–27)*

The story of the crucifixion continues; Jesus dies. Sabbath was drawing near, and the crucified men had to be removed before its start. To hasten the victims' death, the soldiers broke the legs of the men on either side of Jesus. The soldiers saw that Jesus was already dead. One of them drove a spear into his side; there came out blood and water. Then comes the comment: *He who saw this has testified to it, and his testimony is truthful, and that man knows that he speaks the truth, so that you, too, might believe* (John 19.35).

Few sentences in the gospel are so heavily emphatic: This is an eyewitness account. John's is the only testimony that includes such a claim. A critical moment has called for it: This account of the death, insists the writer—in particular those details of blood and water—should be believed. So far, so good. But who was that eyewitness?

"It is notorious," wrote a great expert on John, "that many biblical scholars are passionate readers of detective stories." The search for John feeds both their passions. The search has an easy start. We link those two passages from the crucifixion's story: The pupil that Jesus loved was standing beneath the cross; he, then, was the eyewitness who declared his own presence at the scene. John's last chapter strengthens the case. It has long been seen as an appendix by another and later author, but this author is likely to have worked within that same pupil's community and to have meant with his claim to embrace the whole gospel. The chapter's story features *the pupil whom Jesus loved, who reclined on Jesus' chest at the supper before he died. . . . This is the pupil who is testifying about these things and who wrote them, and we*—his own pupils, who preserved his work—*know that his testimony is true* (John 21.20).

By the end of the second century this pupil has a name: John. A sequence of long lives is under way. John, we are told, lived at Ephesus until the reign of Trajan, emperor from 98 C.E. St. Polycarp, who died in 156 C.E., spent time with John as a young man. And St. Irenaeus, writing toward the end of the second century, heard Polycarp speak of him. John, Polycarp, Irenaeus: These three figures take us from the scene of Jesus' death to the end of the second century.

It is Irenaeus who gives us these details and whose evidence fueled all later stories about John: "Later John the Lord's pupil," he wrote, "who reclined on the Lord's chest, himself published the gospel while staying at Ephesus in Asia." But a good many years had passed; we know Irenaeus muddled his other memories of Polycarp. He may well have been right about the name John; but was this John really the close pupil and missionary of Jesus, the "John the son of Zebedee" recorded by our other witnesses?

We have seen already, in trying to pin down an author for each of our gospels, how elusive such a single, named figure can be. We will refer to "John" in all that follows; whether John the missionary was the first to record the traditions in our gospel, whether some other John was responsible for its final edition, whether the missionary did indeed survive and oversee the text to its completion, we cannot now be sure.

More telling, perhaps, are the stories that link this fourth gospel with Ephesus. At least part of the Seer's Book of Unveiling (Revelation) was written on Patmos, off the coast of Ephesus. The book's complex series of visions contrasts, it seems, with our gospel's style and understanding as starkly as any text from the early church. But we are keeping an eye on this Seer's work. There is more linking his text and our John's than at first meets the eye. In the Seer's unveiling we have been discovering a central clue to the aims and strategies of John himself—and of all our other witnesses.

To do justice to our earlier witnesses, we have explored the contexts in and for which they were writing: What sort of communities did they know, facing what pressures and needs? Similar questions are prompted by John: Did his gospel take on its present form chiefly to help inquirers, as they made their first moves toward his church? Or for that church's committed members? Yet again the readers would be immeasurably helped if they knew the Old Order and the rituals that it laid upon the Jews. It would be natural to think of our gospel taking shape among those who had experienced these rites for themselves. But our gospel is likely, we shall see, to have been completed in the 90s C.E. By then the Temple had been in ruins for twenty years. The younger Jews of John's community and all its gentiles would already need tutoring if they were to see the point of the Temple's rituals.

Such teaching was certainly available. The synagogues took enormous trouble to record the Temple's rites; such accounts could well have been preserved in John's church, too. The church's teachers would have been equipped to explain the Temple's role in Jesus' life. Did most of our gospel's readers, then, first meet it—or first make sense of it—within the church's supervised instruction?

John's readers needed from such teaching more than background information. Other ideas were in the air that all too easily infected the church, as John saw it, and unsettled its members. Our author may well have had particular opponents in his sights, whose views must be rebutted for his readers' safety—antagonists within his own or his neighbors' churches, in local synagogues or among derisive pagans. We will keep our ears open for the sound of such battles. As ever the text itself is our principal guide. But this time we have one further clue. Irenaeus records a story told of Polycarp: "Some heard him say that John the pupil of Jesus was going to the public baths in Ephesus when he saw Cerinthus inside. John jumped out without bathing, saying that he feared the baths would fall down since Cerinthus, enemy of the truth, was inside."

Irenaeus has more to say about Cerinthus: He taught that Jesus was born as an ordinary human; the Anointed descended into Jesus after his baptism, stayed in him to perform his miracles, and then returned to heaven before Jesus died. This is a drastic solution, of which a good many versions are known, to the problem of Jesus' suffering. Jesus the man is occupied by the divine Anointed for the work of his preaching and power. But the divine must not suffer, and on the cross there was no Anointed, just the man: *"My God, my God,"* says such a Jesus with good reason, *"why have you deserted me?"* Were John and Cerinthus natural opponents? Such a battle of beliefs may well play its part: John insists that *the Word came to be flesh* and clearly believes that the Jesus of the miracles is the Jesus that dies.

One sadder note of opposition tolls throughout the gospel. John finished his story in the 90s C.E. The synagogue and church had split apart; each was angrily resisting the other. John's horizon was filled with the synagogue, where his people were expelled, his master mocked, his reading of the Old Order rebutted at every turn. John fights back and uses "the Jews" without fail to speak of Jesus' enemies. He has written the trauma of his own time into the drama of his story. The Jesus who was himself a Jew, whose pupils and all of whose first followers were Jewish, has become in John the target and victim of "the Jews." As in Matthew's case, so in John's: The defense of a single church at a single time has been enshrined in a "universal" gospel—and then used to stir hatred for two thousand years. In the next two chapters we will translate *the Jews* as "the (local) authorities."

We speak of John, but we have in mind a community. Not least, a community of editors, one following another and forever refining his predecessors' work. The final gospel is beautifully composed, but its story has odd breaks and loops. Successive editors have clearly moved some passages from place to place. Stranger still: The gospel appears to relay beliefs in tension—perhaps in direct contradiction—with each other. Have those various editors been clumsy? We need to look again. Here is our evidence of John's all-important plan: to discover the real meaning in what has so far been believed and to bring that discovery, strange and threatening as it may sometimes seem, within the reach of the ordinary, faithful people of his church.

From Mark's Jesus to John's: Man or God?

FROM MARK'S JESUS . . .

Our inquiry is at a turning point. It will be helpful to take stock of the evidence we have already heard and of the remarkable testimony, quite unlike the others, that lies before us now. There is much in the variety to value that we have met so far. Our first three witnesses share stories, titles, and themes; on these each has his own perspective, vigorously pursued. Their contrasts, we might conclude, are strange but exciting. John's Jesus, however, strains such a felt coherence already stretched to breaking point. We may have been ready to plot on a single map the coordinates from which our first three pictures are drawn, but on this map John seems to occupy no coordinates at all. Precisely for this reason John's is our most valuable deposition. He offers a trenchant warning: The character of the map itself may still be, to our surprise, beyond our view.

"Who do you say I am?" Jesus' question has echoed through our other gospels. John poses it in different terms; to do him justice we must reach our answer in these new terms and along the new—and very different—route they call on us to follow. But along this route the Jesus we have met before may seem to disappear. John, we may think, inherited the story of a man; he has passed on the story of a god. Is this fair? Let us start by drawing this contrast as starkly as we can. We will put two witnesses one after another on the stand: Mark and John.

Mark's Jesus is not easy to grasp. Anyone to whom such powers are ascribed will defy easy comparison with ourselves and those we see daily around us. As we have seen in chapter 4, he is the Son of Man, alien and strange; here is no ordinary figure to be gauged as we gauge our neighbors and ourselves. Nonetheless, there is an appealing limit to Jesus' power. He knows that strength has left him when the woman is healed who touches him (Mark 5.30); there is a hint here (no more) of a finite power tapped and drained. In his homeland he can heal just a handful of invalids, for the people have no trust in him (Mark 6.5); as our effect on others depends upon their openness, so, it seems, does his. These limits make Jesus seem familiar; he uses his (extraordinary) abilities much as we use our own (very ordinary) powers.

Not that Mark was drawn to Jesus' psychology or state of mind. Mark tells his story briskly. Only occasionally does he mention Jesus' feelings. Right at the start of Jesus' work we hear that a leper came up to him, begging to be healed: Jesus *was struck by pity* for him (Mark 1.41). We hear of pity once more at his sight of so many hungry, aimless people resembling *sheep without a shepherd* (Mark 6.34). Once only we hear of Jesus' feelings in the face of opposition. A man with a crippled hand was in synagogue one Sabbath. Jesus had him come forward, and he asked those around, *"Is it right to do good on the Sabbath or to do harm, to save life or to destroy it?"* Answer came there none. Jesus *looked around him with anger, deeply upset by their hardness of heart*—and healed the man's hand (Mark 3.5). We hear once, too, of Jesus' response to incredulity. The Pharisees were asking him to perform some sign, something that would confirm his status: Jesus *groaned in himself* and refused to comply (Mark 8.11).

But far more often we must read into the story any view of Jesus' character and motives that we might hope to read out of it. We can imagine him angry when he attacks a shallow legalism or the Temple's misuse (Mark 7.9, 11.15), disappointed when he must again correct his friends' errors (Mark 8.13), frustrated by their lack of trust (Mark 9.19), touched by pity every time he heals. But Mark does not explore such themes; his interest is elsewhere.

Mark's Jesus knows he is to suffer, and we see further glimpses of such foreknowledge scattered through the gospel. Jesus knows that James and John will meet deaths as violent as his own (Mark 10.39), and he tells his innermost circle of the destruction threatening Jerusalem and of the cataclysm, worldwide, of which this disaster will be part (Mark 13). The knowledge of this Jesus, though, is not complete. Rounding off his account of the disasters to come, Jesus faces one crucial question with a simple disclaimer: *"About the day* on which this will happen *or the hour, no one knows: neither the angels in heaven nor the son, only the father"* (Mark 13.32). Nor has Jesus been invested with untrammeled power: It is not for him to decide upon James's and John's request: *"To sit at my right hand or at my left* when I am enthroned in splendor *is not within my gift—it is for those for whom it has already been prepared"* (Mark 10.40).

At just two moments in the gospel's climax, Mark introduces us to Jesus' feelings. These moments come without warning. Jesus is in turmoil, and Mark's readers are deeply unsettled. This Jesus is ultimately as vulnerable as we are. *"Father,"* he pleads before his arrest, *"all things are possible for you. Take this cup away from me. But. . . not what I want . . . but what you want . . . be done"* (Mark 14.34).

The moment passes; Jesus is strong again. The posse arrives, Mark lets the action flow. The friendships surrounding Jesus are very frail, but even here Mark deploys no novelistic touches. It is Judas, one of the innermost circle of Jesus' pupils, who hands him over to his enemies. Judas agrees a signal with the posse: *"The man I greet with a kiss, that's him."* Judas has good reason to fear his plan's failure—or just the angry resistance of Jesus' other and more loyal followers. *"Overpower him,"* he insists, *"and take him away safely"* (Mark 14.44). The encounter is briskly described. It is Luke who sees how poignant the moment is and sharpens it: *"Judas,"* asks his Jesus in the tumult, *"do you betray the Son of Man with a kiss?"* (Luke 22.48).

And then Mark's story turns again. His Jesus draws upon the psalmist as he dies. In despair? Or in the psalmist's confidence that victory will be his? The words with which this Jesus leaves the world drag a deep scar across all that has gone before: *"My God, my God, why have you deserted me?"* (Mark 15.34).

We can recognize Mark's Jesus as human: exceptional, with powers and knowledge beyond our own, but at the last as vulnerable as we are to betrayal, violence, and fear. He is the Son of Man and does not "belong" on earth. But for as long as he is here, he gives his pupils the solidarity and friendship that only "one of us" can offer.

. . . TO JOHN'S

And John's Jesus? We might well ask if this Jesus has lost the limits under which Mark's lived and worked and died—and with those limits, all trace of his humanity. For John's Jesus, it seems, never loses control of his situation or of those around him.

He maintains this control, above all, by his knowledge. We see it from the very start. Among the first people to meet him is Philip's friend Nathanael: *"Look,"* says Jesus as Nathanael draws near, *"there is a true Israelite: there is no deceit in him."* Nathanael is unsurprisingly confused: *"Where do you know me from?" "Before Philip spoke to you, I saw you beneath the fig tree"* (John 1.47–48). Nathanael is awed by this second sight; he acknowledges Jesus then and there as *son of God, king of Israel*. In the next set of stories Jesus gives two signs: He turns water into wine and expels the traders from the Temple in Jerusalem. The people's response is the mirror image of Nathanael's: *Many trusted in his name when they saw the signs that he was doing. But Jesus himself did not entrust himself to them: for he knew everyone, and had no need for anyone to testify about people; for he himself knew what was in them* (John 2.23–25).

The most telling refrain in the gospel is Jesus' own. For all that must happen, he knows the proper *hour*. Before his first miracle, Jesus is reluctant to intervene. His mother and he are guests at a wedding; the wine, she tells him, has run out. She makes no direct request for his help, but her approach is enough, as it seems, to earn a stark rebuff: *"Woman, what have you to do with me? My hour is not yet come"* (John 2.4). He nonetheless supplies the feast with (a vast quantity of) extra wine: *this was the start Jesus made of his signs in Cana of Galilee, and he displayed his splendor, and his pupils trusted in him* (John 2.11). Here is glory or radiance, the term used to speak of the dazzling, unapproachable splendor of God's self-disclosure.

But what form will this splendor take when the hour does come at last for its shining? John himself takes up the theme: Jesus' opponents twice failed to arrest him, *for his hour was not yet come* (John 7.30, 8.20). The hour John speaks of is the hour of Jesus' suffering—and this, it turns out, is precisely the hour of his most brilliant glory.

Raised up on a cross to die, raised up to the glory he had enjoyed with the father before the world began. Two such different raisings become in John's hands one and the same. He looks back to Moses. The Jews had grumbled against God; a plague of poisonous serpents had been sent in punishment to invade the Jews' encampment. Moses was ordered to raise a bronze serpent on a stake; all those who looked on the image would be healed. John's Jesus promises,

> *"Just as Moses raised up the serpent in the desert,*
> *so must the Son of Man be raised up,*
> *so that all who believe in him may not die,*
> *but have the new aeon's life."*
>
> *(JOHN 3.14–15)*

Here is the central paradox of our gospel. John is a poet, to have seen the unity of these two exaltations, and he must be a greater poet still to express it to his readers.

"NOW IS MY HEART DISTRAUGHT"

It is when John's Jesus is most like Mark's that the distance between them is most striking. For John, too, knows of Jesus' turmoil. But where Mark's Jesus had been distraught on the last night of his life, John's resolves his hesitation before the story is halfway through. John knew of Jesus' prayer to be saved from the hour of suffering, and he has his Jesus renounce the wish before it is even spoken. This Jesus appraises and dismisses his own urge to escape. It is the pupils who will be told on that last evening, *Let not your hearts be distraught* (John 14.1). Mark's Jesus, in turmoil himself, strengthens the reader's resolve by his own example; John's offers a victory already won.

There is an important clue here to the character of John's gospel. He is not slipping casually into a different view of Jesus. He is deliberately reframing the story. There are sides to Jesus that he is determined to bring out, sides to which the story's earlier treatments had not yet, he believed, done justice. There is more to Jesus than any one telling of this story can reveal, and John, self-conscious to the core, casts purposeful, well-aimed light on those aspects of Jesus that had remained too long unseen.

"Now is my heart distraught." Jesus' public work is ending, and his opponents are preparing for their final attack. We hear echoes of the themes we know well from our other witnesses. But the key of these motifs has changed. John's is a self-reflective Jesus, standing back from the turmoil in which our other writers had immersed him:

> *"The hour has come* [he says] *for the Son of Man to be glorified.*
> *In God's truth I tell you,*
> *unless a seed of corn falls to the earth and dies, it remains alone;*
> *but if it dies, it bears much fruit.*
> *All who love their own life lose it,*
> *and all who hate their life in this aeon*

will preserve it for the aeon to come.
If anyone would serve me, let them follow me,
and where I am, there will my servant be also."

(JOHN 12.23–26)

Jesus, as so often, resorts to the psalms to sum up his position:

"'Now is my heart distraught'—
and what am I to say?"

(JOHN 12.27; PSALM 6.4)

He imagines adapting to his own use the psalmist's plea for rescue:

"'Father, save me from this hour'?
But it just for this that I have reached this hour.
Father, glorify your name."

(JOHN 12.27–28; PSALM 6.5)

This is the hour for Jesus' return to the father (John 13.1): the hour for his death. By the end of his farewell to his friends they are ready to recognize in Jesus' exaltation the father's exaltation as well. But the connection is not easy to see. *"Walk while you have the light,"* said Jesus, *"so that the darkness may not overtake you"* (John 12.35). The light is fading. We should be moving toward the darkest hour of all. But precisely in this darkness, we learn, was the greatest glory. The darkness was not mere background, a night sky from which some stellar triumph would scintillate more brightly. The darkness was the brilliance. Deep seers in the later church asked if the darkness was the darkness we see at the source of a light when its brilliance is too much to bear.

On the evening of his farewell, Jesus has spoken at length with his pupils. Before they head out to his arrest and death, he turns finally to prayer:

"Father, the hour has come.
Glorify your son,
so that the son may glorify you;
just as you have given him power over all flesh,
so that, for all that you have given him,
he may give them the life of the new aeon.

And this is the new aeon's life:
to acknowledge you the one true God
and the one you sent, Jesus the Anointed.

I have glorified you on earth by completing the work you gave me to do;
and now give me glory, father, next to you,
with the glory next to you that I had, before ever the world was."

(JOHN 17.1–5)

John's Jesus does not pray in Gethsemane; neither does Judas touch him. There is no poignancy in this betrayal. Jesus, in complete control, lets the drama take its course. His death is no defeat, no invasion of Jesus' person or supremacy by the forces of evil. Jesus himself has already made this quite clear:

This is why the Father loves me:
because I lay down my life, so that I might take it up again.
No one takes my life from me, but I lay it down of my own accord.
I have the power to lay it down,
and I have the power to take it up again.
This is the command I have received from my father.

(JOHN 10.17–18)

This is an extraordinary claim. How will John describe the Jesus who has the right to make it? What titles can he use? To find words adequate to his Jesus, John takes us back to the start of things: to the glory that Jesus had with God before ever the world was.

In the Beginning

"In the Beginning God Created the Heavens and the Earth"

In the beginning God created the heavens and the earth. With these words the Old Order begins. Most of its pages are dedicated to the history of Israel and to its place in God's plan. The first chapters of the first book, however—the book of the Beginning or Genesis—set the scene for all that follows. More than just Israel's relationship with God is at stake; in Israel's rescue from allegiance to alien powers and alien gods, the rescue of all creation is involved. This is the scale on which the book of Isaiah works. Here is the part of the yearning promise at its end:

Look, I am creating new heavens and a new earth, says the Lord;
and the old shall not be remembered nor ever come to mind.
But be glad and rejoice for all aeons in what I am creating:
for I am making Jerusalem a joy, and her people a delight.

(ISAIAH 65.17)

This is a far cry from that bleak prelude to the first creation, the hollow rhythms of the Beginning (Genesis):

And the earth was wildness and waste; and darkness was over the deep.

                                                        (*BEGINNING* [*GENESIS*] *1.2*)

The Hebrew text strengthens the one word for *wildness* with a second word of similar sound but uncertain meaning: *tohoo* and *bohoo*. "The deep" echoes the first element of this sinister pair: *t'hom*. To evoke such a world is to send a shiver down the
spine.

And an almighty wind moved over the waters.

                                                        (*BEGINNING* [*GENESIS*] *1.2*)

Darkness and storm: Here is the picture with which the Beginning imagines the
unimaginable. Some readers, ancient and modern, have seen in that wind the first sign
of creation itself, *the Almighty's breath* fluttering over the chaos, ready to breathe life
into everything that will take shape at the command of God: all the animals of creation and, last of all, humanity, Adam and Eve, created *in the image and likeness of God*
himself. If we can see such a glimmer of hope in those opening lines, then we glimpse
here in this primeval breath of God, brooding and alert, the origin of all that follows:
the Garden of Eden and Adam its gardener, all the creatures named by Adam, and the
serpent who deceives Eve and sets in train the history of the world we know.

Our first three witnesses told stories exciting in themselves. We have shared the ups
and downs of Jesus' pupils, enjoyed the triumphs, felt the tension mount. By the time
of Jesus' death we know well what is to come. But the drama in Jerusalem still grips us:
On the one hand, Jesus' awesome but uncanny claims, and on the other, the palpable,
practical authority of the Jewish and Roman powers that be.

John moves the drama's stage. The sets still show us Galilee and Jerusalem, but the
crucial action drawing our hearts and minds does not take place there. It takes place
within ourselves, the readers. The drama to watch is our own response to the story—
a drama in which we are the chief actors. In this quite different theater, the characters
around us have new functions, their actions meet new needs. Jesus' pupils, those he
helps and heals, those who challenge and oppose him—central to their roles is their
relation to ourselves.

We do not expect when reading a drama to find ourselves center stage. More of our
questions, hopes, and fears will have the spotlight turned upon them in John's story
than we dare attend to in our humdrum, daily lives. To play our part in the drama we
need first to hear for ourselves the great questions at stake in the play. They are laid out
in the Beginning (Genesis). These are our own questions, too, of the beginning and
end of all things, of an universal order underlying all we see, of our place in such a
scheme and the knowledge we can have of it. These questions face us nowadays in different terms, but they face us still. They are in themselves as exciting as any more obvious drama, and the answers given two thousand years ago are as moving as any more

straightforward story of that time. The answers, as we shall see, are as gripping as the story itself that John inherited and transforms, to resolve for himself and for his readers these ancient, unavoidable questions.

When those opening lines of the Beginning reached the Greek-speaking world, they raised queries foreign to the ancient Hebrew text. Greek thought had for centuries been fascinated by the *logic* of creation and the conditions that made it possible. How could nothing become something? How could one thing become another? To be embraced by this way of thinking, the dark and fearsome had to be defined. Had God created the heavens and earth from nothing? Or from some formless "soup"? By John's time the questions were familiar within the Jewish world as well; so was a range of answers. They were not idle speculations. New beliefs were growing, which gave rise to stark and vital questions in their turn, questions that took thinkers all the way back to the start of creation.

We have heard in our chapters on Luke of a mother of six Jews who urged them on to martyrdom. We know their story in two versions. The longer and later account speaks, as we have heard, of their death as reparation for the Jews' wrongdoings. In the earlier version, composed some fifty years after the events themselves, this theme is hardly heard. But that generation had been occupied with new thoughts and concerns of its own. Belief in the body's resurrection was still new. Some explanation was needed if these martyrs' hope of such reward was not to be a foolish fantasy. God, it was said, would raise them up to live again forever. But the sons were being mutilated and fried alive. How could they be envisaged in heavenly glory? "I do not know," says their mother, "how you appeared in my womb; I did not give you the breath of life. It is the creator of the world, who molds human birth and presides over the origin of all things—he will give you back the breath of life in his mercy, since you now despise your own lives for the sake of his laws." What God has done at their birth, he will do again for their resurrection; each is a mystery. And so, too, the mother urges her seventh and youngest son to die alongside his brothers: "God made heaven and earth not from existing things; so, too, he made humankind. Do not fear the executioner, so that in God's mercy I may receive you back in your brothers' company" (Story of the Maccabees, Book 2, 7.22–28).

Such answers were not spun from air. As the Old Order could be invoked, so could a great tradition of Greek thought. The poet of Wisdom, writing in the same decades as our author of the Story of the Maccabees, Book 2, imagines God's punishment on those who carved exotic monsters and worshiped—as the author thought—these lifeless images. The God whose all-powerful hand created the world from formless matter could have created, had he wished, just such beasts as these and used them to punish the idolaters (Wisdom 11.17). This poet is drawing on a tributary of the great river that sprang from Plato. "Let us then say," said Plato, "that the mother and receptacle of everything visible and in any way perceptible is neither earth nor air nor fire nor water, nor anything that comes from these, nor anything from which these come. If, rather, we say that it is some pattern or form, invisible and without shape, able to receive everything, sharing in the greatest difficulties to which everything gives rise which is conceived by the mind alone, extraordinarily hard to understand, then we shall not lie."

How might we start to imagine chaos? To think or speak of any thing is to know it as distinct from the other things surrounding it, as uniquely defined in space and time. Similarly, beyond the realm of physical things, to understand *courage* or *love, blue* or *round, walk* or *sit* is to know to which people, things, or actions the words apply and to which other things they do not. A world wholly without such distinctions cannot be imagined; it would have no up or down, no before or after, no objects, character, or contrasts. There is nothing to be spoken of, nothing to be named. It would not be a world at all. Our thought can get no grip on such chaos. The Old Order's sinister language of rhyming synonyms and of darkness would be well chosen to evoke it.

We believe there is an order to the world outside us. What we see and hear out there may reach us only through the sifting and sorting of our own mind, but we believe it is there nonetheless. We are not responsible for the creation of all we survey and understand. It would be oddly unreal—and unsustainable in practice—to claim that we define and organize that world from scratch, that the raw material on which our minds work is mere formless matter. We discern and learn from an order outside us. A source of wonder and of science is the recognition that our creative, ordering minds perceive in their working something of the truth about the world outside them and that we act upon that world with generally assured and predictable results.

How do we recognize that order in the world outside? We might answer in the Old Order's terms: God imposed, at creation's start, the first of all further distinctions— the separation that brought the first form to chaos—and met the first condition for its sight. The poet of the Beginning already has human needs and ways in mind. *There was darkness over the deep:* There were no distinctions to be known and no light to know "them" by. For before all else, we need light. It is this that makes all subsequent distinctions "visible," accessible to our eyes or minds. It is not surprising, in turn, that for the proper process and result of right thinking we speak of light. The sun casts light on the world; our reasoning and imagination cast light on its working. The first source is a daily symbol of God's creative work; the second is our finite, fallible copy of that activity. We make distinctions by the sun's light and our mind's together. When are these distinctions of our own secure? Our poet might have answered, when they conform to the distinctions made and illumined together by that first creative blaze.

Light makes it possible to discern differences. To discern differences brings light. To speak of judging, the Greeks used a more general word than ours: They would "distinguish" or "discern" between two things or opinions. It is no accident that John links light and the judgment that it makes possible and that brings light in its turn. Judgment and discrimination: of physical objects, of relations, and of the moral world. John sees them all as inextricably linked:

God said, Let there be light.

(BEGINNING [GENESIS] 1.3)

There is order outside us. But that is not the only order to be found. We are not mere sponges, soaking up, when we see or hear, impressions already neatly packaged into objects, connections, feelings, and the words we will use for them; neither are we infants when we think, fitting ideas together in the preset patterns of a child's toy. We order what we see, we assess what reaches us, we interpret and arrange our world. And nothing is more powerful evidence of our ordering, interpreting activity than the *language* we use to undertake and express it. We use words. We distinguish the world's different objects in words. We develop in words new ways of thought when the old leave us still confused by the world. We are creative by thinking and speaking in words, and with them we discover new connections, new orders never recognized before.

Let us now turn back to that unimaginable chaos without form, with no order, categories, or distinctions of its own at all. What power would be able to impose order on that chaos out there, from scratch? There would be no prior order to discover. Everything must be imposed: the objects of knowledge as well as the conditions under which they could steadily, consistently, and predictably be known. It is beyond us even to envisage in detail such a power. But we might well look for a comparison, for some activity of our own in whose terms we might imagine its work.

God said, Let there be light.
In the story of the Beginning, God *spoke.*

"In the Beginning Was the Word"

FANFARE

As our first three witnesses set the tone of their testimony in their opening lines, so does John. He alerts our ears to a sound and structure that we have hardly heard before. What we learn here illumines all that follows; so does the outlook, the attitude to the text, into which these extraordinary lines invite their readers. Here at the start of John's story is the most famous poem of the Christian world. It is more than just a poem. These lines have a solemn rhythm; motifs appear and reappear in an intricate, slow dance; a term from one line is picked up at the start of the next. We have before us a *hymn.* John's readers, then, would have been drawn into the sense and sensibilities of worship, that strange midway state between the earthly and the heavenly that is so powerfully evoked in the Book of Unveiling (Revelation). The following version attends to the poem's details, word by word; it does scant justice to the poetry itself.

In the beginning was the Word,
and the Word was with God, one to one,

and the Word was God.
He was in the beginning with God.

All things came to be through him;
and without him came to be not a single thing of all
that which had come to be.
In him was life;
and the life was the light of men.
And the light shines in the darkness;
and the darkness never overcame it.

There was a man sent from God,
whose name was John, the Baptizer.
He came for a testimony, to testify to the light,
that all humankind might believe through him.
He was not the light,
but was sent to testify to the light.

This was the true light, which enlightens everyone,
coming into the world.

He was in the world
and the world was made through him;
and the world did not know him.
To his own he came;
and his own people did not accept him.
But to all those that accepted him,
to them he gave power to become children of God,
to those believing in his name,
who were conceived not by blood,
nor by the desire of flesh, nor by the desire of man,
but by God.

And the Word came to be flesh,
and set up his shelter among us.
And we saw his glory,
glory as of an only son from the Father,
full of kindness and truth.

John the Baptizer *testifies about him and has proclaimed aloud,*
"This was he of whom I spoke:
The one coming after me is ranked ahead of me,
because he was before me."

_____

For from his fullness we have all had a share,
and kindness upon kindness.

For the Law was given through Moses;
this kindness and truth came to be through Jesus the Anointed.
No one has seen God, ever:
it is God the only son,
who is at the father's side,
that has made him known.

(JOHN 1.1–18)

The Word came to be flesh. It is an extraordinary claim: apparently a stark, almost childish, confusion of categories. Opponents could dismiss it as false and, more dangerously, as meaningless. Three hundred years after John wrote, it was as difficult to grasp as ever. The opening sentences of the gospel were acknowledged to be an apt and powerful statement of God's action. Pagan philosophers found here some common ground, a basis for dialogue with the church. But with that climactic line, all hope of such rapprochement was undone. St. Augustine, one of the great teachers of the church, heard "from old Simplicianus, later Bishop of Milan, that one Platonist philosopher used to say, 'The opening passage of John's gospel should be written in letters of gold and hung up in all churches in the most conspicuous place.' But the proud scorn to take God for their master, because *the Word came to be flesh.*"

It is worth dwelling on John's opening hymn. It has much to tell us of his own community, its background and developing needs. We must sharpen our ears to *all* the notes that sound in this poem. Some of these harmonies are faint and uncertain; to others we have no room here to give the attention they deserve. One surprising insight will emerge: This poem developed over the years and decades of its use in John's community; for different generations it was expanded to meet different needs. Our texts of the Bible are long since fixed, our hymns are printed and their authors acknowledged. Modern churches, therefore, respond to new insights with new hymns, new prayers. Our four witnesses, by contrast, were working with traditions that were still fluid; if new needs arose and new disclosures, the texts current in the community would be adapted to embrace them. John's opening hymn has evolved because his community was *alive.*

In the beginning: The poem opens before creation is even under way. We hear clearly of creation: *All things came to be through him.* Within a few lines we reach John the Baptizer: *There was a man sent from God,* just months or years before the Jesus to whom he testifies. And then comes Jesus himself: *the Word came to be flesh,* here on earth. Our witness John was writing within decades of Jesus' life; in covering this range he has in view all the time that had yet been. The poem's movement *through* that time, however, is not presented as we might expect. Between those clear references to the Baptizer and to Jesus, John describes a time hard to pin down:

The Word *was in the world*
and the world was made through him;
and the world did not know him.

(JOHN 1.10)

The Word was rejected by those among whom "he" came. The lines might be jumping forward to speak of Jesus' rejection by those who came across him, but Jesus appears only later in the poem, and such a break in the story's order would be strange. Is there an alternative? These lines might instead be jumping backward, past the Baptizer, to the rejection that has confronted the Word throughout history. Ever since creation, the Word had been as present as light itself but was ignored even by Israel, the Word's own people. In this second case it is the reference to the Baptizer that interrupts the poem's natural progress, and the lines run more smoothly, it might be thought, without reference to the Baptizer at all. Here is how these verses would then read:

In him was life;
and the life was the light of men.
And the light shines in the darkness;
and the darkness never overcame it.
This was the true light, which enlightens everyone,
coming into the world.
He was in the world
and the world was made through him;
and the world did not know him.

This reads fluently and well. Why, though, would any poet insert such a mention of the Baptizer and so interrupt the poem's flow? An answer lies near, in the life of John's community. From this one quirk there emerges, step by step, a dramatic view of our writer and his church's needs.

The Baptizer is mentioned over and over in the early chapters of the gospel. Each time he insists that he is only the witness to one far greater than himself. Why should such an emphasis be needed? As we have seen, there were (and still are) followers of the Baptizer. Powerful questions had been raised: Luke recalls the people's excitement when the Baptizer appeared and their hesitant thought: *"Might this be the Anointed?"* (Luke 3.15) We have encountered the song of Mary at the start of Luke's gospel: *"My soul doth magnify the Lord."* The song celebrates Jesus' conception. A few manuscripts have it sung by Elizabeth, the Baptizer's mother (Luke 1.46); had it once been found in a different context—to mark not Jesus' conception but the Baptizer's? Strange rumors had been current in Jesus' Galilee and been believed by Herod himself: The Baptizer had risen from the dead (Mark 6.14–16, 8.28). Such a story could not be derided by a group that claimed as much for Jesus himself.

Had the Baptizer acquired something of the extraordinary status that John's church believed to be Jesus' alone? Some of the Baptizer's followers clearly changed their allegiance, even before the Baptizer's death; they came to follow his pupil Jesus. They brought with them knowledge of the Baptizer's claims and of the claims his pupils made for him. Among their own beliefs they may have clung to those claims when they moved.

Or had Jesus inherited some of the dignity—even some of the titles—once ascribed to his master, the Baptizer? There was real room for confusion: Which of these leaders was of such high standing in God's eyes? The leaders of John's church had good reason to insist that these honors are Jesus' own and Jesus' alone; they are not the Baptizer's. Imagine this poem in danger of being misunderstood. Readers might hear in it a description not of Jesus but of the Baptizer. John must make the position clear.

Why, though, would he insert the warning right here, where it will disrupt the poem's flow? Our clue lies in the very next line:

This was the true light, which enlightens everyone,
coming into the world.

(JOHN 1.9)

The Greek has two meanings. It is either referring to *the true light, which enlightens everyone who comes into the world* and has done so since the start of humankind; this is the light that shone upon John's forebears and upon him and his community in their turn. This is probably the sense once intended for the clause. Or the line is about *the coming* into the world *of the true light, which enlightens everyone.* Here, then, would be John's opening reference to the light's special arrival: to the presence on earth of Jesus. This is the sense in which our poem's final editor has taken the text. Now the master is naturally introduced before the pupil. If Jesus is to be mentioned, the Baptizer is duly mentioned first, but the author makes clear right away that the pupil is the one to watch. The master's lower status is made clear from the start. Misunderstanding is nipped in the bud.

Once we see the role of the Baptizer's first mention, we can better understand the second, his spoken disclaimer near the end of the hymn.

John the Baptizer *testifies about him and has proclaimed aloud,*
"This was he of whom I spoke:
The one coming after me is ranked ahead of me,
because he was before me."

(JOHN 1.15)

Is that an insertion, too? It has long been noticed how smoothly the poem would run without this second reference:

And we saw his glory,
glory as of an only son from the Father,
full of kindness and truth.
For from his fullness we have all had a share,
and kindness upon kindness.

Here, too, the hymn in our finished gospel provides a well-placed warning: It is to the only son that we must look, and the Baptizer is not he. Now these two stanzas on the Baptizer are carefully placed: They balance each other on either side of the poem's center, to which they attract our attention. Anyone familiar with the poem—and hymns become familiar in the communities that sing them—would have been drawn to this center as the poem's climax. And this center of the finished poem is not where we might expect. For this center is not where Jesus takes flesh, but in those earlier lines, reinforced by a series of negatives that lead up to the final crescendo:

To all those that accepted him,
to them he gave power to become children of God,
to those believing in his name,
who were conceived not by blood,
nor by the desire of flesh, nor by the desire of man,
but by God.

(*JOHN 1.12–13*)

The rhythm of these lines is distinctive; they may well have taken their present form at the hand of our final editor whose vision of the gospel they fit so well. *To them he gave power to become children of God*. Our finished gospel is constructed precisely to bring its readers to new birth, to induce their progress. They were once people defined by their human origin; they are to become people conceived by God.

We can be grateful to the editor who expanded this hymn. For he was surely responsible also for the final shape and dynamic of the gospel as a whole. The movement of Jesus in the hymn is the movement of Jesus in the gospel. The finished poem comes full circle: The Word, we hear at its start, was with God in the beginning; the only son, we hear at its end, is at the father's side. He had descended to earth; his task done, he has returned to the "place" he had occupied since time began.

And more important still: The editor calls attention in the climactic center of his poem to the climax of Jesus' work at the very center of the gospel, the summons to new life from the tomb of the old.

This hymn had once moved from a beginning before time, through creation, to Jesus' arrival. Here was the climax, where Augustine would later find it, in the line that so appalled his philosopher: *the Word came to be flesh*. It invited the audience to wonderment, to awe. Humankind had been blind to the light's presence through all of history. Now a sight was offered, dazzling and complete, in a man of flesh and blood. Here was a poem of meditation.

But the church's situation has changed. John's community has a history, and so has its poem. Those first stanzas to be composed were far too valuable to be discarded; what they said must be said. But they served a living community with shifting crises and insights. A hymn that becomes open to misunderstanding must be revised. It takes on new emphases, new shape. A new melody is added to the old; new harmonies are sounded by their combination.

In its new form the hymn moves quickly from creation to the appearance of John the Baptizer and so to the challenge and the offer with which Jesus confronts the gospel's readers: *the true light, which enlightens everyone,* was *coming into the world.* Two responses to this gospel are possible. They are laid out without compromise.

> *To all those that accepted him,*
> *to them he gave power to become children of God.*
>
> *(JOHN 1.12)*

Here is the present poem's first climax. Of course our final editor keeps the tremendous line, *The Word came to be flesh.* But what inspires him is the sight that this offers of the Word's glory. For when the Word became flesh, the father himself was revealed. Our final editor is enthralled by this disclosure and has shaped the whole gospel, as we shall see, to bring it within the reader's grasp. Some people, we have heard, did accept Jesus: "They" were given power to become children of God. The author returns to them: as "ourselves," John's own community. Here is a poem of encouragement and assertion.

> *And we saw his glory,*
> *glory as of an only son from the father,*
> *full of kindness and truth.*
>
> *(JOHN 1.14)*

Our editor has molded the poem's final lines to make clear his most dramatic claim. When the son was revealed, the father was revealed as well. On the very last night of Jesus' life on earth, his pupils and closest friends will still not grasp the truth that our poet makes clear to his readers.

> *For the Law was given through Moses;*
> *this kindness and truth came to be through Jesus the Anointed.*
> *No one has seen God, ever:*
> *it is God the only son,*
> *who is at the father's side,*
> *that has made him known.*
>
> *(JOHN 1.18)*

The poem's motifs echo through the whole gospel: Over and over John recalls this movement of the Word, of the only son. He moves down to earth and will move back at the end to the place he occupied before. But where, ask Jesus' opponents over and again, is he from?

The poem's shape and the gospel's are the same. *Kindness and truth*, we hear at the poem's end, *came to be through Jesus the Anointed.* Only once more will John use that combination of Jesus' name and title, *Jesus the Anointed:* in Jesus' very last prayer for his followers, as he prepares for his death and return to the father's side: *This is the new aeon's life, to acknowledge you the one true God and the one that you sent, Jesus the Anointed* (John 17.3).

John enjoys coming full circle, both in the poem and in the gospel as a whole. *It is God the only son*, we hear, *that has made him known.* Jesus is declared, in the last of these opening lines, unambiguously to be *God the only son*. Jesus as God; in the body of the gospel this bold assertion fades from view. Why is this great claim not John's permanent refrain? He knows the value of reticence. In the very last scene of John's Easter stories we hear that one of Jesus' pupils, Thomas, was not in the group to which the risen Jesus appeared. He refused to believe that the others had seen Jesus: *"Unless I see on his hands the place of the nails and put my finger there and put my hand into his side, I will not believe."* A week later, John tells us, those pupils were once more together. This time Thomas was among them. Jesus appeared. He addressed Thomas: *"Put your hand here and see my hands and stretch out your hand and put it into my side, and be no longer unbelieving, but believe."* There is a pause. We do not hear that Thomas takes up Jesus' offer. If he needed that much proof he would have needed more, and more again. John's next words are Thomas's reply. Thomas acknowledges who it is that stands before him: *"My Lord and my God"* (John 20.24–28).

Jesus' closing words follow Thomas's confession. They might be John's motto for his whole work. In and through the story of those who have seen Jesus, he must foster the belief of those who never have. The gospel must achieve in his church what the sight of Jesus achieves in his story: *"Because you have seen me, do you believe? Blessed are those who do not see and believe"* (John 20.29).

FROM WISDOM TO THE WORD

By the Word of the Lord, says the psalmist, *were the heavens set fast* (Psalm 33.6). What, for the Old Order and for John, is this Word? Or, to use John's terms, *who* is this Word? We must attune our ears to the poetry of the Old Order and its offshoots, poetry in which John and his readers were steeped. How God worked at creation, what aspects of himself were in use, how these have worked in the world ever since— these are the questions beautifully answered in the poetry that John knew and answered afresh by John himself. John has inherited a world of the imagination and has transformed it by his own.

We have encountered Wisdom already. Sira's Son evoked her to do justice to the Temple's morning sacrifice. Matthew has explored her relation to Jesus and so, in turn, to the gospel's readers. In the book of Proverbs, the poet has Wisdom describe herself. Here is a new version of the story that opens the Beginning, told from the viewpoint of God's creative, organizing power. Wisdom is at work, the center of planning, foresight, care:

> *The Lord created me for his works, the first of his ways,*
> *before the aeons he established me, in the beginning.*
> *When he was preparing the heavens, I was there with him,*
> *and when he was making strong the foundations of the earth.*
> *Daily, without ceasing I took pleasure in his presence,*
> *when he took pleasure in the world's completion,*
> *when he took great pleasure in humankind.*
>
> *(PROVERBS 8.22–31, GREEK VERSION)*

Once more in the poem of Sira's Son, in his grandson's translation, the opening lines of the Beginning are in view: The primordial wind and word together have become a mist from the mouth of God, the moisture that fertilized a barren earth (Beginning [Genesis] 2.6). Here again Wisdom "speaks" and in the last verses, as we know from our chapters on Matthew, reveals the identity in which she can be known on earth. This claim will influence all future thought about God, Jewish and Christian alike:

> "I came out from the mouth of the Most High,
> and like a mist I covered the earth.
> Among every people and nation I sought a resting place,
> one in whose inheritance I might lodge.
> Then the creator of all things assigned a place for my shelter:
> 'Set up your shelter in Israel, receive there your inheritance.'
> Before the aeons began, in the beginning he created me,
> and to the aeons' end I shall endure.
> In the holy shelter I served before him,
> and in Jerusalem I was established.
> Come to me, you who desire me,
> and eat your fill of my produce.
> Those who eat me shall hunger for more,
> and those who drink me will thirst for more."

> All this is the book of the order of the Most High God,
> the law which Moses commanded us
> as an inheritance for the congregations of Israel.
>
> (WISDOM OF SIRA'S SON [BEN SIRA] 24.3–24)

Different readers approach the New Order today with different expectations; some assess its claims from scratch, as they might any other claims to truth; others acknowledge an allegiance to the text and look to it for instruction whose truth is already known and utterly secure. We have all but lost the excitement with which it was first heard, as a text that directly developed, challenged, and rebutted familiar claims—some of them as sacred to Jews or to other Christians as the New Order's claims are to the church today. Every line in John's gospel sets out to unveil, as if for the first time ever, the "real" truth in the Old Order's most precious teaching; those who guarded that truth, whether in synagogue or church, had good reason to resist the twists and turns that John discovered or imposed.

John takes over the language that Sira's Son used of Wisdom and heightens it to describe the Word. The Word, too, was from the beginning and was not created at all; the Word had a natural home but "his own" did not accept him. A similar, sad note is sounded in a book well known to John's generation and still treasured today as part of the Bible in the church of Ethiopia:

> Wisdom could not find a place in which to dwell,
>   but a place was found for her in the heavens.
> Then Wisdom went out to dwell with the children of the people,
>   but she found no dwelling place.
> So Wisdom returned to her place
> and she settled permanently among the angels.

This Wisdom can find no home on earth, no nation that will value her. Sira's Son declares that God's Wisdom is embodied in Israel's Law, for in Israel God gave her a lodging. For John, by contrast, the Word is embodied in Jesus. Wisdom is the basis on which John describes the Word, but the boldest claim of Sira's Son, that Wisdom's disclosure is "embodied" in the Law, is trumped by John's coda:

> *For the Law was given through Moses;*
> *this kindness and truth came to be through Jesus the Anointed.*
> *No one has seen God, ever:*
> *it is God the only son,*
> *who is at the Father's side,*
> *that has made him known.*
>
> (*JOHN 1.17–18*)

All the terms in which John speaks of Jesus were already familiar in Judaism; much of what John's Jesus offered had been offered by the Law. The Law's roles, John insisted, had been transferred to Jesus and radically enhanced in the move. This was neither an open question nor an obvious truth: It was a brave, unforgettable—and polemical—claim.

Let us hear some snippets from the music of Judaism's love for the Law. Before the world was made, said Jewish scholars, the Law was written and lay in the bosom of God and with the ministering angels uttered a song, for as the Old Order says, *I was with him, his master craftsman, I was there, and he rejoiced in me* (Proverbs 8.30). Again: The Law gives life to them that observe it, life in this aeon and in the aeon to come. And with a further reference to the book of Proverbs, we are told, *If your enemies are hungry, feed them with bread*—that is, with the bread of the Law; *if they are thirsty, give them water to drink* (Proverbs 25.21)—that is, the water of the Law. The theme of food and drink recurs: As water is life for the world, so also the words of the Law are life for the world; as the Old Order says, *My words are life to those who find them* (Proverbs 4.22). The analogy was taken further: As water is to be had for the world without price, so are the words of the Law to be had without price; as the prophet Isaiah says, *Every one that is thirsty, come to the waters, and he that has no money* (Isaiah 55.1).

A sequence of sayings ascribed to Rabbi Akiba (who was killed in 135 C.E.) rejoices in the knowledge that the Law brings and, most tellingly, in the knowledge that this *is* knowledge, firm and unshakable. We can recognize this emphasis on knowledge and on the consciousness it brings of ourselves and of our standing. To bring such knowledge within the reader's reach has been the task of all our witnesses.

It was great love for humankind, that they were created in the image of God.
It was greater love, that they should know they are created in the image of God:
In the image of God he made man (Beginning [Genesis] 9.6).
It was great love for Israel, that they are called children of God.
It was greater love, that they should know that they are called children of God:
You are children to the Lord your God (Second Law [Deuteronomy] 14.1).

It was great love for Israel, that the precious instrument was given them with which
the world was made.
It was greater love, that they should know the precious instrument was given them
with which the world was made:
I have given you a good teaching; do not forsake my Law.
(PROVERBS 4.2)

For here is the heart of the Law's truth: the eternal fidelity of Israel's God to his people. What he has promised, he will fulfill: *For all aeons, O Lord, your Word stands fast in heaven* (Psalm 119.89).

So much for the Word set fast for all aeons. But what does this make the Jesus who lived and worked and taught on earth? It is time to return to the Jesus whose life John has set out to describe and in particular to explore the rich, allusive titles with which John tries to do him justice.

"I and the Father Are One"

THE ENVOY OF GOD

John's Jesus, we shall see, is a riddle. And nothing is more riddling than the fact of this riddle itself.

After that opening declaration of Jesus' origin and standing we might expect a calm, clear exposition of his life on earth. To any particular question, after all, we already know the overall and overriding answer: Jesus is the Word of God. Questions and confusions may unsettle the story's other characters; they have not heard this opening hymn. We may acknowledge their confusion and may sometimes feel with pleasure or with horror the irony of their ignorance, but this irony works only because we ourselves have more knowledge than they.

All our knowledge, however, leaves us muddled in our turn. Jesus speaks of himself many times and in many ways. But are these claims consistent? Isolate various sayings from around the gospel, and we can see how odd they are in combination. We need to view not just the climactic line in Jesus' various self-descriptions but the spiraling argument that in each case leads to it and the place of that argument in John's steady, progressive enlightening of his readers.

Jesus first describes himself in full when the authorities claim he is making himself equal to God. Here is the balance between father and son, power and dependence that John works so hard to maintain. The balance can seem confusing enough: *"I and the father are one,"* says this Jesus, but he later declares, *"The father is greater than I"* (John 10.30, 14.28).

We turn to Jesus' opening dialogue with the powers that be. Here are two objects of hope and fear, put side by side, that echo each other through the gospel: the moment of judgment looming over creation, when God will declare his verdict and sentence on the world, and the judgment that lay in the hands of Jesus, even as he spoke. The church had seen in Jesus the agent and viceroy of God's future judgment; his return would mark the great inquest, the punishing of God's enemies, and the rescue of his people from oppression. *Of those who lie asleep in the dust of the earth,* the prophet Daniel had been told, *many will awake: some to the new aeon's life, others to dispersion and shame for all aeons* (Daniel 12.2). Jesus himself would be the advocate and rescue of those who believed in him; he would protect them from the anger of God that was about to engulf the world. John knows this scenario well and gives it due space in his gospel. But he includes such a vision only to transform it. For his Jesus has all authority here and now: *This* is the moment of judgment and of the rewards and punishments that duly follow.

We will follow this opening argument of Jesus as a whole. He starts by claiming for himself, as the father's gifts, the two powers that were most definitively God's alone: the power of life and death and, closely connected, the power of judgment and its execution. Jesus' position is first stated without any reference to time more specific than this: that the son has these powers now.

> "In God's truth I tell you,
> the son can do nothing of himself, nothing,
> unless he sees the father do it.
> For the father loves the son
> and shows him everything that he does himself,
> and will show him greater things than these,
> so that you will be amazed.
> For just as the father raises the dead and gives life,
> so does the son too give life to those he will.
> For the father judges no one,
> but has given the power of judgment to the son,
> so that all might honor the son just as they honor the father."
>
> (JOHN 5.19–23)

Jesus now becomes more precise: In this judgment, it is the person's response to the son himself, and nothing else, that determines that person's standing.

> "Whoever does not honor the son does not honor the father who sent him.
> In God's truth I tell you,
> all who hear my word and believe in the one who sent me have the new aeon's life,
> and do not come to judgment,
> but have passed from death to life."
>
> (JOHN 5.23–24)

As the person's response to the son is under way here and now, so is its effect. What, then, of the future and the threatened judgment of the whole world? John's Jesus next applies the terms of his present judgment to this imminent execution. Here is a warning as immediate as anything heard in our first three writers or in Paul. But its imagery is narrowly focused—on those who will hear the son's voice and come out of their tombs. Is this all? There is no language here of God's cataclysmic intervention such as Mark's and Matthew's readers had been prompted to expect. John's readers are left with a strange, cryptic hope. It is within the text itself that this hope will be explained and within this text's reception that the hope will be fulfilled.

> "In God's truth I tell you,
> the hour is coming and is now,
> when the dead shall hear the voice of the son of God
> and those who hear shall live.
> For just as the father has life in himself,

so he has given life to the son, too, to have it in himself.
And he has given him the power of judgment, because he is son of man.
Do not be surprised, that the hour is coming
when those in their tombs shall hear his voice and will come on out:
those who did good shall rise to life,
those who did evil shall rise to judgment."

(JOHN 5.25–29)

We know of principles, well established at Jesus' time, that granted a man's son or agent the power to act in the master's name. When no message could travel faster than a horse or a ship, the agent must be given plenipotentiary powers. He stood in for the master and represented him; his person was as honored as the master's own. Traces of the same principle survive to this day in the dignity given to a nation's ambassadors abroad.

Jesus has declared himself, throughout the gospel, son and emissary of God and has claimed all the rights that such a role afforded him. He has claimed to act as God's envoy plenipotentiary and so to have powers that are God's alone: the power of judgment and of life and, not least, the power over his own life and death. This is to arrogate to himself so much authority, such autonomy, that his listeners are reduced to confusion. The son's total obedience involves the exercise of total power. As he makes clear toward the end of his public teaching, the authority given to this envoy is there to be used:

"I have the power to lay my life down,
and I have the power to take it up again.
This is the command I have received from my father."

(JOHN 10.18)

Surely, his audience claims, this is madness? But Jesus is not finished yet. He is once more spiraling to a climax: Discussion of the theme whirls slowly around, rising in pitch, until Jesus closes it with an extraordinary claim:

"My father—what he has given me, it is greater than anything,
and no one can take anything from the hand of the father.
I and the father are one."

(JOHN 10.29)

Has John finally forsaken the balance so carefully sustained throughout the gospel? Has his Jesus lost all sight of obedience? Far from it. John follows the trajectory first of one dialogue, then of another. On the night of his arrest Jesus speaks at length with his pupils. The traitor, Judas, has left; he will soon be lying in wait with troops. The first part of Jesus' talk, a long meditation on Jesus' and the father's relation, comes to its climax as follows:

"If you loved me you would be pleased that I am going to the father,
because the father is greater than I . . .
Just as the father commands, so I do."

(JOHN 14.28, 31)

John's Jesus declares himself both one with the father and less than him. It may be easier to walk such a tightrope than to explain how it is possible. An ambassador may fill such an ambiguous role, and a son, it was widely accepted, would function often enough as just such an ambassador. But John looks for more: a tighter, more intimate link between father and son that does not depend upon their public role and legal relation. To say what he needs to say, John digs deep into the Old Order's most mystical poetry.

THE NAME OF GOD

Agents, emissaries, and sons: Jesus' role stretches their logic to the limit. For he is presented as agent, emissary, and son *of God;* and this is not the principal for whom such agents generally worked. The categories, then, are familiar; it is God's role as principal or father that strains their application. But John does not confine himself to terms such as these. A further category is shaping our story that John's Jesus never discusses or defines but that over and over he uses, and to dramatic effect: This Jesus is the "name" of God, the active presence of God that can be discerned and spoken of. When Isaac bade farewell to his sons in the book of Jubilees that we have encountered before, he called on them to make an oath "by the glorious and honored and great and splendid and amazing and mighty name which created heaven and earth together." The "name" of God lived in the Temple; it was inscribed on the headdress of the high priest and spoken only in the Temple itself, by the priests, at the climactic blessing of the daily service. So what is this "name" of God that for Jubilees' author created heaven and earth? The Old Order knew of more such names than we have yet seen.

In one of the most solemn moments of the Old Order, God appears to Moses in the desert. A bush blazes with fire but is not burned. Moses draws near. He is given his great commission: to rescue the Jews from their slavery in Egypt. Moses tries to avoid the task:

"When I come to the children of Israel, and say, 'The God of your fathers has sent me
to you,' and they say, 'What is his name?' What shall I say to them?"
And God said to Moses: "I am He—who Is." And he said: "You shall say to the
children of Israel, 'He who Is has sent me to you.'"

(ESCAPE [EXODUS] 3.13)

"I am He—who Is." This is a name like no other. John is writing in Greek. Any normal speaker would use the Greek for *"I am He"* as informally as we would use its equiv-

alent, *"That's me"* or *"It's me."* It is an everyday, innocent term. But put it in the mouth of God, and we see how much weight can be carried by this simplest of all expressions.

> *The people shall know my name in that day, says the Lord,*
> *that I am He—am he who speaks.*
>
> (ISAIAH 52.6)

"It's me." Three times in one dispute John's Jesus sounds this motif. The drama of its use is consummate. The first mention sets up a challenge: *"If you do not believe that I am He, you will die in your wrongdoings."* As it stands, the claim is just bemusing. The authorities ask the good question, *"Well, who are you?"* Jesus is offering more than any description they could have in mind. We have already heard lines from Isaiah whose Greek translation sounds this resonant chord. *I am He* can evoke all the power and presence of Isaiah's God:

> *Know and believe and understand, says the Lord, that I am—He,*
> *before me there is no other god nor will there be with me.*
> *I am God, and there is none other that saves besides me.*
> *I am He—am he who wipes out your wrongdoings,*
> *and will not bring them to mind.*
>
> (ISAIAH 43.11, 25)

John's Jesus continues his dispute. He uses the term a second time but only, as it seems, to confirm that he is the Son of Man. John is relaxing the tension. Our attention is lulled. The expression is being used to mean less than we might have begun to suspect.

> *"When you lift up the Son of Man, then you shall know that I am He;*
> *and of myself I do nothing, but as the father has taught me, that is what I say."*
>
> (JOHN 8.28)

This is as delicate a summary of Jesus' standing as any in the gospel. Nothing is explicit that declares him to be more than God's obedient agent. This dialogue brought a good many of his hearers to believe in him. Among them were Jews, and to these Jesus turns for the rest of the scene. He speaks—as we have heard the Baptizer speak and Matthew and Paul—of the Jews' descent from Abraham. By its end Jesus' audience is appalled by his claims. And in a final, climactic exchange that strange term sounds again. This time there is no mistaking Jesus' sense:

> *"Abraham your father was overjoyed to see my day, and he saw it and was glad."*
> *"You are not yet fifty years old,"* said the authorities, *"and you have seen Abraham?"*
> *"In God's truth I tell you, before Abraham came to be,*
> *I am He."*
>
> (JOHN 8.56–58)

We shall hear these words again. When the posse arrives to arrest Jesus, he knows, as ever, exactly what is to happen, at whose hands, and when (John 18.2). The tumult of Mark's story has been stilled. Far from Jesus being overpowered, he must rein in his power before the soldiers can lay a hand upon him. Do they get any inkling of their victim's real identity? Their understanding is not even an issue. One sentence from Jesus is enough to drive them back. He has challenged the troops: *"Who are you looking for?" "Jesus,"* they say, *"of Nazareth."* Jesus replies:

"I am He."
The soldiers fell backward to the ground (John 18.4–5).

THE WORD OF GOD

Agents and sons, God's messengers and seers, the name and the Wisdom of God himself: We have cast from each some light upon the relation of father and son. One term, however, we have so far left unexplored, the very term with which the gospel's prelude starts: *the Word*. To create the world, the Old Order says, God *spoke*.

The Greek term for *word* is *logos*. From it are derived our words for reasoning: *logic* and *logical*. This is telling. *Logos* is both the thought and its expression, idea and word together. It is used for just such patterns and vehicles of thought as we, two thousand years after John, might think of as "logical." A word with clear meaning is a *logos;* a scream is not. The idea behind that clear word is a *logos;* the panic impelling the scream is not. A *logos* provides order and expresses it.

In the beginning was the Word. That one, special, incomparable word: the Word of God. This is God's plan and its expression together. Now, any plan of ours is just a small part of our whole identity; how much of God is caught up in this plan, his Word? As we have seen, our opening poem speaks of the Word as the Old Order speaks of God's Wisdom. *The Word was with God, and the Word was God.* The Word was not just divine or godly. *Divine* in Greek is very similar to *God* (just one letter distinguishes the words, *theios* from *theos*), but not a single ancient copy slips into this less dramatic and contentious claim. There are certainly nuances in the Greek to which our ears are ill attuned, but the poem appears to be adamant: the Word was God himself.

The Word is both the plan of God and its expression. Now the plan of God is not an incidental extra to his real nature. God is eternally consistent; his plan is assured and unchanging. If he creates at all, it is because he is intrinsically a creative God. And further still: John does not introduce God's plan as just one of God's projects, a single item in a long curriculum. Against all ambiguity and all concessions John insists, *the Word was God.* The Word expresses all that God is. When the Word takes on human flesh, he transcribes into human form all and everything that God is. And in turn: Nothing that he expresses is other than God; there is no remainder that in this one human figure is other than the perfect expression of God. John's is a vehement, polemical claim. Jesus' pupils fail to see what is offered; so, we might expect, did some in

John's own church. Does John confuse us in our turn? So he should. We have no terms in which to speak clearly of such things. Perhaps the closest analogy is from math: The Word that came to be flesh is an isomorphism of God. Such a figure stands strangely between God and humankind, embracing both within himself—and so as well the insurmountable differences between them. No wonder John's Jesus slips between our fingers.

John is not alone in his focus on the Word. The first-century C.E. Jewish philosopher Philo writes over and again of it. He, too, finds the Word represented in a single person: in the high priest at work in the Temple. The whole created order must be seen as a temple, which the Temple in Jerusalem represents. The high priest of the universal temple is the Word of God, his active and ordering plan, which in turn the high priest in the Temple represents. The high priest in Jerusalem—dressed in his robes that symbolize the universe and standing as he does midway between God and humankind—can himself be described as the firstborn of the universe, the divine Word. In the high priest is the axial point uniting all creation and humankind, heaven's worship and earth's. We have heard of such beliefs before, in the poem of Sira's Son on the morning sacrifice:

> When the high priest went up to the altar there was majesty,
> until the arrangement of the Lord was completed,
> and they had perfectly finished his service.
>
> (WISDOM OF SIRA'S SON [BEN SIRA] 50.19)

The current high priest represented the Word by reason of his office, when vested and at work in the Temple. Jesus' office knew no such restriction. He was, John maintains, the Word by his very nature, throughout his life on earth—and way beyond. To know what is being claimed for Jesus, we must do more justice to this Word, of which John and Philo speak in such exalted terms.

There are times when we long to express all that we are, totally and without distortion. When we are in love, we want to be transparent to our partner: We want him or her to know us as we are. But we soon learn that to express ourselves completely is way beyond our power. Vast parts of our own past and of our own subconscious are unknown to us. Of what we do know we can only ever put a small part into words. We resort to looks, gestures, and touch, and still we express only a fraction of our "real self." And in turn: We may think we have said exactly what we mean, but we can still be misheard and misunderstood; even those who love us have a separate viewpoint of their own, from which they see a different angle of the world and us and in a different light.

But imagine this as possible: to provide a complete and perfect self-expression of ourselves, as lively and complex as we are in real life. Whatever language we adopted for this self-expression, the effect would be a curious "double" to ourselves. Of course we can imagine such *physical* doubles, molded in clay or carved in wood. But these fail on both the important counts. For a start, they do not express all that we are, for they are dead. Such languages of clay and stone can capture only a small part of ourselves: our appearance, our expression perhaps, but not our hopes, plans, and drives. We need a far livelier language. And in turn: These languages of art express much that we are *not*. They have a character of their own, merits and beauties that are not ours. Clay bears an enormous range of textures, wood as wide a range of grains and colors. But these attract us to the artists' skill and their material; they are alien to ourselves, the subject of their work.

For our imagined double the language must either be neutral, without any resonance of its own (in a way no human language ever is), or it must have a tone identical to the tone of our own person and character (in a way no human language ever does). We need a language that can bear a perfect likeness of ourselves.

Let us for one moment assume that such a double could be created. A strange conundrum then confronts us: This double would be distinct from us and yet in every characteristic the same. It would be the perfect transcription of ourselves, saying all and only what we mean, expressing all and only what we are. It would exhibit our liveliness, our character, our laughter and tears, our abilities, loves, and dislikes. Of course it would only be our double, and yet for as long as we were alive it would be as alive as we were ourselves. It would have nothing that was not our own, but all that we had, it would have, too. It would be nothing that we were not ourselves, and could do nothing that we did not do, but all that we were and did, it would express to those who saw it. How *odd* this double would be: identical with us but distinct, wholly dependent but equal in all abilities and power.

And now what happens if we raise the stakes? If we try to imagine the language in which God himself could come to total and perfect self-expression? Here would be the plan of God wholly revealed, the life of God wholly lived. What possible language could bear God's image? And what relation would that double bear to God?

Creation's story in the Beginning tells of different creatures made by God on successive days: light divided from darkness, the heavens from the earth, the waters from dry land; then vegetation of all kinds; then fish to fill the sea, birds the heavens, and animals the earth. Last of all, as the story's climax, *God said, Let us make humankind in our own image, in the likeness of ourselves. And God created humankind in his own image, in the image of God he created them, male and female he created them* (Beginning [Genesis] 1.26–27). Created in God's image from the first, *humankind* is the language that can bear God's image if any language can at all.

So is this where we would first look for such a perfect double of God—in a single person, one flawless vehicle for God's self-expression, molded to be his perfect image? There is no such person to be found. Adam was made in the image and likeness of God, but this Adam could never be confused with his maker. We need an Adam of a quite different kind, in which that image and likeness of God is perfect: God's total self-expression, without gaps, remainder, or flaw.

The status of this figure will be hard to define. Will he be identical to God, or distinct? Equal in power to God, or his subordinate? But define the figure we must, as best we may. For we have not understood all—or any—of the content of this figure until we have understood its relation to God. Here is the "Word" of God. And the key to its comprehension is precisely that it is the Word. Only when we recognize the figure as the Word do we see for ourselves that God's plan and life really do include that Word's—and so God's own—unimaginable unveiling in human form.

The language that we can best hope to understand is the language of humanity: a *person*. And yet we have already seen: Even if we were able perfectly to translate ourselves into the most familiar shared language, those around us would grasp only a fragment of what we have to show them. We have difficulty not only saying what we mean but understanding what is meant. How could we hope to grasp, to *understand*, such a total disclosure of God if it was ever offered? Our powers of expression and our powers of understanding: *both* need to be transformed. If John is successfully to show us what he would have us see, he must transform our sight. And that is precisely what he sets out to do.

We have thought of a single figure, an Adam way beyond the Adam of which the Beginning tells, who would be the expression, total and without distortion, of God's plan and will. So far so good. And yet we will soon move on. For no person is self-contained; a single figure in isolation is not yet wholly human. If humanity is God's chosen language, he will use the full language of humanity. We will hear the full symphony of God's self-expression when we hear it sounding where relationships exist and love flourishes: *in a community.*

As the father has loved me, so have I loved you;
stay in my love.
If you keep my commandments,
you will stay in my love,
as I have kept my father's commandments
and stay in his love.
I have told you this so that
my joy may be in you
and your joy may be fulfilled.
This is my commandment:
love one another as I have loved you.
No one has greater love than this:
to give up their life for their friends.

(JOHN 15.9–12)

CHAPTER 10

The Trial

Hearing the Evidence

We may look in John—as in our first three witnesses—for excitement in the story's plot and characters. Yet John tells a far more stately story. So much has been hinted and claimed by the end of its opening hymn that we may wonder what remains for John to do. He has inspired his readers, awed them, answered all the questions that Jesus' enemies will raise. So what in turn remains for these readers to do?

To answer this one question is to open with a single key the mystery of John's narrative. The drama of this gospel lies precisely in its readers' response: As Jesus' pupils, his mother, Nicodemus, and Pilate are all protagonists in the story, so are we. And we are to be just as attentive to our own responses as to theirs: How much bemuses us that we then come to understand, what errors we make and then come to see. We are to watch this progress and so to learn from it in turn.

And this was the testimony of John, the Baptizer, *when the authorities sent priests and attendants to him from Jerusalem, to ask him: "You, who are you?"* (John 1.19). We shall hear such questions again; throughout the rest of the gospel they will be addressed to Jesus. The authorities watch and listen for themselves, they cross-examine witnesses, quizzing their own servants and those whom Jesus heals. Evidence is being amassed and assessed from the very start. When Jesus is arrested at last and brought before the Jewish authorities, the hearing is soon over, for his "trial" has been under way from the opening scene.

> *The high priest asked Jesus about his followers and about his teaching. Jesus answered him: "I have spoken openly to the world, I have always taught in the synagogue and in the temple where all the Jews gather, and in secret have I said nothing. Why do you ask me? Ask those who heard, What did I say to them? Look, they know what I said."*
> *(JOHN 18.19–21)*

His challenge is well aimed. As he and the high priest both know, there have been witnesses enough. The investigation of Jesus has lasted throughout his public work, and the reader has heard it all: a full account of the events themselves, the charges they prompt, the process they launch. We, too, are on the jury and must make a decision. For Jesus or against him? All sides of the argument have been presented, the strengths and weaknesses of Jesus' position laid bare. For the case is not open and shut; John knows of Jesus' opponents well enough, but he knows, too, of inquirers who never quite make up their mind and of followers who find this Jesus' claims too much to bear and fall away. John's readers will encounter them all.

John's Jesus flouts the Law. Of this there is no doubt. He works on the Sabbath typically and fragrantly: *this is why the Jews prosecuted Jesus, because he would do such things on the Sabbath.* The special plea that he adduces in defense makes his apparent offense more serious, not less: *"My father goes on working right through, I go on working, too"* (John 5.16, 17). Moses had relayed God's Ten Commandments to the Jews. They were and are foundational to Jewish life. The Jews, insists the first commandment, are to acknowledge no other god than God himself; they are, commands the fourth, to keep the Sabbath holy and to rest on it from work. But Jesus? To defend his breach of the fourth commandment he seems to break the first: *the Jews sought* not just to stop but *actually to kill him. For this reason: he was not only breaking the Sabbath, but was calling God his personal father, making himself equal to God* (John 5.18).

Faced with such behavior, the authorities must reach a verdict and so must the reader. Is this Jesus a blasphemer? Or is he who he says he is? The stand of the authorities sets up a valuable foil. The readers know all that is stacked against Jesus; a decision in his favor will be made in full knowledge of the prosecution's arguments and evidence. Here we will look just at some of the opening scenes in this trial; by their end John has introduced all the themes that will then sound and sound again through his investigation.

John's Jesus berates his opponents for refusing to believe his claims. But they have a point: How and why would God's power and perfection be contained in human form? It was not possible and was not needed. God had given his people what they needed in the Law and the Temple. Who would forsake these gifts, palpably endorsed by God, to rely instead on Jesus—endorsed only (it seemed) by himself? John works hard to provide the witnesses that Jesus needs, the independent backing that will support his claims. For without such backing Jesus' opponents have every reason for their view: He is a madman—or worse.

THE CASE BEGINS

First witness on Jesus' behalf is John the Baptizer. Tradition gave him a standing that ensured respect—as the Elijah who would return, perhaps even as God's Anointed. But the Baptizer renounces all such claims: He is a voice, no more. The next and chief witness invoked by Jesus is God himself. Here is the ultimate vindication of Jesus' claims. But God's "testimony" is channeled through Jesus himself. Here is no independent support; Jesus' appeal to God can be trusted only if Jesus is trusted himself—and he has to make that appeal only and precisely because he is not.

At one crucial moment a voice from heaven speaks out. Here should be evidence that no one could ignore. *"Father,"* says Jesus, *"glorify your name." So there came a voice from heaven, "Yes, I have glorified it, and will glorify it again."* John is clear: The words are God's endorsement of Jesus. The crowds, however, are far less sure: Some heard the voice as thunder, others as an angel's words to Jesus. Jesus has to explain: *"This voice did not come for my sake, but for yours"* (John 12.28, 30). He then offers an explanation: It is by the death of Jesus that God will *glorify his name:*

"Now is the judgment of this world,
now the ruler of this world will be thrown out.
And if I am lifted up from the earth,
I will draw to myself all humankind."

(JOHN 12.31–32)

This is an account of God's *glorified name* but in an explanation as cryptic as the term to be explained. It refers, too, to Jesus' death but so indirectly that John helps the reader with a further comment: *He said this, indicating the death by which he was going to die* (John 12.33). The moment is numinous but obscure. The voice speaks out from heaven, and Jesus must instantly recast its words—into another promise as elusive as those he has been making all along. Such evidence will convince none of the bystanders who are not convinced already. Some modern readers have even wondered: Is John undermining any use of such "evidence" by its failure here? The crowd understands neither the words from heaven nor Jesus' explanation. Such "new" support as this will not put Jesus' standing beyond doubt.

We will hear in the pages to come of more usual witnesses, summoned before this court, and of those who cross-examine them. Of them all John asks: How much did they understand of what they saw? And in every case the question confronts the readers, too: How much do they understand of what they hear presented in this enigmatic story?

Final witness on Jesus' behalf is Jesus himself. There are moments when a defendant has only his own word to give. And there will be times when the defendant is in such high standing that the court will accept a claim he makes on his own behalf. But this is precisely the standing that in Jesus' case is under challenge. If he is mad or wicked, nothing can be taken at face value that he says of his relation to God. The authorities may be blind, but John knows that the readers, too, need help if they are open their eyes and see. For we too are members of this court. We can either stand back as jurors and assess the evidence as we might any other argument that comes before us or come to see that this is a hearing like no other. Judge and jury in this trial are not where they seem to be. The judge is in the dock. Who, then, are the defendants? We, the readers, are the accused, and as John would have it, we are on trial for our lives.

MEMBERS OF THE COURT: "COME AND SEE"

The first witness is in place: the Baptizer. His opening task is to clear away any mis-understanding about himself: He is not the Anointed or the Elijah whose coming would herald the Day of the Lord or the prophet foretold by Moses. But he, too, has a positive testimony to offer: *"Look: there is the lamb of God, that takes away the wrong-doing of the world"* (John 1.29). We heard in chapter 2 and 8 of the role that lambs played in Jesus' world of ritual and sacrifice. We will hear of one such role again at Jesus' crucifixion, timed by John to coincide with the slaughter of the Passover sacri-fice. Here is the first marker of many that John puts down in this opening scene.

John rounds off the Baptizer's first testimony with a clear assertion: *"I have seen and borne witness that this man is the son of God"* (John 1.34). The Baptizer now turns the focus upon Jesus with the title that will be most relevant of all: the son of God. We shall hear more of all these terms that the authorities and Baptizer have used. What John is not, Jesus is. In this same first scene Andrew tells his brother Peter that Jesus is the Anointed. The next day their neighbor Philip tells Nathanael about Jesus: He is the man predicted by Moses in the Law and by the prophets. Nathanael himself com-pletes the series: He declares Jesus to be the son of God, the king of Israel.

This opening scene has its natural pair at the end of Jesus' public work, at his last and greatest miracle, when he raises his friend Lazarus from the dead. The dead man's sister Martha speaks of these same roles when she answers Jesus' challenge:

"Yes, Lord, I have come to believe that you are the Anointed,
the son of God,
the one coming into the world."

(JOHN 11.29)

Those first pupils each saw just a part and took up one strand in the rope. Martha, at the story's end, has seen their interweaving. Only kingship is beyond her horizon, and that will be the subject of the gospel's final scenes.

But more divides the pupils and Martha than the words of their belief. The pupils are quickly convinced; Martha is struggling against despair. They freely discuss their allegiance to the Baptizer or his pupil, to their brother's or neighbor's new master; Martha has just one person on whom to rely—the friend of her dead brother. The pupils will have the same faith at the story's end that they have at its beginning; they will have heard more, learned more, seen more, but they show no signs of progress. And Martha? Her story is driven by a deeper urgency: here is a more pressing need and reliance of a different kind. It is in Jesus' miracles that John looks for real change in the story's characters—and in its readers, too.

John maps briskly the route of these first followers to Jesus. Two pupils of the Baptizer transfer their allegiance; here is a move that John would have others make for themselves. They follow Jesus. *"What,"* he asks them, *"are you looking for?"* It is a question to be asked of anyone who seeks to enter John's own community. Their response is a deeper question than it sounds—deeper, too, than they themselves can know: *"Teacher, where are you staying?"* (John 1.38). In the gospel's second half we will hear much of Jesus' return: He will then *stay with* his followers. John's readers within the community know how apt is the inquirers' question. To know the real answer is to know where to find Jesus: where he is *staying* now—in John's church.

Jesus says: *"Come and see."* Within a few lines Nathanael refuses to believe that anything good can come from Nazareth. But Philip repeats the summons: *"Come and see."* A caucus of followers is gathering round: Andrew who told his brother Peter, their neighbor who told Nathanael. The pattern is laid down by which the word will spread. Here is John's invitation to any reader brought by another to read his testimony: Come and see.

THE COURTROOM: "THIS IS THE GATE OF HEAVEN"

This first sequence ends with Nathanael's dramatic turnaround. Jesus reveals his second sight; Nathanael's doubts vanish. It is little enough to trigger such a change.

"Because I told you I saw you under the fig tree, do you believe? You shall see greater things than these." And he says to him: *"In God's own truth I tell you, you shall* all *see the heaven opened and the angels of God ascending and descending upon the Son of Man."*

(JOHN 1.50–51)

This last saying is abruptly introduced. It is almost an appendix to the dialogue. But there is no accident in its position. On the contrary: This saying is the climax of John's first scene. Jesus is making an extraordinary claim. It is all the more striking in retrospect, as we draw to the gospel's end, for remaining unfulfilled. No one in the gospel ever sees what Jesus promises.

Everything about this vision—of heaven opened and the Son of Man—is odd. Where exactly in its scenario is the Son of Man himself? The messengers of God will be seen going up and coming down. Is he then in heaven? Or on earth? Or, in some remarkable way, in both? Or (to have before us every possibility) the Son of Man himself could be envisaged as the ladder. This is a bemusing picture, and it is meant to be.

John has not left us without clues. One of the Old Order's heroes is Jacob. Among all the ancestors of the Israelites, Jacob becomes in the most vivid way the father of the nation, for in a dramatic encounter with heavenly power, Jacob was renamed "Israel." Successive generations sought significance in the name; one of its possible renderings is "a man seeing God." If John takes this rendering of *Israel* seriously, then Jacob's name sets him from the start at odds with our gospel. For *no one,* John's opening poem insists, *has seen God, ever.* Yet again, it seems, John is reworking a venerable tradition in the light of Jesus, casting new light on the tradition and on Jesus alike. Of one thing we can be sure: Thanks to John's narrative, Jacob is already in John's mind and his readers'. For Jacob was renowned for his trickery; it is on Jacob's name and character that John's Jesus is playing when he describes Nathanael, *"Look, here is a true Israelite, there is no deceit in him"* (John 1.47). John has evoked the most famous of all "Israelites" and now dwells on the privileged insight he was given: on the story of Jacob's famous and mysterious vision:

> *Jacob dreamed: A ladder was set up on the earth, and its top reached to heaven; and the angels of God were ascending and descending on it. And the Lord stood above it, and said, "I am the Lord God of Abraham your father, and the God of Isaac. The land on which you lie, I will give it to you and to your children." And Jacob awoke and said, "Surely God is in this place, and I did not know it." And he was afraid, and said, "How dreadful is this place. This is none other than the house of God, this is the gate of heaven." And he called the place Bethel, the house of God.*
> (BEGINNING [GENESIS] 28.11–13, 16–17, 19)

Later generations thought long and hard about this vision. Such a strange event must be important; its every detail must matter. That oddest option in Jesus' promise, that the Son of Man would himself be the ladder, has its basis here. For *the angels of God,* we read in the story of Jacob, *were ascending and descending on it* or *on him.* This text is ambiguous: The angels could be read as ascending and descending on the ladder or on Jacob himself; the Lord, then, could be standing on him, too. But what would this mean? Jacob himself would now be the vehicle for such journeys between heaven and earth. And as he makes possible the angels' journeys downward, so he would make possible the journey of a seer into heaven. This reading is less arbitrary—and less bizarre—than it may at first sight seem. It presents Jacob—and in turn the Son of Man—as the intermediaries that future visionaries need.

The story of Jacob's vision was retold in more elaborate forms and was linked (we shall see) with other incidents in Jacob's life. Such reworking of stories was well known. John's gospel itself may have evolved into its present form by just such a process: A short saying or story of Jesus attracted his followers' attention; they saw in it implications and connections that its earliest telling left unexplored. For their own readers' sake they must record these insights. They had no textbooks or commentaries; the story itself had to be retold. Sixty years of such retelling lie behind our present gospel: Jesus' own immediate followers, their successors, and their successors in turn, at work on the stories by which they had determined to define their lives.

What effect did such reworking have upon a story? We have several versions of Jacob's dream in Jewish tradition. Here are two. They were developed for quite different purposes and so take quite different forms; our gospels were not the only texts whose stories were varied to meet varied needs. Glimpses of these variants help us understand John's own procedure and cast invaluable light on the ways in which such central stories were relayed. The two versions illustrate more than just methods familiar to John's world. We will see here the care for details that John shares. We will see, too, a focus on the very same details that John has in mind and on the very same, central question: What form might God's self-disclosure take on earth, and how might we discern it? There must be an interchange between the earthly world and the heavenly, but who will discharge such a role, and how? The language for such reflection used in this story is not ours, but the question it confronts is as vivid now, for anyone seeking or claiming a "knowledge" of God, as it was two thousand years ago.

Here, then, is the story of Jacob's dream in the first of our two revisions, a free translation of the Old Order's story into Aramaic. This was designed for public reading and had to be a story as continuous as the Old Order's own. We have met with these translations before: They were used in the synagogues, and some of them (by no means all) go back as far as Jesus' and John's day. For any Jews who spoke no Hebrew, these versions were vital.

The angels that had accompanied Jacob from the house of his father ascended to inform the angels from on high, saying, "Come and see the just man whose image is engraved on the throne of God, the man you were longing to see." And the angels of the presence of God were ascending and descending and gazing on him.

Some later rabbis would explore this thought: that Jacob was himself on earth while his portrait was in heaven. Jacob's image is on the throne of God. But engraved there, according to ancient tradition, was the image of God himself. If that same image on the throne is Jacob's, too, then Jacob stands in a strange, privileged relation to God. From Adam to Jacob: We are faced once more with the forms that disclosure can take, of the knowledge we are offered of God and the conditions under which we can grasp it. This Jacob is on earth, but to see him is to see the image of God preserved in heaven. Here is a sight that the dazzled angels had been longing to see—and now they can.

Not that all the angels admired him. Some were said to be jealous. We hear of this envy from our second rendering of the story in a text known as Joseph's Prayer and recorded in the third century C.E. In this text appears a speech ascribed to Jacob. He draws out the double nature implied by his having two names, *Jacob* and *Israel*. The technique is one we know well from John: The speaker must explain his own standing to the reader; the Old Order's story must be retold and its implications unfolded within the new telling of the story itself:

"I, Jacob, who am speaking to you, am also Israel, an angel of God and a ruling spirit. Abraham and Isaac were created before any work. But I am the one whom God called Israel, 'a man seeing God,' because I am the firstborn of every living thing to whom God gives life. . . . "

At our distance from that tradition of the Aramaic translation, we might wonder whether the figure of Jacob engraved in heaven was a mere token, eternal but lifeless, of Jacob's privilege. Far from it. Jacob's heavenly counterpart is a key figure in God's creative order. This was not easily seen, either by those about him on earth or by the Old Order's later readers. The "earthly" Jacob must reveal how much lies behind his own (apparently normal) human figure. To do so the Jacob of Joseph's Prayer appeals to another dramatic encounter between himself and the heavenly world.

The Old Order tells how Jacob wrestled with God or with his angel all one night. Jacob demanded that his adversary reveal his name. Instead, the mysterious figure renamed Jacob: *Israel,* "a man seeing God." Here, by contrast, is the version that we hear in Joseph's Prayer. In this reworking of the story, Jacob is entitled to his second name for far greater reasons, deep in his place in God's plan. The speech in Joseph's Prayer continues:

"Uriel the angel of God came out and said that I had descended to earth and had taken up my shelter among men and had been called by the name of Jacob. He envied me and wrestled with me, saying that his name was to be above mine. I told him his name and the rank he held: 'Are you not Uriel, the eighth after me, and am I not Israel, the archangel of the power of the Lord and the chief captain among the children of God? Am I not Israel, the chief minister before the face of God?' And I called upon my God by the inextinguishable name."

This Jacob is both in heaven and on earth. A heavenly conflict is fought out in Jacob's mysterious struggle on earth. The distinction between the two is blurred. For in Jacob the heavenly and the earthly meet. His dream of the ladder reveals, perhaps even to Jacob himself, his own double role; it discloses, too, the holiness of a single, special place where the two realms converge. For *Jacob was afraid, and said, "How dreadful is this place. This is none other than the house of God, this is the gate of heaven." And he called the place Bethel, the house of God.*

And when John's Jesus recalls that dream? He is making more than a promise of some future vision. This is a declaration: that heaven and earth are linked, here and now, as they were at Bethel. Such a union was not strange in itself to the Jews of Jesus' day: The point of contact was the Temple at Jerusalem, the center of the center of the world and the house of God himself. The drama in John's claim is the role it gives to Jesus: He himself, in his own person, is the point of meeting between heaven and earth. This Jesus is the vehicle for disclosure to humans and to angels; he is that disclosure's content as well. In John's very next chapter this suggestion will be followed through: The true Temple is not the building in Jerusalem; it is the body of Jesus himself.

What then of Jesus' promise, that his pupils would see the heaven opened? *"In God's own truth I tell you, you shall* all *see the heaven opened and the angels of God ascending and descending upon the Son of Man"* (John 1.51). We have met the notion before, of heaven opened to human gaze: It was spelled out at the baptism of Mark's Jesus, predicted at his trial, and all but realized as the veil of the Temple was split open to reveal the Holy of Holies beyond. Disclosure is under way, an unveiling of truths normally locked far from human sight in heaven. John's Jesus promises a vision without apparent limit, but it remains unfulfilled.

Or does it? Over and over we shall see John reinterpret the hopes and words of the church's early faith. To see in these hopes what John would have his readers see was not easy, no easier than it was to see in Jesus the Old Order's prophecies fulfilled. Old meanings unfold into new. To see the clash between them is to start wondering how they might be reconciled. Here is the path along which John would have his readers walk: to see what is strange and so to seek its explanation.

What exactly will John's characters see? What will his readers see? Far less, it seems, than they have been given grounds to hope for. They hope, they grow worried, their worry turns to disillusion. But the gospel offers, too, the mirror image of this movement, its exact opposite: movement into a deeper understanding of what Jesus really promised. The words themselves are Jesus' spur to set such movement under way. That ancient language of disclosure and of heaven's link with earth must be interpreted: The disclosure is here and now, in the presence and person of Jesus, who is himself the link between heaven and earth. What for centuries had been described as heaven's opening and angels' journeys was happening here and now in the life of a Galilean teacher. Seers no longer have to undertake their strange journeys into heaven. To learn this was already to learn the crucial lesson: how to learn. It was to catch a first glimpse of the heavenly ladder itself.

To recognize the unveiling for what it is—this is already to start seeing past the veil. In Mark's terms, the readers must open their eyes and see, a task that it takes Mark's whole gospel to achieve. In John's terms, the reader must be born again: an even clearer indication that the task is not within the reader's unaided, independent power. Help is needed. The gospel's own arrangement and strategy are well-crafted technical aids. But no number of such devices will guarantee their successful application. How can John be confident that his strategy will work, that his readers will be radically reborn into the knowledge that they need?

John is an unfailingly self-conscious author: He is always assessing what will make his text effective, what will make it *work*. He would have his readers be self-conscious, too, to ask themselves, How are they to attain this new life? What is really at work in them to make it possible? Such inquiry is not just an optional extra, tacked on to a process that would continue as successfully unobserved. Part of the gestation is the reader's growing awareness of just what is involved in the process. John recalls the reader over and over to the strange, elusive power that is at work, as John would have it, whenever his gospel is read with any understanding. This is the power that Jesus will give his pupils at the gospel's end: the Breath of God.

Mark's Jesus asked, *"Do you still not understand?"* John, too, knows how elusive the good news of his gospel can be. He starts his account of Jesus' work with two stories told in quick succession. Their moods contrast sharply. First Jesus turns water into wine at a wedding. His mother has asked his help. He rebuffs her strangely: *"Woman, what have you to do with me?"* (John 2.4). But he responds nonetheless; the celebration is revived. The intervention of Jesus has transformed the old into the new. We next hear of him in the Temple of Jerusalem amid the traders. John tells at the start of Jesus' work the story placed by our other gospels in his last climactic week: Jesus makes a whip out of cords and drives the animals and their handlers from the Temple.

Who among those present at these incidents—who among the readers who learn of them—understand what is under way? John rounds off the first story: *This was the start of the signs that Jesus made in Cana of Galilee and he disclosed his glory, and his pupils believed in him* (John 2.11). His pupils have believed. But from the miracle's chief beneficiaries we hear just one response: The master of ceremonies is surprised by the quality of this new supply. It is the servants who know the wine's source, and it is Jesus' followers, strengthened by the sign, who become the "servants" offering the new wine to John's community and beyond. John is offering just such a warning as Mark gave in his image of sown seed. But John's is the starker of the two: Those to whom the new wine is brought will take what is offered, a handful will be gratefully bemused, most will not notice the change in the party's supplies, and none at all will understand what has really happened among them.

Nicodemus: "Born Again from Above"

There are those in John's story who believe, those who seem to understand—and those who admit themselves bemused. John now introduces Nicodemus: He is sympathetic to Jesus, baffled by him, anxious to know more. We will meet him three times in all: here at the start of Jesus' work, once when the opposition to Jesus is growing, and again when Jesus is already dead. He never admits that he is for or against Jesus, and John is far too subtle—and far too sensitive—to judge him for his indecision. But in Nicodemus a sharp question confronts John's readers: whether they, too, will play the part of Nicodemus or will they step beyond the tentative, reasonable inquiry that Nicodemus pursues. Such an approach as his will lead the reader no further than it led Nicodemus. John leaves the reader to decide how far along the road Nicodemus ever travelled to the rebirth by whose very mention he is bemused.

It was night. Nicodemus, *one of the Pharisees, a leader of the Jews,* came to Jesus. No reason is given for his choosing the darkness. Later in the gospel we will hear of opposition, of threats and of fear among would-be followers of Jesus. But Nicodemus's timing has a wider significance:

> *"For God so loved the world* [says Jesus] *that he gave his only son,*
> *so that all who believe in him should not die,*
> *but should have the life of the new aeon.*

For God did not send his son into the world to judge the world,
but that through him the world might be saved.
All who believe in him are not subject to judgment;
but all who do not believe are already judged,
because they have not believed in the name of the only son of God.
And this is the judgment:
that the light has come into the world,
and people preferred the darkness to the light;
for their deeds were wicked.
All who do wrong hate the light, and avoid the light,
so that their deeds might not be open to scrutiny.
But all who do the truth come to the light,
so that their deeds might be seen to be done in God."

(JOHN 3.16–21)

The darkness threatens throughout John. The light that dispelled the darkness when God first spoke must forever hold it at bay. If the light weakens, the darkness will return. And if the light were ever to be extinguished? Then all that the light brought with it would sink once more into chaos; creation would be undone.

Light was the subject of God's first distinction: light over darkness. This is a distinction unlike those that follow. God's thought brings order to chaos; out of mere confusion comes what we in turn can think and think about. On that creative power our own thinking is modeled and depends, our own meager version of God's thought as the interpreting, ordering, creative beings that we are. Light makes possible our judgment, our discrimination; that judgment brings more light in turn. To shirk the light is willfully to muddle and obscure not just matters of mind and intellect, but of right and wrong, good and evil. To seek the darkness is, as John would have it, to condemn oneself.

Jesus says: *"I am the light of the world"* (John 8.12). And in the very next story Jesus warns of the darkness drawing in. Jesus brings light to a blind man. Once more he breaks the Sabbath law and strengthens the opposition of those that will kill him. The man had been born blind, says Jesus,

"so that the works of God may be made known in him. We must work at the works of him who sent me while it is day. Night is coming, when no one can work. While I am in the world, I am the light of the world."

(JOHN 9.3–5)

Jesus has brought light to one man. But the night is closing in all the darker and more threatening for that one miracle of "light."

The next and greatest miracle is given a similar preface. Jesus' friends discourage him from going to Jerusalem for Passover: *"Just now the authorities were trying to stone you, and you are going back there?"* Jesus' reply raises as many questions as it settles:

*"Are there not twelve hours in a day? If people walk in the day, they do not stumble,
because they see the light of this world. But if they walk in the night, they stumble—
because the light is not inside them."*

(JOHN 11.9–10)

How far advanced are "the day's" twelve hours? Will Jesus stop walking as the
night draws on? Or does one figure in this story have the light within him as he
walks through the surrounding darkness, that will keep him safe from stumbling?

No one ever stumbled worse than Judas Iscariot. At supper with his closest friends
Jesus knew what was to come. He predicted his betrayal by the friend to whom he
offered a choice tidbit of food, almost certainly a particular mark of favor and friendship. It was handed to Judas. Straightaway *Satan entered him.* Judas took the tidbit—
and left. *It was night.*

(JOHN 13.30)

We might feel some sympathy for Nicodemus. He sets the conversation off to a gracious start: *"Master, we know you have come as a teacher from God; for no one can do these
signs that you do, unless God is with him."* Jesus' reply is brisk enough:

*"In God's truth I tell you,
unless people are born again from above,
they cannot see the kingdom of God."*

Nicodemus says to him, *"How can people be born when they are old? They can hardly
go into their mother's womb a second time and be born!"* Jesus answered,

*"In God's truth I tell you,
unless people are born from water and breath,
they will not enter the kingdom of God.
What is born from flesh is flesh,
and what is born from Breath is breath."*

(JOHN 3.1–6)

Nicodemus has good reason to be confused. The phrase *again from above* translates
from Greek one word that can mean "again" or "from above" (rather like "from the
top" might mean today). As part of a phrase for "conception from heaven" its meaning is obscure enough; once Nicodemus has in mind rebirth from the womb, his
imagination founders.

Such confusion is frequent in John. In this case the key word's two meanings are
quite familiar, and Nicodemus would have had good grounds to ask which of the two

gave better sense—or any sense at all. John's next story revolves once more around a pun; this time just one sense is natural. The scene is set at a well. Jesus speaks to a Samaritan woman of the fresh, living water he has to offer:

> *"All who drink of the water I shall give shall not thirst, not for all aeons,*
> *but the water I shall give them will become a spring in them,*
> *welling up to the new aeon's life."*
>
> *(JOHN 4.13–14)*

The woman is as confused as Nicodemus. The Greeks spoke of running water as "living"; Jesus can imagine the "life" of his words transferred to those who accept them. A spring within the drinkers will slake their thirst for all aeons, "for eternity," and so will provide the new aeon's "eternal" life.

First Jesus offers this strange drink; then he offers food. Unexpected nourishment is again at issue in the Feeding of Five Thousand: There is more important food to be had from Jesus than the loaves sufficient for a hungry afternoon. The crowd seems worse than obtuse, to ask for a *sign* so soon after the feeding that John himself describes as such. But Jesus has raised the stakes: He has spoken of *food that abides to the new aeon's life*. In answer to their challenge he claims more still:

> *"The bread of God* [said Jesus] *is the one who comes down from heaven and who gives life to the world." So they said to him: "Sir, give us this bread." Jesus said to them:*
>
> *"I am the bread of life.*
> *Those who come to me shall never hunger,*
> *And those who believe in me shall never thirst."*
>
> *(JOHN 6.33–35)*

How is the crowd to understand? How, we might wonder at our distance from the story, is anyone to understand? First condition is the yearning of which the Old Order knew. It was a longing as basic as our most basic instinct of all. Isaiah cries,

> *You that are thirsty, come to the waters;*
> *and you that have no money, come, buy, and eat, without money and without cost.*
> *Why do you spend money on what is not bread?*
> *Listen well to me, and eat what is good.*
> *Pay attention, come to me;*
> *hear, and you shall live.*
>
> *(ISAIAH 55.1–3)*

We have already heard the promise of Sira's Son, that those who fed on Wisdom would hunger for more. Those who are nourished by John's Jesus are filled for all aeons to come.

Nicodemus is an honorable man. He has heard Jesus speak and would have the authorities hear him before they judge his claims (John 7.50). His own encounter with Jesus had been confusing enough. Jesus' words had been elusive and strange; they had offered no direct reference to Jesus himself at all. Nicodemus, when he reappears among the authorities, is making no commitment of his own, but in this limbo of his doubt he wants justice and due process. Here is a voice the reader can be glad to hear—not least the reader who shares Nicodemus's doubts and looks for more time and information.

Two men tend the body of Jesus after his death, Joseph of Arimathaea and our Nicodemus. Joseph is described as *a pupil of Jesus, but in secret, for fear of the authorities.* John has spoken of such fear before and always with disdain for those who felt its pressure: *for they loved human glory more than the glory of God* (John 12.43). John offers no judgment on Joseph: He has, after all, at least gone to Pilate and made his loyalty known, if only at his master's death. Nicodemus is more ambiguous. Not a word is spoken of his allegiance. He brings a vast amount of spices, far too extravagant for a single body—and for a body that will leave the tomb, a waste. Is this still the uncertain figure that we met at the gospel's start?

He and Joseph may well represent groups among the readers John expects: fearful believers on the one hand, inquirers hesitant and still uncomprehending on the other. Nicodemus has not made progress. Even at the gospel's close he is still identified by his first appearance: *the one who came to Jesus by night, right at the start* (John 19.39). The aftermath of Jesus' death is as poignant and ambiguous as anything in this extraordinary testimony: Jesus' body is consigned to two men who have failed to declare or failed to reach the faith for which John calls. Is this the tenderness for which his community is still grateful after sixty years, or is the dead body all that such men will ever have of Jesus?

Of Good and Evil: John and Qumran

Light and darkness, good and evil, one of the most ancient links in human thought. Such connections are not ours alone. All the questions that we ask about evil were asked by our forebears two thousand years ago; the symbols in which they found they could say what they needed to say are the symbols we still use today. But Jesus' words to Nicodemus focus sharply on the division between those who come to the light and those who avoid it, those who do good and those who lurk in the darkness that suits and hides their evil. We find such a resolute, fierce distinction in just one other community of Jesus' time: at Qumran.

The John who edited this dialogue with Nicodemus is a John steeped in the teachings of the Qumran sect. That strange community was destroyed, its library hidden, its members scattered or killed. All that we have to remind us are ten thousand scraps of parchment and a range of buildings that may even have housed a different community altogether. But here in the tradition of our fourth witness their influence lives on, in John's own version—a typically deep, careful version—of their stark, defensive view of the world.

What is the basis of good and evil? The questions asked at Qumran are our questions, too.

Evil seems a power as active as good, to have a drive within it that sweeps up individuals, crowds, and nations. Is this evil superficial, a blister on the surface of a beautiful world? Or is it set deep within creation, a cancer from which nothing—and no human being—is ever free? Only when we let our own questions be heard can we do justice to the answers reached at Qumran.

Good and evil: The stark distinction known in Qumran can take various forms. A good table might be readily explained as one that could be used in every role in which we wish to use a table. So, perhaps, might a good person, if we could once be clear what is a person's proper role. But such a role is far from clear, and we speak nonetheless of good and evil in people, their actions, and the world. We might attempt further comparisons: Do we use *good* and *evil* as we use *large* and *small, transparent, blue,* or *square?* One factor in good and evil is missing from these other attributes. We might be drawn to think of an abstract world—in a greater, all-encompassing mind, perhaps—in which all such qualities have an existence of their own. We use these words to describe them and are confident that those with whom we speak mean by them what we mean, perhaps (as some thinkers proposed in the ancient world) precisely because we and those around us share some part in such a greater mind.

But this does not yet capture why we think of good and evil as existing in themselves. We think of them as powers, as active, urgent forces in our lives, just as love can be, or jealousy. If we think of good and evil as existing at all, it is in large part thanks to the assurance or the fear inspired by such "powers," inside and around us, acting upon us and apparently beyond our control.

Strong instincts attract us to this view—and perhaps to the hope—that good and evil are not just categories with which we dignify our likes and dislikes, ambitions and needs, that there are "real" good and evil that exist beyond our humdrum world and (even unknown to us) inform our minds and hearts. We can never be sure, of course, that we have genuinely discovered any such reality. We inherit and generally accept the conviction that the good lies in our own and our culture's values and that evil lurks in the lives and ideals of those that our culture despises, hates, or fears. But our generation is not the first to look back on those that have gone before and wonder how they can have been so certain of rights and wrongs that look quite different to ourselves. Our grandchildren will be bemused in their turn by the certainties that shape our lives.

These "real" distinctions, nonetheless, help us make sense of the world around us. We can invoke the good to vindicate our actions, point to evil to explain and condemn our enemies'. The distinctions give us strength. We believe ourselves under the influence of good, or evil, or both, sometimes as willing allies, sometimes as captives dragged along against our will, and sometimes as victims torn one way and the other in painful indecision. In the thought of such "powers" we have left mere labels far behind.

Once we see good and evil as powers outside us, such conflict in ourselves seems to echo and exemplify a battle raging in creation as a whole. The whole created order is at war. We can draw further strength from such a sharp divide: There is right and wrong and no common ground between them; we are fighting for the right and have God on our side. But this gain comes at a cost: The image of such war is all the more frightening when a single, all-loving, and all-powerful God is thought to have made the world. Is there some second god, responsible for evil and straining to flout God's will? How could such a power have ever entered God's creation? To ask about evil's origin is soon to ask about the world's origin too.

And then in turn: How much freedom are we left to make decisions for ourselves, once we see such powers around us, shaping our lives and calling for allegiance? We imagine ourselves to be independent agents. But we see ourselves and those around us growing, one by one, into just the character that has been visible since childhood. We can well wonder if good and evil have been given to each of us in advance, in proportions that will determine our fate in this life—and, if there is one, in the next.

In the Community Rule is the boldest, fullest statement of the beliefs on good and evil held by the Qumran sect. It was written as instruction for the sect's instructor.

Everything, he is told, is under the control of God; there is no danger of a second power responsible for evil. Why God ordains evil, we are not told. Each person's destiny is settled in advance: We have a portion of good and of evil, and the balance between them—however viciously the evil angels may try to unsettle it—determines our standing in this life and the next. A teacher, of course, may well be most effective by telling his pupils that success is out of their hands: To hear that our destiny is fixed, can spur us to vindicate the place in heaven that is assigned to us already if we are to have it at all. The sect's members could not know if their failings were a sign of the Dark Angels' activity licensed by God or of their eternal condemnation. All the more reason to resist temptation. The instructor, of course, knows their fate no more than they do themselves, and he has already been warned that some who have no loyalty to the sect will pretend it. Here is the instruction he is to give:

> The Master shall instruct all the children of light in the nature of all the children of men about their different breaths [or spirits] with their signs, about their deeds during their lifetime, their visitation for chastisement with their final rewards.
>
> From the God of Knowledge comes all that is and shall be. Before ever they existed he established their whole design, and when, as ordained, they come into

being, it is in accord with his glorious design that they accomplish their tasks, and they cannot be changed.

He has created humankind to govern the world, and has appointed for them two breaths in which to walk until the time of his visitation: the breaths of truth and injustice. Those born from truth spring from a fountain of light, but those born of injustice spring from a well of darkness. All the children of righteousness are ruled by the Prince of Light, but all the children of darkness are ruled by an Angel of Darkness. The Angel of Darkness leads all the children of righteousness astray, and until his end all their wrongdoing is caused by this Angel's dominion in accordance with the mysteries of God. For all the Angel's allotted ministers seek to trip up the children of light.

But the God of Israel and his Angel of Truth will help all the children of light. For it is he who created the breaths of light and darkness and founded every action upon them.

These are their ways in the world: to lighten the heart of man and to make straight before him all the paths of goodness, and to instill in his heart the fear of God's laws: a breath of humility, patience, abundant charity of mighty wisdom which trusts in all the deeds of God and leans on his great loving-kindness of faithful concealment of the mysteries of truth.

God's visitation on all who walk in this breath, shall be healing, great peace in a long life, together with everlasting blessing in life for all aeons, a crown of glory, and a garment of majesty in unending light.

But the ways of the breath of falsehood are these: greed, wickedness and lies, pride, a blind eye and dull ear, a stiff neck and heavy heart, so that a person walks in all the ways of darkness and guile.

And God's visitation on all who walk in this breath shall be a mass of plagues everlasting damnation, torment for all aeons, and shameful extinction in the fire of the dark regions. The times of all their generations shall be spent in sorrowful mourning until they are destroyed without remnant.

The nature of all humankind is ruled by these two breaths, and during their life all people have a portion of their divisions and walk in both their ways. And the whole reward for the person's deeds shall be, for everlasting aeons, according to this: whether his portions in these breaths' divisions are great or small. For God has established the breaths in equal measure until the final age. But in the mysteries of his understanding, God has ordained an end for injustice and at his visitation will destroy it for ever.

Then truth, which has wallowed in the ways of injustice, shall arise in the world forever. God will purify every deed of men with his truth. He will cleanse them from all wicked deeds with the breath of holiness; like purifying waters he will shed upon them the breath of truth, to cleanse them of all injustice. And they shall be plunged into the breath of purification, that they may instruct the upright in the knowledge of the Most High.

For God has chosen them for an everlasting Order, and all the glory of Adam shall be theirs.

Food for the People

Jesus has spoken with Nicodemus about flesh and breath; Nicodemus is not the last to hear this contrast. It is brought vividly before us when Jesus has just fed with bread and fish five thousand people in the desert. Anyone who knew the church's Service of Thanksgiving would have seen beneath this narrative the Thanksgiving's central rite: a meal of shared bread, just a mouthful each, such as Jesus and his pupils ate on the last night of his earthly life. John does not tell the story of that meal; it is in the story of the feeding and the following dialogue that these themes of the Thanksgiving are explored. It is no surprise, then, that John places the feeding at Passover, for Passover will be the season of that last meal and Jesus' death.

Jesus has fed the crowd. The crowd pursues him. He speaks of bread:

> *"The bread of God is the one coming down from heaven and giving life to the world."*
> *"Sir," they said, "give us that bread always."*

> *"I am the bread of life.*
> *Whoever comes to me shall never hunger,*
> *and whoever believes in me shall never thirst."*
>
> (JOHN 6.33–35)

John's readers knew what was muddling the crowds and why: how little they understood—how little they could possibly understand—of the bread about which Jesus was instructing them. The crowd speaks of Moses and the manna given to Israel in the desert. The readers hear the invitation that Jesus really offers: to hear his word and to eat bread and drink wine at the Thanksgiving's meal. But the readers, too, are in for a surprise. Many knew the Thanksgiving Service well. We have heard in Pliny the echoes of dark stories about the Christians' services. But these rumors were wild and unfounded; ordinary food was eaten at these meals by ordinary people. Why, then, does John's Jesus uses the most vivid, earthy language he can?

> *"In God's truth I tell you,*
> *unless you eat the flesh of the son of man and drink his blood,*
> *you do not have life in you.*
> *For my flesh is the true food and my blood is the true drink."*
>
> (JOHN 6.53, 55)

Is Jesus demanding cannibalism after all, as the church's opponents claimed? Certainly not. But how, then, are his words to be understood? His pupils are dumbfounded: *"This is a hard saying. Who can grasp or accept it?"* Jesus provides a cryptic interpretation. We have encountered this technique of John's before: to juxtapose one saying with another and let the echo sound from one to the other and back again:

> *"Does this shock you?*
> *What then if you saw the son of man ascending where he was before?*
> *It is the Breath that gives life;*
> *the flesh is of no benefit at all.*
> *The words that I have spoken to you are breath, and they are life."*
>
> *(JOHN 6.61–63)*

It is the command to eat his flesh that shows how little the flesh helps; it is these words about flesh and blood, as brutally physical as any in the gospels, that Jesus can describe as living breath. All that the hearers had understood by the contrast of flesh and breath must be redefined. It is too much to ask. So terrible is this demand to eat his flesh and drink his blood that many of his pupils leave off from following him. There is real tension here. The pupils of Jesus and the pupils of John's community are all alike in danger of seceding. No reader could have read this chapter without a frightened pang. As fearsome as anything is the need to admit: some teaching, it seems at this stage—some central, indispensable teaching—is not for understanding.

The range of possible responses is put starkly before us. Jesus turns to the Twelve, his innermost circle:

> *"You don't want to leave, too, do you?"*
> *Peter replied, "Sir, who would we go away to? You have the words of life, and we have come to believe and to know that you are the holy one of God."*
>
> *(JOHN 6.67–69)*

Our first three witnesses made Peter's declaration the high point of their narrative, the watershed between the triumph of Jesus' miracles and the suffering to which he now turns. John, by contrast, has Peter state the pupils' faith at a moment of confusion. Just a page before, the crowd was stirring to make Jesus king. And now? Only a handful of followers remain. The miracle that roused the crowds has scattered them. Peter's is a brave, strong claim. But its terms are touching: *"Who would we go away to?"* The Twelve are searching, just as John's readers will be, sixty years later. Against the offense of Jesus' latest teaching stands not only the triumphs that have gone before; there is simply no alternative to Jesus.

"You are the holy one of God": Peter is more right than he knows. In his final prayer Jesus will ask the father,

Make them holy in the truth;
your word is truth.
Just as you have sent me into the world,
so I, too, have sent them into the world;
And on their account do I make myself holy,
so that they, too, might be made holy in the truth.

(JOHN 17.17–19)

On the one hand, Peter, but on the other hand, the traitor. In this story we hear for the first time of Judas Iscariot and—in emphatic repetition—of his later betrayal. *"Didn't I choose you myself? And one of you is a devil"* (John 6.70). In our earlier witnesses it was Peter who mistook the character of Jesus' mission and was bitterly put down: *"Off with you, Satan, get out of my sight! For you think in men's ways, not God's."* (Mark 8.33). But John brands Judas himself. We may wonder why John looks forward to the betrayal here. One answer lies in the timing of Judas's eventual treachery: during the last evening of Jesus' life, spent with his pupils and devoted, as our other writers tell us, to that meal whose themes John has explored throughout this chapter. But why does Judas betray his teacher? John's Judas is a thief, a man of no honor. But behind this story of the feeding there lie old memories of a worldly hope: that Jesus would reign on earth as God's own agent, the Anointed that Mark's Peter declares him to be, the king that John's crowd tried to make him. Jesus was not to satisfy this longing. He spoke instead, as John relays the story, of the Breath of God—in abhorrently fleshly terms.

Here was a danger to Jesus' pupils, in his own day and in John's, worse even than secession: that this strange teaching might trigger Jesus' betrayal by one of his closest friends. John knows of disappointment, confusion, scandal—and danger.

Moses gave the Jews manna from heaven to eat in the desert. Later tradition asked what this manna had been. One answer shows the rabbis' concern to do justice to God's blessing: The manna was the food that Adam and Eve had once enjoyed in Paradise. There would have been good reason to think of Paradise at Passover: The synagogues' readings for the week told the story of Adam and Eve and their expulsion. God warns Adam and Eve, *"You shall not eat the fruit of this tree of the knowledge of good and evil, or you will die"* (The Beginning [Genesis] 2.17). Once they have eaten, God sees they might take fruit from the tree of life and eat and live for all aeons. So he drives them out.

We can set this beside the dialogue that follows the crowd's feeding. Here Jesus explains his role. In the Beginning (Genesis) the father forbade, preempted, drove out; Adam and Eve are kept far from the fruit of the tree of life and resolutely subject to death. In John's testimony the son is sent to invite, to offer, to welcome in *so that anyone may eat of this bread and not die:*

"This is the bread that comes down from heaven,
so that anyone may eat of it and not die.
I am the living bread that comes down from heaven;
anyone who eats of this bread will live for all aeons.
Anyone who comes to me, I will never drive them out."

(JOHN 6.50, 37)

The door into Paradise is opening once more. By the gospel's end the readers themselves will have been invited through.

Light for the World

Lord, remember David [pleads the psalmist],
how he made a vow to God the Almighty:
"I will not come within the sheltering of my own house,
nor let my eyelids slumber;
Until I find a place for the temple of the Lord,
a sheltering for the mighty God of Israel.
Arise, O Lord, into your resting place;
and let your servants sing with joy."

(PSALM 132.1–5, 8)

Autumn has come. The grapes and olives have been harvested, the last great festival of the year is under way. Jerusalem is once more crowded with pilgrims. All over the city, shelters are being built of branches and foliage, in which the pilgrims will live for a week. This Festival of Shelters (Sukkoth) is second only to Passover for the numbers of people gathered in Jerusalem; it is a festival, Josephus confirms, observed with special care. Thanksgiving for one season's end merges with prayers for the October rain and the next year's crops. Around this ancient festival had gathered further celebration, for God's guidance of Israel through the desert to the Promised Land. *You shall live in shelters, to remind your generations: I made the people of Israel dwell in shelters when I brought them out of Egypt* (Laws of Ritual [Leviticus] 23.42–43).

And more: It was at the Feast of Shelters that King Solomon dedicated the Temple in Jerusalem, the Temple planned by his father, David, and completed at last. A dramatic set-piece in the Old Order describes the ceremony and Solomon's speech (First Book of the Kings 8.23–53). We have good reason to believe that this story was read aloud in synagogues in the festival's week: *"Keep faith,"* prayed Solomon, *"with your promise to my father David: 'There shall never fail you a man to sit before me on the throne of Israel, if only your children take heed to their way, to walk before me as you have walked before me'"* (1 Kings 8.25).

No wonder a later tradition saw in this festival the promise of God's Anointed. In the rebellion against Rome in 135 C.E. the Jews' general was acclaimed as God's Anointed by the Akiba that we have encountered before, the most famous rabbi of his time; on the rebels' coins were symbols of the Festival of Shelters.

"Now, therefore [continued Solomon], *"O God of Israel, let your word be confirmed, which you spoke to David my father. But will God really dwell on the earth? The highest heaven cannot hold you: how much less this house which I have built! Yet hear the prayer of your servant, O Lord my God: that your eyes may be open day and night toward this house of which you have said, 'My name shall be there.'"*

(1KINGS 8.27–29)

Halfway through the festival Jesus goes to Jerusalem and to the Temple. He begins to teach. Into the celebrations of Shelters comes a sense of foreboding. We have seen Jesus in the Temple before: He expelled the traders at Passover and warned that the real Temple was not the building in which they were standing at all. *Many of the crowd* who heard him teach *believed in him: "The Anointed, when he comes, will he really do more signs than this man has done?"* (John 7.31).

On each morning of the festival a procession went south from the Temple to draw water, down the hill to the spring of Gihon, which fed the Pool of Siloam. Flutes played in celebration: "Those that have never seen the joy of the Place of Drawing," ran a proverb, "have never in their life seen joy." Later rabbis saw in the place name a hint of the ceremonies' deeper meaning: "from the Place of Drawing they drew the Breath of God." A golden flagon was filled with water. The choir sang from the prophet Isaiah, *With joy you shall draw water from the wells of salvation* (Isaiah 12.3). The procession turned back toward the Temple. As they reached the Water Gate the ram's horn sounded: a long note, a quavering note, another long note. The pilgrims followed, a frond of myrtle and willow in one hand, in the other a lemon as a sign of harvest. They sang the praise psalms as they went. A priest walked up the ramp toward the altar and poured the water into a silver bowl. A spout at its bottom let the offering drain away. Among the passages read aloud at the Festival of Shelters was Isaiah's prophecy,

I shall pour water on the thirsty land,
and streams on the dry ground;
Upon your descendants I shall pour out my Breath.

(ISAIAH 44.3)

"Help me now," sang the crowd from the psalms as they waved their fronds, *"O God, send us now prosperity."* On the seventh day the procession went seven times around the altar. The rite closed with a confession, "Praise to God and to the altar! Praise to God and to the altar!"

On the last and greatest day of the Festival Jesus stood up and cried out:

"If anyone is thirsty, let him come to me and drink,
whoever trusts in me,
as scripture says,
'Rivers shall flow from his stomach,
rivers of living water.'"

This he said about the Breath which those were going to receive who trusted in him.
(JOHN 7.37–39)

From the prophet Zechariah we have a vision of the final Festival of Shelters, when God's people are finally gathered together, free from oppression, and free to serve God in his Temple.

On that day living waters shall flow out from Jerusalem,
half of them to the eastern sea and half to the western sea.

On that day even the bells on the horses shall be inscribed "Holy to the Lord,"
and every pot in Jerusalem shall be holy to the Lord,
and there shall no longer be any trader in the house of the Lord on that day.
(ZECHARIAH 14.8, 16, 20, 21)

This festival of the last times is here and now: The water flows from the real Temple, now here in Jesus himself; Jesus has already driven the traders from the house of the Lord. Not all of Zechariah's prophecies are yet fulfilled: The king is still to enter Jerusalem, humble and riding on an ass; the city is still to see his rejection:

I will pour out on the house of David and on the inhabitants of Jerusalem
a breath of compassion and of prayer:
they look on the one whom they have pierced,
they shall weep over him as over a firstborn, over an only child.

On that day a fountain will be opened for the house of David
and for the inhabitants of Jerusalem,
to cleanse them from evil and impurity.
(ZECHARIAH 12.10, 13.1)

On the festival's first evening a procession led down the steps from the courtyard in the Temple that held the altar eastward to the Court of the Women. There stood huge golden candlesticks, said to have been seventy-five feet high. At their tops, reached by ladder, were golden bowls for oil and wick. Once they were lit, there was not a courtyard in Jerusalem, we are told, that did not reflect the light. "Men of piety and great powers used to dance and sing before these candles with torches in their hands." On the steps between the two Temple courtyards stood musicians; harps, cymbals, and trumpets were played. Zechariah wrote, of the final Shelters,

> *On that day,*
> *there shall be continuous day, not day and not night,*
> *for at evening time there shall be light.*
>
> (ZECHARIAH 14.7)

At cockcrow two priests, stationed at the top of the steps, blew three notes on their trumpets. Down five steps, and again three notes. Down the rest of the steps, and the same again. And so they moved gradually eastward, away from the Temple's heart and toward the rising sun, trumpets sounding. At the outermost gate of the Temple they turned about. They faced the Temple itself: "Our fathers," they called out, "turned with their backs toward the Temple of the Lord and their faces toward the east, and they worshiped the sun toward the east. But *our* eyes are turned to the Lord."

> *Again Jesus spoke to them:*
> *"I am the light of the world.*
> *Those who follow me shall not walk in darkness.*
> *They shall have the light of life."*
>
> (JOHN 8.12)

Water was poured onto the Temple's ground in a prayer for water for the coming year; the ritual recalls the Old Order's most famous promise for the Temple's future. The prophet Ezekiel had seen a vision of God's departure from his Temple; here is a sense of sad desolation. But this is not his story's end. Toward the close of his prophecies he records a vision, given him at the Feast of Shelters, of that Temple's restoration and of God's return: *The messenger of God brought me to the door of the Temple. And water was pouring from beneath the threshold of the temple toward the east* out of Jerusalem and into the desert. The messenger takes Ezekiel along the water's course. Going on eastward for five hundred yards, Ezekiel tests the water; it is ankle deep. Five hundred yards further, and the water reaches his knees. A thousand yards still further into the desert, and the river has become too deep to ford. Where the water goes, life follows: The water is bordered by trees and is filled with fish. The river's eastward course takes it to the Dead Sea, whose saltwater it turns to fresh. Fishermen will ply their nets along this barren shore as richly as on the shores of the Mediterranean itself. Along the river, on both banks, grows every kind of fruit tree with leaves that never wither and fruit that never fails; they bear new fruit every month, because the water that feeds them flows from the sanctuary. (Ezekiel 47.1–12)

We hear from the Beginning that a river flowed from Eden to water the garden, and from there it divided to make four streams: the Pishon, the Gihon, the Tigris, and the Euphrates (Beginning [Genesis] 2.10). We have already heard lines from the poem of Sira's Son about Wisdom, the agent of God that served him in Jerusalem's Holy "Shelter," the Temple.

All this is the book of the order of the Most High God,
the Law which Moses commanded us
as an inheritance for the congregations of Israel.
This Law fills them with Wisdom like the Pishon with water,
like the Tigris in the season of fruits;
the Law fills understanding like the Euphrates, to the brim,
and illumines instruction like a light,
like Gihon at the time of vintage.
(WISDOM OF SIRA'S SON [BEN SIRA] 24.23–27)

The Law flows from Jerusalem as the four rivers flow from Paradise. The streams of the Law bring wisdom as the rivers bring life. For the Temple is described throughout Jewish tradition on the model of Eden. The Feast of Shelters looks back to Eden, long lost, and looks forward to its restoration.

As in Ezekiel, so in the Book of Unveiling (Revelation). The Seer sets his heavenly worship at the final Festival of Shelters, when all the nations shall be gathered to Jerusalem (Book of Unveiling [Revelation] 7.9). He has a vision of the new Jerusalem: There is no Temple, for God himself and the Lamb are the Temple; there is no sun or moon, for the whole city is alight with the glory of God and the Lamb. The Seer next sees a river, as Ezekiel had seen and as Sira's Son described:

The river of the water of life, bright as crystal, flowing out from the throne of God and of the Lamb. Down the middle of the street and on either side of the river were the trees of life, bearing twelve fruits, one fruit for each month of the year, and their leaves were a cure for the nations.
(BOOK OF UNVEILING [REVELATION] 22.1)

The new Eden and the new Jerusalem are one. And in John's testimony they are no longer a place or a building:

"If anyone is thirsty [said Jesus], *let him come to me and drink,*
whoever trusts in me,
as scripture says,
'Rivers shall flow from his stomach,
rivers of living water.'"

(JOHN 7.37–38)

CHAPTER 11

Dark Splendor

Born Again?

NEW QUESTIONS

Jesus said to Nicodemus:
"In God's truth I tell you,
unless people are born again from above,
they cannot see the kingdom of God."
"How can people be born when old?" said Nicodemus. "Can they go back into
their mother's womb and be born?"

(JOHN 3.3–4)

We have held John's text before us as a whole, a single and complete composition, all of whose elements can be surveyed at once, any of whose details can be compared with any other. It is precisely this overview that reveals John's favored themes and the unity they give to his story. Confronted with a masterpiece of painting, we would do the same; the more carefully we look at the whole, the more clearly we see shapes, colors, and angles recur in its different parts. These patterns unite the composition and draw our eye to its chief elements. The painting may have a beautiful subject, but it is the translation of that subject into the artist's language of paint and style that attracts our eye.

Any book may, if we wish, be read as a giant painting, across whose surface we move slowly but freely. It is too large a canvas for a single overview, but we can flick from page to page, back and forth, remind ourselves of forgotten details, and (if the tension is too much) read the final chapter in advance.

This is not, however, how we expect to read. A book's contents are presented in a careful sequence: A narrator builds up the plot, and a thinker rests one idea upon another. A book's story is constructed as a house is built—the order of its construction matters—not as the assembly of a jigsaw, where that order is irrelevant and it matters only that the pieces are correctly combined.

Readers generally adhere to the author's order when they hold a book; listeners have no option when they hear it. We have seen how likely it is that our gospels were first read aloud in public, and we have discovered the drama that our first three authors wrought by their highly crafted ordering. What, then, of John? We shall discover in John's order the single most important clue to his gospel. For there is a process through which John sets out to draw his reader, a process in which every element has its proper and only place. John takes the reader through gestation to the new birth of which Jesus speaks to Nicodemus.

As Mark called for a revolution in the readers' understanding, so does John; they must undergo a transformation whose very description Nicodemus could not begin to understand. We have seen Paul at work on the Romans' mind, having to use the very organ that needs renewing to effect the renewal: A corrupt mind must see and correct its own corruption. John has just as deep and paradoxical a task: to effect a rebirth for which an embryo such as Nicodemus cannot see the possibility or the need. Riddles and contradictions face the story's characters and the reader alike; these are the devices with which John sets out to confound his reader into new birth and its consequence— the life of the new aeon. John is the midwife of this new life.

The oddities in John's testimony have been given many explanations. Most invoke familiar developments in the thoughts and insights of the church's first decades. And quite rightly. Yet John does not preserve these fragments out of loyalty to leftovers, as primitive beliefs outweighed by the newer insights with which they jostle in his text. Readers are ready for new birth precisely when they can see the new insights in the old.

Mark's gospel has been successful if the reader recognizes as disclosed on earth what we would expect to be unveiled only in heaven. The forms of unveiling have been turned upside down. So, too, in John, with a sharper focus: Mark's Jesus discloses the Son of Man; John's discloses God himself. John is clear from the start that God has never been seen. Only a handful of privileged seers had been given even a glimpse of his splendor. We need not be believers to see the force of such images; the sight of infinite power and perfect goodness would overwhelm us. It will be John's most striking claim that the splendor shone most brightly in the deepest darkness of all. Betrayed by his friend, rejected by his people, buffeted, and killed: Jesus does not enter the dark setting so that a contrasting triumph might reveal God's power. The darkness itself is the disclosure of God and his perfect triumph.

We heard at the start of John's story how Jesus spoke of the Temple: *"Destroy this sanctuary and in three days I will raise it up."* When Jesus was raised from the dead, John tells us, *his followers remembered that he had spoken* of the "sanctuary's" destruction (John 2.19, 22).

John gives his reader the clues he knows they need. Here, in the story of Jesus in the Temple, which John places right at his gospel's start, he is alerting the readers to the timescale over which his disclosure is spread: Some riddles will be solved only after Easter—the time in which John's audience lived and read. We must expect some things to be clearer to us than to the story's own characters. Jesus is the one *baptizing in the Breath of God* (John 1.33), and yet we will hear that the Breath is given only, as a climactic legacy, right at the gospel's end. On the one hand, *there was not yet Breath* (John 7.39), but on the other, there were baptisms performed by Jesus' pupils (John 4.1). John sets up a double timescale from the outset: This earthly Jesus whose story is only getting under way is the risen Jesus that John's readers know from the rite of baptism that most of them have themselves undergone or asked for at his later pupils' hands. Jesus is to speak in both characters from the outset and throughout.

Such clues continue. Characters invoke previous conversations at which they were not present. The figure present at them all, who has heard Jesus throughout and has good reason to ask the next question and the next, is the reader.

When Jesus is speaking with the Samaritan woman, he contrasts the water he is offering with the water she is drawing from a well: *"All who drink from the water that I will give them will not thirst, not for all aeons, but the water I will give them will become a spring of water welling up for the new aeon's life"* (John 4.14). Jesus' pupils then return. They have brought him some food, but he tells them he has food of which they do not know: *"My nourishment is to do the will of the one who sent me, and to complete his work"* (John 4.34).

Two chapters later, Jesus has fed a huge crowd in the desert.

> *Jesus said to the crowd: "Work not for the food that perishes, but for the food that lasts for the new aeon's life, which the Son of Man will give you. For he is the one on whom the father, God himself, has set his seal."*
> *So they said to him, "What shall we do to perform the works of God?"*
> *(JOHN 6.27–28)*

The crowd's question is a good one but is apparently unconnected with what the people have ever seen or heard. Why do they ask it? John has the crowd connect two foods and two donors: The food given to others by the Son of Man is the nourishment that Jesus has for himself; and the Son of Man who gives the food is the Jesus who gives the water, too. So to share in the food *that lasts for the new aeon's life,* the nourishment off which Jesus lives, is to do the father's work as he does. Quite rightly, then, the crowds ask, *"What shall we do to perform the works of God?"* But these crowds did not hear those earlier dialogues with the woman and Jesus' pupils. It is the readers who can make these links, and they should.

Who, then, is John writing for? As these readers absorb his story—for the first time, second, or third—what might he expect of them? That repetition is important. As a story becomes more familiar, we see in it things we have not seen before; among the thoughts that we bring to a second reading are insights gleaned from the first. John writes in puns and riddles. He teases the reader just as Jesus teases his pupils, questioners, and disputants. To most of these riddles a solution is clear, at the latest, by the time the gospel is ended. Even those readers who know the story and the church's claims for Jesus could be bemused at first. By the second reading they will have seen the point. Now they have the advantage over John's figures, who flounder still as they themselves once did.

John, however, has no time for complacency. His riddles are not exhausted by their apparent solution. John himself provides due warning against any such reduction. In chapter 10 we met Nicodemus. Jesus told him of the need to be born *again* or *from above*. Nicodemus, as the reader quickly sees, misunderstood. Jesus was speaking of spiritual birth "from above," while Nicodemus asks how we can reenter our mother's womb and so be born "again." By the end of Jesus' miracles the reader will have thought afresh. Jesus' climactic action brings Lazarus to life from death: to "rebirth." It is no longer obvious that the rebirth Jesus called for was precisely and only spiritual or that Lazarus' rebirth is significant only because it is so dramatically physical. Both senses are before us, inextricably entwined. Nicodemus was more nearly right than he knew and far closer to the truth than the reader who had smiled at his naïveté.

NEW ANSWERS

John warns his readers against easy answers that are no answers at all. What, then, will count as a solution to his own and Jesus' riddles, puns, and ironies? The deepest solution is not to seek their resolution at all. Each of John's strange double meanings offers the reader, as John presents it, an unveiling about Jesus, the sight of a deeper truth. The disclosure lies in the double meaning itself, in the two senses and the fact of their combination, not in a handful of disentangled terms and meanings. These double and triple meanings take time and attention before they unfold and reveal their secrets. Their value lies in their complexity, slowly unfolded, like the beauty of a rose; no one will thank us, however impatient they or we may be, for dismantling its bud into a pile of petals.

Why is the disclosure so hard to grasp? Its oddity starts in that relation of father and son. We are likely to stumble first over the very possibility: Can God really be disclosed in human form? When we have accepted the disclosure, its content becomes an issue. What does Jesus actually reveal? The reader must see the father in the son. And a large part of what the son reveals about the father lies precisely in this: that the father has sent him. The father sent the son to unveil the father: This already speaks volumes about the father and his plan for humankind. That plan involves judgment now, at the son's assize. The son has all the father's authority and is exercising it here on earth. But this is not the form in which John's readers had expected God to work his judgment. Old hopes must be recast.

John, then, does not want us to abandon the search for understanding. He is transforming the object of the search and so the way we search for it. John teases us into thinking about Jesus in a different way. He is not showing us just what to know but how to know it. A sort of knowledge is at stake that, as his strategy makes clear, stretches our daily language and logic to breaking point and beyond. The need is not just for different thoughts but for a different way of thinking. How are John's readers to attain this new way? And how will it function when they have?

"*Unless you are born again from above, you cannot see the kingdom of God.*" Nicodemus blunders through the dialogue. But we have already seen how strangely right he then turns out to be: A man is "born again." After the healing of a cripple, Jesus answers the charge that he makes himself equal to God:

"In God's truth I tell you,
all those who hear my word and believe in him who sent me
have the new aeon's life and do not come to judgment,
but have passed from death to life.
In God's truth I tell you,
the hour is coming and now is
when the dead shall hear the voice of the son of God,
and those who hear shall live."

(JOHN 5.24–25)

Here again is a hint that will find fulfillment in the gospel itself—in that same story of Lazarus. "*Lazarus,*" *cried Jesus in a loud voice:* "*Come on out*" (John 11.43). The need that Jesus made clear to Nicodemus is matched by a promise of Jesus that Jesus then fulfills—and all within the course of the story.

The dialogues, as we shall see, turn and turn around; each is a slow, expansive exploration of its distinctive theme. Within the story line the readers hear a sequence of discussions: with Nicodemus, the Samaritan woman, Jesus' own pupils, the crowds, and, over and over, the delegations from Jewish authority. But John is offering his reader just one discussion, a giant fugue on the son's relation to the father and to humankind. The reader shares Nicodemus's confusion, the woman's surprise, the pupils' disgust. On each reading, of course, the reader's knowledge is deeper. More variations are heard, but the most obvious continue to sound. A symphony is not a symphony if we hear its orchestra's instruments played separately, one by one; their combination makes the music what it is.

From these dialogues stems no sure progress in Jesus' pupils or the reader. Insights are offered, purposefully and in order. But they seem so obstinately beyond our grasp. John shows the readers they need a new form of understanding, but does he give them any help to reach it? We should not be surprised that Jesus' pupils flounder; within the story line they have no help from the Breath of God, the final gift of Jesus *that will lead them,* he says, *into all truth* (John 16.13). But the readers can have that help.

"Rivers shall flow from his stomach,
rivers of living water."

This he said about the Breath which those were going to receive who trusted in him.

(*JOHN 7.37–39*)

The Breath has now been given, and John's readers know the ritual that makes real the gift: baptism. In the series of miracles John creates an unstoppable momentum: wholeness, sight, new life. These are the effects of baptism: light, rebirth, and above all the gift whose power it represents, the gift of the Breath of God.

John lays before his readers the "process" through which a candidate for baptism is invited, trained, and expected to undergo. And more still: The readers are invited to "undergo" that process for themselves in the reading of his text. The text itself offers the reader new birth, the gift of God's Breath, the understanding that Jesus' first pupils could not have. The Breath was to lead those pupils *into all truth* and will now lead the readers in their turn. A reader might well have asked then, as we can ask now: What does the language of new sight and new birth really signify? The grander such claims are, the more carefully we will check them, for the most awesome words can be the most hollow. John shows his readers what this rebirth amounts to by taking them through it for themselves.

John aims high. But his text's success does not depend on all his readers' transformation as they read. The ideal of such change has shaped the gospel overall and in every detail, but it left the text open for use by the baptized and unbaptized alike, by the committed and the unsure, the deep-set member of John's church and the interested outsider. Some readers already knew the story well; others heard little more than the invitation, "Come and see." Some encountered this gospel on their own way to baptism. Others had been baptized already, and the text reminded them of the offer they had already accepted and encouraged its renewed acceptance. The need for such reminders did not fade; as we have seen in chapter 9 from Paul's Letter to the Romans, high claims and ritual could leave the "reborn" Christian all too clearly untransformed. Neither Paul nor John was fooled by his own rhetoric.

John expects some readers to understand more than others. Jesus' own pupils were the ones—and only ones—to hear their master's final teaching on the night before he died. They were still half blind and stumbled through the dialogue. Of all Jesus' teaching, the words of this last dialogue are the most strange and surprising. No wonder it follows the raising of Lazarus and the disappearance of the crowd. For those who are really ready to hear it are those who have been brought to new life. The gospel lays out what needs to be heard—and what the readers need to undergo if they are genuinely to hear it.

John is not alone in such a strategy. Paul undertakes no less in his Letter to the Romans. John evokes the movement toward and through baptism; Paul looks back on his readers' baptism and sets out to realize within them its latent, transformative power. Most of John's readers, we may suspect, were already baptized, just as Paul's were. They may well have heard such a sequence of stories and instruction for the first time on their own way to baptism and have heard it in others' preparation, year by year, ever since. So much the better, for as John would have it, this is a story that must be heard again and yet again if it is to unveil all that it has to offer the reader. The rosebud must be given time to unfold; those who see it must take time to recognize just what beauty is opening before their eyes. As Paul writes,

> *All of us who have been baptized into the Anointed have been baptized into his death. So we were buried with him through baptism into his death, so that, just as the Anointed was raised from the dead through the father's glory, so we, too, might walk in newness of life. And if we died with the Anointed, we believe that we will live together with him, too. For we know that the Anointed, once risen from the dead, dies no more; death has no more lordship over him.*
>
> *(ROMANS 6.3–6)*

John takes his readers through baptism's death before the death of Jesus, which makes it possible, so that the readers might understand that enabling death when its story is finally told. They must first be brought to new life; only then (as John would have it) can they hope to grasp its origin.

NEW LIFE

John's readers can recognize within themselves the questions of his different figures, their errors and confusion; they are also to recognize within themselves the needs of those that Jesus heals or helps. A nobleman and the desert crowd, the cripple and blind man, Martha and Mary: These as well are offered to the readers as images of their past experience and as models for their future. Here, too, is a single theme. We do well to follow its course through the first half of the gospel.

The nobleman has asked Jesus to heal his son. Jesus challenges the father: *"If you do not see signs and wonders, you will not believe."* The nobleman presses on. *"Sir, come down with me, before my little boy dies." Jesus says to him: "Go back yourself. Your son lives"* (John 4.48–50). The nobleman takes up the challenge. He turns and leaves and goes back to his sick son—and finds him healed. The boy's father has come to Jesus only because he had heard of his miraculous powers, but nothing in Jesus' work so far has made it reasonable for the father to have such trust as he shows. The reader has more reason to believe than the father has, for the nobleman has seen no miracles; the first wonder he will see is the miracle to which his own faith is about to give rise. Here is a blank, uncomprehending faith. But faith it is, stirred by his son's impending death. John never loses sight of such urgency and its power.

And so to the next healing, of the cripple in chapter 5. He does not even know who commanded him to walk. When the authorities quiz him, he has no answer. The stranger had simply asked him: *"Do you want to become well?"* (John 5.6). He, too, had long had faith, if only in the magic healing power of a bubbling spring.

Jesus tells him nothing and requires nothing of him. He is simply healed. We have then seen Jesus, over the following chapters, once more in Jerusalem for the Festival of Shelters. He applies to himself all the celebration's rites: The water drawn from Siloam is replaced by the water of God's Breath; Jesus himself lights Jerusalem and the world. During this scene his claims rise to that extraordinary crescendo:

> *"In God's truth I tell you, before Abraham came to be,*
> *I am He."*
>
> *(JOHN 8.58)*

And now the man born blind. The story, in John's chapter 9, is well placed: right after that claim so dramatic that anyone might doubt their ears or their understanding. *"While I am in the world,"* says Jesus, *"I am the light of the world"* (John 9.5). He anoints the man's eyes with a paste of mud and sends him to wash in the Pool of Siloam, the Pool of "One Who Has Been Sent." This beggar knows the name of Jesus but has no idea, when Jesus asks, who is the "Son of Man" to whom he owes his sight and his allegiance. This story becomes comic in the authorities' failure to understand. They cross-question the man himself, his parents, the man again. First they will not believe in the healing, then they look to the man to disown his healer. John presents them as absurdly, culpably "blind":

> *Jesus said: "I have come into this world for judgment, so that those who do not see may see and those who see may become blind." Some of the Pharisees who were with him heard this and said, "You are not saying we are blind?" Jesus said, "If you were blind, you would bear no guilt. But as it is, you say 'We can see,' and so your guilt remains."*
>
> *(JOHN 9.39–41)*

There is a dark note beneath the irony. The beggar's parents evade the officials' questions; *they were afraid of the authorities, for these had decreed that anyone who acknowledged* [Jesus] *to be the Anointed was to be expelled from the synagogue* (John 9.22). The opposition is gathering strength. Jesus may be unafraid, but his followers were more frail; we are hearing, in this threat, of the danger faced by John's own church. There is good reason for the mention of this danger here. The claims of John's Jesus are becoming more open and more extreme; those who hear and accept them are growing nearer to the church's own beliefs. "Truly" to accept these beliefs is to be ready for baptism into John's community, and so for public admission to a church in open opposition to the synagogues.

The themes that echo through John's gospel are sounded elsewhere in the New Order, loud and clear. The baptized, we are told in these other books, have been brought into the light; they have tasted the gift from heaven and been given a share in the Breath of God. They have an anointing from the Holy One. For God has anointed them and sealed them and given them the pledge of his Breath in their hearts. Reads a hymn from the first decades of the church,

> *Wake up, sleeper,*
> *and rise up from the dead,*
> *and the Anointed will shine upon you.*
>
> (*EPHESIANS 5.14*)

The last scene of hostile questioning is under way. *"I am—the gate to the sheep-fold,"* says Jesus, *"I am—the good shepherd"* (John 10.7, 14). The authorities quiz him yet again: about being the Anointed, about being son of God. We have heard how this dialogue spirals to its climax. *"If you are the Anointed, tell us openly."* Jesus' answers are never that easy: *"I and the father are one"* (John 10.24, 30). This is too much for the authorities; once more they take up stones to stone him. But the scene is not quite over yet. For Jesus asks, why are the authorities not swayed by the good works he does? John's next story will pose the question more force-fully than ever, for Jesus is about to work the greatest of all miracles: He will raise his friend Lazarus from the dead. In this one story all the motifs of Jesus' teaching come to expression at once. They are resumed, rounded out, and drawn together at this climax of his public work. We may almost say that the story of Lazarus itself starts far back in the gospel, when Nicodemus came to see Jesus by night. Jesus had told Nicodemus,

> *"In God's truth I tell you,*
> *unless people are born again from above,*
> *they cannot see the kingdom of God."*

Nothing in the narrative has made this claim any easier to grasp. It was the first of many warning promises from Jesus: of life and death, what made them possible, and what they made possible in turn. And most central to such a scene as this, with Lazarus in his tomb and his sisters surrounded by mourners, is the fear of the Last Day when God would judge the world—a fear from which, Jesus promises, those are released who believe in him.

> *All who believe in the son are not subject to judgment;*
> *but all who do not believe are already judged,*
> *because they have not believed in the name of the only son of God.*

Jesus himself had spoken of the Last Day as that future when those would win their reward at last who had been loyal to his strangest command:

"In God's truth I tell you,
if you do not eat the flesh of the Son of Man and drink his blood,
you do not have life in you.
Those who eat my flesh and drink my blood have the life of the new aeon,
and I will raise them up on the Last Day."

(JOHN 6.53–54)

The prelude to this story of Lazarus pits Martha's faith against her sister's inconsolable despair. They are confronted with the death of one they love, and here, at both extremes, is humanity's response to such loss. In earlier miracles the action has been followed by questions and dialogue; here all that needs to be said is said before the miracle. Yet again John confronts a traditional belief with its transformation at his Jesus' hands.

Martha said, "Sir, if you had been here my brother would not have died. But even now, I know that whatever you ask God, God will give you."
"Your brother," says Jesus, "will rise again."
"I know that he will rise again on the Last Day."

(JOHN 11.21–24)

Yes, but with an extraordinary twist. The old understanding of the Last Day and the new are starkly bolted together. Martha must see in Jesus himself the Last Day on which she knows that Lazarus will rise again. Jesus does not contradict Martha; he shows her the real truth of what she believes. He answers:

"I am the rising and the life:
all who believe in me, even if they die, shall live;
and all who live and believe in me shall not die, not for all aeons.
Do you believe this?"

(JOHN 11.25–26)

Martha gives a full answer. All the terms that we met at the gospel's start, around which the dialogues have turned and turned again, are acknowledged at last. All the characters have asked, who is this Jesus? They have looked for an answer in old titles and old expectations. But titles are helpful only when the claims they make are first agreed on and understood. At issue are not the names chosen for Jesus but the new weight that any such name must bear. Here is the understanding to which Martha's turmoil is bringing her. *"Yes, sir. I have come to believe that you are the Anointed, the son of God, the one due to come into the world"* (John 11.27).

The sisters speak for themselves, and they speak for their dead brother, too. Mary has little to say. She falls at Jesus' feet and repeats just the first words of her sister: words almost of reproach. *"Sir,"* she says, *" if you had been here my brother would not have died"* (John 11.32). Martha's belief and Mary's despair: The two impulses are rarely separate at bereavement and have long been familiar to those who know of John's Jesus and who wonder at his enigmatic promises. Jesus is as humane here as in any story of the gospels. Martha's voice or Mary's: One will lead to life, the other to self-condemnation. It is Martha's voice that Jesus hears, the voice of sorrow, incomprehension—and trust. For Jesus, too, loved Lazarus, and at the sight of his sister's tears and of those crying around her, Jesus is deeply moved. He weeps.

But what does this do for his friend?

"For God so loved the world [we have heard this Jesus say] *that he gave his only son,*
so that all who believe in him should not die,
but should have the life of the new aeon."

(JOHN 3.16)

At Jesus' strange words about rebirth, Nicodemus had been bemused: *"How can people be born when they are old? They can hardly go into their mother's womb a second time and be born!"* (John 3.4). It is not from his mother's womb that Lazarus needs rebirth. A rock has been used to close the mouth of the tomb. It is rolled away. Motifs come to mind that the text does not need to mention: A shaft of light breaks into the tomb; a gust of warm air spreads through the chamber.

"All those [Jesus had said] *who hear my word and believe in him who sent me*
have the new aeon's life and do not come to judgment,
but have passed from death to life.
In God's truth I tell you,
the hour is coming and now is
when the dead shall hear the voice of the son of God,
and those who hear shall live."

(JOHN 5.24–25)

Where there is darkness, the Word is again to be spoken. The Almighty's breath is moving once more over chaos. The readers have heard the cripple ordered to walk and the blind man to wash. The commands were given as directly to the readers themselves. They have been restored to health, brought to sight. Now Lazarus sees the light outside the tomb. Darkness or light: Both are before him.

This is the judgment:
that the light has come into the world,
and people preferred the darkness to the light;
for their deeds were wicked.
All who do wrong hate the light, and avoid the light,
so that their deeds might not be open to scrutiny.

But all who do the truth come to the light,
so that their deeds might be seen to be done in God.

(JOHN 3.19–21)

"The dead shall hear the voice of the son of God." It is a voice that will echo down the years. For John's readers, too, are buried in darkness, can see the light of day outside, and hear the voice of the son of God:
"Lazarus, come on out" (John 11.43).

Jesus is more upset at the tomb of Lazarus than in any other scene of our gospels; when he meets Mary and sees her despair, he weeps. We may think of this as the most telling and dramatic sign of his humanity. Here is no god, immune to sympathy. But perhaps, after all, nothing in Jesus' public work reveals God more clearly than this: that he weeps at the death of a friend—and at Mary's despair, who sees no hope in the presence and promise of God.

THE END OF THE BEGINNING

John's overarching trial is coming to an end. The readers have been given all they need—to make a decision in this trial and for the rebirth that will make possible their sight of the kingdom of God. The ground is prepared. The readers can now join Jesus' own pupils for the instruction reserved, in the story, for those pupils' ears alone. It is a touching thought, that the readers can hope to understand this final teaching of Jesus better than those pupils themselves. The readers have been told they need the Breath of God and have been offered a way to the rebirth its presence brings about.

But within the story? Jesus brings Lazarus to life and so triggers the maneuvers that will lead directly to his own death. The Jewish authorities declare their decision: Jesus must die. They are afraid: *"If we let him carry on like this,"* said the high priests and Pharisees, *"everyone will believe in him, and the Romans will come and will destroy us— the place and the nation together"* (John 11.48). It was no foolish fear, and by the time John wrote Jerusalem was in ruins. Caiaphas, the presiding high priest, intervened. In right of his office he could speak as a prophet; Josephus records two other high priests whose pronouncements were acknowledged to be from God. *"You,"* said Caiaphas to those gathered for this nervous conversation, *"you know nothing. Do you not realize that it is better for you to have one man die for the people, than for the whole nation to be destroyed?"* (John 11.49). Caiaphas's assessment is both less and more accurate than he knows. The death of Jesus will not save Jerusalem; neither will it save the Jews from the brutal efficiency of the Roman army. But Jesus will indeed die for his whole people, and more: *so that those children of God,* comments John, *who are scattered far and wide, might also be gathered into one* (John 11.52). John's high priest is the mirror image of Jesus, the true priest of his "Temple" and true victim together. When this arch opponent prophesies, he speaks a far deeper truth than he knows, for he confirms in God's name what he would deny in his own: that Jesus is the lamb of God whose death takes away the wrongdoing of the world.

John brings Jesus' public teaching to a close with a summary from Jesus that evokes all the themes of the gospel so far:

> *Those who trust in me do not trust in me but in the one who sent me,*
> *and those who see me see the one who sent me.*
> *I have come as light into the world,*
> *so that all who believe in me may not remain in darkness.*
> *And as for those who hear my words and do not hold to them,*
> *I do not judge them;*
> *for I have not come to judge the world,*
> *but to save it.*
> *Those who reject me, and who do not receive my words,*
> *they have a judge:*
> *the word that I have spoken,*
> *that will be their judge on the last day.*
> *For I have not spoken on my own account,*
> *but the father who sent me,*
> *he has commanded me to say what I have said and what I am yet to say.*
> *And I know that his command is the life of the new aeon.*
> *What I myself say, then, it is just as the father has told me:*
> *that is what I say.*
>
> *(JOHN 12.44–50)*

Jesus as priest and victim together: John has reworked the themes of sacrifice as deeply as all the other motifs to which we have seen him turn. Others dwelt on sacrifice as well. Centuries before Jesus' death, the Old Order tells us, Abraham was ordered by God to sacrifice his beloved son Isaac (Beginning [Genesis] 22.1). We heard in chapter 5 how important the story became in Jewish thought. By the first century C.E. its details had been reworked and expanded. The sacrifice, it was said, took place at Passover, and on the site of the future Temple. The Old Order told of Isaac's rescue: At the last moment God's angel interrupted the sacrifice and told Abraham to kill instead a ram, caught in a nearby thicket. This resolution is less clear in our story's later versions. We hear there of Isaac's blood being shed. We hear, too, of Isaac's readiness to die: "If for the wicked deeds of the world," he says in one of these later versions, "animals are appointed to be killed, but humans are designed to inherit the world, how then do you now say to me, 'Come and inherit life without limit?' Have I not been born into the world to be offered as a sacrifice to him who made me?"

Such details were ever more carefully drawn. Versions from later centuries tell that Isaac had a vision of the angels in heaven, that he was the Servant of whom Isaiah speaks, that thanks to Isaac's merit God will bring the dead to life. But the most poignant of details was already known to the Old Order: Abraham had Isaac himself carry the wood for the sacrificial fire. The young man, at his father's command, carried the fuel for his own burning.

The Beginning of the End

The Farewell

"In God's truth I tell you [says Jesus],
those who eat my flesh and drink my blood have the life of the new aeon,
and I will raise them up on the Last Day."

(*John 6.53*)

John's readers had good reason to fear the Last Day. There was the aching question, how God's judgment on any one person would fall. As time went by, further questions arose: about loved ones who had trusted in Jesus but had died before he returned in glory and exercised this judgment. Anyone who loved them might be confident of their vindication but could well wonder why Jesus had not returned already to claim and reward his own. Most of us today express differently our worries for those we love who have died. We no longer have a burning sense that a final judgment has been longer delayed than those early Christians (for good reason) expected it to be. But in Paul's reassurance to the Thessalonians we hear an answer to questions as plangent then as they are for us all, whether Christian or not, at every death that affects us now. Paul was writing to a church that looked forward fervently to Jesus' return:

I tell you this in a word from the Lord: We who are still alive, who are being left behind until the Lord's return, will not precede those who have died. The Lord himself at the word of command, at the voice of an archangel and in the blast of a trumpet, will come down from heaven; and those who have died in the Anointed will rise first, and then we who are still alive, who are being left behind, will be snatched up together with them in the clouds to greet the Lord in the air. And thus we shall always be with the Lord.

(*1 Thessalonians 4.15–17*)

But John's Jesus has transformed this expectation. The Last Day is not a horizon far ahead; it is present in the person of Jesus. All expectation has been transformed.

We move to that last evening spent by Jesus with his pupils. The crowd has dispersed; Judas has gone. Jesus is left with just his loyal friends. Now starts the longest dialogue of all, another spiraling discussion that ends with Jesus' own prayer for his followers—for those gathered around him at the time and for those who will come to faith through those pupils' words. The farewell is solemn; difficult truths are unveiled. It is a fitting time for such disclosure. The synagogues' Aramaic version of the Beginning saw disclosed in Jacob's farewell to his sons the secrets of all time: "I will show you the mysteries that are hidden," says Jacob, the Israel whose visions have shaped John's opening chapter, "the appointed times that are concealed; what is the recompense of reward in store for the just, the punishment in store for the wicked, and what the joys of paradise are."

Halfway through this dialogue, at the end of John's chapter 14, Jesus appears to round off the discussion: *"I will no longer talk much with you, for the ruler of the world is on his way. Get up, let's go"* (John 14.30). But the conversation, far from coming to an end, takes us through three further chapters. It has been shrewdly asked if the dialogue as we have it represents two versions of the same scene, developed in different ways and reunited near or at our gospel's final revision.

There may well be more turns to the spiral now, with two versions combined into one, than had been expected by the author of either. The versions, however, share their central style with each other and with the rest of our gospel: to reread familiar sayings, from the Old Order and from Jesus himself, in the terms and sense in which John believes they must be understood. The Last Day has already been taken up into John's understanding of Jesus; Martha's hopes for the Last Day have been starkly juxtaposed with Jesus' action here and now. Such expectation mattered, and it took many forms. Here John returns to the theme more boldly than ever. The aim closest to John's heart is to unveil God for his readers. He translates the language of the Last Day and of Jesus' return into the language of present, immediate disclosure. Once readers understand these promises aright, they will see their fulfillment in the presence of Jesus and in the legacy he leaves to his friends. The readers, reborn as Lazarus was, are now ready to hear what this rebirth implies for themselves.

To make room for these answers, John has the pupils redraft their questions: They, no less than John's readers, are looking for the disclosure of God.

> *"Do not let your heart be distraught* [said Jesus]: *"You believe in God and believe in me. In my father's home are many rooms. If there were not, would I have told you 'I am going to prepare you a place'? And if I go and prepare you a place, I will come back and take you to myself, so that where I am you may be, too."*
>
> (JOHN 14.1–3)

The words refer naturally to Jesus' return in glory at the Last Day. Forty years before, Paul had evoked the moment vividly in his First Letter to the Thessalonians. Paul calls on his *"word from the Lord"* to reassure those who feared for their dead. It was a worry that grew more insistent as the years went by, as the faithful died and still the Lord delayed. Questions of Jesus' return were not idly asked.

John sees in Jesus' promise the door to the same hope. But here it is quite differently cast, focused on a different expectation and to be met in different ways. At issue once more, as ever in John's gospel, is disclosure: how to attain the knowledge, the total clarity that is held before the reader in this promise of a home in God's house.

Peter had just asked where Jesus was going and was told only that he and the others could not follow there for now. Jesus' friends have no clearer sense where he must go than had the authorities who imagined him off to the Greeks (John 7.34) or on the point of suicide (John 8.21). Jesus redirects his friends' focus: Where they are to go matters less than the way they are to get there.

> *"And where I am going, you know the way there."*
> *"Lord," said Thomas, "we do not know where you are going; how can we know the way?"*
>
> *(JOHN 14.4–5)*

They know the way better than they dare believe or understand:

> *"I am the way, the truth, and the life.*
> *No one comes to the father except through me.*
> *If you have got to know me, you will know my father too.*
> *And from this moment on you do know him and have seen him."*
> *"Lord," said Philip, "show us the father; that is all we need."*
>
> *(JOHN 14.6–8)*

It is an extraordinary request: for a sight of God, the disclosure never granted and is almost too dangerous to ask for. John's opening hymn reminded us: *"No one has ever seen God."* But it is a request as well that shows how little Philip has yet understood. Jesus' reply is emphatic: He repeats the request and his own response. Here, in the closest circle round John's Jesus on the last evening of his life, is a fundamental error. No heavenly journey is needed. The sight of God is before their very eyes.

> *"Have I been with you for so long and you have not got to know me, Philip?*
> *Whoever has seen me has seen the father.*
> *How can you say, Show us the father.*
> *Do you not believe that I am in the father and the father in me?*
> *The words that I speak to you I do not speak from myself,*
> *but the father—who dwells in me—is performing his own deeds.*
> *Believe me: I am in the father and the father is in me.*
> *If for no other reason, believe because of the deeds themselves."*
>
> *(JOHN 14.9–11)*

It is a dramatic claim, but it leaves open a raft of questions. There will be talk of Jesus' departure and return, of his leaving these friends' sight and his reappearance soon. *"A little while yet and the world sees me no longer; but you see me, because I am alive and you will be, too"* (John 14.19). *"A little while and you no longer see me, and again a little while and you do see me"* (John 16.16). Are we to think of that going as his death and then of the return as his appearances at Easter? So far, so good—for those gathered at that last meal. But John has not forgotten the quite different viewpoint of his readers. Between that supper and any occasion at which John's account was read or heard lay Jesus' death and rising. The Jesus who speaks for John's readers has already gone, returned, and once more disappeared from view. Stories of a few strange Easter meetings will not satisfy their understanding—and their hope—of his return. If the Last Day had become real in Jesus' presence on earth, if judgment had already been bypassed or undergone and yet the world went on the same, then what lay ahead to hope for?

"In the world you will have dire trouble," Jesus warns. *"But take courage. I have con-quered the world"* (John 16.33). John's community needed all the assurance it could get. Expelled from the synagogues and neglected by the world, its members might well have looked for heavenly confirmation of that victory from heaven. John has no doubt: This is quite the wrong place to look.

Everything in this gospel comes full circle. Philip told Nathanael at the story's start, *"Come and see."* By the end of Jesus' public life, the news of Jesus is spreading. Philip has a Greek name; when the Greeks want to *see* Jesus, Philip relays their request. He is with Jesus, too, on this last night, and now it is for him to ask to see the father. *"Have I been with you for so long, Philip, and you have not got to know me? Whoever has seen me has seen the father."* Even Jesus' closest friends have no easy or assured route to the insight that they need. There is nothing naive in John's portrayal of the new life into which his gospel leads his readers or in his guidance along the route that he believes will take them there.

Over and over we have heard of the Breath of God. Now John gives the Breath a new and striking guise: as the Advocate, the Breath of Truth. John could not take even its name for granted; at almost every mention he explains this Advocate's standing as the Breath of God. So useful was the Greek term *Advocate* that the word was borrowed into Hebrew to speak of a representative at court, an ally—a function familiar among Greeks and Romans but unknown to Jewish law. Here, then, was a spokesman in the readers' defense, a foil to Satan, the great accuser, who had entered Judas. Here, too, is the readers' guide: *"The Advocate will guide you in all truth"* (John 16.12). What must the community do to be given this attorney? *"If you love me,"* said Jesus, *"you will keep my commandments. And I will ask the father and he will give you another advocate, to be with you for all ages: the Breath of Truth"* (John 14.15). This is the form in which John's readers will "see" Jesus again. In the Breath's presence John finds, too, the key with which he can decode that language of a heavenly dwelling. Jesus' pupils had expected to be taken away to be with him. But far from it: He will come to dwell with them. This is the intimacy that he promises, among himself, his father, and his pupils. *"Those who love me will keep my word, and my father will love them, and we will come to them and make our home with them"* (John 14.23).

Here, too, was a saying that held out hope for Jesus' final return and the end of history. It has been interpreted afresh. Life on earth will carry on; it is within that life that the transformation will be wrought, that the father will make his home within the believer. We have seen the gospel at work on sayings from the Old Order; here John has undertaken a similar task on a saying of Jesus himself. We might almost say that John's Jesus has his Jesus anticipate the work of the Breath that he himself will send, the work of guiding John's community in all truth: *"the Advocate, the holy Breath, which the father will send in my name—it will teach you everything and remind you of all that I have told you"* (John 14.26). John and his community have the Breath that Jesus promised; John writes and they read with the benefit that Jesus' pupils did not have when he spoke. It is John's task to ensure that the Breath is passed on and that its effect is shared with his whole community.

The Breath is to function in John's day as Jesus did in his. But here the gospel's central function comes into view. For the gospel itself, as we have seen, is to function in John's church as Jesus "functioned" in the story among those he met. Jesus healed, brought sight, called to new life; so in its turn does the gospel itself, the text itself, as it is read and received. And now the Breath is promised that will bring to fruition the function of the gospel in which the promise is made. The gospel needs the Breath's work and is in turn its perfect vehicle. As for Jesus, so for the Breath he has sent: The presence of Jesus with John's church is the gospel's text; the activity of the Breath is the text's effective reception.

John has reworked the expectations that a reader would have had of such an Advocate. Everything in this reworking is by now familiar. John's Advocate is busy on earth, but this is not the court in which he was expected to work. Yet again John enacts on earth what should be happening far from normal sight and understanding, for in Jewish thought the Advocate belongs—with his adversary, Satan the great accuser—not in our humdrum life on earth, but in the counsels of the court of heaven. No privileged journey is needed now to hear this Advocate's plea on our behalf, and the Advocate in turn needs no more evidence to mount his case than the relation that defendants bear to Jesus.

The question of Jesus' return arises yet again, in the second version of our dialogue, this time with even greater prominence. Here starts the climax of Jesus' words to his pupils. It is a most telling section. Awareness and ignorance, faith and incomprehension—we see all sides of Jesus' closest friends.

Jesus knows his going grieves them.

> *"But I tell you the truth, it is to your benefit that I go away.*
> *For if I do not go away, the Advocate will not come to you;*
> *but if I go, I will send him to you. . . .*
> *I am going to the father and you see me no more."*
>
> *(JOHN 16.7, 10)*

Around and around goes the promise: John has Jesus repeat it, the pupils echo his words, Jesus echoes theirs. The subject is crucial for John's readers. The pupils know that they do not understand the promise, and they discuss it among themselves. Jesus uses that power we have seen in him from the start to read the thoughts of others. *He knew that they wanted to ask him, and he said to them: "You are wondering among yourselves about this, my saying 'A little while and you see me no longer; and again a little while and you will see me'"* (John 16.19).

Jesus deploys the comparison of which we have heard already: His going is like the pain of childbirth and the joy that follows. This moment of departure will mark a change in his role. His pupils will no longer ask him for anything; they will ask the father in Jesus' name, and the father will grant their requests. Jesus then stands back from his instruction and speaks of its style. It stands as a reflection on his whole style of teaching from the gospel's start:

> *"I have said this to you in riddling stories.*
> *The hour is coming when I will no longer speak to you in riddles,*
> *but I will speak out to you openly about the father.*
> *On that day you will ask in my name;*
> *and I do not say I will ask the father on your behalf—*
> *for the father himself loves you,*
> *because you have loved me*
> *and have believed that I have come out from the father.*
> *I have come out from the father and have come into the world;*
> *now I am leaving the world and going to the father."*
>
> *(JOHN 16.25–28)*

Jesus has ended his instruction. Such has been his followers' faith that they and Jesus are now one in the father's eyes; the father will give them at their request what he would give Jesus at his. This is a fitting climax to their time with him; their faith has its due reward. And how do they respond?

John sees here a most poignant moment. These pupils have seen and heard all that Jesus had to teach and do; they and they alone have spent this last evening with their master. And after all this, they are brought to their final, climactic statement of faith simply by his knowledge of their thoughts. But this is the same power that had impressed the first of them to join him at the story's start. Nothing has changed. The story has come full circle, and these closest friends, not yet with guidance from the Breath of God, are exactly where they were on that first day. There is nothing caustic or dismissive in John's tone; this most humane and sensitive of writers just lets the circle stand. *"Look,"* they say,

> *"now you are speaking openly and not telling any riddle. Now we know that you know everything and that you do not need anyone to ask you anything. Because of this we believe that you have come from God."*
>
> *(JOHN 16.29–30)*

Jesus has just spoken of their long friendship and faithfulness, but he knows how fragile it will prove to be. Mark's Jesus knew this, too; his pupils promised loyalty to death, but he knew they would be scattered, like sheep once the shepherd is killed. John's pupils do not claim courage; they claim belief. But one guarantees no more than the other: *"Do you now believe?"* He answered: *"Look, the time is coming and has come when you will be scattered, each to his own home, and will leave me alone"* (John 16.31–32). For all their time with him and all the insight to which they lay claim, their faith will not keep them with him when the traitor comes.

John's Jesus seems ever further removed from the world's contexts and crises. He becomes a timeless figure who speaks as directly to John's church—and to all churches since—as to his own close friends. This distance is most marked in the prayer with which Jesus ends this last evening with his pupils.

Jesus seems already on his way. In one sentence he has already left this world: *"I am no longer in the world, and I am coming, father, to you."* But a few lines later his departure still lies ahead: *"Now I am coming to you, and I am saying this in the world"* (John 17.11, 13). If his presence on earth has suggested any distance from the father, this impression now evaporates.

Within this prayer, however, eternal and universal though it is meant to be, lie traces of the crises that John shaped it to meet. *"May they all be one,"* asks Jesus: *"one"* or *"a single thing,"* a term for community familiar from Qumran. Earlier in this same dialogue Jesus had spelled out his new commandment with emphatic repetition: Love one another. We might well wonder what deep division called for such instruction and prayer, an appeal placed at this final hour and invested with supreme solemnity. Unity was threatened, but when and where?

Within the gospel itself we hear of some among the Jews and possibly among their leaders, who believed in Jesus but not in John's appraisal of his status. It is against such Jews that John has Jesus launch his (fierce) assault in his chapter 8: he claims for himself a status higher by far than Abraham's. Jesus' standing, John insists, was of a kind and dignity that some of his own adherents failed to see, and his offer was one they needed far more than they acknowledged in the claims they made for him. So fierce is Jesus' attack that these adherents eventually declare him mad and try to stone him. They are not the first that we have watched "come and see" and then leave.

John, then, was not working for unity at any price. What was the creed or life around which he would have believers gather? His Jesus starts that final prayer with a clear summary: *"This is the life of the new aeon: to acknowledge you the only true God and the one that you sent, Jesus the Anointed"* (John 17.3). The importance of God's sending Jesus is stressed throughout the gospel. This is the knowledge that establishes his pupils' claim on God's attention. It featured in that (surprising) attack of which we have heard on the believing Jews. Such a stated, clear conviction may well have been one key to membership of John's community. Here, then, would have been an added weight, on this last evening, to the final exchange between Jesus and his friends, for this would be his chief claim and the heart of their confession of faith. It would then be no surprise that this is the climax of their dialogue:

> *"I have come out from the father and come into the world;*
> *now I am leaving the world and going to the father."*

> *"Now* [they reply] *we know that you know everything;*
> *because of this we believe that you have come from God."*
>
> (*JOHN 16.28–29*)

John knows how difficult belief can be, knows it better, perhaps, than his confident story lets on. Faith dominates the gospel and brings it to its end. John's first and chief account of Easter—the set of stories that may once have rounded off the gospel as a whole—is completed with a flourish: *Jesus performed many other signs before his followers' eyes, which are not recorded in this book. These are recorded so that you might be believers: that Jesus is the Anointed, the Son of God; and so that by believing you may have life in his name* (John 20.30–31).

It is all the more telling that John shows his readers so many sides of such belief: how likely it is, as he sees it, to be frail, cowardly, misdirected, or two-faced. All that the word suggests of conviction, trust, and self-entrusting are not enough to guarantee it error free or honest. The new aeon's life depends finally on a movement within that belief that cannot be deceiving or deceived: *"Unless people are born again from above, they cannot see the kingdom of God"* (John 3.3).

John's Jesus says farewell to his closest friends as Moses said farewell to his people just before his death. In a first section Moses sang of God, the Rock of Israel; in a second he prayed for God's blessing on each of its twelve tribes. We hear next of his death: He is given just a glimpse of the Promised Land to whose borders he has led the nation but that he himself will never enter. The theme of farewell has echoed through this final evening of Jesus' life on earth. Jesus tells his friends not to be afraid: He is going to prepare a place for them, to which he is himself the way. Moses had reminded Israel of his earlier encouragement and its vindication: *"Then I said to you, 'Do not be afraid of the enemy.' Yet in spite of this you did not believe the Lord your God, who went in the way before you, to choose for you a place to pitch your shelters in"* (Second Law [Deuteronomy] 1.29). Moses saw from the mountaintop their destination in the distance. It was his successor who led the people across the Jordan and into the Promised Land: Joshua, the first Jesus. The second Jesus, for John, is himself the way that leads into the presence of God.

More, though, is evoked by John than just those final hours of Moses. Jesus seems almost to be leaving as he speaks, to be already on his way back to the father. Those within his inner circle hear of his ascent before it happens. Here is the most remarkable unveiling of all. The way to God, it seems, is opened before the readers' eyes.

When the Jewish philosopher Philo speaks of "understanding" the Old Order, he uses the language of the "mysteries," religions into whose rites and teachings the new-comer had to be initiated by an instructor or mystagogue. Philo appeals to Moses for aid. Moses' ascent of Sinai to receive the Law has been seen throughout the Jewish and Christian world as enlightenment of the highest kind, reserved for the rarest and most privileged of seers. This involves intellect, emotions, and behavior together: "Even if we have closed the eye of our inner being" says Philo, "and do not care or are not able to look up, lift up your voice yourself, Moses, take command of us, go on and on anointing our eyes, until you lead us, our mystagogue, to the hidden light of sacred words and show us the beauties that are fenced off and invisible to those not initiated in these rites."

Such a tone is alien to us. We do not think of texts available to all as locked from the understanding of all but a favored few; still less do we know of texts preserved for the sight or hearing of a few initiates alone. But a culture that valued a closeness to God valued also the routes to it, and these routes were as sacred as the closeness they made possible. Some things were too precious, too easily degraded, to be exposed to general gaze or understanding. We hear from Matthew's Jesus: *"Do not give what is sacred to the dogs, nor throw your pearls in front of pigs, in case they trample them beneath their feet and then turn and gore you"* (Matthew 7.6). We need not be surprised, then, if this last prayer of John's Jesus echoes with ideals whose sound is strange. At this stage in John's story the world has been closed out and left behind. The innermost circle of pupils is gathered to hear the last words of their master; his return to the father is already under way.

We may feel at a far remove from this notion and hope of such union with God. But it is evoked in other texts both from Judaism and from the gentile world. We have already encountered Joseph's Prayer, in which Jacob speaks of his heavenly counterpart, Israel. At stake was not just a mystical version of Jacob's venerable story; to "see God" was an aspiration, drawn from the great visions of Ezekiel, that offered to transform the seer. He would become an angel, semidivine; he would be "saved" from the turmoil of mere humanity. We might wonder at this strange cosmos of two worlds and a passage between them. But the language of such hope is perhaps more alien than its substance; we, too, know the hope for clarity and insight and the sense that such knowledge offers freedom from the tawdry muddle of our own and our culture's daily life.

Such longing was not confined to Judaism and the early church. A dialogue between the mythical teacher Thrice-Greatest Hermes and his pupil Tat evokes in one short text, as solemn and hymnlike as John's own, the whole process of rebirth to which John dedicates his gospel. The collection of dialogues to which Hermes' and Tat's talk belongs was composed in Greek over one hundred years after Jesus died and is clearly influenced by the Old Order. And by John's gospel itself? Probably not. Hermes refers over and again to the Word, never to such a vehicle for its work and unveiling as Jesus (let alone to Jesus by name). We need suppose no direct link between Tat's tradition and John's.

Tat recalls to Hermes their earlier and more public conversation. Here is a summary of his next request:

"You spoke in enigmas when you discussed the divinity of humans. You said we cannot be saved until we have been born a second time. You told me that you would instruct me further only when I had distanced myself from the world's deceptions. And now I have. So I entreat you to supply what I need. I do not know from what womb a person can be born a second time or from what seed." Replies Hermes, "The womb is wisdom, conceiving silence; the seed is the true good; and the father is the will of God. And the mystagogue, by whom the rebirth is brought to be, is a child of God, working in submission to God's will." Hermes then describes the effect of his having himself become divine. Tat is (unsurprisingly) driven to distraction by his teacher's impossible claims. "This cannot be taught," says Hermes, "and you cannot see it with your eyes. I can tell you nothing but this: I see that by the mercy of God (*theou*) an uncreated vision (*thea*) has come to pass in me. I have passed out of myself and entered into an immortal body. I am not now the person I was; I have been born again in mind, and the bodily shape that was mine has been pulled away from me. I am no longer an object colored and solid and of three dimensions. I am distanced from all this and from all that you perceive when you gaze with bodily eyesight. To all such eyes as yours I am not now visible."

This riddling, paradoxical style is carefully crafted. Its target is as much the reader as Tat. What we hear of Tat is offered to ourselves. To read such a text as detached observers is to miss its point. Tat insists that he still sees Hermes, just the same as ever. Not so, says Hermes. What is real is not bodily and by the body cannot be perceived. The senses distract us. With a solemn formula Hermes invites Tat to gain the crucial power: to perceive what the eyes cannot see.

> "Draw it into yourself, and it will come.
> Will, and it happens.
> Silence the senses of the body, and the birth of deity will be."

Hermes tells how God's mercy will free Tat from the irrational torments of matter: first among them ignorance, then grief, lust, desires, injustice, greed, trickery. Lists of such evils are familiar from the New Order; the early church shared its demands for new and purer morals with other movements of its time.

Tat is ready. We are to imagine the silence for which Hermes calls.

> "Now be silent, my child, and speak not,
> and so mercy will not cease from God toward us."

"Rejoice now, my child," the teacher continues, "as you are purified by the powers of God for the installation of the Word. Knowledge of God has come to us, my child, ignorance is driven away." Hermes calls upon the powers to expel the irrational torments of matter. Among them goes injustice: "for we have been made just in God's sight without judgment, for injustice is no longer here." Once the torments are dispelled, "to join the truth, the good has come to us, together with life and light."

"So has the mind's birth been formed in us,
and by this birth we have become gods."

Tat is becoming divine, whether by the birth into a wholly new form or by the recovery of a state his soul had once known before. Jesus, by contrast, is revealing the status he has had from all eternity. But Jesus is also himself the way for his friends to follow. In this closing approach to the father the son lays out the path for those who will come after him. John's readers, like Tat, are to be reborn; summoned from the tomb with Lazarus, they have been instructed as neophytes, newborn initiates who are entitled to hear Jesus' most secret teaching with the members of his inner circle. Now they are ready to hear of and to share the final intimacy of father and son.

There is a striking contrast between the unity called for by Jesus and the promise of Hermes. To take up John's offer is to be member of a community:

"I do not ask [says Jesus] *only for the benefit of these around me,*
but also for those who will come to believe in me through their word,
so that they may all be One,
just as you, father, are in me and I in you,
so that they as well may be in us,
so that the world might believe that you sent me.

And I have given them the splendor that you gave me,
so that they may be One as we are One:
I in them and you in me,
so that they may be fulfilled into One,
so that the world might know that you sent me
and that you loved them just as you loved me."

(JOHN 17.20–23)

Tat gazes upon the divine and becomes divine. His mystagogue is Hermes. No other person is mentioned. And when we envisage a community in which the text was used and authorized? We do hear of others' instruction: It is to make possible just such insight for them, one by one, each through his or her own gaze in turn.

John's gaze, by contrast, is forever on his community. Here is the place of unveiling and of rebirth: Within the community of those bound together by Jesus' command, *"Love one another as I have loved you."* Jesus' return to the father does not portend heavenly journeys for his followers or a lonely insulation from the dangers and crises that John himself knows only too well. On the contrary:

"I have given them your word, and the world has hated them,
for they are not from the world just as I am not from the world.
I do not ask you to take them from the world,
but to keep them from the evil one."

(JOHN 17.14–15)

It is within the community that everything is offered that its members need and hope for. John's Jesus throughout the gospel has deflected the readers from those hopes—and fears—for which the church had primed them: of a cataclysmic judgment and then a world transformed. The alternative offered by John's Jesus is under way. He has spoken of the new aeon's life, begun here and now. He has summoned Lazarus from the grave. It is on this last evening with his pupils—his friends in his own time and in John's, initiates together in the mystery of new birth—that Jesus spells out the conditions of this new life and its consequence in the life of their community.

All that his Jesus has said and done has not engendered in those pupils the insight and steadiness to which Jesus invites them. John would have had pupils of his own, who were just as slow to see the point and just as fast to let it slip. That range of people is the point: different readers at different stages returning over and again to this text to see there both acknowledgment of their present state and a model of the change the gospel offered them, all of it gauged by their relation to Jesus. In the drama of John's gospel, the paradox of Jesus' death and glory mounts to a crescendo. The excitement of this drama is one of recognition. It is a source of unfailing and rising awe through the story's course, that Jesus' death is the brightest display of all.

We heard at the start of light and darkness: of light as the first distinction of all, which makes all the knowledge possible that brings "light" in its turn. The brightest of all light is the darkness of Jesus' death. We look for clarity thanks to the light; we know where we stand and where we are going, and we are in no danger of stumbling. But the splendor before us now is the victory of darkness. Here is no such clarity as we long for, such as makes us safe and sure. John prepares his readers to be confused, to be "in the dark." Such darkness, at this stage in the story and even among well-primed readers, is not their fault or weakness. Far from it. The Breath does not clear away the darkness; it enables the reader to recognize it for what it is. Precisely in this dark the brightness lies. Only as darkness will it ever be seen.

But in such a drama Jesus himself is oddly "undramatic." His progress from an obvious glory to its paradoxical climax is steady. We gain little sense of his personality; for John's purpose such detail would only be distracting. The focus is on the paradox and its recognition by those around Jesus and around the text. The drama is in the pupils and antagonists of Jesus and ultimately in the gospel's reader. To be offered this paradox and to judge it aright, to see the unimaginable and to know it for what it is: Here is a drama that can be repeated in every reader at every reading. And as in every good story, its outcome is not clear in advance. For *many of his pupils left off from following him, and no longer went around with him* (John 6.66).

How far this seems from the testimony of our first three witnesses! What underlay Mark's drama has now become the drama itself. The pathos of Jesus' betrayal and death has been distilled into a slow waltz whose every movement and whose closing tableau are known and controlled from the start. The strange, uncanny figure that has lurked in all our texts has come to the surface—and in a distinctively static form. This Jesus has lost the battle-scarred engagement of Mark's Son of Man. The humanity of the story is now our own, the readers': our judgment, our insight, and ultimately our rebirth. The assumption of our first three witnesses has become John's leading theme: What matters in the story's telling is the readers' response.

Within this new purpose, however, this new lens on the landscape of Jesus' life, more is familiar than at first sight catches our eye. Jesus' long dialogue with his pupils prepares us for the story's final movement. Our other witnesses as well, in Jesus' last week in Jerusalem, have him speak at length with a small group of his closest friends: He predicts his followers' persecution, the city's fall, and the return in glory of the Son of Man. *"They will hand you over to the courts and to the synagogues and you will be flogged and brought up before leaders and kings on my account, to bear witness before them"* (Mark 13.9). So, too, John's Jesus frames the promise of his own return with a reassurance offered to John's followers no less than to his own.

> *"I have told you this so that you may not be made to stumble. They will expel you from the synagogues. But more: there comes a time when all who kill you will think they do a service to God. . . . In the world you will have dire trouble. But take heart: I have conquered the world."*
>
> *(JOHN 16.1, 33)*

Jesus speaks to John's readers from the past. They heard in his voice the prayers, too, of their own present church. Important knowledge of those prayers has reached us in the so-called Teaching of the Missionaries, written within a few years of John's completion and closely related to the instruction we know from Matthew. The Teaching lays down the prayers to be used at a Thanksgiving Service. John speaks only indirectly, and early in the gospel, of the service, in the dialogue that follows the Feeding of Five Thousand. All the more remarkably, he gives no details of that last meal itself from which, it seems, the service took its rise. From the Teaching we may learn why. It gives directions for a Thanksgiving to follow the ritual meal of wine and bread. Clause after clause recalls the final prayer of John's Jesus.

John evokes in Jesus' words the prayer that John's own readers knew. In this most solemn moment the words of the church and the words of its Lord drew close to merging. Here in practice, in John's text itself, is that unity of father, son, and church of which John's Jesus has already told: *"I in my father and you in me and I in you"* (John 14.20). Many scholars have wondered if this section of John was read aloud during his church's Thanksgiving, where, as the church believes, the prayer of the church on earth and the prayer of Jesus in heaven become one.

Here is the prayer that the Teaching of the Missionaries records for use at the great Thanksgiving:

> We thank you, holy father, for your holy name, that you have sent to shelter
> in our hearts,
> and for the knowledge and belief and immortality that you have made known to us
> through Jesus your child.
> To you be glory for all aeons.
> You, almighty master, have created all things for the sake of your name,
> you have given food and drink to humankind for our enjoyment
> so that we might give you thanks,
> and to us you have granted a spiritual food and drink and the new aeon's life
> through your child.
> Before all we give you thanks that you are powerful.
> To you be glory for all aeons.
> Remember, Lord, your church to deliver her from every evil and to fulfill her in love;
> and gather her from the four winds,
> the church made holy, into your kingdom which you have prepared for her.
> For yours is the power and the glory for all aeons.
> May grace come and may this world pass away.
> Hosanna to the God of David.
> All who are holy, let them draw near; all who are not, let them change their heart
> and their ways.
> Lord, come. Amen.

Jesus' prayer and the community's Thanksgiving echoed each other across heaven and earth and across the decades that divided them. We, too, can catch a sense of this effect for ourselves from the most famous prayer to have reached us from the New Order, the prayer with which Jesus taught his pupils to acknowledge and to ask the help of God:

> *Our father in heaven,*
> *make known the glory of your name*
> *. . . Your will be done.*
> *. . . Do not bring us to the time of testing,*
> *but rescue us from the evil one.*

(MATTHEW 6.9–13, LUKE 11.2–4)

John never mentions the "Our Father." Yet in that closing prayer of his Jesus there lies a commentary on its words. For here is the version of such prayer to the father that precisely and only the son can offer: It makes clear how much is already done and how much in the world there remains to do. In Jesus' prayer John's readers would have heard a transfigured, all-knowing version of their own:

> *"Father, glorify your son, so that the son may glorify you; . . .*
> *I have brought glory to your name*
> *by completing the work that you gave me to do; . . .*
> *Keep them in your name, the name you have given to me; . . .*
> *I ask you to keep them from the evil one."*
>
> (*JOHN 17.1, 4, 15*)

John's church clearly knew some version of the "Our Father" that we know today. Did his readers know as well the plea with which, for our other witnesses, this part of Jesus' last night ends? Mark's story, like John's, lacks the "Our Father," but Mark, too, links the events of this last evening with the words of the prayer that Matthew and Luke record. John's Jesus absorbs the prayer into the declaration of his victory. Mark's echoes the plea of his frightened church.

"*Stay awake,*" Mark's Jesus told the innermost circle of his friends, "*and pray that you do not come to the time of testing.*" Mark's Jesus knew such trial well. This Jesus, *troubled to death,* fell to the ground in Gethsemane. Three times he begged his father that this hour, if it were possible, might pass him by. "*Father, all things are possible for you. Take this cup away from me. But . . . not what I want . . . but what you want . . . be done*" (Mark 14.38, 35, 36).

John does not look to Jesus' hopes or fears. His eyes are fixed on the larger battle that is about to be fought out. Judas the traitor has brought the posse; Satan is in the garden.

THE VERDICT

The witnesses have been heard, the evidence amassed. A verdict must be reached. The hearing before Annas, as we have seen, is short and sharp. His agents have done their work; there is nothing to add. John alerts the readers to our one important privilege over those who have led the prosecution: These antagonists have not opened themselves to the prospect of rebirth and so have not heard the private teaching given, this last evening, to Jesus' pupils alone. It is the readers who can confirm Jesus' claim, "*I have spoken openly to the world, I have always taught in the synagogue and in the temple, and in secret I have said nothing*" (John 18.20).

Morning comes. In the Temple the priests stoke the altar fire and prepare the morning sacrifice: a single lamb. There are more to follow. In readiness for Passover, thirty thousand lambs will be slaughtered in the Temple on this single afternoon; crowd after crowd of fathers will bring their family's lamb to shift after shift of priests.

Jesus is brought by the Jewish priests before Pilate, the Roman governor. The hearing is elaborately staged. We are to imagine two settings. The first is inside Pilate's headquarters; here he interrogates Jesus. To enter this home of the gentile power, however, would contaminate the Jews with ritual impurity. For how long? In one account of the Jerusalem festivals, Josephus tells how the high priest's vestments were kept in these Roman headquarters; the priests had to retrieve them a whole week before the festival began. The Jews, then, remain outside; to speak to them—with or without Jesus—Pilate comes out, too. The movements are striking: four short dialogues outside the fort and three within. From the private circle of those who long to understand him, Jesus has moved into an arena whose actors have all-consuming and conflicting motives of their own. The trial is a nightmare in which we know enough to know that nothing is what it seems to be. Here parody is truer than the real world it sets out to mock. Jesus becomes a plaything in other actors' sport. His own subjects deny the claims that their chief enemy declares for him, and that enemy is more right than he knows.

The prosecution has mounted its case and Jesus his defense; now for judgment. Here is a new perspective from which readers can see Jesus and watch their own response to him. The readers know far more than Pilate. They have the distance that they need to compare the judge's movements with their own. For Pilate moves in more ways than one, whether through weakness, tactics that misfire, or a genuine uncertainty. Inside the headquarters Jesus stands alone, face-to-face with the readers and ostensibly "in their power." Outside are ranged authorities demanding Jesus' blood, powers that be who corner Pilate and—if we once take Pilate's routes—will corner us, the readers, as well. It is not easy to read out of Pilate's words a consistent line of thought or action. John has less concern with Pilate's psychology than with different ways his own readers might evade what lies before them. They, too, have a decision to dwell on, make, or reinforce. Compromise, complaisance, impatience, and just a weary inability to understand: All these affected John's generation no less than they affect our own.

We are not in Pilate's shoes and are not bound to follow where he leads. This crucial distance is maintained by the governor's worldly power, in which most readers have no share. John's Pilate has been briefed about Jesus: Kingship is his chief concern. *"Hosanna!"* the crowd cried as Jesus entered the city less than a week before, *"Blessed is he who comes in the name of the Lord, and the king of Israel"* (John 12.13). Pilate's interrogation is not a success. Jesus is enigmatic, speaks of kingship of a different kind, makes clear he has no army in the wings. *"For this I have come into the world,"* says Jesus, *"to bear witness to the truth."* But Pilate was a busy man: *"What is truth?"* (John 18.38). Pilate has in mind the emperor's kingship and Jesus'. John and his readers know of another: the dominion of God. To such dominion Pilate is, at this stage in the story, quite blind; once Jesus is absolved from any challenge to the Roman order, Pilate would gladly let him go.

The local authorities, however, have other plans. They sidestep their governor's suggestions. He offers them Jesus for special release; instead they choose Barabbas. He accedes to their demand for punishment. Jesus is robed in imperial purple and crowned with a wreath of plaited thorns. The soldiers do him mock obeisance: *"Hail: the king of the Jews"* (John 19.3). Here indeed is the king of Israel, dressed up by Israel's enemies and taken out for presentation to his subjects with Pilate's strange, ambiguous declaration, *"Look, here is the man"* (John 19.5). Is this an expression of cynical or genuine pity? A mockery of Jesus that the authorities are to enjoy as well, or an insult aimed at Jesus and the priests together to show how easily Pilate can deride their hopes for independence? Here is a king that Pilate would have let them have and keep; little does he know that he is offering them their real king—and his. Dressed in purple, with crown and scepter, Jesus has never appeared before his people with such clear tokens of his real majesty as when he is made a plaything for their conquerors' sport. John has more in mind than he ascribes to any of these characters, not least a coronation by the prophet Zechariah, who had written of another Jesus long before, once more a chosen agent of God, a branch sprung from the stump of David's tree. God commanded the prophet:

Take silver and gold and set them on the head of Joshua, son of the high priest, and say to him,

"Thus says the Lord:
'Look, here is the man whose name is the Branch,
and he shall build the Temple of the Lord,
and he shall bear the glory and shall rule upon his throne.'"

(ZECHARIAH 6.12–13)

If Pilate hoped that scourging and mockery would satisfy the priests, his maneuver fails. *"Crucify him! Crucify him!"* For the third time Pilate declares, *"I find no ground for a charge against this man."* John's Pilate is losing control of the scene. At last the Jews state what for them had always been the root of the charge: *"He has made himself the son of God"* (John 19.6–7). Here in their eyes are clear grounds for execution, in Pilate's, cause for real fear. Who is this defendant? He had brushed aside too quickly Jesus' enigmatic answers about kingship of a different kind. Back once more into the fortress, and this time a closer enquiry. But Jesus will not answer. The moment has passed. The tide of worldly power and cares is rising and will wash away those traces of a deeper questioning.

Pilate had good reason to nurse his power. To be entitled a "Friend of the Emperor" would be known by John's time as a special privilege, one that no governor could afford to lose. To release a rebel king was for Pilate to endanger every favor he enjoyed at Rome. He had introduced the claim of Jesus' kingship and had mocked it, but in that mockery he had confirmed he knew the claim was current. He had parodied the Jews' hopes in a pantomime and given Jesus the very role that would in real life have made him dangerous. With such tricks Pilate has worked all morning to have Jesus released, and it is just these maneuvers that have put the defendant's death beyond all doubt. *"If you release him,"* argue the authorities, *"you are no friend of the emperor. Everyone who makes himself a king becomes the emperor's rival"* (John 19.12). Pilate's options are at an end.

It was midday. Passover, starting at sunset, fell this year on a Sabbath. Its lambs must be slaughtered after the regular evening sacrifice and before Sabbath began. To provide enough time, the evening sacrifice, counterpart to the morning sacrifice and offered every day without fail, was brought forward to the early afternoon. That service would start in half an hour.

"Hear, O Israel," the priests would say at the service, in the words of the Old Order's most famous declarations:

> *"The Lord our God is one Lord;*
> *and you shall love the Lord your God with your whole heart,*
> *and with your whole being and with your whole strength.*
> *Take heed, that your hearts be not deceived,*
> *and that you do not turn aside,*
> *and serve other gods and worship them."*
>
> (SECOND LAW [DEUTERONOMY] 6.4, 11.16)

Pilate brought out Jesus for the last time, and he got seated on a seat of judgment. Our roundabout translation catches something of John's double meaning. Who sat down? Surely Pilate, about to deliver sentence? But is John thinking, too, of the role that Jesus should be playing in this surreal trial—of the role, way beyond the recognition of those other actors on the stage, that he has in fact been filling all along?

Pilate turns the tables at last. If loyalty to the emperor is the issue, he will secure a declaration from the priests to match his own. He presents their "king" to the Jews, confident of their response. John's readers yet again know more than the story's own protagonists. "No king but God" would be the Jewish rebels' cry in the war against Rome's rule in 66–70 C.E.

> *"Take him away, take him away, crucify him!"*
> *"Am I to crucify your king?"*
> *"The emperor is our only king!"*
>
> (JOHN 19.15)

As the evening sacrifice came to an end, the attendants in the Temple sang, the trumpets sounded, and the people bowed to the ground. The attendants sang the psalm set for the day before the Sabbath:

> *The Lord is king and has put on glorious garments,*
> *the Lord has put on his garments*

and has wrapped himself around with strength.
Ever since the world began has your seat been prepared.

(PSALM 93.1–2)

The priests' acclamation marks the most poignant moment in John's narrative. This is the day on which those priests will celebrate God's kingship in his Passover victory; before them is the Jesus to whom God has entrusted all his power. *"The emperor is our only king!"*

Readers may hope to take some reassurance from the scene: John, after all, is no neutral reporter and has written all he has to keep his readers from the same mistake. But yet again John turns a mirror on ourselves. He has invited the reader to join the court, to hear the evidence, to shadow—and correct—the weak, impatient calculation that reduced his Pilate to a compromising impotence. And at the close the readers, too, sit in judgment.

Or do they? At the very last John brings his actors back to the role that they were born to fill. Just one person in this court has the right and power to sit in judgment, and he is in the dock. We have been judging the judge of the whole world. And in a final paradox: that judge's stand toward the reader is based solely on the stand that the reader takes to him.

"God did not send the son into the world that he might judge the world,
but that through him the world might be saved.
Those who believe in him are not subject to judgment;
those who do not believe are already judged,
because they have not believed in the name of the only son of God."

(JOHN 3.17–18)

The Return

THE PANGS OF CHILDBIRTH

The evening sacrifice is over. The priests in the Temple, in their thousands, are robed for their Passover work. The father of each family brings a lamb. The priest holds back the lamb's neck while the father wields the knife. Rows of priests relay the blood to the altar and sprinkle it against the steps.

Jesus took up the cross by himself and went out to the so-called Place of a Skull.

(JOHN 19.17)

A young man, centuries before, had picked up the wood for a sacrificial fire at his father's command. Little had Isaac known, in the Old Order's story, that he was the chosen victim. Jesus knew well what lay ahead. This time there would be no escape, no angel's voice to deflect the blow. So obedient was Abraham that he was willing to sacrifice his son. Later rabbis saw in the Jews' rescue at Passover a reward for their forefather's faith: "When I see the blood of the Passover lambs, says the Lord, I will pass over your houses: for I see there the blood of the sacrifice of Isaac."

Pilate also wrote a placard and put in on the cross. On it was written,
Jesus the Nazarene the King of the Jews.
And it was written in Hebrew, Latin, and Greek.

(JOHN 19.19–20)

The local authorities protested: Pilate was endorsing the pretender's claim; he should have written, "This man said, "I am King of the Jews.'" *"What I have written," said Pilate, "I have written"* (John 19.23). Here is Pilate's last ambiguous move. Is he mocking the Jews' hopes for a king, or does he see that these hopes have been fulfilled—and the chance for the kingdom thrown away? John leaves unanswered any question of such motives. His concern is elsewhere, in the final unity of themes and their fulfillment. Every instrument in his symphony is still playing: understanding and blindness, knowledge and ignorance, love and fear. And their effect? To sound the ultimate splendor of God.

"Can anything good come out of Nazareth?" asked Nathanael at the story's start (John 1.46). His Jesus from Nazareth is now dying in disgrace; Nathanael's question stands. One kingdom, long hoped for, is lost; another, far stranger, is revealed. The king is lifted up, his throne is a cross.

"Just as Moses raised up the serpent in the desert [promised Jesus],
so must the Son of Man be raised up,
so that all who believe in him may not die,
but have the new aeon's life."

(JOHN 3.14–15)

Jesus' subjects have denied his kingship and so have brought about his greatest glory. Rejected by his own people, Jesus' rule is proclaimed by their Roman oppressor in the languages of all the world.

The soldiers divided up the victim's clothes between them.

They took his clothes and made four portions, one for each soldier, and there was the tunic, too. The tunic had no seam, it was woven in one piece from top to bottom. So they said to one another, "Let us not tear it, but let us gamble for it, to see who gets it." So that the Old Order might be fulfilled,

They divided up my clothes among them,
and for my clothing they rolled dice.

(JOHN 19.23–24, PSALM 22.19)

On such a feast day the high priest himself would preside at the Temple's sacrifices. Says Josephus,

> The high priest is dressed as the other priests. Then over and above these clothes he puts on a tunic of blue, reaching to the feet, secured with a sash woven with flowers and gold thread. To its lower border are stitched tassels and bells. But this tunic is not made from two pieces, stitched at the shoulders and down the sides. It is one long woven cloth, with slits for the neck and the arms.

John records three sayings of Jesus from the cross; none of them is preserved by our other witnesses. Each saying in turn is connected—by John as narrator or by his Jesus—with the completion of all that is to be done. Any personal needs of Jesus are taken up into this larger program. A care for his mother, a thirst of his own—John may expect us to dwell on these reminders that Jesus was human, but not a word in his account invites us to do so. His focus does not waver: Here God's plan is coming to fulfillment.

> *And there stood by Jesus' cross his mother and his mother's sister. So Jesus, seeing his mother and the pupil standing by whom he loved, says, "Woman, look: there is your son." Then he says to the pupil: "Look, there is your mother." And from that hour the pupil took her into his own home.*
>
> *(JOHN 19.25, 26–27)*

We hear of Jesus' mother only twice in John's account: at the marriage that launched Jesus' public work, and here at its very end, when she stands beside the cross on which her son is dying. Both times he calls her "Woman," a term with which a man might well address most women, but certainly not his mother. We have encountered this Woman elsewhere, too, in the visions of the Seer.

> *There was seen a woman clothed with the sun, and the moon was beneath her feet, and on her head was a crown of twelve stars. And she had a child in her womb, and she cried out in her pangs and strained to give birth. And there was seen another sign in heaven, look, a great fire-red dragon, and its tail swept away a third of the stars of heaven and hurled them to the earth. And the dragon stood opposite the woman about to give birth, that when she gave birth he might eat the child.*
>
> *(BOOK OF UNVEILING [REVELATION] 12.1–4)*

Jesus' hour is come at last; so has the dragon's hour, the hour of the serpent of Eden. But the worst pangs of this childbirth are giving way, against all expectation and all human understanding, to a new mother's joy. The woman has her son. Jesus had said on that last evening with his pupils,

"When a woman is in labor,
she is in distress,
because her hour has come;
but when the child is born, she no longer remembers the agony,
because a person has been born into the world."

(JOHN 16.21)

Jesus is now nearing death.

After this Jesus, knowing that everything was now finished, so that the Old Order
might be brought to final completion, says: "I am thirsty." There was a vessel there,
full of sour wine; so fixing a sponge full of the wine on a stick of hyssop, they put it to
his mouth.

(JOHN 19.28–29)

Jesus had once been tired and sat at a Samaritan well. The woman there offered him water, but she needed the water that he could give far more than he needed hers:

"All who drink of the water I shall give shall not thirst, not for all aeons,
but the water I shall give them will become a spring in them,
welling up to the new aeon's life."

(JOHN 4.14)

Here on the cross Jesus needs the water he had not needed before. Is this a glimmer of the agony through which Mark's Jesus went? Or is this his longing to finish the task he had undertaken: *"Am I not to drink the cup,"* he had asked, *"that the father has given me?"* (John 18.11).

For my thirst, says the psalmist, *they gave me sour wine* (Psalm 69.22). Jesus is given the sponge on hyssop; at the very first Passover the Israelites used hyssop to wipe their doorposts with the blood of lambs. Their descendants were in the Temple now, thousands upon thousands surrounding the high priest and his colleagues, each with a knife to the neck of his family's lamb. The victim's blood must not congeal; to be sprinkled on the altar it must be free flowing. To ensure a flow of blood, the victim's heart would be slit.

When he had taken the wine Jesus said: "It is completed." And bowing his head he
handed over his breath.

(JOHN 19.30)

This is a striking phrase. Jesus hands over his breath: to God? Yes. But not only to God. Jesus must leave his followers if the Breath of God is to be given them. Here at the moment of death is a hint of the legacy that will follow formally at Easter. Zechariah had prophesied of the final Festival of Shelters,

God will pour out on the house of David and on the inhabitants of Jerusalem,
a breath of compassion and of prayer:
they look on him whom they have pierced
they shall mourn for him as for an only child,
they shall weep over him as over a firstborn.

On that day a fountain will be opened for the house of David
and for the inhabitants of Jerusalem,
to cleanse them from evil and impurity.

(ZECHARIAH 12.10, 13.1)

Jesus has hinted, all through his teaching, at this gift: as John himself explained, when he recorded that extraordinary promise:

"If anyone is thirsty, let him come to me and drink;
whoever trusts in me, as scripture says,
'Rivers shall flow from his stomach,
rivers of living water.'"

(JOHN 7.37–38)

Jesus has died. *One of the soldiers pierced his side with a spear, and straightaway there came out blood and water* (John 19.34). The victim's blood flowed. And at the moment of this death there flowed the living water, too—the water that John sees welling up in all those who drink of it.

We have come full circle. Our witness has told his story: *He who saw this has testified to it, and his testimony is truthful, and that man knows that he speaks the truth, so that you, too, might believe* (John 19.35).

"It Is Completed"

Jesus has died. The last testimony is before us of his earthly life. Here is no despairing death such as we encounter in Mark's and Matthew's stories, or the example for Jesus' followers that Luke records. John has seen God's plan coming steadily to fulfillment. And now, at the moment of Jesus' death, *it is completed*.

> *As the rain and the snow come down from the heavens and do not return without watering the earth, that it might give seed to sow and bread to eat, so shall my word be: it shall not return to me empty, but it will complete my will and prosper in the task for which I have sent it.*
>
> *(ISAIAH 55.10)*

We have come a long way since that story of Jesus' entry to Jerusalem, surrounded by the singing crowds. Jesus knew well enough the hopes that were stirred by Passover; so did John. They were not alone. In that simple ballad, anonymous and undated, of which we heard in chapter 2, are set the seeds that grew in John's church into the richest, deepest poem that has reached us from the ancient world. We will never know when those longing verses were first sung or where. But to share such hope was to be open to John's offer to transform it. To sense the depth of that hope is to be open to John's offer still.

The First Night: when the Lord was revealed over the world to create it.
The world was without form and void,
and darkness was spread over the face of the abyss,
and the Name of the Lord was the light, and it shone.
And he called it the First Night.

The Second Night: when the Lord was revealed to Abraham and to Sarah his wife.
And Isaac was thirty-seven when he was offered up on the altar.

The heavens were bowed down and descended, and Isaac saw their perfection,
and his eyes were dimmed because of their perfection.
And he called it the Second Night.

The Third Night: when the Lord was revealed against the Egyptians at midnight.
His hand slew the firstborn of the Egyptians
and his right hand protected the firstborn of Israel
to fulfill what the scripture says:
"Israel is my firstborn Son."
And he called it the Third Night.

The Fourth Night: when the world reaches its appointed time to be redeemed.
The iron yokes shall be broken
and the generations of wickedness shall be blotted out,
and Moses will go up from the midst of the desert
and the king the Anointed from on high.
One will lead at the head of the flock,
and the other will lead at the head of the flock,
and his Name will lead between the two of them,
and I and they will proceed together.

This is the night of the Passover to the name of the Lord:
it is a night reserved and set aside for the redemption of all Israel,
throughout their generations.

Epilogue

CHAPTER 12

The Last Act

Jesus has died. Our four stories have converged on the cross; the order and detail of the events they narrate is closer here than in any other passage of such length. The tone of their narratives, however, is further apart than ever before. Mark's Jesus dies like a man in terrible desolation, and John's Jesus like a God who controls all that happens to him, not least his death's "completion." Matthew lets Mark's view stand; Luke offers his Theophilus the story of an innocent martyr. In the face of such stark differences that first question echoes again: "Who do you say I am?" Must we finally admit defeat and concede that our four witnesses have such different viewpoints and are addressing such different needs that we can find no answer to Jesus' question shared by all?

One last movement remains: Easter. This is our last chance to find the key uniting all our four instruments in harmony. Yet here the evidence becomes more confusing still. Our four witnesses themselves tell the story of Easter in wildly divergent ways. These different stories may be consistent with one another. Some scholars have certainly stressed what they have in common and have sought to thread those incidents into a single string of events. Others by contrast have wondered if the church wove stories here more freely than in any other section of the gospels.

Our own purpose is not to peer through the stories to see the events beyond but to let each account discharge its function in its writer's story as a whole. Each fills the closing, climactic pages of its gospel. We might expect each to be the keystone of its gospel's structure: to keep in place all that has been built before and to enable the gospel's parts to fulfill their function in its completed arch. If in *The Four Witnesses* we prize the Easter stories open, it is to look more closely at their construction—and to look for the solution to our own search, which seems ever further from our grasp. We must look back over our own narrative for further, unrecognized clues if our detective story is to have any solution at all. They have been before us all along: in those two further "witnesses" that have accompanied us throughout: Paul and John the Seer.

To understand Mark and John we have already turned to the unveiling offered by the Seer. The Seer describes a heavenly vision and so makes its disclosures available to readers who themselves have enjoyed no such privilege. Mark and John turn the expected setting for such disclosure upside down: It is now on earth that the battle is acted out and that judgment is faced. A figure that belongs in the court of heaven confronts his contemporaries—and so his evangelist's readers—here on earth. The challenge to the reader is to see the point, to recognize what was under way in Jesus' life and is offered to the readers in turn. Mark's Jesus heals a blind man just before Peter struggles to his understanding of Jesus' standing and role; John's Jesus heals a blind man on the readers' way to rebirth. Our authors, by opening readers' eyes to the nature and significance of the events they narrate, are teasing those who have never seen a vision into the benefit that such a vision gives. The readers, our authors insist, do not need the gift of such heavenly visions, but modern readers cannot be offered, in their place, any account of the events, in more modern terms, that makes their status clear. We can feel baffled. For we are likely to ask questions that our authors do not address. Did our authors think of their texts as sufficient, when read with normal human faculties, to tease open their readers' understanding? Or was some further gift required from the subject of the disclosure itself, from God, his Anointed, or the living Breath that gave the church life and that would lead John's readers into all truth?

Now Mark and John both think in terms of "unveiling," but they deploy the motif in different ways. Mark has it that the battle was being fought there and then in Jesus' presence on earth; John has it that the judgment is now. We need not be surprised that the two traditions have diverged. Our writers are exploring the outer limits of narrative and its use; each is stretching the form of the story to the breaking point. So what happens when overt instruction is preferred to narrative? It is time to turn again to Paul.

Paul

Paul's message, as we have seen, is not taken on board just by grasping an argument or accepting proofs. His readers must learn to contemplate a wonder too great for normal speech. Paul had been exposed to this wonder in the most dazzling and immediate form: in his sight of the risen Jesus on the road to Damascus. Paul, in turn, must make it present in and as a person. The form in which that Jesus is made present to Paul's churches is the person of Paul himself. His presence is open to dire misunderstanding—but is vital.

We know most about Paul, however, precisely from his absences: from the letters he had to write when he could not be with his churches. They are intensely personal. His churches' response to Paul himself will affect their response to the Jesus that he represents to them. There are times enough when he cannot be with correspondents that he already knows well. His absence upsets them. He has changed his plans, has failed to arrive. But if they grow to distrust their missionary, they will distrust the gospel that he proclaims—and the Jesus that he represents. Paul must reassure them: his love for them and theirs for him. His pride in them and theirs in him unite the church and their missionary in unbreakable unity: *We are your boast just as you as well are ours, in the day of the Lord Jesus* (2 Corinthians 1.14). To be sure of this, they must know Paul with the personal, intimate knowledge that dissolves (in particular) their suspicions of his duplicity or lack of care. Now to speak of such knowledge Paul invokes, above all, the imagery of sight; the Corinthians must look upon him, and they will see in his face the reflection of God's glory. They will apprehend from such contemplation of Paul what he received from the vision of Christ himself. He will still offer arguments to remove the suspicion that clouds or distracts their gaze and will explain what the gaze offers and why, but the arguments are no substitute for the knowledge afforded by the contemplation itself.

One letter survives, however, to Christians that Paul had never seen, over whom he could claim no authority, who would not recognize in him the representation of Christ: the Letter to the Romans. At its start Paul paints a picture of communal delinquency that has borne evil fruit. He does not claim that his addressees themselves are sunk in this dire spiral of crime and matching punishment. We will speak in the next few pages of "the Romans" or of Paul's addressees. But Paul is writing to a church or churches that he has not visited; how much he knows about their state or how much he presumes, we cannot now be sure.

The letter opens with a general condemnation; it moves ever closer to the Romans' own case, as Paul understands that case to be: *As they have not reckoned to keep God in their awareness, God himself has consigned them to an unreckoning mind, to do all kinds of wrong* (Romans 1.28–32). This mind is healed by the letter's end: *Stop your conformity to the present age. Keep up your transformation in the renewal of your mind, so that you might reckon aright what is the will of God: what is good and well pleasing and perfect* (Romans 12.2). Paul is not just persuading, teaching, informing. He is setting out to heal the Romans by and during the reception of his own letter. At the letter's start he describes a uniform delinquency of mind, will, and flesh. By its end he can urge the Romans *to present their bodies as a living, holy sacrifice, well pleasing to God* (Romans 12.1). The willful blindness of the wicked that underlay the opening scenario is no longer a threat to the Romans; their bodies—their living, concrete humanity—can be presented to God as *their reasonable service* (Romans 12.1). Their minds are healed, and they are conscious of their own health. Paul expects the key change in the readers to have taken place precisely by the letter's midway point. In a vivid plea, cast in the voice of an autobiographical "I," Paul looks back on the progress made possible by the letter so far: *So then I myself serve the law of God with my mind—but with my flesh the law of sin* (Romans 7.25).

Paul sets out not just to describe his gospel, to ground it or defend it, but to make it effective, within the letter itself, as God's power at work on his readers as they read and on his listeners as they hear. Paul has to answer charges that his gospel is a disgrace: He is said to belittle the Law and to encourage wrongdoing; such a gospel—as Paul is the first to maintain—would be shameful. But such is not his gospel: *I am not ashamed of the gospel, for it is the power of God to salvation for every believer, first for the Jew and then for the Greek. For God's way to have us just in his sight is being unveiled: from faith to faith* (Romans 1.16).

God's way to have us just is being unveiled. So is its counterpart: a spiral of crime and punishment, vividly described. *For the wrath of God is being unveiled from heaven against every impiety and injustice of those who hem in the truth with their injustice. For that which can be known of God is clear for them to see; for God had made it clear to them* (Romans 1.18). Paul aims to trigger the power that will move his readers from the downward spiral of God's wrath to an upward spiral of obedience. The gospel, activated here and now in the letter's reception, is God's present *power to salvation;* the Romans are to grow, even as they read or hear the letter, into a self-conscious determination to obedience and to faith.

A downward spiral at the letter's start, an upward spiral at it end. The underlying crime at the letter's start was a willful failure of knowledge and understanding. This is an odd state but carefully and perceptively described. Paul is constructing for the Romans a mirror image of the state to which he hopes to bring them; everything in Rome that he will address at the letter's end is already in his mind at its beginning. In the letter's closing section Paul draws first the contrast with overweening pride. He then recalls the whole list of evils from the letter's start and expounds their contraries. Love works for good, not for evil; lives in friendship; honors others; serves the Lord; and succors saint and stranger alike. For all in all, the love that is the fulfilling of the law stands over against the discord whose punishment is death. This is a far cry from the agents of evil evoked at the letter's start, who are filled with injustice and evil, with envy, trickery, and spite; who are libelers, hate God, and are devoid of love or pity. The evils that he has in mind are social; they will tear a community apart. Their contraries are social, too, and will be the strength of this "body," the church.

How will the readers' state look, once their mind is restored to health and the gift of the Breath inspires them? Paul contrasts their old delinquency with the demands and offers of their new state in a characteristic trilogy: love, faith, and hope (Romans 12.9–13.10, 13.11–15.6, 15.7–13). The three stand in close relation: Those who love rejoice in hope; we can claim nothing as done in faith that breaches love; love fuels the endurance through which we have hope. Paul demands that the strong in faith support the weak and so reminds them of the hope supported by Christ. The God of hope, Paul promises, will give the peace whose pursuit defines the rights and wrongs of faith. Above all is peace: the church's divisions must be healed. The harmony of the body's limbs, the catalogue of love's effects, the business of peace and of building, the unanimity of mind and of praise—all these converge at the climax of Paul's exhortation: *May the God of hope fill you with all joy and peace in your believing, so that you may excel in hope in the power of the Breath of God* (Romans 15.13).

The Romans' response to this very letter will be a benchmark of the gospel's power among them; they have in themselves, here and now, the chance to break the cycle of evil and to recognize for themselves the sign of their healing in their own response to Paul's words. There is an offer here; there is a warning, too. If they fail to heed Paul's letter, they will confirm that they are caught in the cycle of evil that leads to death.

Only and precisely at the letter's end can the church take on Paul's command: *Stop your conformity to the present age. Keep up your transformation in the renewal of your mind, so that you might reckon aright what is the will of God: what is good and well pleasing and perfect* (Romans 12.2). The community that was collapsing into bitterness can now recover the life to which it was called: as a single body of many limbs. It is Paul's letter itself, through the course of its reception, that has healed the corruption of the church's moral judgment.

The church as a whole has been healed. Communal breakdown at the start, the church in unity by the end, and in between, Paul's most famous teaching on the individual's standing before God. The movement is as important as its parts: The community is nothing without the individuals that make it up, and only within the church, in turn, can those individuals fulfill God's will as limbs of the Anointed's single, united body. Parts of Paul's teaching on the individual we have already heard: Christians are baptized into the death of the Anointed and buried with him, *so that just as the Anointed was raised from the dead through the father's glory, so we, too, might walk in newness of life* (Romans 6.4). If Paul's gospel is distorted, that new status can be made an excuse for renewed wrongdoing, and we have heard Paul's condemnation of those who so drastically misrepresent his gospel. But we must be clear: The deep subject of Paul's teaching is not human behavior itself, but the most basic terms in which humans are to be described and their behavior understood.

Much in the letter's central section is searingly personal. Paul seems so clearly to have an individual in his mind's eye, very possibly, himself. But at stake is more than a single "I." Echoes sound of baptism, of the Law's gift on Sinai, and of Adam and Eve themselves. Within Paul's "I," all humanity is being redefined. And so, for Paul's purpose, it must be. For this focus on the "I" is framed by the letter's still more central concern: with a community, delinquent and divided at the letter's start, restored and united at its end. Every limb in this community's body must be healed so that the body as a whole can function as it should.

The letter reveals as subtle an understanding of human self-correction, its possibilities and limits as we find in any text of the New Order. Paul appeals over and again to the readers' *mind*, their moral judgment—precisely the sense that is "diseased" in Paul's opening scenario. This judgment, then, must become the agent of its own healing. Paul must work with the greatest care: It is sound judgment that will heal the Romans' delinquency, but it is precisely that judgment that is delinquent. How can a diseased awareness heal itself?

Our limits are as important as our capacities. Paul describes us as dying by wrongdoing and so losing life, then through baptism dying to wrongdoing and so coming to life anew. Baptism's effect is not our achievement; it is not under our control. Far from it. Paul describes the "real" process undergone at baptism and then evokes the tension that this transfer can involve. For the Romans are still in gestation, still coming to the new life for which baptism equips them. The process is not wrought by magic; there is slippage, misunderstanding, moral sleight of hand. It is only after half the letter is past that Paul can be confident that he speaks with and for his readers as he declares his moral judgment to be healed. This is still only half the battle:

As for my inner man, I joyfully agree with the Law of God; but I see another law in my limbs, fighting against the law of my mind and taking me prisoner in the law of wrong-doing, the law that is in my limbs. Wretched man that I am: who will rescue me from the body of this death?—But thanks be to God through Jesus Anointed our Lord!—So then: I myself serve the Law of God in my mind, but in my flesh the law of wrongdoing.
(ROMANS 7.22–24)

The mind is healed. The flesh is beyond the power of Paul's therapy. *But thanks be to God through Jesus the Anointed our Lord!* Paul has anticipated the power that can sub-due this most recalcitrant element in human life: *So now there is no condemnation for those in Jesus Anointed. For the Law of the Breath of the life in Anointed Jesus has freed you from the law of wrongdoing and death* (Romans 7.25, 8.1–2).

And as with God's wrath, so with his gospel. The Romans have accepted the gospel. But without the help of Paul their understanding has been imperfect or incomplete, liable to misunderstanding—and not least, misunderstanding of Paul's own gospel. Paul needs to declare the character and content of the gospel as divine disclosure to a church already within the gospel's call; the unveiling is available—the Romans need only see the point, but this is what they have spectacularly failed to do. They need Paul to show them the truth that they have not understood or even recognized—Paul, the missionary who reveals the true gospel, expounds their prior misunderstanding, and provides the means for their correction.

Here already, in the gospel's character as divine disclosure, lies a first reason for the Romans' failure: The unveiling is now pointed out to them by such a privileged recip-ient and interpreter as they have not had among them. As with Mark, so here: God's verdict, action, and purpose are being enacted on earth. For *now, without the Law, God's way to have us just stands exposed* for all to see (Romans 3.21). The unveiling is not dependent on any heavenly journey; it is close at hand. But the readers need help to see the point. The gospel can be understood only thanks to the missionary who unfolds it. The problem lies not only in the Romans but in the character of the gospel itself as divine disclosure. As Paul works to restore the Romans through their mind to the proper service of God, he is asking throughout why his intervention should be needed and what is its status. Here is the underlying theme of Paul's letter: what makes possible and effective the unveiling of God's will.

Paul's letter and the power of God, baptism recalled and represented, the mind's openness to healing and the obstinacy of the flesh—these are observed and acknowledged by Paul with the greatest care. In every case we might compare his acuity and his purposes with John's.

John has told a story; Paul has offered teaching. They use terms as different as the forms in which they present their "gospel." But each has an extraordinary sense of human capacity and its limits, of the insights within our reach, and the frailties that keep us from seeing them. And most important of all, they share an overarching strategy: Paul must heal his readers and their church; John must bring his readers to new birth. Each uses his text to transform the readers during and through their reception of the text.

So much in common and yet surely so far apart. Paul uses his letter to transform the reader only when he cannot offer the memory of his own presence and person to achieve his aim. His Letter to the Romans gives us invaluable insight into the course and conditions that he envisages for such renewal, but only because Paul reveals here the anatomy of a process that he would sooner—and perhaps more effectively—direct by quite different means. For John, by contrast, the use of narrative was not second best; it was not, as far as we can tell, a poor "substitute" for the writer's or church leaders' personal representation of Jesus.

But these two documents are more similar than they seem. Paul's strategy centers on his own person and resorts to a text when need be. John's uses a text precisely to present a person. For as John's Jesus heals in the story, teaches, and brings new life, so does John's gospel set out to heal, teach, and bring new life within the community that hears it. The effect of Jesus in the story spurs the readers to recognize the text's function among themselves; and that function is exactly parallel to Jesus' presence, power, and effect within the gospel. Paul represents Jesus in his own person. Here in the presence of the gospel itself is Jesus' representation by John.

Unveiling the Mystery

We are on the track of our solution: Four traditions are working to effect here on earth, among ordinary readers of any time, the understanding that (as our authors believe) eludes all unaided human endeavor. The gospels themselves, texts read and heard, must make possible that understanding.

Each of our four witnesses uses a strategy that achieves its effect only at his narrative's end. These accounts of Easter are precisely the coda to which each gospel has been heading from its start. Only now do we see what *sort* of stories we have been reading all along. They are mysterious, elusive narratives. To tell the story is only half the battle; the story must carry, within its telling, the key to its own comprehension.

MARK: THE RETURN TO GALILEE

On Easter morning Mark has the women come to Jesus' tomb. Jesus' body is not there. A young man is in the tomb, dressed in white.

> *"Don't be amazed," said the young man, "you are looking for Jesus the Nazarene, who was crucified. He is up and risen. He is not here. Look, there is the place where they laid him. But go and tell his pupils and Peter, 'He is going ahead of you into Galilee. There you will see him, just as he told you.'"*
>
> *Trembling and bewildered, the women went out and fled from the tomb. They said nothing to anyone, because they were afraid.*
>
> *(MARK 16.6–8)*

And with that, it seems, Mark has finished. What a strange way to end: more fear, disobedience, everything still open. The women, the only followers who had not run away as danger drew near, understand as little about Easter as the men had understood about the suffering that went before it. Why do we not hear of the meeting between Jesus and his followers? Why does the story not follow them to Galilee and their reunion and his pupils' comprehension at the last?

At our distance we look for some familiar and reassuring distinctions: between the earthly and the risen Jesus; between his power when on earth and his power after Easter; and between his presence with his pupils and any presence his followers may claim for him since. But the Jesus of Mark's story was already in his own person and in his days on earth the Son of Man. And more: He was the visible presence of God in action. The veil between heaven and earth is a veil on the eyes of those around Jesus who cannot open their eyes and see. It takes Jesus' death to tear the veil apart.

Jesus' pupils could not understand him before his death; Mark knew that the gospel's readers would still need help to understand him after it. It is time to start the story again: to go *back to Galilee* where it all began, to the first appearance of Jesus and his summons to Peter. Mark would have us see beneath the surface this time around and then to start to story yet again, over and over, at an ever-greater depth. Jesus tells riddling stories whose point does not lie open for all to see. Gradually we get clear the riddling story that is the whole gospel, and we can grasp who is really speaking in this narrative from long ago—and who he is really speaking to. The encouragement and warning that Jesus gives to those who hear his stories apply no less to those who hear Mark's story as a whole: *To you the secret of the Kingdom of God has been given* (Mark 4.10).

There were those who heard Jesus' stories and saw nothing more in them than charming—and perhaps confusing—fables. Such listeners were *those outside,* who failed to see the point behind the stories. There would be others, too, who would read Mark's whole story of Jesus as a straightforward narrative: Here were striking, dramatic events such as were told of emperors, sages, and other claimants to the favor of heaven. Such readers, too, would be *those outside.* Mark's whole narrative is as cryptic as the stories it records in the mouth of Jesus. The gospel is a giant parable. To fail to see beneath its surface is to be in dire danger, to be one of *those outside.*

This is history as it has never been before: history disclosing far more than itself. The readers, too, are to follow the young man's command and to be given the sight that he promises Jesus' pupils: They will return to Galilee and see the risen Jesus. But where is this "Galilee"? Readers must go back to the story's start, where they will hear of the Jesus at the start of his work, long before his death and rising. *Jesus came into Galilee preaching the gospel of God* (Mark 1.14). Can *this* be our sight of the risen Jesus? Yes, and of the earthly Jesus too. Mark flouts once more the distinction on which any history of Jesus must rely. To look for the earthly Jesus in Mark's story, as a figure distinct from the risen Jesus of his church, is already to miss his story's point and so to be among *those outside.* Of course historians of Jesus, ancient and modern, have a duty to pry apart these aspects of Mark's Jesus; historians deal in the business of earthly figures living earthly lives. But historians of the text and of the church that used it are called to a stranger and more elusive task: to grasp the insights, purpose, and methods that drove Mark's denial of the one basic distinction that could make of his story a straightforward history of Jesus.

And what of those who returned to "Galilee" and the story's start, and who saw ever deeper beneath its surface? What of Peter's harassed church and the final victory that its members longed for? Has the Son of Man, as Mark portrays him, assured us of this triumph yet to come? Or has this history achieved what it discloses? Deep down in the truest structure of things, has Mark's Son of Man won the final victory already?

Mark is far too wise to answer these questions for his readers. To ask them is already to be on the way to understanding. For those who would look deeper and ever deeper, Mark has just one command: *"Go back to Galilee; there you will see Jesus, just as he told you"* (Mark 16.7).

For centuries following Bishop Papias, whom we met in our "Introduction to Mark," Mark's gospel was thought a clumsy compilation, a string of pearls unsorted and ill matched. The gospel's ending is the oddest thing of all; later manuscripts add fuller conclusions in which Jesus is actually seen. Here is the most common version. It has drawn most of its details from the stories that we have heard in the other gospels:

> When Jesus rose early on the first day of the week, he appeared first to Mary Magdalen, out of whom he had driven seven daemons. She went and told those who had been with him and who were mourning and weeping. When they heard that Jesus was alive and that she had seen him, they did not believe it.
>
> Afterward Jesus appeared in a different form to two of them while they were walking in the country. These returned and reported it to the rest, but they did not believe it, either. Later Jesus appeared to the eleven as they were eating; he rebuked them for their lack of faith and their stubborn refusal to believe those

who had seen him after he had risen. He said to them, "Go into all the world and preach the good news to all creation. Whoever believes and is baptized will be saved, but whoever does not believe will be condemned. And these signs will accompany those who believe: in my name they will drive out daemons; they will speak in new tongues; they will pick up snakes with their hands; and when they drink deadly poison, it will not hurt them at all; they will place their hands on sick people, and they will get well."

After the Lord Jesus had spoken to them, he was taken up into heaven and he sat at the right hand of God. Then they went out and preached everywhere, and the Lord worked with them and confirmed his word by the signs that accompanied it.

We may recognize this ending as a later compilation of Easter stories. But if we remove it from the text, have we really recovered the shape of Mark's story? Or had Mark intended and perhaps written a fuller ending of his own? Scholars have tested every possible explanation for its absence. Was Mark prevented from finishing the gospel by persecution or death? Was a closing chapter lost from the first (and at that stage the only) manuscript of the story? Or was the story's conclusion provided by the next stage of the church service in which the gospel was (we may surmise) read aloud?

In *The Four Witnesses* we let the ending stand, abrupt and jagged as it is. Perhaps the explanation is straightforward: Mark just gave his narrative a strange, dark close to match the days of its completion. As we heard the rest of our witnesses, however, we found that their texts, too, were informed by the need to ensure their readers' genuine—and difficult—*understanding*. Into this pattern Mark's present conclusion finds its place. It is precisely in these last lines that we are steered back to the gospel's start with the knowledge we need if we are to open our eyes and *see*.

Mark's text is at an end. The women and Jesus' pupils are to head back to Galilee. Passover has been and gone; it is high summer now. The fields are golden with wheat. It is time for harvest.

Now in my vision [wrote John the Seer thirty years later] *I saw a cloud and on it one like a son of man, with a gold crown on his head and a sharp scythe in his hand. Than an angel called aloud to him, "Put in your scythe and reap. Harvest time has come and the harvest of the earth is ripe." Then he set his scythe to work on the earth, and the harvest of the earth was reaped.*

(BOOK OF UNVEILING [REVELATION] 14.14–16)

MATTHEW: "I AM WITH YOU ALWAYS"

From Mark to Matthew: from one distinctive strategy to another. *And they will call his name Emmanuel, With-Us-God* (Matthew 1.23).

From the time of Jesus' conception we know he is to act as God's agent working on his people's behalf. As Isaiah's Emmanuel did, so Jesus is to do. Now the story comes to an end. And Jesus' pupils, obedient to the angel's command, have gone to Galilee.

The eleven pupils went to Galilee to the mountain at which Jesus had told them to be. And when they saw him they fell prostrate before him, but some hesitated. And Jesus came up to them and spoke to them saying, "All authority has been given to me in heaven and on earth. Go out, therefore, and make pupils of all the gentiles, baptizing them in the name of the father and of the son and of the Breath of God, teaching them to keep all the commandments that I have commanded you. And look, I am with you always, every day, until the aeon's completed end."
(MATTHEW 28.16–20)

Once more the readers look forward: to their own time and beyond. But Matthew's closing words set up questions as tantalizing as Mark's: With-Us-God has been Jesus through the story, before this overwhelming authority had been his. On the mountaintop he had refused the devil's offer; on a mountain he had taught his pupils and the crowds; and here on a mountain he declares his investiture with unprecedented power. The angel had named him for his earthly presence and task; how much more directly and vividly this name must describe him now. But where and how, then, is "Jesus-with-Us" to be found?

God was "with us" in the life of Jesus, and as those very last words of the gospel make clear, that is the same Jesus who is with us still. From With-Us-God at the gospel's beginning to "I am with you" right at its end: Everything between these two poles describes the Jesus who was With-Us-God and the Jesus who is with us still. It was the life described in the gospel that was With-Us-God and the description in the gospel that is with the readers now. The presence of Jesus with us is the text of the gospel itself.

Matthew's whole strategy falls into place at last. Matthew's Jesus had so often seemed to speak to Matthew's church even more than to the audience around Jesus himself. And so he did, for underlying Matthew's earthly Jesus is the Jesus that after Easter he will be declared to be. Matthew's Jesus speaks, then and now, as Wisdom itself.

This strategy prompts questions that Matthew did not need to face: What change in Jesus' standing is marked by the gospel's closing lines? What is the authority that Jesus is given at the gospel's end that was not already Wisdom's entitlement at its start? Has Matthew been consistent in his view of Jesus then and now? We would be untrue to ourselves if we did not raise such questions, but we lose sight of Matthew's purpose if we press them. The transition from the earthly to the Easter Jesus is not Matthew's chief concern; he is looking back on Jesus then and now, the single figure presented in his single story who was With-Us-God and is now Jesus-with-Us. Only at the gospel's end can the reader see the force of that opening "Emmanuel": All Jesus' words and deeds bear the imprint of his "new" authority, from the gospel's opening chapter to its close. Here, then, is the presence of With-Us-God—in the words Matthew puts before us in the text of his gospel itself.

Matthew's practical gospel, its eye always on the standards and rules of daily life, may seem suddenly to have changed its character. But the same Matthean voice speaks to us with the same concerns. Matthew tells in detail how an angel removed the stone from the tomb's mouth; the guards shook with fear *and were as if dead* (Matthew 28.4). Matthew's love of portents and angelic intervention is as strong in his story's closing pages as at its start. The guards tell the high priests what happened and are bribed to confirm instead that Jesus' pupils had stolen the body. *And this story has been spread abroad among the Jews, right up to the present day* (Matthew 28.15). Matthew knows his readers and the stories circulating in their synagogues; yet again the church and synagogues are making angry moves and countermoves.

Perhaps most striking is Matthew's unbroken silence on the central problem, as we might think of it, to face a church that was drawing gentiles to its door. Did gentile males need to be circumcised to become full members of the church? Matthew does not mention circumcision once. And in these closing lines his Jesus makes missionaries of his pupils: missionaries to every nation under the sun. Matthew had given due space to the doubts harbored by his church's conservative leaders; he knows how strange and improper its developments could seem. He has steered these leaders to this climactic moment through his story's course. They are now ready to hear Jesus' final command. At last the most significant control on the church's life—and its most dramatic contrast with the synagogues'—are laid down: the rule and rituals for admission. Circumcision is not at issue. *Go out, therefore, and make pupils of all the gentiles, baptizing them in the name of the father and of the son and of the Breath of God, teaching them to keep all the commandments that I have commanded you* (Matthew 28.19–20).

LUKE: "OPENING THE MIND"

Mark and Matthew use the story of one time to drive home its effect on another. Jesus' past and their readers' present are equally in focus; the story, then, of Jesus' past becomes the disclosure of his present—and of the readers', too. Past and present are laid one on top of the other. If we fail to recognize our authors' strategies, Mark's teasing story is simply confusing and Matthew's subtle story a textbook case, almost dull in its rigor, of organizational care. Once we see their purposes, however, their every detail comes alive. Mark takes us at his story's end back to its start, to have us read this giant parable over and over and at each rereading to see more deeply into the *mystery of the kingdom of God*. Matthew keeps his whole narrative before our eyes: everything is embraced by the statements, at start and finish, of the roles Jesus played, then and now.

What, then, about Luke? He lets the times of his story stand as they might in a conventional narrative, one after the other. He has no need to double back, to describe the risen Jesus in terms of the earthly or the church in terms of Jesus' own pupils. He has the Mission (Acts) in which to tell of Jesus risen and of his church and so can use the gospel to tell of the earthly Jesus alone. Mark and Matthew laid their account of Jesus' present power onto their story of his past; we get to know the risen Jesus by hearing of the earthly and can understand the earthly Jesus only and precisely in a story that tells at the same time of the risen. Luke, by contrast, lays Jesus' past and the church's present one after another and uses the latter to give us the understanding we need of the former. The layers of Luke's story are laid out before us and so read far more like history as we know and read it. But we should not be misled into naïveté. Luke tells a beautifully controlled story, shaped so that we can see the pattern in God's plan and take up its rhythm for ourselves. As the story unfolds we come to expect its mirrored motion. Expectations are set up and then unsettled on an ever-longer swing and broader arc. We have ever more to see and ever more time to see it.

Over and over we hear in Luke's account of Easter: Jesus opened the eyes and minds of his pupils to understand the Old Order and Jesus' own earlier words. The women come to the tomb. They find the stone rolled away from the tomb's mouth; the body of Jesus is not there. Two men appear to them:

"Why are you looking for the living among the dead? He is not here, but has been raised. You remember how he told you when he was still in Galilee, talking of the Son of Man, that he must be handed over into the hands of wrongdoers and be crucified and on the third day rise again." And they remembered his words.

(LUKE 24.5–8)

The women return to Jesus' closest group of followers and tell them what has happened; *and this story seemed to the others like nonsense, and they did not believe the women* (Luke 24.12). Peter goes to the tomb; he finds just the graveclothes and goes home in amazement.

Now we join the two members of Jesus' circle who were walking to Emmaus. We have heard how they were deeply despondent. They failed to recognize Jesus and told him of all that had happened, right up to the report of the women.

And he said to them, "How foolish you are and slow in your hearts to trust in all that the prophets said. Was it not necessary for the Anointed to suffer and to enter into his glory?" And beginning from Moses and from all the prophets he explained to them the passages in all the scriptures that were about himself.

(LUKE 24.25–27)

When they reach the village the two pupils persuade Jesus to stay with them.

And it happened in his having dinner with them that he took the bread and gave the blessing and broke it and gave it to them, and their eyes were opened and they recog-

nized him; and he disappeared from their sight. And they said to each other, "Weren't
our hearts burning in us as he spoke to us on the way, as he opened the scriptures to us?"
(LUKE 24.30–32)

We should keep an eye on these two followers. They return to the main group and
are among them for all that follows. The readers who have shared their awe can follow
and share the slowly growing insight of the group as a whole. Jesus appears at the very
moment that the two are telling of their encounter at Emmaus *and how he became
known to them at the breaking of bread.* The group is terrified by Jesus' appearing. They
think they are seeing a wraith, a "breath." And he says to them,

*"Why are you distraught, why do queries arise in your hearts? See my hands and my
feet: it's me myself. Touch me and see, for a wraith does not have flesh and bones as
you see me have."*
(LUKE 24.38–40)

Now they are incredulous for joy and simply amazed, so he eats some fish before
their eyes. Then the interpretation of the Old Order starts once more.

*Jesus said to them, "This is just what I said to you when I was still with you: everything
must be fulfilled that is written in the Law of Moses and prophets and psalms about me."
Then he opened their minds to understand the scriptures. And he said to them, "Just so
it is written that the Anointed must suffer and must rise from the dead on the third day."*
(LUKE 24.44–46)

Over and over strange evidence is followed by explanation. Over and over this priv-
ileged group of followers needs more. The women see angels, who remind them of
Jesus' words. Then two followers, who by now have heard the women's story, meet
Jesus and have the Old Order explained. The group as a whole hears how Jesus has
appeared twice: once to Peter and once to those two followers. At this very moment
Jesus appears to them all—and once more the scriptures are explained.

When we first encountered the group its members thought the women's story was
nonsense. Peter went to the tomb and was amazed to find it empty. The two followers
on the way to Damascus were anxious, confused, and thoughtful. At last all the
threads are woven together: The group hears that Peter and the two followers have
seen Jesus. They accept that Jesus really has been raised. But when he appears? The
group is first terrified, then incredulous from joy. Their recognition is slow, roundabout, stumbling. The pair did not recognize Jesus on the road; *their eyes had been prevented from knowing him.* Their eyes must be opened, in turn, for them to know him
over the meal. And at the last encounter, Jesus himself opens the minds of those who
have now heard of his rising, touched him, and seen him eat.

All the doubts and worries and excitement of this first group are as likely to be part
of Luke's readers' response. Luke is as humane and perceptive as ever: He gives space

to all the turmoil that readers might feel and steers them from an opening bemusement to the confident faith to which those first witnesses had come. He echoes the forms of the church's worship: the exposition of scripture was followed by the meal of Thanksgiving; Jesus explained the scriptures and then broke bread—and at this moment the two followers know him for who he is.

Then he opened their minds to understand the scriptures. How are the readers to come upon this knowledge and its understanding? It is in the Mission (Acts) that Luke expounds to the readers the passages that he refers to Jesus. The missionaries who had heard Jesus explain the scriptures explain them, in turn, to Luke's readers. Luke's Easter stories take the reader by the hand. At their end we are ready to recognize the "presence" of Jesus in the gift of power with which his followers will be invested at the outset of the Mission. Luke's sequel takes us onward, forward: beyond the gospel itself. He does not need to turn his readers back upon their tracks to find the risen Jesus in the story of his earthly life.

The *hearts* of two travelers *burning,* a group terrified and within minutes *incredulous from joy,* the search for a natural explanation, and a *surge of conflicting thoughts:* Luke's descriptions are as delicate as ever. He may be exploring for its own sake the effect of such appearances on Jesus' despairing followers. But just as important is their effect on Luke's own readers. Theophilus had good grounds to be skeptical and good reason to value an advocate who did justice to his doubts and questions. Luke's story has a particular setting with particular characters, but the readers are invited to share the turmoil of those first witnesses.

Few scenes are so evocative as that walk to Emmaus: the fading light, the mysterious traveler, the restatement and revival of hope. The two followers were enthralled.

And they drew near to the village to which they were going, and he himself made as if to travel onward. And they prevailed upon him, "Stay with us; it is nearly evening and the light has already gone." And he went in to stay with them.

(LUKE 24.28–29)

It was a close call. The stranger so nearly journeyed on. The two followers would never have known who had walked with them and would never have understood why their hearts burned as they heard him speak. Luke is the most humane of all our witnesses. He knows how doubts and worries affect his readers. There will be times when dull despair will be all they know. But there is a place even then for listening, for persistence, for wanting to hear more from the mysterious stranger beside them in the dusk.

For he might otherwise walk on and be for ever lost from view.

"WHO DO YOU SAY THAT I AM?"

Our story is coming to its end; the strategy that unites our witnesses is coming steadily into view. We have just one account of Easter still to read. This may well be the best moment to take stock, to acknowledge how far our authors' strategies are from those that we had expected to find—and yet how close to our own concerns the questions are that have shaped their extraordinary stories.

"Who do you say I am?" First and foremost, our answer to Jesus' question is likely to be "a historical figure." Most of us would approach the gospels now with this basic answer already in mind. The scholarly and popular search for fuller details has lasted a hundred years and more. Dominant among current proposals are variants of the following:

Mark's is the earliest of our gospels and offers a Jesus who is still recognizably human. The underlying figure of "the historical Jesus" was a "prophet," perhaps, with an extraordinary charisma; it could have been at his baptism that he recognized for himself some God-given task. For Matthew and Luke, writing a decade or more after Mark, Jesus' special status calls for a special conception: He must be born from a virgin. In John, the last gospel to be completed, Jesus has been God for all eternity before his birth and in the story is still God, now striding the earth, with hardly a pretense of humanity.

Further search can be made for a Jesus more "original" than Mark's. We can invoke the Collection of Sayings (probably) used by Matthew and Luke and (for example) a further gospel of sayings ascribed to Jesus, the Gospel of Thomas, which was found at Nag Hammadi in Egypt in the 1940s. With their help we can perhaps place Jesus in a tradition of teachers familiar at his time: Jesus himself condemned moral and social degradation in Israel; his followers dwelled on its—spectacular—consequence in God's impending judgment. Such a Jesus is not only credibly "human"; he is also sympathetic. Too much was heard in the twentieth century of destruction; biblical warnings of a great enemy and its defeat have been too readily recruited to serve human ends. We might welcome the wise, trenchant cast of this rediscovered teacher.

Such hypotheses, unsurprisingly, have had as many adversaries as proponents. It was in the very years that the Nag Hammadi texts were becoming known that Qumran as well gave up its secrets. Here were texts completed within a generation of Jesus' death from a sect with which the Baptizer or Jesus himself could well have had personal links. We have drawn amply on passages from Qumran; readers will have seen how freely they speak of a coming cataclysm and the sectarians' victory—political and military—under God's guidance and protection. These are not the hopes of which we hear at Nag Hammadi. But which of these two streams, if either, offers the context in which we can best understand Jesus and his teaching?

Underlying the dispute is our view of ourselves, as modern readers, and of our own resources for understanding. We are looking for a Jesus who is historically credible. It is natural to believe that the terms in which we think are adequate for understanding all the world around us. Our witnesses expected the same of the terms in which they thought. Those terms, however, encouraged our authors into beliefs that many of us find hard to share: beliefs in miracles, magic, a heaven above the sky, and a creation of the universe in six days. Such a worldview might have been almost universal then; it certainly is not now. Faced with these accounts of Jesus that take for granted such a view, we can follow either of two routes. Either we will insist that we know better about the world, with the benefit of our modern knowledge, than did our witnesses. If, then, we are to understand Jesus, it must be within the terms of modern knowledge and not of an ancient and misplaced credulity. Or we will admit that our ancient authors knew better, in this if in nothing else, than we do now. Jesus did defy what we take to be the laws of nature. And further still: If he and his evangelists all spoke of heaven and hell in geographical terms, we should in all humility do the same.

Such defense of the gospels' truth against the claims of modern knowledge is almost always a defense of a truthfulness whose conditions modern knowledge has defined. Such defendants are using their opponents' weapons on ground of those opponents' choosing. They accept the opponents' claim that the nature of knowledge and of truth is clear. What conditions must be met, then, if a claim is to be accepted as true or rejected as false? Here, too, the defendants accept the conditions that their opponents specify. At dispute, then, is only the truth or falsity of certain apparently clear-cut claims.

In *The Four Witnesses,* however, we have found how far are the evangelists from these battles of our own. Of course our writers and their age thought their categories adequate to ordinary life. But they write precisely in the conviction that Jesus was no part of that ordinary life and that their categories were inadequate to describe him. So our writers set out—each in his own way—to turn our understanding upside down. A disclosure is under way that our usual ways of learning and seeing cannot apprehend. It is not particular truths that are at issue but the nature of history and of the truths that it can bear.

We may still seem, as modern readers, to be on the wrong foot. We have no such tradition of a disclosure, of an unveiling granted to an occasional seer; we cannot then benefit when the tradition is invoked and inverted. But we have now encountered the traditions behind the gospels and might find that the Bible as a whole, the Old and New Orders together, is extraordinarily self-contained. For each writer ensures that precisely in his text's reception the conditions are fulfilled that make possible that disclosure. The gospels have different ways of making Jesus present to their readers, and different needs, concrete and specific, must be met by that presence. Our witnesses are united by the certainty that a new route must be found for the readers' understanding. *"Who,"* asks Jesus, *"do you say I am?"* We have solved the mystery of our four witnesses at last: not in what they say but in the ways they say it and in what they expect those ways to achieve. Of all our four witnesses, John offers the most dramatic challenge. The reborn readers, called out of the tomb of Lazarus, at last see the origin of their new life. And what has brought them to it? The gospel itself. John's text functions for his reader as the figure of Jesus functions in its story: Here is the summons to new life.

The pupils in Mark were told, *"Go back to Galilee; there you will see him,"* The same invitation could be offered by all our gospels: Only when we have reached their end can we see what they have been telling us right from the beginning. The Jesus whose story the gospels tell is the Jesus whose "presence," here and now, they themselves are for the reader. Luke need only hint at the motif; for his story of the early mission shows Jesus' presence throughout his church. All the more striking is the theme's importance for Mark, Matthew, and John. Their Jesus is present now in the text as he was once in Galilee and Jerusalem; and he discloses God now through the text as he did then through his presence on earth. Our writers know how much help we need if we are to see what their stories are really written to disclose. And they give us that help, page by page, as they draw us through a change of perspective so radical that John describes it as a new birth.

JOHN: THE BEGINNING AND THE END

And Nicodemus came—the one who had come to him at first by night—bringing a mixture of myrrh and aloes, twelve hundred ounces. So he and Joseph of Arimathea took the body of Jesus for burial. There was in the place where Jesus was crucified a garden, and in the garden a new tomb in which no one had yet been laid. There they laid Jesus.
(JOHN 19.39, 41–42)

From the garden of betrayal to the garden of burial. A third garden is recalled through these closing pages of John's story: a garden of love.

I come to my garden, my sister, my bride,
I have gathered my myrrh with my spices.
(SONG OF SOLOMON 5.1)

The Old Order's great love song, the Song of Solomon, records the songs of bride and groom, first one singing, then the other, sometimes to each other and sometimes to those around. Over and over we hear of spices:

How sweet is your love, my sister, my bride.
A garden locked is my sister, my bride,
a garden locked, a fountain sealed.
Your shoots are an orchard with all choicest fruits,
with all trees of frankincense, myrrh, and aloes,
a garden fountain, a well of living water.
(SONG OF SOLOMON 4.10, 12-15)

Myrrh and aloes were the spices in the garden of love, and now at Jesus' burial, myrrh and aloes are the spices of embalming. The fragrance of love has become the smell of death. Solomon had entered the garden to find his beloved; Jesus was met instead by his enemies. Solomon had approached with the mighty ones of Israel to be crowned:

Come out, daughters of Jerusalem,
and look on Solomon the king,
on the crown with which his mother crowned him
on the day of his marriage,
on the day of the joy of his heart.

(SONG OF SOLOMON 3.11)

Jesus entered the garden with his pupils, and his crown would be a crown of thorns: *"Look,"* said Pilate, *"here is the man"* (John 19.5).

A garden outside Jerusalem. Early morning, *on the first day,* the day that began the week and that had begun creation at the very start. The priests were gathering in the Temple for the morning sacrifice. It was still dark.

In the beginning, we read in the Old Order, *God created the heavens and the earth. And the earth was wildness and waste; and darkness was over the deep.*

Mary Magdalen came to the tomb; she found it empty. She ran to tell Peter and the pupil that Jesus loved. They came to the tomb in turn. Peter entered first. John gives us a precise description of the graveclothes he found there. Then the other pupil entered, too, *and he saw and believed. For they had not yet grasped the scripture, that he must rise from the dead. So the pupils went back home* (John 20.8–10). John takes care over this scene; the pupils saw the tomb empty and could describe it in detail. But from the sequence of events themselves, nothing, it seems, need follow. They believed: The tomb was empty. And no more. The pupils simply go home.

One figure remains outside the tomb.

Mary stood at the tomb, outside it, weeping. As she wept, she stooped down facing the tomb. And she sees two angels, in white, sitting where the body of Jesus had lain, one where his head had been and one where his feet. And they say to her, "Woman, why are you weeping?" She says to them: "Because they have taken my lord, and I do not know where they have put him."

(JOHN 20.11–13)

The light is rising. *God said, "Let there be light." And the light,* John told us in his opening hymn, *shines in the darkness, and the darkness has never put it out.*

Mary turns round and sees Jesus standing there, and does not know that it is Jesus. "Woman," says Jesus, "why are you weeping? Who are you looking for?" She thinks he is the gardener and says, "Sir, if you have taken him away, tell me where you have put him and I will take him away."

(JOHN 20.14–15)

Searching, still searching: Jesus had asked two of the Baptizer's pupils right at the gospel's start, *"What are you looking for?"* They wanted to know where Jesus was staying. The posse came upon Jesus in the garden: *"Who,"* he asked them, *"are you looking for?"*

> *The bride of Solomon sang,*
> *Upon my bed by night I looked for him,*
> *him whom I love with all my soul,*
> *I looked for him and did not find him.*
> *I will get up and will walk round the city*
> *and will look for him whom I love with all my soul.*
>
> (SONG OF SOLOMON, 3.1-2)

Mary had found what she sought, but she has lost him. The scene is extraordinarily sensuous: Mary, too, will long to touch Jesus, to have him as the human presence that she loved and misses.

> Sang the bride,
> *The watchmen found me as they went round the city;*
> *"Haven't you seen him whom I love with all my soul?"*
> *I had scarcely left them*
> *when I found him whom I love with all my soul;*
> *I took hold of him and will not let him go,*
> *until I have led him to the house of my mother,*
> *to the chamber of her who conceived me.*
>
> (SONG OF SOLOMON, 3. 3-4)

Mary, in turn, will reach out for Jesus. Here is such love as all Jesus' pupils have not shown. But such is not the love that Mary must have for Jesus now. He refuses her touch: *"Do not hold on to me"* (John 20.17).

The gardens of Jesus' betrayal and burial, the spice garden of the Song of Solomon. And underlying them all is the very first garden of which the Old Order knows. We read in the Beginning (Genesis), after the story of man's creation:

> *And God planted a garden in Eden, in the east, and there he put the man whom he had formed. And out of the ground God made to grow every tree that is pleasant to the sight and good for food. God took the man and put him in the garden of Eden to till it and keep it.*
>
> (BEGINNING [GENESIS] 2.8, 15)

The day has dawned. Strange echoes are sounding: What is this garden, in which Mary meets the gardener at first light, on the day when all creation had begun? The garden of creation became the garden of love; the garden of love has become the garden of death. Spices hang heavy in the air, spices that perfumed Paradise and the bower of Solomon and that Nicodemus brought in huge quantities to honor the corpse of Jesus. All that the reader might expect of such a garden has been overturned. But the tomb is empty. The corpse is gone. Everything is out of place; not even the contrasts, drawn to mirror love with death, are any longer secure.

If we wonder at this dream world in which Mary stands, we might wonder, too, how Jesus compares to the Solomon sought by his bride. John was not alone in drawing on Solomon's song, where Solomon sings to his bride,

> Your navel is a rounded bowl,
> that never lacks mixed wine;
> your belly is a pile of wheat
> encircled with lilies.

> (SONG OF SOLOMON 7.3)

Of these lines, as of so much in the Old Order, we have an Aramaic translation, central to the synagogues' life. The translators apply these verses to the leader of the Jewish Council. The translators, then, turn attention to their present; they look back, just as John does, to the Beginning's primordial themes: the maintenance of the world and the garden of Eden. Here is their rendering of those lines. The simplest love song has become elaborate praise of the community's leader. Every image must have a function, must illumine and instruct the synagogues. John draws on every strand of the Old Order to cast light on Jesus; the Song of Solomon's translators work no less hard to do justice to their text and to the hopes it must express and fortify. Here, according to their translation, are the scholars of Israel in the Garden, gathered around their leader:

> It is through the head of the Council,
> through the influence of his merits,
> that the whole world is sustained,
> as a fetus is sustained by the navel in its mother's womb.
> He sparkles with the knowledge of the Law.
> The words of the Law are never lacking from his mouth,
> just as the waters of the Great River, which issued from Eden, never fail.
> (SONG OF SOLOMON 7.3, ARAMAIC VERSION)

The Aramaic song has Eden forever in view. It presents the Song of Solomon as ten canticles: The first is Adam's song of praise when he is forgiven his wrongdoing; the last is to be sung on the great day of deliverance, when God's Anointed triumphs at last. From beginning to end: John is not alone in seeing, in the songs of Solomon and his bride, the arc on which creation moves from its first days to its last. But where will the course of John's creation come to rest?

> Then God said, "It is not good that the man should be alone. I will make him a helper suitable for him." So out of the ground God formed every beast of the field and

every bird of the air, and brought them to the man to see what he would call them. And whatever the man called every living creature, that was its name.

(BEGINNING [GENESIS] 2.18–19)

In Eden the serpent had lurked and deceived humankind. A "serpent" had entered the garden to guide the posse that would arrest Jesus and take him to his death. And in this garden on Easter morning? There is no serpent here; Satan's power is undone. We are watching the first day of a new creation. Here is once more an Adam, an Adam who can express perfectly and without remainder all that God is and wills and plans. This new Adam is again to name a "creature" of God and so to complete creation. Adam and Eve are once more in Eden; all creation is restored.

The austere disclosure of Jesus' power, riddling and strange, has tested the understanding of his followers from the start. The search on which John has launched his readers is as deep and abstract as any line of thought in the Old Order or the New. At its end his closest pupils see the empty tomb, believe, and go home. Left behind and disregarded is a woman. In John's gospel we have not heard of her before. She has misunderstood the empty tomb, she looks still for Jesus' body, she fails to know him when he stands before her, she longs for an earthly love and a human touch.

Those knowing pupils have checked the evidence, believed, and left. But it is not to them that Jesus first appears. It is to Mary. For in that inconsolable weeping is the voice of love. The Song of Solomon ends,

Let me as a seal upon your heart,
as a seal upon your arm.
For love is strong as death.
Many waters cannot quench love,
neither can the floods drown it.

(SONG OF SOLOMON 8.6–7)

Jesus says to her, "Mary" (John 20.16).

The sun has risen. The Temple's morning sacrifice is over, and the bustle of Jerusalem is once more under way.

And I saw a new heaven [writes the Seer] *and a new earth. For the first heaven and the first earth were passed way. And I saw the holy city, new Jerusalem coming down from heaven from God, prepared as a bride adorned for her husband. And I heard a great voice from the throne saying,*

"Look, the shelter of God is with men, and he will shelter with them, and they shall be his people, and God himself will be with them. And he will wipe away every tear from their eyes, and there will be death no more neither mourning nor crying nor pain any more, for the first things have passed away."

And he who was seated on the throne said, "Look, I am making all things new."

And one of the seven angels showed me the holy city Jerusalem coming down from the throne of God. And I saw no sanctuary in her. For the Lord God Almighty is her sanctuary, he and the Lamb. And the city has no need for sun or of moon to shine on her, for the glory of God illumined her, and her light is the Lamb. And the angel showed me the river of the water of life, bright as crystal, flowing out from the throne of God and of the Lamb. Down the middle of the street and on either side of the river were the trees of life, bearing twelve fruits, one fruit for each month of the year, and their leaves were a cure for the nations.

And the throne of God and of the Lamb will be in her, and his servants will worship him and will see his face, and there will be no more night and they will have no need of the light of a lamp or of the light of the sun, for the Lord God will shine on them and will reign for all aeons.

(BOOK OF UNVEILING [REVELATION] *21.1–5, 10, 22–23, 23.1–5*)